Elias of Thriplow

Serium senectutis

MEDIEVAL & RENAISSANCE TEXTS & STUDIES

VOLUME 116

Elias of Thriplow
Serium senectutis

Edited and Translated

by

Roger Hillas
Howard University

Medieval & Renaissance texts & studies
Binghamton University
1995

Library of Congress Cataloging-in-Publication Data

Elias, of Thriplow, 13th cent.
  [Serium senectutis. English & Latin]
  Serium senectutis / Elias of Thriplow ; edited and translated by Roger
Hillas.
        p. cm.— (Medieval & Renaissance texts & studies ; v. 116)
  Originally presented as the author's thesis (Ph.D)—University of Virginia.
  Includes bibliographical references (p.) and indexes.
  ISBN 0-86698-169-1
  1. Satire, Latin (Medieval and modern)—England—Translations into
English. 2. Satire, Latin (Medieval and modern)—England. I. Hillas, Roger,
1953– . II. Title. III. Series.
PA8310.E54S47 1993
871'.03—dc20   93-37751
                                                                    CIP

Contents

Parentibus optimis

Preface

This is the first edition of the *Serium senectutis*, an Anglo-Latin Menippean satire of the thirteenth century. Little is known of its author, Elias of Thriplow, who takes his *cognomen* from a small village, outside Cambridge, where he held land from the Bishop of Ely. The *Serium senectutis* survives in a unique manuscript, British Library, Sloane 441, which was copied in the early fifteenth century. It is a difficult work. Inventive and idiosyncratic in its diction, its complex syntax often obscure and sometimes faulty, the *Serium senectutis* does not so much articulate a continuous argument as hint at one. Few people will master its literary design in one or two readings, and there can be little doubt that the author intended things to be this way.

I have tried to make as much sense as possible of the *Serium senectutis*. The editorial principles I have adopted to this end are addressed in the introduction. Particularly difficult passages are discussed in the commentary; readers will also want to consult the translation and *index verborum* for implicit commentary on such passages. Often Elias's style is so periphrastic, even vague, that passages not obviously corrupt are hard to comprehend; in such cases, the plot summary which appears in section 5 of the introduction, "Contents," is worth consulting. Many readers will want to begin there. All translations from the Bible are from the Douay-Rheims version, except where it diverges from Elias's Latin text. All other translations are my own.

I am extremely grateful to Dr. Nigel Palmer for introducing me to Elias, and to Professor Paul Gerhard Schmidt for encouraging me to edit a work which he first brought to the attention of scholars. For help with specific points I am indebted to Dr. Chris Lewis, Dr. Margaret Nickson, Mr. J. M. Farrar, Dr. D. M. Owen, Professor James Carley, Professor Eleonore Stump, Dr. M. C. Davies, Professor Sten Ebbesen, Dr. D. R. Howlett, Mr. R. Sharpe, Dr. R. W. Lovatt, Mr. M. G. Underwood, Dr. Charles Burnett, Professor Daniel Kinney, and Professor A. G. Watson. Their individual contributions are noted in the appropriate places, but I cannot pass over here the extraordinary interest and kindness with which they answered my inquiries, served me coffee, sharpened my thinking, and covered some of the gaps in my research.

For kindly permitting me access to their collections, I wish to thank the Master, Fellows, and Scholars of St. John's College, Cambridge, and the keepers and librarians of the British Library, Lincoln College, Oxford, the Bodleian Library, Cambridge University Library, Alderman Library, Founders Library and the Library of Congress. Thanks are also due to Anne-Véronique Gilles of the Institut de Recherche et d'Histoire des Textes and Dr. Julian G. Plante of the Hill Monastic Manuscript Library for verifying that the *Serium senectutis* does not occur in any of the manuscripts which come into their purview. Michael Pavese and Judith Sumner, my editors at Medieval and Renaissance Texts and Studies, have displayed the ideal combination of patience in allowing me to complete my work and dispatch in completing their own. And I owe a more than personal debt of gratitude to MRTS and its general editor Professor Mario Di Cesare for their commitment to publishing scholarship with such limited commercial prospects. Publication of this book was aided by a subvention from the Graduate School of Arts and Sciences, Howard University.

The dissertation upon which this book is based was read by Professors Hoyt Duggan, V. A. Kolve, Gordon Braden, and Thomas Noble at the University of Virginia. I thank them in equal measure for their criticism and encouragement. The Latin text of the *Serium senectutis* presented here has benefited considerably from close readings by Professors Marvin Colker and Paul-Gerhard Schmidt and two anonymous readers for the press. As third reader for the press, Professor A. G. Rigg supplied a set of extraordinarily detailed and perceptive comments which have improved every aspect of this work. I shall be glad to acknowledge all remaining errors and omissions as my own, if they provoke others to study further this difficult but interesting author and his works.

Introduction

INTRODUCTION

I. The Life and Works of Elias of Thriplow

1. *The Rediscovery of Elias*

Elias of Thriplow was first brought to the attention of modern scholars by Beryl Smalley, who included him in the Appendix of Lost or Previously Unknown Works to her *English Friars and Antiquity in the Early Fourteenth Century*.[1] He figures there as a source for Thomas Ringstede's fourteenth-century *Commentary on Proverbs* and the mid fifteenth-century *Pabularium poetarum* compiled at St. Albans under the aegis of Abbot John Whethamstede. Both Ringstede and the *Pabularium* cite a prosimetrum by Elias, *De vita scolarium atque sua*, or "On His Own Life and That of His Students"; in addition, Ringstede paraphrases material from another work by Elias, *Contra nobilitatem*, or "Against Empty Nobility." Working only from the prose and verse fragments available to her in Ringstede and the *Pabularium*, Smalley offers a brilliant reconstruction of Elias's aims and style in *De vita scolarium*:

> He must have admired Pseudo-Boethius, *De disciplina scolarium* and set out to imitate him. Pseudo-Boethius wrote entirely in prose; Elias improved on him by adapting the alternate prose-and-verse form of the true Boethius to the subject-matter of Pseudo-Boethius.[2]

So apt is Smalley's characterization that in Olga Weijers's edition of *De disciplina scolarium* it becomes historical fact:

> Au XIVe siècle le Ps-Boèce a aussi été imité par un certain Elias Tripolanensis, dont l'ouvrage *De vita scolarium atque cura* est perdu sauf quelques citations par deux autres Anglais.[3]

As we shall see, Elias of Thriplow's works are contemporary with, or earlier than, the *De disciplina scolarium*, which Weijers dates to 1230–1240.[4] And despite the similarity of subject matter, there is no evidence

---

[1] Beryl Smalley, *English Friars and Antiquity in the Early Fourteenth Century* (New York: Barnes and Noble, 1961), 218–19, 351–53.

[2] *English Friars*, 351.

[3] Pseudo-Boèce, *De disciplina scolarium*, ed. Olga Weijers, Studien und Texte zur Geistesgeschichte des Mittelalters, 12 (Leiden-Cologne: Brill, 1976), 33.

[4] For the dating, see Pseudo-Boèce, *De disciplina scolarium*, 10–13.

for direct influence in either direction. Unfortunately, this is not the last time we will see a literary historian turn a predecessor's speculation about Elias of Thriplow into fact.

The study of Elias's life and work reaches maturity in Paul Gerhard Schmidt's exemplary paper "Elias of Thriplow—A Thirteenth-Century Anglo-Latin Poet."[5] Schmidt argues, correctly I believe, that *De vita scolarium* and *Contra nobilitatem* are two separate works, not two titles for the same work as Smalley had thought;[6] even so, he more than manages to double the number of works attributable to Elias. Besides discovering Whethamstede's own *tabula* or subject index to *De vita scolarium* in British Library, MS Arundel 11, Schmidt has also drawn attention to paraphrases and excerpts from Elias's *Semidiales*, or "Demigods," in the second edition of Matthias Flacius Illyricus's *Catalogus testium ueritatis*, or "Witnesses of the Truth" (Basel, 1562).[7] Most importantly, he has located a complete work by Elias, the *Serium senectutis*, or "Grave Thoughts in Old Age," which is preserved in a unique manuscript, British Library, Sloane 441. According to its colophon, the *Serium senectutis* was copied in the Dominican convent at Brecon, Wales by Bartholomew Texerii, O.P. Schmidt argues convincingly that since Texerii was Master General of the Dominican order from 1426 to 1449, he probably copied Elias's work before 1426.[8]

More recently, Marvin Colker and I have independently concluded that Elias is probably also the author of a work which Colker has edited as *A Collection of Stories and Sketches: Petronius rediuiuus*.[9] The *Petronius rediuiuus* is a prosimetrum in fourteen books which survives without attribution in Dublin, Trinity College, MS 602, an English manuscript of the early thirteenth century.[10] If its attribution to Elias is accepted, the Trinity College manuscript becomes by far the earliest surviving copy of a work by our author and so a potentially important witness to his language and style, as well as his early readership.[11]

---

[5] In *Papers of the Liverpool Latin Seminar, Third Volume*, ed. Francis Cairns, ARCA Classical and Medieval Texts, Papers, and Monographs, 7 (Liverpool: Cairns, 1981), 363–70.

[6] "Elias of Thriplow," 364.

[7] "Elias of Thriplow," 364, 368–69.

[8] "Elias of Thriplow," 366.

[9] In *Analecta Dublinensia: Three Medieval Latin Texts in the Library of Trinity College Dublin*, ed. Marvin L. Colker (Cambridge, Mass.: Medieval Academy of America, 1975), 181–257.

[10] For the dating and provenance of this manuscript, its contents and bibliography, see Marvin L. Colker, *Trinity College Library Dublin*, 2 vols. (Aldershot: Scolar, 1991), 2:1051–55.

[11] For the evidence for the attribution, see appendix 2 below and Colker, "New Light on the Use and Transmission of Petronius," *Manuscripta* 36 (1992): 200–209.

2. Reconstructing a Life

Schmidt has also shown that Elias was not so much previously unknown as long forgotten. In fact, Elias was known to the Tudor antiquarians John Leland (c. 1506–1552) and John Bale (1495–1563) and their followers.[12] Among the manuscripts possessed by the Augustinian priory at Barnwell just outside Cambridge, Leland records in his *Collectanea* a work "Helias Rubeus Tripolaunensis contra inanem nobilitatem."[13] This is all the mention Leland makes of Elias,[14] so it comes as a surprise to find that Bale claims the *Collectanea* as his authority for the account of Elias he includes in the first volume of his chronological *Scriptorum illustrium Maioris Brytannie ... Catalogus*, or "Catalogue of Illustrious British Writers." Given the paucity of external evidence for Elias's life and works, Bale's account is worth translating in full:

> Helias Rubeus, a native of Thriplow in Cambridgeshire, having successfully devoted his youth to the proper studies, at length turned his mind to greater and loftier subjects and, it is said, totally dedicated himself to the mysteries of theology at Cambridge. He was a man, as Leland testifies in his *Collectanea*, outstanding for humanity and prudence, nobly instructed in many branches of knowledge. Having often frequented the royal court, he saw many men vainly boasting not virtue itself but a noble name and fleshly lineage, although he knew they had fallen far short of their ancestors' nobility. Attacking them with heroic spirit and the daring of Hercules, he revealed their shallowness with lively reasoning, demonstrating that genuine nobility is to be reckoned according to virtue, not blood.
>
> He wrote *Contra inanem nobilitatem* in one book and certain other works of which, however, I have not thus far seen the titles.
>
> Leland does not say at what time or under which king he either lived or died; Leland does, however, make honest mention of him. So he will stay here until he finds his proper place.[15]

---

[12] "Elias of Thriplow," 366–67.

[13] John Leland, *De rebus Britannicis collectanea*, ed. Thomas Hearne, 6 vols. (Oxford: E theatro Sheldoniano, 1715), 3:15 (= Oxford, Bodleian Library, MS Top. gen. c. 3, p. 12).

[14] Elias appears nowhere else in Leland's autograph, Oxford, Bodleian Library, MSS Top. gen. c. 1–4, or the editions based upon it.

[15] John Bale, *Scriptorum illustrium Maioris Brytanniae ... Catalogus*, 2 vols. (Basel: Oporinus, 1557–59), 1:338 (hereafter *Catalogus*). For the *Catalogus*, see W. T. Davies, "A Bibliography of John Bale," *Oxford Bibliographical Society, Proceedings and Papers* 5 (1936–39): 210–79, at 268–70, 272–73. Despite its title, Davies's study remains the best biography of Bale; it can be brought up to date by consulting Peter Happé, "Recent Studies in John Bale," *English Literary Renaissance* 17 (1987): 103–13.

Admitting his uncertainty about Elias's dates, Bale places him between two writers, Gilbert the Great and Walter the Hermit, who died within a year or two of 1280.

If we take Bale at his word, we gain an appealing portrait of Elias as man of virtue, polymath, theologian, and courtier. But, as Schmidt remarks, Bale has merely piled moral commonplaces on top of the one hard fact he found in Leland, namely, that the *Contra inanem nobilitatem* of one Helias Rubeus Tripelaunensis was still to be found in a convent near Cambridge.[16] Furthermore, Bale makes no mention of Elias in his two earlier catalogues of British writers, the chronological *Summary of Illustrious British Writers* of 1548 and the alphabetical notebook, compiled from 1548 to 1557 as Bale revised the *Summary*, which R. L. Poole has published as the *Index of British Writers*.[17] Nor does Elias appear in either Bale's autograph epitome of Leland's *De viris illustribus* or the "Regystre of the names of Englysh Wryters" which Bale appended to his edition of Leland's *Laboryouse Journey*.[18] It is, in any case, disturbing to notice that according to the *Catalogus* Bale had not seen the *titles* of Elias's other works, as if that were all he had seen of the *Contra nobilitatem*. But as Schmidt points out, Bale did at least interpret Elias's cognomen correctly. The adjective Tripolaunensis, Tripolanensis, or Tripolawensis denotes a native of Thriplow, a village eleven kilometers southwest of Cambridge, and not of Tripoli in Outremer.[19]

The manor of Thriplow was held by the bishop of Ely from the creation of that see in 1109 until 1600. There were several other manors in Thriplow, including the rectory, which remained with the Ely priory after 1109 and was appropriated to the Pittancer, whence its name, the Pittensaries, or Pigeons.[20] British Library, MS Cotton Tiberius B. ii contains a

---

[16] "Elias of Thriplow," 367.

[17] John Bale, *Illustrium Maioris Britanniae scriptorum ... Summarium* (Wesel: Plataneum, 1549 [recte 1548]); *Index Britanniae scriptorum*, ed. Reginald Lane Poole and Mary Bateson (Oxford: Clarendon Press, 1902), hereafter *Summarium* and *Index*, respectively. For the former, see Davies, "Bibliography," 218–19, 258–59.

[18] John Leland, *The laboryouse journey and serche of Johan Leylande, for Englandes Antiquitees, geuen of hym as a newe yeares gyfte to Kynge Henry the viii. in the .xxvii. yeare of his reyne, with declaracyons enlarged: by Johan Bale* (London: Bale, 1549), signature G. ii. ff. The epitome of Leland's *De viris illustribus* is now Cambridge, Trinity College, MS R. 7. 15. I am grateful to Dr. M. C. Davies for checking this manuscript for me.

[19] "Elias of Thriplow," 367. In *English Friars*, 218, Smalley suggests "Elias of Tripoli," a mistaken deduction she seems to have arrived at by incorrectly transcribing "tripolensis vel tripolanensis" in the Ringstede Commentary (MS Bodley 829, fol. 61vb, wrongly cited as Lincoln College, MS latin 86, fol. 185rb) as "Tripolanitorum vel Tripolensis" (352).

[20] S. M. Keeling surveys medieval and later holdings in Thriplow in his article on "Thriplow" in *A History of Cambridgeshire and the Isle of Ely*, vol. 8, The Victoria History of the Counties of England (London: Institute of Historical Research, 1982), 239–42. The medieval holdings are summarized and analyzed briefly by Edward Miller and John

survey of lands belonging to the bishop in 1222; among those holding land in Thriplow it names "Helyas le mastre" as the farmer of one cotland (fol. 220ᵛ). This small holding, probably one acre in extent,[21] would not have sufficed to feed an individual, let alone a family.[22] It was, moreover, burdened with the heavy obligation of furnishing the bishop two days' work per week. As a result, it would not have served as a benefice rewarding Elias for service to the bishop or See of Ely and must, instead, be considered a family holding, although it is unlikely that Elias would have farmed it himself.

> Elias would either have been leasing the land to an undertenant or if resident and running the farm himself (which is very unlikely given his other interests) would presumably not have stooped to labour in the fields himself.... Elias held his cotland exactly as they did, but only in that he was responsible for seeing that the services were performed.[23]

Thus, one major piece of evidence for Elias's authorship of the *Petronius rediuiuus* is the author's claim, at the end of that work: "it is from farmers that I took my birth."[24]

We have seen that Bale placed Elias among a group of writers who died about 1280 "until he finds his proper place." In fact, that place must

---

Hatcher, *Medieval England—Rural Society and Economic Change 1086–1348* (London and New York: Longman, 1978), 20, 185. For landholding in Cambridgeshire, see Fredrick William Maitland, *Township and Borough* (Cambridge: Cambridge Univ. Press, 1898). The rectory of Thriplow was later granted by Bishop Hugh of Balsham to the scholars of what became Peterhouse, first to be shared (1280) with the Hospital of St. John, where the scholars were located, then for the sole use of the scholars when they relocated to two hostels outside the Trumpington Gate in 1284; see H. Butterfield, "Peterhouse," in *The Victoria County History of the County of Cambridge and the Isle of Ely*, vol. 3, ed. J. P. C. Roach (London: Institute of Historical Research, 1959), 334.

[21] Keeling, "Thriplow," 243.

[22] For the social status and economic condition of peasants in general, see Christopher Dyer, *Standards of Living in the Later Middle Ages: Social Change in England c. 1200–1520* (Cambridge: Cambridge Univ. Press, 1989), 109–40, 151–87. For cottagers in particular, see Miller and Hatcher, *Medieval England*, 22–25, 54–55; Edward Miller, *The Abbey and Bishopric of Ely* (Cambridge: Cambridge Univ. Press, 1951), 48–49. There seems to be a consensus, at least among members of the Cambridge school, that a minimum of ten acres was needed to support a family; see M. M. Postan, *The Medieval Economy and Society* (1972; repr. Harmondsworth: Penguin, 1975), 144–46; J. Z. Titow, *English Rural Society 1200–1350* (London: Allen and Unwin, 1969), 78–93; Miller and Hatcher, *Medieval England*, 147–48. Those with smaller holdings would have been forced to seek non-agricultural sources of income; see Dyer, *Standards of Living*, 131–34.

[23] Personal communication from Chris Lewis of the Victoria County History (Cambridgeshire). For subtentants on Ely lands, see Miller, *Abbey and Bishopric*, 132–33, 144–47.

[24] "A talibus [sc. ruricolis] natiuam natus originem traho" (*Analecta Dublinensia*, ed. Colker, 234).

be at least thirty years earlier than Bale suggests. We might have guessed as much from his appearance in the Cotton survey of 1222. We can be sure of this when Elias fails to appear in a similar survey from 1251 contained in the Ely Old Coucher or *Liber R*. Although this later survey makes no mention of Elias, it does name Albric, son of Elias, and Willelmus le Maistre as *cotarii* in Thriplow.[25] Most likely, the cotland had passed to Albric at the death of his father Elias, confirming the claim that the cotland was a family holding, and providing a clear *terminus ad quem* of 1251 for Elias's death.

Elias's full name, as we know from Ringstede and the Sloane manuscript of the *Serium senectutis*, was Helias Rubeus Tripolanensis.[26] Both of the Ely surveys list other landholders in Thriplow named Ruffus (le Rus or Russel): Robertus Ruffus, who also held land elsewhere from the bishop, in 1222 (fol. 219^v), and Coteman le Rede and Willelmus Russel in 1251 (72^v). And various members of the Ruffus (le Rus or Russel) family were prominent citizens in Cambridge before or at mid-century.[27] They were, furthermore, connected to several men who played central roles in the development of the University of Cambridge. Richard de Leycestria, who may have been the first chancellor of the university, witnessed a charter for Maurice Ruffus or le Rus before circa 1232,[28] and while regent master in civil law circa 1254–1257 Simon de Asceles lived in a great stone house on Trumpington Street owned by John le Rus.[29] The latter is particularly suggestive, since in 1257 Asceles became an Augustinian canon at Barnwell, where he was prior from 1267 to 1297. Some network of friendship and blood relation between Simon, John le Rus, and Helias Rubeus might explain how the copy of *Contra nobilitatem inanem* noted by Leland found its way into the library of Barnwell.

But we will search in vain for any confirmation of a link between the heads of the Ruffus family—Alberic, Maurice, John, Aunger, and Alice—and our Elias. They appear in entry after entry in the Cartulary of St. John's Hospital and the early records of Peterhouse as donors or witnesses; nowhere are they joined by Elias Ruffus or le Rus. We should not altogether dismiss the possibility that Elias was a poor relative of this

---

[25] Ely Diocesan Record G. 3. 27, fol. 73^v. I am indebted to Dr. D. M. Owen, formerly Keeper of the Archives, University of Cambridge, for bringing this reference, as well as the manuscript references to le Rus and Ruffus below, to my attention.

[26] Schmidt, "Elias of Thriplow," 365–66.

[27] H. P. Stokes, *Outside the Trumpington Gate before Peterhouse Was Founded*, Cambridge Antiquarian Society, octavo series, 44 (Cambridge: Cambridge Antiquarian Society, 1908), 35–43.

[28] M. B. Hackett, *The Original Statutes of Cambridge University* (Cambridge: Cambridge Univ. Press, 1970), 48–49 and 49 n. 1.

[29] Hackett, *Original Statutes*, 30–32 and 32 n. 1.

well-connected family, especially as his education would, if nothing else, have required some form of patronage from family or other sources.[30] However, we do have enough evidence to conclude that he was not an important member of the family and that he was perhaps not a family member at all.

Elias's title *le mastre* in the 1222 survey is hard to interpret exactly. By the thirteenth century the title *magister* (*maistre, master*) is more likely to specify the status accorded recipients of university training than it is to indicate the occupation of grammar master (*magister scolae*) or elementary teacher (*ludimagister*).[31] But as "Helyas le mastre" in the Cotton manuscript can be identified confidently with the Helias Tripolaunensis whose *De vita scolarium atque sua* is cited by Ringstede and Whethamstede, we may consider it quite likely that Elias was active as a grammar master in or before 1222. In those excerpts that survive from *De vita scolarium* Elias makes frequent reference to what Schmidt labels "the *miseria* of the teaching profession."[32] Smalley quotes a passage from Ringstede in which Elias complains of masters who are so incompetent that they must bribe students to attend their lectures.[33] In Whethamstede's *tabula* we find under *magister* a similar complaint about masters who set about flattering their students like parasites at a rich man's table. Under *parens* Elias complains of those parents who provide so magnificently for their children at school that the excess distracts them from their studies.[34]

It is tempting to imagine Elias as a grammar master in Ely or Cambridge, but the records which might prove or disprove such a thesis are lacking for both places.[35] Even so, there can be little doubt that such

---

[30] For the crucial importance of family support, see T. H. Aston, G. D. Duncan and T. A. R. Evans, "The Medieval Alumni of the University of Cambridge," *Past and Present* 86 (1980): 9–86, at 47–50. For a vivid evocation of the hard choices which faced those who lacked such support, see R. W. Southern, *Robert Grosseteste: The Growth of an English Mind in Medieval Europe* (Oxford: Clarendon Press, 1986), 52–53.

[31] R. W. Southern, "The Schools of Paris and the School of Chartres," in *Renaissance and Renewal in the Twelfth Century*, ed. Robert L. Benson and Giles Constable (Cambridge, Mass.: Harvard Univ. Press, 1982), 134–35; idem, "From Schools to University," in *The Early Oxford Schools*, ed. J. I. Catto, The History of the University of Oxford, 1 (Oxford: Clarendon Press, 1984), 11, 27–28.

[32] "Elias of Thriplow," 365.

[33] *English Friars*, 352.

[34] British Library, MS Arundel 11, fol. 174ʳ (*magister*) and 174ᵛ (*parens*). It should, however, be noted that the former betrays a strong indebtedness to Petronius, *Satyrica* 3.1, and may derive from Elias's reading rather than his personal experience. See below, appendix 2.

[35] Ethel A. Hampson, "Schools," in *The Victoria County History of the County of Cambridgeshire and the Isle of Ely*, vol. 2, ed. L. F. Salzman (London: Institute of Historical Research, 1948), 319–56. Nicholas Orme, *English Schools in the Middle Ages* (London: Methuen, 1973), 169–70. On the dangers of arguing from the silence of the quite fragmen-

schools existed. As a bishopric Ely was under obligation to maintain a grammar school; indeed, it had long been known for the education "of princelings and nobles."[36] And while there were no "cloister children" at Ely after the mid-thirteenth century, there was a school in the almonry where poor boys were taught by a secular clerk. But the first known master appears only circa 1541.[37] Likewise, our earliest evidence for any specific grammar school in Cambridge dates only from 1276.[38] But the foundation and growth of the University of Cambridge must have led to a proliferation of schools which taught grammar, that is, Latin language and literature, to the high standards required for entry into the university.[39] Moreover, while Elias lived at the time when university curricula were being restructured around Aristotelian philosophy, grammar remained a subject of intense study in the arts faculty.[40] In fact, the Angelica manuscript which contains the original statutes of Cambridge University is, as its editor M. B. Hackett has recognized, a grammarian's book from the first half of the thirteenth century which would have appealed to a master of arts such as the Cambridge grammarian Nicholas of Breckendale.[41] Nor would connections in Ely have failed Elias if he sought to teach grammar in Cambridge, since even after the establishment of the university the head of the grammar schools or "master of

---

tary records we possess that there was no school at a given place and time, see Orme, *English Schools*, 172.

[36] Orme, *English Schools*, 174; Hampson, "Schools," 321. Both rely on the work of James Bentham, *The History and Antiquities of the Conventual and Cathedral Church of Ely from the Foundation of the Monastery, AD 673 to the Year 1771* (Cambridge: Cambridge Univ. Press, 1771).

[37] Dorothy M. Owen and Dorothea Thurley, eds., *The King's School Ely: A Collection of Documents Relating to the History of the School and Its Scholars*, Cambridge Antiquarian Records Society, 5 (Cambridge: Cambridge Antiquarian Records Society, 1982), 1–15.

[38] Hampson, "Schools," 324.

[39] Orme, *English Schools*, 133; *The Early Oxford Schools*, 68, 373.

[40] For the study of grammar in general, see Charles Thurot, *Notices et extraits de divers manuscrits latin pour servir à l'histoire des doctrines grammatical au Moyen Âge* (Paris: Imprimerie Impériale, 1868), and Richard W. Hunt, *The History of Grammar in the Middle Ages: Collected Papers*, ed. G. L. Bursill-Hall (Amsterdam: Benjamins, 1980). For Oxford, see P. Osmund Lewry, "Grammar, Logic and Rhetoric, 1220–1320," in *The Early Oxford Schools*, 401–33. For Cambridge, see Hackett, *Original Statutes*, 13–14, 316–17, 340–43.

[41] Hackett, *Original Statutes*, 14. For Breckendale, see A. B. Emden, *A Biographical Register of the University of Cambridge to 1500* (Cambridge: Cambridge Univ. Press, 1963), 90, Hackett, *Original Statutes*, 14 n. 1, and Tony Hunt, *Teaching and Learning Latin in Thirteenth-Century England*, 3 vols. (Woodbridge: Brewer, 1991), 1:153–56. Hackett also points out that Oxford, Bodleian Library, MS e Musaeo 96, which contains the earliest Oxford statutes, is of similar constitution, including as it does "Huguccio, Hildebert [of Lavardin], a treatise on versification and a tract on grammar and kindred subjects" (14 n. 3).

glomery" for Cambridge was appointed by the archdeacon of Ely.[42] Wherever he taught grammar, Elias would have derived his living primarily from students' fees rather than the insufficient income of the cotland in Thriplow.[43]

In the *Serium senectutis* Elias displays at least a layman's knowledge of the new Aristotle and the canon law concerning marriage. The *Serium senectutis, De vita scolarium,* and *Petronius rediuiuus* all betray a familiarity with civil law.[44] Is there then any likelihood that Elias studied law or, as Bale claims, theology at Cambridge? Probably not, as the lack of external evidence here is more damning than in the case of Elias as grammar master.[45] If he did attend a university, Elias is more likely to have pursued an arts course; that, along with his teaching of grammar, would account for all but his knowledge of the new Aristotelian theology and the two laws.[46] Perhaps the best way to square Elias's manifest erudition with the silence of the records is to speculate that Elias did pursue an arts course, most likely at Cambridge, but terminated his studies some time before incepting as M.A.[47] Such a course would have been sufficient training for a career as grammar master, since the masters at the leading endowed schools normally held the M.A., but most of the masters elsewhere were not university graduates.[48] If he failed to complete the requirements for the M.A., Elias would have been unable to proceed to formal study in the higher faculties of theology and canon law, but that would not have prevented him from achieving some knowledge of both laws on his own from the conversation, teaching, and even manuscripts which would have been available at Cambridge or

---

[42] M. B. Hackett, "The University as Corporate Body," in *The Early Oxford Schools,* 68, and *Original Statutes,* 23, 43–44, 90 n. 4.

[43] Orme, *English Schools,* 156–57, 175.

[44] See *Serium senectutis* 6.60–70 (and commentary *ad loc.* below); Whethamstede's *tabula* to the *De vita scolarium,* s.v. *animus* and *malus* (British Library, MS Arundel 11, fols. 171ᵛ, 174ᵗ); and *Analecta Dublinensia,* ed. Colker, 185.

[45] "There is no sign of Elias as an alumnus of Cambridge under any possible forms of his name, and until we have full texts available of such topographical sources as the cartulary of St. John's hospital, I do not think we can hope to associate him with Cambridge" (D. M. Owen, personal communication of 12 October 1984). Elias does not appear in Emden's biographical registers of Cambridge and Oxford or in any of the other printed sources for university history.

[46] Service at Ely as a grammar master or in some other capacity could have brought Elias into contact with the Oxford masters who congregated in the *familia* of Bishop Eustace as a result of the Oxford migration of 1209 (Hackett, *Original Statutes,* 45–47).

[47] Aston et al., "The Medieval Alumni of the University of Cambridge," 25–27, conclude from their computer assisted analysis of Emden's biographical record that shortage of funds, death, and other obstacles prevented as many as a third or a half of all students at Cambridge from completing their studies.

[48] Orme, *English Schools,* 151–54.

elsewhere.[49] It may also be that Elias joined a religious order such as that of the Dominicans, which would have afforded him an opportunity for further learning before writing the *Serium senectutis*.

Did Elias frequent court? Again there is no external evidence to corroborate Bale's claim that he did, and nothing in the surviving works to indicate Elias's acquaintance with any particular court as opposed to moral or satirical commonplaces about courts.[50] If we again entertain the suspicion that Bale's account of Elias's career is really an embroidery on the title of the one work known to Bale, *Contra nobilitatem inanem*, we will find corroboration in the admission of Bale's biographer that "where he has few definite details at his disposal he does not hesitate to expand his scanty facts by the addition of 'purple passages' which have practically no value save that of tradition."[51]

But while we may doubt whether Bale's claim that Elias was "outstanding for humanity and prudence, nobly instructed in many branches of knowledge" derives from any great acquaintance with the man and his works, it would be unfair to leave the matter there. For despite the inevitable errors of fact, the purple passages, and the acerbic Protestantism which earned him the sobriquet "Bilious Bale," Bale established with his *Summarium* and *Catalogus* a basis for the study of British writers for two centuries. He and Leland worked at a time when manuscripts were perishing wholesale in the aftermath of Henry VIII's suppression of the monasteries. And Bale did his work without Leland's royal backing or the connections and wealth Matthew Parker possessed as archbishop of

---

[49] A faculty of canon law was founded at Cambridge as early as the chancellorship of Richard of Leycestria (circa 1222–1232) who was himself a canonist. Civil law was taught there *extraordinarie* as an adjunct to canon law before 1250 (Hackett, *Original Statutes*, 130–31). The civil law faculty probably dates from the late 1230s or early 1240s and was organized circa 1250. It may be that John de Cadamo and Walter de Tyrington, who served at Ely circa 1225–1238, later lectured as regents in civil law at Cambridge (32 and n. 4). In any case, the requirements of administering a diocese in a litigious age would have ensured a force of lawyers at Ely at all times.

[50] The only mention of an Elias Ruffus in the holdings of the Public Record Office printed or calendared thus far occurs in an entry in the Curia Regis rolls for Essex in 1206:
> Matillis filia Gaufridi queritur quod Willelmus le Bedellus et Elias Ruffus et Rogerus frater Clementis et Gaufridus Serviens et Robertus le Bacheler in pace domini regis eam robaverunt et abstulerunt in felonia i. chevise et i. tunicam et duas ulnas linee tele et sotulares suos et quod Willelmus Bedellus predictus in rapo eam defloravit. (*Curia Regis Rolls Preserved in the Public Record Office*, 16 vols. to date [London: H. M. S. O., 1922–], 4:232.)

This is not the sort of behavior we would have expected of the future author of the *Serium senectutis*, although it does recall a notorious entry in Geoffrey Chaucer's police blotter.

[51] Honor C. McCusker, *John Bale: Dramatist and Antiquary* (Bryn Mawr, 1942; repr. Freeport, N.Y.: Books for Libraries, 1971), 50–51. This work is particularly useful because McCusker prints extensively from Bale's manuscripts and correspondence.

Canterbury.[52] No wonder then that sometimes Bale could hope to do no
more than record titles, dates, and incipits. Describing the research he
undertook after he set about revising the *Summarium* in 1549, Bale writes
that between visits to libraries in Oxford, Cambridge, London, and
Norwich,

> Among the stacyoners and boke binders, I found many notable
> Antiquitees, of whom I wrote out the tytles, tymes and begyn-
> nynges, *that we myghte at the leaste shewe the names of them,* though
> we have not as now, their whole workes to shewe (my italics).[53]

Bale did, after all, record Elias's full name and interpret his cognomen
correctly. Nor can I claim that my attempt to locate Elias in the daily and
learned life of Cambridge and Ely by means of a few scattered hints and
documents is altogether different in kind from Bale's account of a career
at Cambridge and court which squared with the one piece of evidence he
possessed.[54]

What sort of life, then, have we reconstructed for Helias Rubeus
Tripolanensis? He held a small parcel of land and was styled "master" in
the survey of 1222; he was dead by 1251. He taught school for at least
part of his career. Elias would not have been licensed master in arts
before the customary age of twenty-one; nor, as is more likely, would he
have completed a partial course of university study and assumed control
of a classroom containing up to sixty or one hundred students at a
younger age.[55] Dating back from 1222, Elias was born before 1200,
perhaps as early as 1180–1190. He wrote at least four works, one of
which, the *Serium senectutis,* survives intact and contains material, drawn
from the new Aristotle, which was the basis for study in the arts at
universities by mid-century but was little known before 1220–1230. So we
should date Elias's death closer to 1251 than 1222, perhaps circa 1240–
1250, and even speculate that Elias returned to his studies, perhaps by

[52] For brief accounts of the three great Tudor antiquarians, see May McKisack, *Medieval History in the Tudor Age* (Oxford: Clarendon Press, 1971), 1–49.

[53] Preface to Bale's edition of Leland's *Laboryouse Journey* (1549), cited by McCusker, *John Bale,* 51–52.

[54] It remains just possible that Bale had seen more about Elias in Leland's literary remains than the Barnwell entry, since some of Leland's material was lost within ten or fifteen years of his death in 1552—long enough for Bale to have had a look before it perished.

[55] For the age at which the M.A. was received, see D. A. Callus, "Introduction of Aristotelian Learning to Oxford," *Proceedings of the British Academy* 29 (1943): 242–43, citing the Paris statutes of 1215 (*Chartularium universitatis Parisiensis,* ed. Henricus Denifle, O.P., and Aemilius Chatelain, 4 vols. [Paris: Delalain, 1889–97], 1:78). For the size of classes, see Orme, *English Schools,* 122.

entering orders, after he had served as a schoolmaster and fathered at least one son, perhaps a family, in his earlier years.[56] Before then Elias earned a living from his students' fees rather than his acre in Thriplow; it is just possible that he was related to a prominent Cambridge family surnamed le Rus or Ruffus.

3. Elias and the Antiquarians

Despite his shaky beginning, Elias entered the antiquarian tradition with the highest possible recommendation, since Bale had written him up in his authoritative *Catalogus*, ostensibly from the exhaustive researches of Leland. Elias makes his next appearance in John Pits's *Relationes historicae de rebus Anglicis*, where Pits explicitly assigns him the *floruit* circa 1280 implied by Bale.[57] Purposing to write ecclesiastical history favorable to the Catholic faith he espoused, Pits was eager to undermine the Protestant Bale's authority and sought to do so by censuring his pilferings from Leland. It may also be that Pits's brazen reliance on Bale for "facts" such as those included in his notice of Elias gave him something of a guilty conscience in this matter. Pits's vignette of Elias as moralizing courtier should not blind us to the fact that he relies completely on Bale for his knowledge of Elias and has no independent authority as a witness to Elias's life and works:

Helias Rubeus was born in the town of Thriplow in Cambridgeshire, England. After acquiring polite letters and the liberal arts in grammar school, he is said to have proceeded to higher studies at Cambridge, where he applied himself strenuously to first philosophy, then theology. Leland praises him highly in his *Collectanea* for his mild disposition, humanity, wisdom and range of learning. Having long frequented the royal court, he perceptively noticed, pondered silently by himself and discreetly wrote down that many who sauntered about puffed up by the empty title of nobility fell short in manner, life and in everything they did, and utterly forfeited the esteem of which they so boasted. He warned them from time to time, in private and with modesty, that true, innate nobility does not derive from someone else's blood but from each person's own worth. According to the tragedian, "He who boasts of his ancestry praises something not his own," to which Ovid agrees when he

---

[56] Orme, *English Schools*, 154–55, provides several examples of schoolmasters who returned to the university for further studies.

[57] John Pits, *Relationes historicae de rebus Anglicis* (Paris: Thierry and Cramoisy, 1619), 363; Schmidt, "Elias of Thriplow," 367.

says: "For I scarce call ours ancestry and forefathers / Whom we did not ourselves create." Thus he warned them either to stop their empty boasting of nobility or to display behavior consonant with nobility, laudable actions and appropriate virtues. Otherwise they would do better to call it fatuity rather than nobility. So along these lines he published *Contra nobilitatem inanem* in one book.

He is reputed to have been still alive in AD 1280, when Edward I sat on the English royal throne.[58]

Pits acknowledges Leland, which is to say Bale's *Catalogus*, as his source, but he goes both Leland and Bale one better by making Bale's provisional dating explicit ("alive in AD 1280"), then treating it as an historical fact worthy of elaboration ("when Edward I sat on the English throne"). As if to emphasize further the petrification of Bale's now traditional account, Pits includes Elias in his index of Cambridge graduates.

Elias appears as one of relatively few Cambridge writers in Thomas Fuller's *History of the Worthies of England*, a topographical collection published after the author's death by his son.[59] Discussing his principles for treating the writers of each county, Fuller prudently dismisses the "trash" Bale and Pits had included in their early centuries and proclaims that he will begin with Gildas.[60] When he comes to Cambridgeshire and Elias, Fuller cites Bale's *Catalogus* "Cent. 4, Num. 48" in his right margin as authority for a by now familiar account:

HELIAS RUBEUS was born at *Thriplow in this County, bred D. D. in *Cambridge*. *Leland* acquainteth us that he was a great Courtier, and gracious *with the King*, not informing us *what King* it was, nor what time he lived in; onely we learn from him, that this *Rubeus* (conceive his English Name *Rouse*, or *Red*) seeing many who were *Nobilitatis portenta* (so that as in a *Tympany* their very *greatness* was their *Disease*) boasted (if not causelessly) immoderately of their high

---

[58] *Relationes historicae*, 362–63.

[59] Thomas Fuller, *The History of the Worthies of England* (London: J. G. W. L. and W. G., 1662). I wish to thank J. M. Farrar, Cambridge County Archivist, for bringing Fuller to my attention. Little could differ more from Bale's fervent commitment to religious reform and dire fears for the survival of England's antiquities than Fuller's genial statement of his own aims as author:

I propound *five ends* to my self in this Book: First, *To gain some Glory to God.* Secondly, *To preserve the Memories of the Dead.* Thirdly, *To present Examples to the Living.* Fourthly, *To entertain the Reader with delight.* And lastly, (which I am not ashamed publickly to profess) *To procure some honest profit to my self* (1).

While one may wish that Bale had consulted his readers' delight at times, we are fortunate indeed that, so far from seeking profit, he spared no expense in his antiquarian labors.

[60] *Worthies*, 26.

Extraction, wrote a Book *contra Nobilitatem inanem*. He is conjectured to have flourished about the year 1266.[61]

Because Fuller acknowledges Leland and Bale's ignorance of when Elias lived, his *floruit* 1266 is a surprise; it may have its ultimate source in a work published a century earlier, the second edition of Matthias Flacius Illyricus's *Catalogus testium ueritatis*.[62]

The title page to his *Bibliotheca Britannico-Hibernica* claims that Thomas Tanner includes writers overlooked by Leland, Bale, and Pits and also supplies omissions, corrects, and illustrates his material with abundant notes,[63] but his entry for Elias is notable, in fact, for its reliance on the earlier antiquarians and for its brevity:

> RUBEUS, [HELIAS] saw daylight in the town of Thriplow in Cambridgeshire, was a graduate of the University of Cambridge, where he spent some years studying philosophy and theology; then a royal chaplain. He wrote *Contra nobilitatem inanem* in one book. He is said to have been alive in 1280.[64]

His claim that Elias was *capellanus regius* is original, but we must not accept it uncritically. Tanner offers no documentation for his claim, and there is nothing in the records which still survive to corroborate it.[65] It is unlikely, albeit not impossible, that a royal chaplain would be father to one or more sons, as is the Elias we know from the Ely accounts. Finally, this claim is all too easily explained as an attempt to make Bale's account of Elias at court look more plausible by making it more circumstantial. While we may prefer Tanner's *dein capellanus regius* to Pits's tedious

---

[61] *Worthies*, 157. According to Fuller, Cambridgeshire is famous for its eels, hares, saffron, and willows (143–44).

[62] See below, 16 and n. 70.

[63] Thomas Tanner, *Bibliotheca Britannico-Hibernica; sive de scriptoribus qui in Anglia, Scotia, et Hibernia ad saeculi xvii initium floruerunt, literarum ordine juxta familiarum nomina dispositis Commentarius* (London: Impensis Societatis ad literas promovendas, 1749). As good as his word, Tanner indexes Elias under his family name Rubeus. His alphabetical scheme betrays a bias towards analytical classification, while Bale's chronological ordering hints at a stronger desire to implicate individual authors in a larger history. For the apocalyptic tenor of that history, see Katherine R. Firth, *The Apocalyptic Tradition in Reformation Britain 1530–1645* (Oxford: Oxford Univ. Press, 1979), 32–68, and John N. King, *English Reformation Literature: The Tudor Origins of the Protestant Tradition* (Princeton: Princeton Univ. Press, 1982), 56–75, 418–29.

[64] *Bibliotheca*, 645.

[65] However, the author of the *Petronius rediuiuus* does mention having frequently seen a certain I— of London: "I quendam sepissime uidi Lundoniensem" (*Analecta Dublinensia*, ed. Colker, 199). But as Colker notes (182), the author does not say where these encounters took place.

account of Elias dispensing moral wisdom to self-important nobility, we should not be any swifter to take it as fact.

4. Baleus and Flacius

In their accounts of Elias, all the English antiquaries are sons of Bale. It is appropriate then that the other branch of Elias studies which established itself among Reformers in Germany was founded by Bale's kindred spirit on the Continent, Matthias Flacius Illyricus.[66] Schmidt has pointed out that the second edition of Flacius's *Catalogus testium ueritatis* includes a chapter *Helias Rubeus Tripelauensis* which summarizes and quotes from the lost *Semidiales,* or "Half Holies," of our author.[67] From there he enters the *Lectiones memorabiles* of Johannes Wolfius, where he figures in the entry for 1264 as a critic of ecclesiastical abuses. Flacius does not say how the *Semidiales* came to his attention, but when he mentions *Baleus in suo scriptorum catalogo,* we may reasonably suspect that Bale himself was involved.

From the length at which Flacius excerpts and quotes Elias it seems likely that he had a manuscript of the *Semidiales* at hand as he wrote. In that sense he knows far more about Elias than Bale had when the first nine centuries of the *Catalogus* were published five years earlier in 1557. He even knows Elias can be prolix.[68] But what he says about Elias the man is easily reconciled with what Bale had said:

> About three hundred years ago a certain Elias, *Rubeus Tripelaniensis* by surname, an Englishman I believe, wrote *Semidiales* in seven books.... Although this writer has not been printed we attribute

---

[66] For a brief outline of Flacius's life and current bibliography, see Oliver K. Olson, "Matthias Flacius Illyricus," in *Theologische Realenzyklopädie* (Berlin and New York: de Gruyter, 1977–), 11:206–14, and " 'Der Bücherdieb Flacius'—Geschichte eines Rufmordes," *Wolfenbütteler Beiträge* 4 (1981): 111–45. The standard biography remains Wilhelm Preger, *Matthias Flacius Illyricus und seine Zeit,* 2 vols. (Erlangen: Bläsing, 1859–61).

[67] "Elias of Thriplow," 368, referring to Matthias Flacius Illyricus, *Catalogus testium ueritatis, qui ante nostram aetatem Pontifici Romano, eiusque erroribus reclamarunt: iam denuo longe quam antea et emendatior et auctior editus ...* (Strassburg: Apud Paulum Machaeropoeum, sumptibus Ioannis Oporini, 1562). A similar imprint appears on signature eee 5[b], after index and errata. This edition also includes an Appendix with its own collation AA[6]–EE[6] and separate pagination 1–58 plus one flyleaf. This appendix contains material, delivered at the last moment, as the introductory *Lectori Typographus* explains, from Alain Chartier and Froissart, among others, but nothing from Elias. It is in a different type than the main volume—clearer, more widely spaced, thinner, and larger—and ends with the colophon: "Basiliae, Ex officina Ioannis Oporini, anno salutis humanae MDLXII. Mense Martio."

[68] *Catalogus testium ueritatis,* 448.

several compositions to him. Moreover, Bale mentions him in his catalogue of writers.[69]

Bale's guess that Elias died about 1280 could easily have suggested Flacius's claim that he wrote the *Semidiales* about three hundred years before the publication of the *Catalogus testium ueritatis*, that is, around 1262. Both writers attempt only approximate dates for Elias; Flacius could have come by his simply by counting back a plausible amount from the date for Elias's death implied by Bale. Since we have already seen how Pits and Tanner made explicit and propagated Bale's *floruit* 1280 for Elias, it should come as no surprise that Flacius's approximate dating of the *Semidiales* was in turn accepted as definitive by Continental scholars, beginning with Wolfius.[70] Flacius agrees with Bale that Elias was the author of several works: "although this writer has not been printed we attribute several compositions to him."[71]

But Flacius's knowledge of the entry for Elias in Bale's *Catalogus* does not go far towards explaining how he acquired a manuscript of the *Semidiales*. In fact, there is abundant evidence that Bale and Flacius had known each other since at least 1554, when Flacius wrote Bale from Magdeburg on 1 July.[72] From the tone and contents of that letter—*Clarissimo viro Joanni Baleo doctori et episcopo*—it is clear that Flacius and Bale had already made contact, probably some time after Bale's arrival in the Netherlands in November 1553 as a Marian exile.[73] Among other matters, Flacius offers to see Bale's enlarged *Catalogus* and Leland (presumably the *Collectanea* or *De viris illustribus*) through the press at Wittenburg or Leipzig. He then implores Bale to help with his *Magdeburg Centuries*, the first Protestant history of the church, and ends by greeting a common friend.[74]

---

[69] *Catalogus testium ueritatis*, 447.

[70] Schmidt, "Elias of Thriplow," 368. Since Wolfius's *Lectiones* achieved wide circulation "as a kind of handbook of Protestant church history" (ibid.), we may prefer them to Flacius's *Catalogus testium ueritatis* as a source for Fuller's *floruit* of 1266 for Elias (above, 14).

[71] Bale says (*Catalogus*, 1:338): "He wrote *Contra inanem nobilitatem* in one book *and certain other works* of which, however, I have not thus far seen the titles" (my italics). English antiquaries from Pits on make no mention of the possibility that Elias wrote works other than *Contra nobilitatem inanem*.

[72] McCusker prints the letter (*John Bale*, 69–70) from British Library, MS Cotton Titus D. x. 2, fol. 180[r-v].

[73] Davies, "Bibliography," 224–25. Bale claims to have spent three weeks in jail on arrival near Antwerp; otherwise, we know little of his whereabouts until 25 September 1554, when his signature appears on the Frankfurt congregation's invitation to John Knox to become their pastor. See Christina Hallowell Garrett, *The Marian Exiles: A Study in the Origins of Elizabethan Puritanism* (Cambridge: Cambridge Univ. Press, 1938), 78.

[74] Although Flacius is best known for conceiving and supervising the research for what

At this time, Flacius was busy collecting literary and historical writings attacking the papacy and endorsing true religion for three collections, all published at Basel, the first two by Oporinus: the *Antilogia papae* (1555), *Catalogus testium ueritatis* (1556), and *Varia ... poemata* (1557).[75] Bale himself was soon to publish his *Catalogus* (1557–59) with Oporinus; its appendices include a *chronique scandaleuse* of the papacy which Bale also published separately as the *Acta Romanorum pontificium* in 1558.[76] In the preface to the *Acta*, Bale names Flacius as one of his sources, and in a letter of July 1560 to Archbishop Matthew Parker, Bale has cause to mention

> The newe ecclesiastycall hystorye, collected by Matthias Illyricus, Joannes Wigandus and others, from whome I have receyued diverse and many epistles, for helpe in the same.[77]

Later in the same letter, Bale answers Parker's query about Protestant church histories by recommending the papal history in his *Catalogus* and

> ii other bokes lately set fourthe by me and Illyricus, the one is called Catalogus testium veritatis, the other beareth this tyttle: Varia doctorum piorumque virorum. Antilogia Papae, wyll also correspond to the same.[78]

---

became the *Magdeburg Centuries* (Basel: Oporinus, 1561–74), it is now clear that the text was written by his coworkers at Magdeburg, Johann Wigand and Matthaus Judex. See Ronald Ernst Diener, "The Magdeburg Centuries: A Bibliothecal and Historiographical Analysis" (D.Th. diss., Harvard Divinity School, 1978).

[75] The full titles indicate the similarity of purpose among these collections. They are *Antilogia papae; hoc est, de corrupto ecclesiae statu et totius cleri papistici perversitate, scripta aliquot veterum authorum ante annos plus minus CCC et interea; nunc primum in lucem eruta et ab interitu vindicata* (Basel: Oporinus, 1555), and *Varia doctorum piorumque virorum de corrupto ecclesiae statu poemata ante nostram aetatem conscripta: ex quibus multa historica quoque utiliter ac summa cum voluptate cognosci possunt* (Basel: Lucius, 1557). For the *Catalogus testium ueritatis*, see above, 15 n. 67.

[76] John Bale, *Acta Romanorum Pontificium a dispersione discipulorum Christi usque ad tempora Pauli Quarti, qui nunc in Ecclesia tyrannizat* ... (Basel: Oporinus, 1558); Davies, "Bibliography," 227–28, 270–72. For Oporinus, see Martin Steinmann, *Johannes Oporinus: Ein Basler Buchdruker um die Mitte des 16. Jahrhunderts*, Basler Beiträge zur Geschichtswissenschaft, 105 (Basel and Stuttgart: Helbing und Lichtenhahn, 1967). Bale's doings in Basel receive exemplary treatment from Manfred Edwin Welti, *Der Basler Buchdruck und Britannien: Die Rezeption britischen Gedankenguts in den Basler Pressen von den Anfängen bis zum Beginn des 17. Jahrhunderts*, Basler Beiträge zur Geschichtswissenschaft, 93 (Basel: Helbing und Lichtenhahn, 1964), 187–95, 203–16.

[77] Quoted by Welti, *Basler Buchdruck*, 190 and McCusker, *John Bale*, 59 from Cambridge University Register Misc. 8.

[78] Quoted by McCusker, *John Bale*, 61–62. For relations between Bale and Parker, see McCusker, 30–31, 58–68, and Norman L. Jones, "Matthew Parker, John Bale, and the Magdeburg Centuriators," *Sixteenth Century Journal* 12, 3 (1981): 35–49.

Bale exaggerates, as the authorship of the *Catalogus testium ueritatis* and *Varia . . . poemata* was Flacius's alone. But there is no reason to doubt that Bale's researches for his *Catalogus* enabled him to contribute texts and commentaries to Flacius's works. As Schmidt notes, Bale had anticipated Flacius's collection of goliardic verse in the *Catalogus testium ueritatis* and *Varia . . . poemata* with his own *Rhitmi vetustissimi de corrupto ecclesiae statu* (1546).[79]

That Bale and Flacius met in person is clear from an exchange of letters between Flacius and Archbishop Parker in 1561, while Bale was still alive. Writing from Jena in search of material for the revised edition of his *Catalogus testium ueritatis*, the edition which contains the excerpts from Elias's *Semidiales*, Flacius asks Parker to send him manuscripts illustrating church history and attacking the papacy. Along the way, he mentions that

> Bale told me that he had many old books which could usefully be placed in the King's public libraries after his death; the same is true of other books except that they easily perish when inherited by ignorant heirs.[80]

Flacius and Bale both moved about on the Continent and could have met in many places, but the most obvious spot would have been Basel, where they shared the same publisher, Oporinus. Bale lived in the Clarakloster there from 1556, when his name appears in the matriculation list for the university, until March 1559.[81] Indeed, he may have made his first contact with Flacius there, as he claims in the preface to his virulent *Declaration of Edmonde Bonners Articles* (London, 1561) that it was "wrytten from Basile in Heluetia, an. 1554,"[82] which would have been before he went to Frankfurt in that year.

It seems unlikely that Bale discovered the *Semidiales* and relayed their contents to Flacius while still in Basel, since in that case he would almost surely have made use of them himself in the second part of his *Catalogus*.[83] Perhaps Parker or one of Flacius's literary agents in England

---

[79] "Elias of Thriplow," 369. For the *Rhitmi vetustissimi*, see Davies, "Bibliography," 216, 251.

[80] For the Latin original, see John Strype, *The Life and Acts of Matthew Parker . . .* , 2 vols. (London: J. Wyat, 1711), 2:31. A letter from Parker to Flacius which its editors date to 1566 looks very much like a reply to this letter and should be redated to 1561. See John Bruce and Thomas Thomason Perowne, eds., *Correspondence of Matthew Parker*, Parker Society, 33 (Cambridge: Cambridge Univ. Press, 1853), 286–88, and McCusker, *John Bale*, 67–68. For the redating, which I arrived at independently in 1983, see Jones, "Matthew Parker," 40–41.

[81] Garrett, *The Marian Exiles*, 78; Davies, "Bibliography," 228.

[82] Welti, *Basler Buchdruck*, 204–5; Davies, "Bibliography," 273.

[83] There is no marginal annotation to the chapter on Elias in Bale's marked copy of the *Catalogus*, now in the British Library. See also Davies, "Bibliography," 269.

found them and forwarded them to Flacius while he was revising the *Catalogus testium ueritatis* around 1561.[84] Flacius may even have found a copy of the *Semidiales* on the Continent in the aftermath of the dispersal of the English monastic libraries, although he writes to Parker that he is unable to get about much himself in search of material. But my best guess is that Bale found a manuscript of the *Semidiales* in England sometime between the publication of the second part of the *Catalogus* 1559 and his death in 1562 and relayed it or its contents to Flacius on the Continent.

II. The *Serium senectutis*

5. Contents

Book One:

In a poem based on the hymn to Hymen which opens Martianus Capella's *Marriage of Mercury and Philology*, Elias first sings of the marriage bonds between pagan gods and goddesses, then laments human vice and the divorce it causes between mind and tongue (i).[85]

Philip, Elias's *confrère*, echoes Martianus's son by objecting that Elias should, at his advanced age, abandon such frivolities for serious concerns (1). A brief second meter states that man's voice uncovers the mind's secrets (ii).

Elias replies with the charge that Philip knows not of what he speaks (2). He provides allegorical explications of the marriage of Saturn and Cybele as the natural cycle which causes crops to grow (3), of Admetus and Alcestis as mind and courage, and of Mercury and Philology as the wise man's union of mind and tongue (4). He then praises the marriage of mind and tongue with several psalm paraphrases (5) and defines lying as saying one thing and meaning another (6). He ends by outlining God's eternal punishment of lies (7).

Book Two:

The opening meter recapitulates Elias's notion that lies result from a disassociation of mind and tongue (i). Philip objects that Elias is a know-it-all (1). Philip knows of God's punishments for lies; even the

---

[84] In his letter to Flacius, Parker mentions "vester Nigerus," who thought Bale's books would be of use to Flacius. See McCusker, "*John Bale*," 67 and Jones, "Matthew Parker," 41.

[85] For the purposes of this summary, Roman numerals represent meters, and Arabic numerals represent paragraphs in the *Serium senectutis*.

pagans mention how their gods avenged lies and other transgressions (2). Philip backs his assertion by excerpting material that treats lies from the Psalms (3–5) and rehearsing the fatal end of the man born of an Egyptian and an Israelite who dared blaspheme against God (6). But an objection arises: is God too harsh in punishing blasphemy with death (7)? Certainly human law does not propose such a stiff penalty for slandering an emperor (8); besides, demons delight in spilling human blood, not God (9).

Philip then offers several Old Testament examples of God's vengeance on the Israelites' apostasy. The murmurs of the Israelites in the wilderness cause God to consume the outer part of their camp with flame (10); soon afterwards they spurn the manna (11), and Miriam revolts against her brother Moses (12). The explorers sent to the Promised Land return with a false report (13–14), and Chore and Dathan lead another revolt (15–16); in every case the malefactors meet a bad end. Another rebellion (17) and the worship of the golden calf (18–19) prove equally fatal. Philip concludes the book by advancing Moses as a model for all judges (20–22).

Book Three:

After a poem urging man to serve God without murmuring (i), Philip enters an extended discussion of the vengeance various pagan gods exacted for blasphemy or other sins against their worship. The gods and the mortals who offend them are Mercury and Battus (1–4), Bacchus and Pentheus (5), Jove and the Syrian king Alexander (6–8), Jove and Cambyses (9–11), Apollo and Xerxes (12–21), Minerva and the Metapontines and Sybaritans (22), Hercules and the Potitii (23), Apollo and the Romans who stole a golden vest from his statue (24), Aesculapius and Turullius (25), Jupiter and Ptolemy of Macedonia (26–34), Apollo and the Gaul Brennus (35–42), Juno and the Censor Fulvius (43), and Juno and Pyrrhus of Epirus (44). Such stories should make us fear lying, says Philip, but they should not pervert our normal manner of speech (45). Talk of a marriage between mind and tongue is patently absurd (46), and Elias should write about topics which mix profit with delight (47).

Book Four:

The opening meter recapitulates Philip's concern that people act as their peers do (i). Elias replies by labelling Philip rash and obstinate (1). He summarizes Philip's argument (2–4), then proposes that it contains an implicit criticism of those who have spoken God's word, as well as pagan philosophers (5). Elias launches a defense of figurative expression by adducing biblical texts and their standard allegorical readings: the Bride and Groom of the Song of Songs (6–7), the Heavenly Jerusalem in Apocalypse (8), and a number of verses from the Psalms (9–15). Having defended God's word, Elias turns to pagan literature in the person of Martianus Capella. Using the standard commentary by Remigius of Auxerre, he allegorizes four passages: Hymen's binding of the elements in the opening hymn (16–17), Mercury's scanty garments (18–19), the caduceus (20–21), and Philology's offering to Athanasia and Apotheosis (22–25). He concludes by suggesting that the next time Philip is tempted to mock something, he should put his finger over his lips (26–28).

Book Five:

After a meter on the dangers of a slippery tongue (i), Philip promises to hold his peace (1–2).

Book Six:

In the opening meter, Philip reiterates his promise to remain silent (i). Elias, in turn, makes a concession to his advanced age by promising to forego his marriage allegory and fancy words (1). In something of an aside, he argues from canon law that the absence of a dowry does not invalidate a legitimate marriage (2–4). He will consider the marriage of mind and tongue without any reference to Hymen, Genius, Juno *pronuba*, or the Muses (5–6).

Book Seven:

The meter argues that since old age is hateful in the marriage bed it should concern itself with virtue (i). Elias continues the marriage discussion by arguing that marriages are legitimized by affection not documents (1). He then repeats Philip's point that, although not everything said by the ancients is true, they do often provide useful examples of honest behavior (2). He repeats the stories of Mercury and Battus (3) and the explorers of the Promised Land (4), and adds the story of Susanna and the elders (5–6). He concludes with a warning that a lying mouth slays the soul (7).

Book Eight:

The meter reiterates Elias's point about the danger a lying mouth poses to the soul (i). Philip revives and advances rather surprising claims that man is not the only animal blessed with an immortal soul, and that God is not alone in possessing absolute power (1). He argues the first point by noting that pagan philosphers disagree as to the composition of the human soul (2–3) while agreeing on its immortality (4). While men are more intelligent than other creatures (5), their nakedness leaves them more vulnerable than other animals (6). Man's excellence arises from the shape of the body and head, not the powers of the soul (7), a point which is confirmed by the ease with which physical injuries impair the workings of intellect or soul (8).

Book Nine:

After a meter urging man to avoid vanity and cultivate virtue (i), Philip argues his second point from the fact that philosophers are not sure that there is only one God (1). Antiquity worshipped a multitude of gods (2); Philip cites the Hermetic *Asclepius* on man's creation of idols to worship (3-4). Even the Israelites worshipped the golden calf in the desert (5) and the two calves at Dan and Bethel (6); Solomon also worshipped a number of gods (7). Rome worshipped the Epidaurian serpent (8) and the Egyptians worshipped Apis in the form of an ox (9). Philip ends by daring Elias to refute him (10).

Book Ten:

A meter warns that the man who refuses to coexist with others is obnoxious to all (i). Elias replies to Philip's dare by asserting that only reason distinguishes man from the animals and makes him like a god (1). The immortality of the soul is proved by the fact that a corpse will bleed in the presence of its slayer (2). All religious sects offer proofs for the soul's immortality (3). Any resurrection of the dead provides an example (4). Elias offers three: Elijah resurrected the son of the widow of Sarepta (5-8); Elisha provided his elderly hosts in Sunam with a son, and revivified him after an untimely death (9-11); and a dead man was brought back to life just by touching Elisha's coffin (12). Elias concludes his Old Testament proofs with a reminder that man is distinguished from the animals by reason in life and an immortal soul in death (13).

Elias then offers some pagan proofs for the immortality of the soul: Plato's vision of Er (15), the restoration of Bacchus after he was torn to pieces by the giants (16), the *Asclepius* on man's return to the stars after death (17), and Seneca on Scipio Africanus's ascent (18). The argument is clinched by Christ's greatest miracles: the raising of Lazarus (20), the prince's daughter (21), and the dead son of the widow of Naim (22). Elias reminds Philip that Christ gave his followers the power to resurrect the dead (23).

Book Eleven:

The meter repeats Elias's reminder that Christ gave his disciples the power to resurrect the dead (i). Next Elias considers Philip's second claim. All men agree that there is one all-powerful God (1); just saying otherwise deserves strict punishment (2). This is because sharing power inevitably leads to conflict (3). Elias pauses briefly to apologize for borrowing his proofs from other writers (4). Those proofs are the Ambrosiaster on knowing God through his visible creation (5), a series of Aristotelian proofs (6–9), Anselm's ontological proof (10), and a claim that two first principles could not coexist (11). Elias again emphasizes that he has not thought up these arguments, but does claim to have adorned them stylistically (12). He reminds Philip that it is onerous to serve more than one master (13), exhorts him to embrace the immortality of the soul, one God, and the marriage of soul and tongue (14), and promises that a faithful servant will be rewarded by sharing his master's joy (15).

Book Twelve:

The meter argues that man can serve only one God—the Trinity (i). Philip replies that he is a changed man and now agrees with Elias (1). The pagans have been refuted (2); no man can love virtue or worship God without marrying mind to tongue (3). The man without friends is the most miserable of men (4).

Book Thirteen:

The meter reiterates that no man can serve two masters (i). Elias rejoices: "Behold how good and pleasant it is for brethren to dwell together in unity" (1). Elias and Philip will live together as friends (2) like Damon and Pythias (3–5). Elias proclaims his desire that they live as friends in charity (6) and ends with a hymn to friendship (ii).

6. Sources

Twice in the course of articulating his proofs of God's oneness, Elias reminds his friend Philip that his arguments are not his own but have been borrowed from others and adorned by verbal and syntactic elaboration. Elias probably felt compelled by the seriousness of the topic under discussion to make such an admission at this point, since it is equally true of the rest of the *Serium senectutis*. Virtually all the material of the work, whether spoken by Elias or Philip, comes from other written sources. Those parts which do not, the meters and prose passages that begin and end books, are the most stylistically convoluted and least substantial of the work. Left to his own devices, Elias tends towards the rhetorical elaboration of moral commonplaces.

Elias's primary sources are not particularly numerous, but they cover an impressive range of disciplines. Part of Elias's account of the legal status of the marriage contract is based on civil law.[86] Elias's discussion of marriage is based on the fundamental accounts in Gratian's *Decretum*, the *Decretales* of Gregory IX, and book 4 of Peter Lombard's *Sentences*. Here, as in the case of his Aristotelian sources, the difficulty of locating exact written sources may well indicate that Elias wrote from memory, relying on knowledge gained from university study or other contact with civil and canon lawyers.[87]

The most certain sources for Elias's proofs of God's oneness are the Ambrosiaster's comments on Romans 1.19, as cited by Peter Lombard in the first book of the *Sentences*, and Anselm's *Proslogion*. The former he follows with enough verbal parallels to indicate a written source; the latter he treats with few parallels, as if from memory rather than the written page. This brings us to the vexing matter of Elias's Aristotelian proofs. Elias claims to be following the authentic Aristotle, but in fact I have not been able to locate one incontrovertible borrowing from any Latin version of the philosopher now available in the *Aristoteles Latinus*. The analogues I have located are mostly from Arab Aristotelians, such as Avicenna, Alfarabi, and Algazel, or their early translators and reworkers, especially Gundissalinus. Such indirect appropriations of the material Aristotle covers in his *De anima* and *Metaphysics* are typical of the intellectual climate of the early thirteenth century. Among British philosophers whose works have appeared in print, Elias seems closest to, although notably less complex than, Robert Kilwardby, who wrote in the second half of the thirteenth century. Given the mountains of philosophical works lost or still in manuscript, it is impossible to argue that Elias had no written source for his material. But his rather vague logic and the parallels noted above are at least consistent with the theory that he studied philosophy as an arts student at Cambridge, or perhaps elsewhere, in the late 1230s or 1240s.[88] This is quite early in the history of

---

[86] For the early study of civil law in Oxford, see R. W. Southern, "Master Vacarius and the Beginning of an English Academic Tradition," in *Medieval Learning and Literature: Essays Presented to R. W. Hunt*, ed. J. J. G. Alexander and M. T. Gibson (Oxford: Clarendon Press, 1976), 257–86; idem, "From Schools to University," in *The Early Oxford Schools*, 8–10, 16–21; Leonard E. Boyle, O.P., "The Beginnings of Legal Studies at Oxford," *Viator* 14 (1983): 107–31; J. L. Barton, "The Study of Civil Law Before 1380," in *The Early Oxford Schools*, 519–30. For early developments at Cambridge, see Hackett, *Original Statutes*, 29–33. For an overview, see Francis de Zulueta and Peter Stein, *The Teaching of Roman Law in England around 1200* (London: Seldon Society, 1990).

[87] For canon law at Oxford, see L. E. Boyle, "Canon Law Before 1380," in *The Early Oxford Schools*, 531–64; for Cambridge, see Hackett, *Original Statutes*, 130–31.

[88] This is a subject of the utmost complexity. For a general orientation, see Martin Grabmann, *I divieti ecclesiastici di Aristotele sotto Innocenzo III e Gregorio IX*, Miscellanea Historiae Pontificiae 5, 7 (Rome: Typis Pontificiae Universitatis Gregorianae, 1941), and the

Latin Aristotelianism,[89] and Elias shows none of the philosophical so-
phistication the study of Averroes and the work of Aquinas and his
contemporaries had brought to the subject by mid-century.

Elias's evidence for the immortality of the human soul comes from the
Bible and a range of pagan authors. Macrobius provides Elias's account
of the vision of Er, as he had provided Philip's summary of what Greek
philosophers had argued concerning the composition of the soul. Bacchus's dismemberment probably derives from Servius's commentary on
Vergil, which Elias would have known well from a career as grammar
master. Elias knows the Hermetic *Asclepius* directly and as it appears
excerpted in Augustine's *City of God*; his account of Seneca's visit to the
tomb of Scipio Africanus comes from the former's *Epistolae morales*.

Elias drew the bulk of his pagan mythology from Remigius of Auxerre's
Commentary on Martianus. In the case of Mercury's caduceus he uses the
Third Vatican Mythographer; his account of Apis may come from the
First Mythographer. But this is a tradition in which authors copied from
each other with the greatest freedom, so until we have modern editions
and some systematic monographs all attributions remain tentative. At the
same time, we should notice that Fulgentius does not figure as a source,
while Elias antedates late medieval mythographic compilations such as
Ridevall's *Fulgentius metaforalis* or the anonymous *Imagines Fulgentii*.

Elias's opening and central conceit come from Martianus Capella,
whom he quotes and explicates at length in his defense of figurative
language. Those explications rely heavily on Remigius's *Commentary*. He
borrows his definition of lying from Augustine's *De mendacio*, perhaps by
way of the *Sentences*. Philip's account of the ideal judge is based on
several passages in John of Salisbury's *Policraticus*. A passage in the same
author's *Metalogicon* probably sharpened Elias's sense of the possibilities
for reworking Martianus's conceit.

Throughout the work, Elias and Philip draw proof texts and stories
from the Bible, especially Psalms, Numbers, and Kings. For the interpretation of those texts they rely on the *glossa ordinaria*. They retell several
stories—most notably the tale of Mercury and Battus—from Ovid's

many works by Fernand van Steenberghen, including *La philosophie au xiiie siècle* (Louvain:
Publications Universitaires; Paris: Béatrice-Nauwelaerts, 1966). For Oxford, the best account
remains D. A. Callus, "Introduction of Aristotelian Learning to Oxford." See also J. M.
Fletcher, "The Faculty of Arts," and J. I. Catto, "Theology and Theologians," in *The Early
Oxford Schools*, 369–99 and 471–517, and an exemplary edition by D. A. Callus and R. W.
Hunt, *Iohannes Blund, Tractatus de anima*, Auctores Britannici Medii Aevi, 2 (London:
British Academy, 1970).

[89] Material from the *libri naturales* is rare before 1250, ubiquitous after. See Bernard G.
Dod, "Aristoteles Latinus," in *The Cambridge History of Later Medieval Philosophy*, ed.
Norman Kretzmann et al. (Cambridge: Cambridge Univ. Press, 1982), 69.

Metamorphoses. But their greatest stock of *exempla* is drawn from Justinus's epitome of Pompeius Trogus's *Philippic Histories* and Valerius Maximus's *Facta et dicta memorabilia*. Valerius must have been one of the authors Elias modeled himself upon, since he cites him with a minimum of verbal alterations or additions. The less convoluted Justinus does not fare so well: Elias elaborates his syntax and frequently moralizes his action, seemingly in an attempt to make Justinus read more like Valerius. Even so, the narratives drawn from the these two authors are among the most straightforward passages in the *Serium senectutis* and contrast strongly with Elias's own syntactically difficult passages of reflection and transition.

While Ovid is the only literary author whom Elias borrows from at length, our author does echo brief passages from Vergil, Horace, Persius, Juvenal, the *Apocolocyntosis* attributed to Seneca, and possibly Petronius. But the *Serium senectutis* does not contain any clear echoes of the *Disticha Catonis* or the other *libri Catoniani*, which we would expect Elias to have been familiar with from his teaching duties.[90] This is perhaps especially surprising in the case of Maximianus's *Elegies*, which would seem to pertain rather directly to Elias's subject matter. But Elias also neglects a far greater treatment of old age, Cicero's *Cato Maior de senectute*. And while there are enough structural and verbal resemblances to suggest that Elias knew the two greatest *prosimetra* of the twelfth-century— Bernardus Silvestris's *Cosmographia* and Alan of Lille's *De planctu Naturae*—there are no direct borrowings from either in the *Serium senectutis*. We can, I think, best make sense of this patchwork of literary borrowings and omissions by viewing Elias of Thriplow as a conscious classicizer, albeit within the limits established by thirteenth-century humanism.

7. Genre

In form, the *Serium senectutis* is what the Middle Ages would have labelled a *prosimetrum*.[91] In the terms of modern genre theory, it is a Menippean satire,[92] although we must heed Joel Relihan's warning

---

[90] For the evolving contents of the *libri Catoniani*, see Hunt, *Teaching and Learning Latin*, 1:66–79, and M. Boas, "De librorum Catonianorum historia atque compositione," *Mnemosyne* 42 (1914): 17–46.

[91] For the medieval origins of this term, see Eduard Norden, *Die Antike Kunstprosa* (Berlin-Leipzig: Teubner, 1918), 756. For critical orientation, Udo Kindermann, *Satyra* (Nuremberg: Carl, 1978), 21–22.

[92] For theoretical accounts of this genre, see Mikhail Bakhtin, *Problems of Dostoevsky's Poetics*, trans. R. W. Rostel ([Ann Arbor]: Ardis, 1973) and Northrop Frye, *Anatomy of Criticism* (Princeton: Princeton Univ. Press, 1957), 309–12. For more historically oriented accounts, see Karl Mras, "Varros Menippeische Satiren und die Philosophie," *Neue*

that this label is modern rather than classical.[93] Its central conceit, style, and contents, as well as form, all betray the fact that Elias has written a work which is not only modeled on classical and medieval exemplars, but seeks to convey meanings in ways similar to those employed by the earlier works. The *Serium senectutis* belongs to the subgenre of Menippean dialogue, of which the outstanding Latin exemplar is Boethius's *Consolation of Philosophy*.[94] It also betrays the modal influence of moralized histories such as Valerius Maximus's *Facta et dicta memorabilia* or John of Salisbury's *Policraticus* in Philip's discussion of divine vengeance on human impiety,[95] and of scholastic philosophy in Elias's proofs for God's unique omnipotence.

How does recognizing the *Serium senectutis* as a Menippean satire contribute to our understanding of the work itself? For as Fowler reminds us: "genres have to do with identifying and communicating rather than with defining and classifying. We identify the genre to interpret the exemplar."[96] In the first instance we should not overlook the practical importance of identifying genre correctly. The *Serium senectutis* lay unknown to literary scholars before Schmidt because Scott's index to the Sloane collection mistakenly registered it as a "Sermon on Old Age."[97] More importantly, recognizing generic affiliation and influences allows us to discover the form and meaning of what must otherwise seem a rather formless and enigmatic work. As we have seen, Beryl Smalley

---

Jahrbücher für Klassische Altertum 33 (1914): 390–420; Joachim Gruber, *Kommentar zu Boethius "De consolatione Philosophiae"* (Berlin and New York: de Gruyter, 1978), 16–19; Jennifer Hall, *Lucian's Satire* (New York: Arno, 1981); Caroline D. Eckhardt, "The Medieval *Prosimetrum* Genre (from Boethius to *Boece*)," *Genre* 16 (1983): 21–38; Joel C. Relihan, "A History of Menippean Satire to A.D. 524" (Ph.D. diss., University of Wisconsin, 1985); Danuta Shanzer, *A Philosophical and Literary Commentary on Martianus Capella's "De nuptiis Philologiae et Mercurii" Book 1* (Berkeley: Univ. of California Press, 1986), 29–44. Eugene P. Kirk, *Menippean Satire: An Annotated Catalogue of Texts and Criticism* (New York: Garland, 1980), covers all periods.

[93] "A History of Menippean Satire," 8–20.

[94] I adopt here Alastair Fowler's distinction between kinds, or historical genres with internal and external characteristics; subgenres, which add further specifications to those of genre; and modes, which retain the internal repertoire of kinds while shedding their external rules. See *Kinds of Literature: An Introduction to the Theory of Genre* (Cambridge, Mass.: Harvard Univ. Press, 1982), 55–56, and more generally chapters 4 and 7. For the dialogue genre in Antiquity, see R. Hirzel, *Der Dialog*, 2 vols. (Leipzig: Hirzel, 1895), and Seth Lerer, *Boethius and Dialogue* (Princeton: Princeton Univ. Press, 1985), 14–93.

[95] See Peter von Moos, *Geschichte als Topik: Das Rhetorische Exemplum von der Antike zur Neuzeit und die "historiae" im "Policraticus" Johann von Salisbury* (Hildesheim and New York: Olms, 1988).

[96] Fowler, *Kinds of Literature*, 38.

[97] Schmidt, "Elias of Thriplow," 366. In fact, the description of the *Serium senectutis* as a "Sermo de senectute" goes back, by way of Sir Hans Sloane's own catalogue, to the earlier catalogue of Edward Bernard. See below, 42–43.

suggested that in his lost *De vita scolarium* Elias adapts the prosimetric form of Boethius to the subject matter of the pseudo-Boethian *De disciplina scolarium*.[98] In the *Serium senectutis*, we might say, he adapts the style and central conceit of Martianus Capella's *Marriage of Mercury and Philology* to the form and *telos* of Boethius's *Consolation*.

With his long periods, his delight in periphrasis, and his frequent use of *rariora*, Elias writes in the Asiatic tradition of which Martianus was one of the chief exemplars for the Latin Middle Ages. Indeed, we may properly speak of a Menippean lexicon at play in the *Serium senectutis*. Again and again one comes across words which do not appear in the standard dictionaries but find their place in the index verborum to any edition of Martianus. For example, three times in the course of his work Elias plays variations on Horace's claim (*Sermones* 1.7.3) that Persius's vengeance on the outlaw Rupilius Rex was "known to every bleary-eyed man and barber in town" (*omnibus et lippis notum et tonsoribus*). One variation involves "the bleary-eyed and those unable to see out of one eye" (*lippis non minus quam luscis lumine cecutientibus*). Elias found the word in Martianus Capella (1.3 [2.21–22]), who writes of "poets who followed the Oeagrian lyre player and the sweet-spoken old age of the blind Maeonian" (*poetae ... praecipue Oeagrium citharistam secuti caecutientisque Maeonii suaviloquam senectutem*). And from Martianus, the word's lineage stretches back to Varro's *Menippeae* and Apuleius's *Florida*.[99]

Elias concerned himself with more than just Martianus's style. The whole first half of the *Serium senectutis* should be read as a defense of literary meaning and figurative expression. That defense culminates in book 4, where Elias saves first a series of biblical verses and then four passages in Martianus's *De nuptiis* from the superficial appearance of blasphemy or absurdity by evoking standard allegorical readings from the *Glossa ordinaria* and Remigius of Auxerre's *Commentary*, respectively. Unlike fourteenth-century authors such as Pierre Bersuire or Smalley's classicizing friars, Elias does not claim any specifically Christian sense for his pagan author Martianus.[100] But his juxtaposition of biblical and

---

[98] *English Friars*, 351.

[99] For documentation, see the *Thesaurus linguae Latinae*, s.v. Elias also uses the word in his *Semidiales*, where according to Flacius, he wrote of the pope viewing the fairness of the law with *oculo ... caecutienti* (*Catalogus testium ueritatis*, 448).

[100] For examples, see Smalley, *English Friars*, passim, and A. J. Minnis and A. B. Scott, with David Wallace, eds., *Medieval Literary Theory and Criticism c. 1100–c. 1375: The Commentary Tradition*, revised ed. (Oxford: Clarendon Press, 1991), 314–72. Early in the twelfth century, Conrad of Hirsau had used Judges 9.8 ("The trees went to anoint a king over them: and they said to the olive tree: Reign thou over us") to justify the use of allegory in secular works, and he even argued briefly for the presence of a fourfold sense in such secular allegory (Minnis and Scott, *Medieval Literary Theory*, 45–48). But neither he nor any

classical allegoresis is intellectually striking and rhetorically effective. While Elias's immediate target is the literal minded Philip, it is clear that he addresses all those who would deny the significance of figurative expressions when he says:

> You seem unafraid ... to vituperate the salutary metaphorical language of Solomon, who was confirmed in the highest spiritual wisdom. Indeed, as can be inferred plainly from your vociferous ravings, scarcely anything could be more absurd or discordant ... than for the Bride to be coupled in marriage with the Groom, and the Church married to the Lamb, or for the Bride to long to be solaced by the kiss of her spouse's mouth (4.85–94).

If Elias begins his defense of figurative expression with examples of biblical allegoresis, he ends it with Remigius's account of the particularly obscure passage which follows Philology's drink from the cup of immortality in book 2 of Martianus's *De nuptiis*. Ultimately, Elias's explication of the "sober ... sense" hidden within Martianus's fiction constitutes his main defense of his own use of figurative expression and fictional narrative.

Elias is all the more eager to defend the significance of Martianus's fiction because it was from Martianus that Elias drew his central conceit of a marriage between mind (Philology) and tongue (Mercury). Elias's first metrum speaks of the god and his mortal bride, but from his first *prosa* on Elias literalizes Martianus's metaphor by speaking of a bond between the wise man's thoughts and words *quo bene conveniant pectus et oris opus*. Pamela Gradon has shown that such literalization of allegory is typical of late medieval literature.[101] At the same time that Elias literalizes Martianus's conceit he also discreetly Christianizes it, so that early in the second *prosa* of his first book he can map out the course his entire treatment will take:

> I reckon that for any rational man the marriage of mind and tongue is no less useful and expedient than any other marriage. What is more, the conjugal confederation of such a well-matched couple leads by a direct route to the tabernacle of the supreme Governor and the infinite dwelling of incircumscribable celsitude (1.100–104).

This theme culminates in Philip's claim, when he accepts Elias's proofs, that

---

other twelfth- or early thirteenth-century writer I am aware of develops this claim at any length or makes the finding of explicitly Christian meanings in secular literature a regular critical practice.

[101] *Form and Style in Early English Literature* (London: Methuen, 1971), chap. 6: "Mannerism and Renaissance."

As I now see for the first time as a result of your edifying discourse, no man who breathes under the sun can love virtue or worship the true godhead purely, unless he constantly praises this matrimonial contract with unchanging will and true emotion (12.69–77).

But to get as far as Elias's proofs for God's omnipotence we must consider his debt to Boethius. Like Bernardus Silvestris and Alan of Lille in the twelfth century, Elias follows Boethius in maintaining a regular alternation between verse and prose. But Elias is unable to rival Boethius's metrical dexterity, so he sticks to the hexameters and elegiac couplets he would have known best. Nor can Elias rival the complex counterpoint of theme and image summarized and anticipated which Boethius achieves in his meters. Elias may place his meters at the beginnings of books, but they serve almost solely to recapitulate earlier themes in abstract and not always memorable moral terms. Like Boethius, Elias organized his satire as a dialogue, but he gives himself the better part of the argument, rather as if Boethius had written the *Consolation* from Philosophy's point of view. Anna Crabbe has written well of the process of Platonic *anamnesis* by which Boethius achieves his reconversion to a properly philosophic attitude towards misfortune.[102] There is no such process here: Philip functions rather baldly as a pupil to be educated, even a straight man to draw out Elias's best lines, before capitulating quite suddenly at the end.

But the overall movement of the two works is unmistakably similar. In working out his dialectic with Lady Philosophy, Boethius moves from a solipsistic imprisonment in error to an awareness of his freedom to act in the sight of God. Elias's implied dialectic starts from Philip's stories of human impiety and misplaced belief in a plurality of gods, and ends with Elias's proofs of the immortality of the soul and the unique oneness of the Trinity. Philosophy's shift from lighter to stronger medicines finds its echo in Elias's switch from figurative language to the technical terms of canon law and scholastic philosophy midway through the *Serium senectutis*. The similarity of their ends clinches the resemblance between the two works. Book 5 of the *Consolation* is Boethius's creative reworking of the whole body of thought surrounding Aristotle's discussion of future contingents in chapter 9 of *De interpretatione*. No work is more important to our understanding of this book than Boethius's own commentary on the *De interpretatione*.[103] Elias uses several proofs to establish God's

---

[102] "Literary Design in the *De consolatione Philosophae*," in *Boethius: His Life, Thought and Influence*, ed. Margaret Gibson (Oxford: Blackwell, 1981), 258–59.

[103] Boethius, *Second Commentary on the "De interpretatione*," in *Anicii Manlii Severini Boethiii Commentarii in librum Aristotelis "ΠΕΡΙ ΕΡΜΗΝΕΙΑΣ*," ed. C. Meiser (Leipzig: Teubner, 1880), 2:186–249.

unique omnipotence, but he clearly showcases arguments derived from Aristotle's *Physics* and *Metaphysics*, the so-called *libri naturales*, which came into general circulation in Europe in the first half of the thirteenth century. In Elias's choice of a source in the new Aristotle, rather than the old logic which Boethius had done so much to transmit, we see the literary and philosophic spirit of the Roman alive in the Englishman. Here, surely, we find startling confirmation of T. S. Eliot's claim that "not only the best, but the most individual parts of [a poet's] work may be those in which the dead poets, his ancestors, assert their immortality most vigorously."[104]

What about Eliot's related claim that, "The existing order [of literature] is complete before the new work arrives; for order to persist after the supervention of novelty, the *whole* existing order must be, if ever so slightly, altered; and so the relations, proportions, values of each work of art toward the whole are readjusted"?[105] Having read Elias, we see that Martianus Capella was still, in the thirteenth century, a rallying point for those seeking a marriage between technical knowledge and literary style as defined by the grammatical tradition.[106] We see Boethius valued primarily for the *telos* of his *Consolation*, not the early books which we tend to favor. We also see Boethius and Martianus as representatives of antiquity (*venerata vetustas*, to use Elias's term) valued above the Menippean satirists of the twelfth century. But this Martianus, so far from being a practicing theurgist, as modern scholars have argued,[107] is a presumptive Christian with an antiquarian interest in the pagan past (4.401–3). Nor can one easily imagine Elias espousing an ironic account of a benighted narrator and deficient Philosophy in Boethius. Both Elias and Philip make light of the former's advanced age (an aspect of the carnivalization Bakhtin writes of), but there is every reason to believe that Elias was in fact an old man when he wrote the *Serium senectutis*. Elias would have ridiculed any attempt to discover an ironic disparity between author and narrator in his own work or in Boethius's. We may even see Elias's frequent echoes of Horace, Persius, and Juvenal as an attempt to heal the breach between Menippean satire and moralizing verse satire in Latin—to see a community of purpose and values between what seem to us antithetical traditions.[108]

---

[104] "Tradition and the Individual Talent," in *The Sacred Wood*, 3d ed. (London: Methuen, 1932), 48.

[105] Eliot, "Tradition," 50.

[106] For this theme, see Gabriel Nuchelmans, "Philologia et son mariage avec Mercure jusq'à la fin du xiie siècle," *Latomus* 16 (1957): 84–107.

[107] See Shanzer, *A Philosophical and Literary Commentary on Martianus Capella*, 21–28.

[108] See Relihan, "Menippean Satire," chap. 1, for a judicious affirmation of this antithesis

Elias also helps us see the modal influence of Menippean satire where we may not have seen it before, in John of Salisbury's *Policraticus* and *Metalogicon*. John's verses are quoted from the classical authors and are not original compositions, but we remember that John read Petronius and tells the Milesian tale of the Widow of Ephesus from the *Satyrica*. Given the strong modal influence of tales from ancient history and literature on the first half of the *Serium senectutis*, we may now suggest that the similar subject matter of the *Policraticus* in particular places that work in the class, for which Petronius is an exemplar, of Menippean satires which use verse incidentally and not as a regular formal feature.[109]

It should, however, be noted that even with Elias's defense of the immortality of the human soul and of God's unique omnipotence, the *Serium senectutis* does not contain the themes which Mras and other scholars have isolated in the Menippean satire of the ancient world. Here we find no heavenly journey, no council of the gods, no journey to the underworld, no thirteenth labor of Hercules, no meeting with the muses, no ὄνος λύρας.[110] But we do find the Menippean juxtaposition of the serious and ludicrous,[111] although the latter takes the form of mockery or verbal and stylistic extravagance rather than genuine wit. And this juxtaposition, visible also in the *Petronius rediuiuus* and what survives of the *De vita scolarium*,[112] is central to the ethos and aesthetic of the *Serium senectutis*.

We may conclude this section by noting the modal influence on the *Serium senectutis* of one of the thirteenth century's most distinctive liter-

---

which also questions some of the assumptions upon which it has traditionally been based.

[109] However, we may note that particularly in the *excerpta vulgaria* the medieval text of the *Satyrica* contained a much higher percentage of verse than the modern text, which conflates O (the *excerpta vulgaria*), L and H. In any case, the advantage of Fowler's distinction between genres and modes is that it allows us to preserve generic boundaries while discussing literary influences which work across those boundaries. In this manner, we can escape the bind of Shanzer, who purchases a bracingly rigorous definition of the Menippean genre at the cost of peremptorily dismissing Petronius's *Satyrica* as "a satyric novel rather than a Menippean satire" (*A Philosophical and Literary Commentary on Martianus Capella*, 31).

[110] "Varros Menippeische Satiren," 393–95; Shanzer, *A Philosophical and Literary Commentary on Martianus Capella*, 33–41.

[111] For classical testimony to this mixture, see the remarks attributed to Varro by Cicero: "et tamen in illis veteribus nostris, quae Menippum imitati non interpretati quadam hilaritate conspersimus, multa admixta ex intima philosophia, multa dicta dialectice, quae quo facilius minus docti intellegerent, iucunditate quadam ad legendum invitati; in laudationibus, in his ipsis antiquitatum prooemiis philosophiae more scribere voluimus, si modo consecuti sumus" (*Academica* 1.8 [ed. Plasberg, 4.10–17], cited by Shanzer, *A Philosophical and Literary Commentary on Martianus Capella*, 30).

[112] See Whethamstede's *tabula* s.v. *fabula*: "Uaria fabularum ludicra et interdum commixta seriosa" (British Library, MS Arundel 11, 172ᵛ).

ary developments, the *compilatio*.[113] As we have seen in surveying the work's contents, Elias justifies his use of other men's arguments for the existence of one God by claiming to have embellished them stylistically. He might also have defended his procedure by pointing out that he had done his readers a service by assembling excerpts from such a wide range of sources under clearly defined moral headings. Ringstede found the historical material assembled in the lost *Contra nobilitatem inanem* and *De vita scolarium* a useful source of classical material for his Wisdom commentary. But Parkes reminds us that *compilatio* served "both as a form of writing and as a means of making material easily accessible."[114] Compilation was Elias's method for composing a Menippean satire.

8. Language and Style

The *Serium senectutis* contains fifteen *metra* or verse passages: one at the beginning of each book, with an extra *metrum* in both the first and last books. The longest meters are those which begin and end the work; they are each twenty-eight lines in length. The shortest meter is the second one in book 1, which is four lines in length. Besides the latter, the work contains seven meters which are between twelve and sixteen lines long, and seven meters which are between twenty-two and twenty-eight lines long. Nine meters (numbers 1–6, 8–9) are written in elegiac couplets, while six (numbers 7, 10–13.2) are written in hexameters. It is worth noting these formal symmetries at the outset, because these fifteen meters may be a conspicuous element in the work's form, but they have little effect on its deeper structure. Elias was, at heart, a writer of prose.

In downplaying the importance of verse in his prosimetrum, Elias followed the lead of Martianus Capella. Here we will find none of the metric virtuosity of Boethius or Alan of Lille, none of their complex interplay between language, image, and argument. Once his work is underway, Elias uses his meters strictly to summarize points already made in the discursive prose passages. As we have seen, he restricts himself to elegiac couplets and hexameters. One might glorify this as a classicizer's conscious rejection of accentual meters, but it would be safer to see here a prudent resolve on Elias's part to stick to the two meters he

---

[113] M. B. Parkes, "The Influence of the Concepts of *Ordinatio* and *Compilatio* on the Development of the Book," in *Medieval Learning and Literature*, 127–30; A. J. Minnis, *Medieval Theory of Authorship: Scholastic Literary Attitudes in the Later Middle Ages* (London: Scolar, 1984), 191–210; Neil Hathaway, "*Compilatio*: From Plagiarism to Compiling," *Viator* 20 (1989): 19–44.

[114] "*Ordinatio* and *Compilatio*," 127.

would have known best from his duties as grammar master. Indeed, all the *metra* in hexameters contain an even number of lines and are, in fact, written for the most part as couplets. Elias no doubt intended his transition from couplets to hexameters to mark the higher seriousness of the work's second half, but the effect he achieves falls short of this intent.

The most conspicuous characteristics of Elias's verses are heavy alliteration and word play. He probably intended the alliteration to tie together verses which are highly paratactic and do not so much flow as erupt in short, staccato bursts. The opening lines of the *Serium senectutis* set the tone for the work as a whole:

> Dum variat studiosus homo sacra coniugiorum
>   ffedera felici federe crebro caret,
> Et superum sacra sponte loquax hominumque reuelat;
>   Copula fine fide federibus verata
> Cum Ioue Iunonem, claudum cum Cipride fabrum
>   Federat, Abderitem copulat atque Team.

The lack of closure in the second couplet is a striking violation of both the classical norm and Elias's usual practice, but it is repeated in the fourth couplet of this same *metrum*. The triple alliteration on *s* and *f* accords with the precepts for *paranomeon* given by Matthew of Vendôme, as the word play (*ffedera, federe, federibus, federat*) does with those for *paronomasia*.[115] In at least one line later in the work, Elias comes close to achieving complete alliteration: *Vix validus volet in viciis vir viuere vanis* (9.7). The meter which this comes from, that prefixed to book 9, also shows the highest density of *paronomasia*; as the final meter in elegiac couplets it is doubtless meant as a bravura showpiece. But little has changed when we arrive at the hexameters which end the work:

> Quam bene iocundum fuerit retro quam sit amenum
> Nunc eciam, scius expertis iam sencio factus,
> Sponte sua sibi concordes habitare sodales,
> Longius et rixas viciumque repellere licis,
> Et sibi sensate vitam solidare quietis
> Vitales variando vices dumtaxat in vnum.

It is as a writer of prose that Elias comes into his own. Concerned with stylistic elaboration and metrical exigency, Elias uses rare words only infrequently in his meters, but he festoons his prose with them. He is

---

[115] *Ars versificatoria* 3.9–10, ed. Edmond Faral, in *Les arts poétiques du xii⁰ et du xiii⁰ siècle* (Paris: Champion, 1924), 169–70. For excessive alliteration and word play as stylistic vices, see Geoffrey of Vinsauf, *Poetria nova* 1928–35 (ed. Faral).

especially fond of a series of adverbs in *-iter* which may be his own coinages: *cachinnabiliter, derisibiliter, diouolariter, horripilaliter, subsannabiliter*, and the like.[116] Both Elias and Philip sprinkle these derisive adverbs liberally through their speeches. By applying them to stories of pagan impiety and Jewish apostasy, Elias and Philip sound a note of learned, Christian detachment. When they hurl them at each other, they achieve at least a faint echo of Bakhtinian carnivalization, although the basis of their humor is mockery rather than wit. Cumulatively, Elias uses these adverbs and their cognates to define a negative pole of folly and futility antithetical to his moral and intellectual ideal of the man who thinks and acts sensibly (*sensatus, sensate*).

Elias is also fond of creating compound verbs beginning with *con-, pre-* and *re-*. Rarely do they mean anything different from the simple verb. Notice also the many adjectives ending in *-iuum*, such as *abanimatiuum* (3.58), *derogatiuum* (4.69), *incitatiuum* (3.753, 4.20, 8.81–82), and *subsecutiuum* (3.25).[117] He creates a range of phrases using *ad* to indicate purpose or use: *ad vsum, ad genituram, ad habundans, ad bene conveniens*. This practice derives from the classical *ad* plus gerund (*gratias ad exibendas*); its strangest fruit is the seemingly adverbial *ad expediens*.

Elias uses medieval forms of classical words (*affectiuus, capesco, capio, conferueo, dissidium, frustratim, itero, lacesco, mendositas, merito, optate, protensus, quamplures, ridiculosus/-e, sanccio, verisimillime*), words which merged or became commonly confused in medieval Latin (*diduco/deduco, endelichia/entelechia, oppugno/expugno, perpropere/prepropere, vernaliter/verniliter*), and words which he himself seems to have elided together or confused (*mansuesco/consuesco, facilitas/vacillitas* [not attested, from *vacillo*]). In a few cases (*mastigo/mastico, paruiloquium/prauiloquium*) it is hard to tell whether one is dealing with distinct words, confusion on the part of the author, or scribal error.

We will also find alliteration and *paronomasia* in the prose passages. A particular variation of the latter involves ringing the changes on personal pronouns: *meo me michi* (12.46), *tu tibi tuis* (1.66–67), *suis se sibi* (2.304–5). Other examples are sprinkled throughout the work: *cauillator arte cauillatoria* (3.42), *Gallos gallorum* (3.528), *rurali rusticus ... rustice vagaretur in agro* (7.40–41), *diuersis diuersorum philosophicis in exerciciis philosophorum* (8.36–37), *molaque molestiarum molestato* (12.44). Nor is alliteration hard to find: *res ridiculosissima sit senes interesse scurrilitatibus, iocarive iuueniliter in thalamis, vanitatibusue vacare veneriis* (1.40–41), *te solum supine scium censeas*

---

[116] See the *index verborum* for documentation of these and other forms.

[117] On the use of adjectives in *-iuus*, see Matthew of Vendôme, *Ars versificatoria* 2.24 (ed. Faral, 158–59).

(2.21), *nemo nempe natus sub sole* (2.353), *est triuialiter trita de transmissis* (7.54).

One of the implicit rules of Elias's prose is to avoid vowels in hiatus at any cost, sometimes including sense, as a number of passages in the commentary will testify.[118] This prohibition extends to the elision of final *-um*: Elias never allows the juxtaposition, common elsewhere, of *-um est*. Note likewise the omission of *est/esse* because of a proliferation of vowels and nasals at word junctures in *cui templum circa litus cocodrillorum Libies et in monte consecratum* (10.231–32). Only in the case of *veritate enunciator* (1.126) is there a good likelihood that the author himself allowed vowel hiatus.

It is not at all surprising, given Elias's probable career as a grammar master, that he betrays a familiarity with the technical language of *grammatica*. The grammatical terms he uses in their technical sense are *antonomasice, figurate,* and *verbalis/-iter*.[119] More frequently, he uses grammatical terms in broader or transferred senses: *anomale, coniunctiuus, continuatiuus, copulatiuus, defectiuus, finalitas, inclinatiuus, infinitiuus, optatiue, retransitiue, subiunctiuus, transitiuus,* and *zinzugia*. To these, we should add the rhetorical terms *positio* and *prediuido*.

Elias also betrays a lesser familiarity with legal language, which sorts well with his extended discussion of marriage law at the center of the *Serium senectutis*. Legal terms and phrases include *cognicionaliter, condempnabilis, coniunctim disiunctimve, indistincte,* and *reproducere*. But Elias betrays the limits of his legal learning by using the grammatical term *transitiuus* ("transitive") with a legal sense ("transferable") at 6.67. And while Elias shows a knowledge of the technical vocabularies of logic and theology when discussing material drawn from those disciplines, he rarely uses them elsewhere in the work.

Elias is a master of circumlocution and the many ways in which one may say the same thing more than once (*interpretatio, expolitio*).[120] Hence the proliferation of adjectives and adverbs in phrases articulated by the construction *ve ... ve*. But at times the result is simple pleonasm: *occisus occumberet* (3.405), *totam ... per vniuersitatem* (3.541–42), *sequitur ... subsequenter* (4.228), *male felices et infausti* (7.93). Furthermore, Elias tends to repeat himself. He repeats Persius's *in udo* and the Horatian *omnibus et lippis notum et tonsoribus* more than once; he repeats his beloved adverbs in *-iter* constantly; he repeats his seasonal allegory of Vulcan, Juno, and Saturn (1.80–84 and 4.270–77); he tends to narrate the

---

[118] For hiatus as a stylistic vice, see Geoffrey of Vinsauf, *Poetria nova* 1923–27 (ed. Faral).
[119] Again, consult the *index verborum* for forms and documentation.
[120] Geoffrey of Vinsauf, *Poetria nova* 1173–75, 1244–51, 1301–46.

same event several times in telling any given story. Leonidas occupies the pass at Thermopylae twice within ten lines (3.215–17, 224–27). Elias even tells several stories, most notably the story of Mercury and Battus, more than once.

Elias has two fairly distinct prose styles. He uses his more ornate style in the bridge passages at the beginning and end of books, where he and Philip exchange charges and counter charges, introduce and summarize their arguments, or effect transitions from one stage of an argument to another.[121] Besides the meters, these are about the only passages in the *Serium senectutis* which are not written from any outside sources, and so they may be called exercises in free composition. These passages are often difficult to understand, and their sense can at times be inferred only from the discursive arguments which lead up to or flow out of them. Elias uses his relatively straightforward style for narration, especially for the many *exempla* he has drawn from Old Testament and classical sources. Elias does not hesitate to recast even his biblical stories in this relatively plain style, which is, in fact, far more ornate than Jerome's biblical Latin. This makes his unwillingness to alter the style of Valerius Maximus all the more remarkable. In fact, Valerius was probably one of the primary models for this plain narrative style, as Martianus Capella was for the difficult style of the reflective passages.

We can best see how ornate even this plain style is if we compare Elias's description of the temple at Delphi with its source in Justinus. According to Justinus,

> Templum autem Apollinis Delphis positum est in monte Parnasso, in rupe undique concurrentes in eo saxo consedere. Atque ita templum et civitatem non muri, sed praecipitia, nec manu facta, sed naturalia praesidia defendunt, prorsus ut incertum sit, utrum munimentum loci an maiestas dei plus hic admirationis habeat. Media saxi rupes in formam theatri recessit. Quamobrem et hominum clamor et si quando accidit turbarum sonus, personantibus et resonantibus inter se rupibus multiplex audiri ampliorque quam editur resonare solet. Quae res maiorem maiestatis terrorem ignaris rei et admirationem stupentibus plerumque adfert.[122]

---

[121] R. W. Hunt draws attention to similar "highflown language" in the transitional passages of works by the fourteenth-century Oxford grammarian Richard of Hambury. See "Oxford Grammar Masters in the Middle Ages," in *The History of Grammar in the Middle Ages*, 177.

[122] M. Iunianus Iustinus, *Epitoma historiarum Philippicarum Pompei Trogi*, 24.6.6–8, ed. Otto Seel (Stuttgart: Teubner, 1972), 197.21ff. I have altered Seel's edition in a few particulars to match the text Elias used.

This is what Elias makes of the account (3.563–77). My italics mark his additions to Justinus:

> Est autem, *sicut (qui magna de magnis fari consueuere) perhibent poete,* templum Delfis Parnasii montis in rupe situm sic Appollinis. Rupes vndique concurrentes in eo saxo conueniunt; sic templum ciuitatemque non muri *manualiter facti* sed precipicia, non artificialia sed naturalia, *murorumque vices supplendo, pro muris ciues et templum ciuitatemque* defendunt, quo sit *uel esse videatur* prorsus incertum munimentumue loci maiestasue *potestatiua* Delii *maioris* sibi fit admiracionis excitatiuum. Media quidem saxi rupes in theatri *similitudinem* formamque cedit, quo fit ut et hominum clamor (et si quando solus acciderit aduenticius, *com*personantibus inter se *con*resonantibusque rupibus audiri videatur multiplicatus) amplior quam *sicut* editur resonare senciatur. Que res terrorem maiestatis *multo* maiorem rei *racionem perfunctorie* considerantibus admiracionemque frequencius incutere solet *insolencia* consternatis.

No doubt Elias is led into a few excesses (*compersonantibus ... conresonantibusque*) by the temptation, arising from his subject, to create a thoroughly conventional echo effect. But notice the opening appeal to the authority of poetry; the *paronomasia* involving forms of *murus*; and the attempt to ornament Justinus's account of the town's natural defenses, which crashes down in the bald repetition of *templum ciuitatemque*. As he does elsewhere, Elias elaborates the copula into putative gradations of reality and appearance: *quo sit uel esse videatur.* His claim that these defenses were *admiracionis excitatiuum* uses a construction (adjective in *-iuum* with genitive object) he is fond of elsewhere. All through the passage we find *interpretatio* (*in theatri similitudinem formamque*) and pleonasm (*frequencius ... solet*).

Perhaps the one salient characteristic of Elias's style which this passage does not illustrate is his fondness for *hyperbaton*, the separation of nouns and their attributes within sentences.[123] Examples, chosen almost at random, would include: *talibus tamque vanis temperare de hinc de racione deberes a deliramentis* (1.37–38), *post tales talium reprobaciones de facto taliter in factoue menciencium* (2.61–62), *Uetustas enim, deorum derisorie delirans ridiculis in aduencionibus commenticiorum* (4.403–4), *subleuatus ab eo suum suo duplicauerat Helyas in Heliseo spiritum* (10.121–22), and *sodales sana sane conuiuunt in sodalitate* (13.49). Elias intended this to increase the suspense or tension of his periods and create in his readers a pleasure derived from resolving difficulties, but his practice tested the mettle of medieval

---

[123] For *hyperbaton,* see Geoffrey of Vinsauf, *Poetria nova* 1051–60.

scribes and continues to test the limits of modern punctuation and comprehension.

A particularly vexing, but representative, example occurs at 3.164–67:

> Uerum suas [suo suas *S*], ut (in tali casu sponte circumscribilis et errabunda) coniectabat antiquitas, arbitrio numinis ulciscente Iouialis iniurias, temeritate sacrilega sic transmissus vi [in *S*] tempestatis totus arenarum molibus letaliter oppressus obiter interiit exercitus.

The complexity of this sentence results first from Elias's placement of one parenthesis (*in tali casu ... errabunda*) within another (*ut ... coniectabat antiquitas*) and secondly from a welter of ablative constructions. One could not blame the scribe(s) if they found this sentence rough going, and it is clearly corrupt as it stands in the manuscript. My second emendation, of *in* to *vi*, is necessary and obvious. However, the deletion of *suo* before *suas* is fraught with difficulty. For *suo suas* is just the sort of *paronomasia* in which Elias indulges elsewhere, and one might take *suo* as modifying *arbitrio* just as *suas* surely modifies *iniurias*. But the possessive *numinis ... Iouialis* renders either *suo* or *suas* not only unnecessary but unacceptable. Perhaps we should emend *suo* to *sua* and take it as modifying *sponte*. In that case we would have one possessive adjective modifying a noun within the double parenthesis *ut ... coniectabat antiquitas* and one modifying a noun outside it. If this is what Elias wrote, then he has allowed adjectives to float almost completely clear of the nouns they modify. Even so, I would hesitate to rule *sua suas* out, were it not that it creates a jingling assonance which does not sound like the sort of thing Elias might have written.

While Elias's difficult style does employ some elements of the pre-conquest Anglo-Latin hermeneutic style, it does not descend directly from the style cultivated by Aldhelm and his followers.[124] Elias does share with that style a fondness for rare adverbs,[125] alliteration,[126] interlaced word order,[127] and for rewriting more plainly worded sources.[128] But Elias displays no fondness for the *cursus*, either the *tardus* or the *velox* beloved of Aldhelm and his followers.[129] My own study of the cadences

---

[124] For the history of the hermeneutic style through the tenth century, see Michael Lapidge, "The Hermeneutic Style in Tenth-Century Anglo-Latin Literature," *Anglo-Saxon England* 4 (1975): 67–111, and Michael Winterbottom, "Aldhelm's Prose Style and Its Origins," *Anglo-Saxon England* 6 (1977): 39–76.

[125] Lapidge, "Hermeneutic Style," 94, 98–99.

[126] Winterbottom, "Aldhelm's Prose Style," 41, 49 and n. 3.

[127] Winterbottom, "Aldhelm's Prose Style," 50–52.

[128] Winterbottom, "Aldhelm's Prose Style," 45–46.

[129] Winterbottom, "Aldhelm's Prose Style," 71–73.

in the *Serium senectutis* shows that the various forms of the *cursus* occur almost exactly as often as we would expect them to by pure chance. Putting my tally of the cadences for the first 123 periods in the *Serium senectutis* in the form employed by Tore Janson,[130] we get the following results:

	Observed	Expected	$(o-e)^2/e$
pp4p	7	5	.40
p4pp	6	5	.20
p3p	6	6	0
other 2–5	81	84	.09
sum	100	100	.69
1 and $\geq$ 6	23		
sum total	123		

x^2 for 0.05 probability = 7.81

Furthermore, Elias's long sentences lack the tight structure of Aldhelm's,[131] he does not employ Graecisms among his *rariora*,[132] and in elaborating his periods he tends towards qualification or generalization rather than the vivid and detailed thematic expansion or stylistic variation of the earlier tradition.[133]

9. The Manuscript

London, British Library, Sloane 441[134]

Collation: 1 (modern). i[16-1]. ii[16]. iii[16]. iv[16]. v[16]. vi[16]. vii[16-1]. 2 (1 old and 1 modern). Catchwords visible on 15[v], 31[v], 47[v] (partially), 63[v], 95[v].

---

[130] In *Prose Rhythm in Medieval Latin from the 9th to the 13th Century* (Stockholm: Almqvist and Wiksell, 1975).

[131] Winterbottom, "Aldhelm's Prose Style," 40–41.

[132] Lapidge, "Hermeneutic Style," 67–68, 79–80, 82, 86–90, 93–94, 97, 100. For the study of Graecisms in the thirteenth century, see Hunt, *The Teaching of Latin*, 1:289–368.

[133] Winterbottom, "Aldhelm's Prose Style," 41–46, 74–75.

[134] The unpublished *Catalogus librorum manuscriptorum bibliothecae Sloanianae* (1837–40) available in the Students' Room of the British Library is worth quoting on this manuscript and the first of the works it contains:
Codex, partim chartaceus, partim membranaceus, in 8vo. minori, ff. 110, sec. xv nitide exaratus; quondam Francisci Bernard, 56.
1. "Helie Rubei Tripolawensis" [Triplow in com. Cantab.] "Serium Senectutis," libris constans tredecim, sermone partim legato, partim soluto, compositis.

Paper (no watermarks) with parchment leaves on the outside and inside of each quire, the smooth side of the parchment facing towards the quire. Paper: 150 X 95 mm.; parchment up to 5 mm. less vertical.

Red capitals throughout, with book or chapter headings rubricated, except for headings to books 1–5 of the *Serium senectutis*, which are in brown ink framed by red lines. Initials at the beginnings of new paragraphs or sections are also rubricated. Secondary headings, such as capitals at the beginnings of sentences or lines of verse, highlighted by yellow-brown wash.

Binding twentieth century.

(1)   1^r–61^v. Elias Rubeus of Thriplow, *Serium senectutis*. 25–30 lines per page; text in one column 95/105 X 65mm. Writing above top line, 7^v–15^r, 18^v–30^v, 48^{r-v}, 52^v–59^r, 60^v–61^r; elsewhere below. Fol. 1^r, initial D in red, decorated with leaves (= 10 lines of text).

Explicit: Explicit Serium senectutis Helye Rubei Tripolawensis per ffratrem Bartholomeum Texerii ordinis predicatorum, Degentem pro eo tempore Brechonie eiusdem ordinis Conuentu.[135]

(2)   62^v–71^v. Pseudo-Dionysius, *De mystica theologia* in the translation of John the Scot, with Eriugena's Prologue (62^v) and list of chapter titles (63^r). Text (100 X 35 mm.) and interlinear glosses flanked by two columns of commentary (100 X 18 mm.), except fol. 63^{r-v}, which has only one column of commentary.[136]

(3)   72^r–76^r. Pseudo-Dionysius, *Epistola de obscuratione solis in morte Christi ad Policarpum Episcopum Smyrneorum* (Letter 7) in Eriugena's translation. Layout similar to (2), but with columns for commentary left empty.[137]

---

[135] For Texerii, see Thomas Kaepelli, O.P., *Scriptores Ordinis Praedicatorum Medii Aevi*, 3 vols. (Rome: ad S. Sabinae, 1970), 1:169–71; Jacobus Quetif and Jacobus Echard, *Scriptores Ordinis Praedicatorum*, 2 vols. (Paris, 1719–21; repr. Turin: Botega d'Erasmo, 1961), 1:776–77; R. P. Mortier, *Histoire des maîtres généraux de l'ordre des Frères Prêcheurs*, 8 vols. (Paris: Picard, 1903–20), 4:141–335.

[136] For the text of this translation, see Philippe Chevallier, O.S.B., ed., *Dionysiaca: Recueil donnant l'ensemble des traductions latines des ouvrages attribués au Denys de l'Aréopage*, 2 vols. (Paris: Desclée, de Brouwer, 1937–49), 1:565ff.; for the translator, Gabriel Thery, "Scot Érigène traducteur de Denys," *Bulletin du Cange* 6 (1931): 185–278. Also, H. F. Dondaine, O.P., *Le corpus dionysien de l'université de Paris au XIIIe siècle* (Rome: Edizioni di Storia e Letteratura, 1953); David Luscombe, "Some Examples of the Use Made of the Works of the Pseudo-Dionysius by University Teachers in the Later Middle Ages," in *The Universities in the Late Middle Ages*, ed. Jozef Ijsewijn and Jacques Paquet (Louvain: Louvain Univ. Press, 1978), 228–41; idem, "The Reception of the Writings of Denis the Pseudo-Areopagite into England," in *Tradition and Change: Essays in Honour of Marjorie Chibnall*, ed. Diana Greenway, Christopher Holdsworth, and Jane Sayers (Cambridge: Cambridge Univ. Press, 1985), 115–43.

[137] Chevallier, *Dionysiaca*, 2:1482ff.

(4)   76^r–79^r. Pseudo-Dionysius, *Libellus de Seraphin*, a collection of extracts from *De ecclesiastica hierarchia*, chapters 4–6, in Eriugena's translation. Text and commentary deployed as in (2).[138]

(5)   80^v–110^v. Fulgentius, *Mitologiae*, with a summary of books and chapters on fol. 80^r. Text only, 102 X 65/70 mm.

Sloane 441 is written in Secretary throughout, but in a hierarchy of three gradations: a bastard Secretary book hand for the text of Ps.-Dionysius, a Secretary book hand for the texts of Elias and Fulgentius, and a glossing hand for the commentaries on Ps.-Dionysius.[139] For his copy of the *Serium senectutis*, Texerii uses an informal Secretary hand, upright and with a minimum of splay. He clearly meant his script to be intelligible but easy to write: he rarely attempts any calligraphic elaboration of individual letters, but he distinguishes precisely between the various letters formed with minims.

With the exception of a more current Secretary hand which appears on the top of fol. 85^v and completes the Fulgentius, the whole volume forms a unit. As the rubrics share a characteristic curved *p* with the text script, it would be sensible to conclude that Texerii wrote the entire volume, except for the last twenty-five folios, then rubricated and decorated it after it had been completed by a second hand. Such a conclusion is strengthened by the rather un-English appearance of the initial on fol. 1^r. As further confirmation, we might note that the rubric to book 6, on the bottom of fol. 37^v, has been corrected by Texerii using the same brown ink he employed for the text.

Texerii's hand in the *Serium senectutis* resembles other Secretary hands of the first quarter of the fifteenth century, and is consistent with the dating before 1426 which Schmidt arrived at on historical grounds.[140]

The manuscript is marked "Bern. 56" in Sloane's hand at the top of fol. 1^r. This indicates that Sloane acquired the manuscript from the library of Dr. Francis Bernard, which was dispersed after Bernard's death in 1698. The number "56" refers to an item number in the catalogue of Bernard's manuscripts contained in Edward Bernard's *Catalogi librorum manuscripto-*

---

[138] *Dionysiaca*, 2:1289–91, 1293–98, 1299–1300, 1316–18, 1403–8.

[139] On hierarchies of book hands, see M. B. Parkes, *English Cursive Book Hands 1250–1500* (Oxford, 1969; repr. Berkeley: Univ. of California Press, 1980), xiv, plates 19–20.

[140] See above, 2. For contemporary hands, see Parkes, *Cursive English Book Hands*, plates 11–12; Andrew G. Watson, *Catalogue of Dated and Datable Manuscripts c. 700–1600 in the Department of Manuscripts, the British Library*, 2 vols. (London: British Library, 1979), plates 300, 317, 337, 341a–b, 343; Andrew G. Watson, *Catalogue of Dated and Datable Manuscripts c. 435–1600 in Oxford Libraries*, 2 vols. (Oxford: Clarendon Press, 1984), plates 228, 231, 232, 246, 273, 285, 324; Viviana Jemolo, *Catalogo dei manoscritti in scrittura latina datati o databili, 1. Biblioteca nazionale centrale di Roma*, 2 vols. (Turin: Bottega d'Erasmo, 1971), plates 60, 82.

rum Angliae ... (Oxford, 1697). The manuscript is also marked at the bottom of fol. 1ʳ:

MS C 797

441   III-A

"MS C 797" is the classification assigned to the manuscript by Sloane's librarian J. G. Scheuchzer sometime between 1726 and his death in 1729.[141] According to Scheuchzer's scheme, manuscripts were catalogued by size (A = folio, B = quarto, C = octavo) and number. "441" is the number assigned to the manuscript when it was catalogued as part of the Sloane collection in the British Museum. I am unable to determine the significance of the marking III-A, which is in pencil and much later than the other markings.

However, it is possible to discover the number assigned to the manuscript when it entered Sloane's collection, although that number is not visible on the manuscript in its current form. In Sloane's own main catalogue of his manuscripts, now British Library, MS Sloane 3972C, our manuscript appears in volume 1 (of eight) at the bottom of page CXCII as MS C 797. This, again, is its classification according to Scheuchzer's system, which is applied to each manuscript in the catalogue. Scheuchzer's numbers are recorded on strips of paper which have been pasted over the original margins, where the manuscripts were numbered according to Sloane's original scheme. Although it is not possible to read the original number of our manuscript, it is possible to read numbers for manuscripts higher on the page and on the following page. By counting forward or backward we discover that our manuscript was MS 506 according to Sloane's original classification when it entered his collection.

As Sloane 441 contains no other marks of provenance, I am unable to trace its history from the time of its copying circa 1425 to it entry into Sloane's library in 1698. But we might hazard a guess that its movement from Brecon to London may have been facilitated by the Welsh book collector Sir John Prise. Although Prise settled in Hereford and did most of his collecting in western England, he was born in Brecon and retained enough interest in that "natali quidem solo mihi charissimo" to purchase the priory there in 1542.[142] It was in Brecon that Prise found his most

---

[141] M. A. E. Nickson, "Hans Sloane, Book Collector and Cataloguer, 1682–1698," *The British Library Journal* 14, 1 (1988): 52–89 at 54.

[142] N. R. Ker, "Sir John Prise," in *Books, Collectors and Libraries: Studies in the Medieval Heritage*, ed. Andrew Watson (London and Ronceverte: Hambledon, 1985), 471–95 at 472, 474.

prized acquisition, a copy of Nennius.[143] And enough of the Prise manuscripts which did not find a home at Hereford Cathedral or Jesus College, Oxford have entered the Cotton collection for us to suspect that the manuscript which contains the *Serium senectutis* may have entered Bernard's collection by a similar route.[144] But having said that much, we must acknowledge that Prise mentions neither Elias of Triplow nor the other contents of Sloane 441 in his *Historiae Brytannicae defensio*.[145] Furthermore, Prise collected works of history and theology. If he did acquire the manuscript which became Sloane 441, he would have done so because of an interest in the Pseudo-Dionysius and not Elias of Thriplow or Fulgentius. As a final caveat, we should note that N. R. Ker personally inspected Sloane 441 while compiling *Medieval Libraries of Great Britain* but nowhere connects the manuscript to Prise, as he undoubtedly would have done if he had noted any sure signs of provenance.[146]

10. This Edition

Sloane 441 was produced carefully, with corrections throughout, but at some remove from the original. Reading Elias against his sources suggests that besides Elias's own stylistic ornamentation or substitutions, numerous corruptions have crept into the text of Sloane 441. In the more difficult passages there are signs that Texerii or scribes earlier in the history of transmission have been alternately baffled by and prone to revise the readings they encountered. Therefore, while I have made every attempt to justify manuscript readings, I have not hesitated to emend them when that seemed called for. I cannot be sure that I have in every case recovered the authorial reading, but I have seen no reason to leave an already difficult work littered with textual absurdities.

Besides providing rubrics for each book of the *Serium senectutis*, Texerii also uses rubricated initials to distinguish subsections, primarily biblical passages and *exempla*, in books 3 and 10.[147] Paragraphs and their nu-

---

[143] Ker, "Prise," 478.

[144] For the Cotton manuscripts, see Ker, "Prise," 486–87.

[145] John Prise, *Historiae Brytannicae defensio* (London: Impressum in aedibus H. Binneman, 1573).

[146] For Sloane 441, see N. R. Ker, *Medieval Libraries of Great Britain: A List of Surviving Books*, 2d ed., Royal Historical Society Guides and Handbooks, 3 (London: Royal Historical Society, 1964), 12. I am grateful to Professor A. G. Watson for relaying to me the contents of Ker's note card for Sloane 441 and for verifying that it is in Ker's own hand (personal communication, 31 July 1989).

[147] These books contain, respectively, Philip's stories of divine vengeance on human impiety and Elias's defense of the immortality of the human soul. It may be that Texerii, or perhaps the author, thought that readers would be particularly likely to consult these two

meration are my own, as is capitalization, except at the beginning of sentences or lines of verse. Texerii is quite scrupulous about marking sentence divisions, and I follow him quite closely in this regard. Like him, I accept as sentences clauses (perhaps authorial) which contain a participle but no finite verb, or which begin with the construction *gnarus* (*ignarus, non bene gnarus*) *quod* but lack a main verb.

Texerii paid close attention to establishing a hierarchy of punctuation for his copy of the *Serium senectutis*. He indicates minor medial pauses with a *punctus* (.) and major medial pauses with a *punctus elevatus* (⸪); they correspond to the modern comma and colon or semicolon. He does not employ a separate mark for questions. I have added brackets and dashes to articulate the structure, or at times lack of structure, of Elias's longer periods. Otherwise, encouraged by Peter Dronke's practice in his edition of Bernardus Silvestris's *Cosmographia*, I have tried to punctuate Elias's Latin as if it were modern English. In practical terms this means that I have punctuated for breath pauses as well as logical articulation or subordination.

Orthography follows Sloane 441. It shows usual medieval variations such as *i/y, i/e, d/t*, doubling of consonants, addition or elimination of *h*, assimilation and dissimilation of consonants. For the most part Texerii distinguishes graphically between *c* and *t, u* and *v*, but then uses them rather interchangeably. I silently expand 9 and $\bar{\iota}$ before *p* as *com-* and *im-*, which are the forms Texerii prefers when spelling them out. However, I retain *con-* and *in-* when they are Texerii's actual spellings. By the same principle, I expand $\bar{\iota}m$- as *inm-*. *Michi* and *sed* are Texerii's spellings. Although Texerii clearly distinguishes between *circa* (*cc^a*) and *citra* (*cit^a*), a glimpse at the apparatus will show that they are often confused. Presumably, a scribe earlier in the chain of transmission abbreviated both as *cc^a*. In the case of ambiguous abbreviations (*nichil/nil, specialis/spiritualis*) I have been guided by context, although this has rarely been unambiguous in the case of the latter.

The most unusual spellings here, *saguis* and *ligua*, are consistent but probably scribal. Indeed, Texerii's treatment of nasals is somewhat idiosyncratic. He adds nasal consonants to *pungnatum* (3.292) and *pungna* (4.199). He transposes them twice in *antimonias* (8.48, 52 *var.*; cf. also *anamolumque*, 4.356). He begins to write *segnificare* (8.14) as *seni-*. And, while these are probably no more than slips of the pen, we might note the spellings *Nuquid* (1.32 *var.*) and *sollepnitates* (2.24 *var.*). Texerii also

---

sections either for their own edification or for material they could easily use in their own writing or speaking. Ringstede quarried *exempla* in this manner from the *De vita scolarium* for his *Commentary on Proverbs*.

wavers some in his treatment of labials. For *f/v* alternation, note *invatuata* (3.88 *var.*), but *facillantis* (4.455) and *facillitas* (from *vacillo?*, 3.171). For *v/b*, note *diouolaris* and *diouolariter*, although this spelling is attested earlier by the *Thesaurus linguae Latinae*. *Merculialis* (4.297 *var.*) and the twin forms *diouolariter/diouolaliter* testify to a slight uncertainty about liquids.

Texerii normally treats enclitic *-ve* as a separate, or rather semi-separate, word.[148] At times he treats the conjunction *-que* in the same manner.[149] So, while a case could be made for printing them as separate words, printing them as enclitics is just as faithful to the manuscript and more in accord with normal editorial usage.

This edition prints names as they appear in Sloane 441 since it is often impossible to determine whether spellings which diverge from those in modern printed editions of Elias's sources are to be attributed to variants in the manuscripts consulted by Elias, to the transmission of Elias's text, or simply to the differing norms of classical and medieval orthography. However, the textual apparatus records source readings and variants on the first appearance of most names. Where possible, the commentary tries to assess which manuscript families Elias worked from.

Numbers are spelled out or left as Roman numerals according to how they appear in the manuscript. Notice, however, *duodecim* (xii^{cim}) at 7.60.

The textual apparatus records all substantive divergences from the text of Sloane 441. But the manuscript also contains corrections in several hands, as well as its share of insignificant slips of the pen. While a record of those slips and corrections would unduly burden the apparatus, its inclusion below in appendix 3 will allow readers to reconstruct every reading and correction in the Sloane copy of the *Serium senectutis*. As that copy is our only witness to a difficult text, serious readers will want to consider this record with care.

All references to the *Serium senectutis* are keyed to book and line in this edition.

---

[148] Note, however, *legittimaue* (1.46) and *animaue* (12.55).

[149] E.g., *superstitibus que* (3.406), *dogmatizandi que* (4.419), and *vniuersaliter que* (6.81).

Conspectus siglorum

R   rubrics in Sloane 441 written by Bartholomew Texerii
S   the text of Sloane 441 written by Bartholomew Texerii
S^1 corrections to Sloane 441 probably in the hand of Texerii
S^c corrections to Sloane 441 by uncertain hand(s)

ad.   adds or inserts
corr.   corrects
del.   deletes
ed.   editor's addition
eras.   erases, erasure
ill.   illegible
marg. margin
om.   omits
var.   variant(s)

[ ]   editor's additions
< >   lost or obscured readings
+ +   corrupt passages
/   folio division or line ending (in the apparatus)

HELIE RUBEI TRIPOLAWENSIS SERIUM SENECTUTIS[1]

Dum variat studiosus homo sacra coniugiorum
    ffedera felici federe crebro caret,
Et superum sacra sponte loquax hominumque reuelat;
    Copula fin<e> fide federibus + verata +
5 Cum Ioue Iunonem, claudum cum Cipride fabrum
    Federat, Abderitem copulat atque Team;
Argionam[2] Iano iungit, dum Philologiam
    Mercurio sociam conciliare studet
Iudicio Iouis, et Peleo Thetis[3] a Ioue iusto
10   Iungitur, idque libens sepe retartat homo:
Admeto sociare suam se segnificare
    Vix volet Alcestem per deitatis opem,
Nec sobolem ceteris cupido coniungere Diti
    Cessat homo dignam tam locuplete viro;
15 Promptus et ad vicium, socialia vincula viuens
    Nisibus intensis querere curat ouans.
Sic secum sua nupta sibi super omnia querit,
    Solaque sepe sibi uota maligna mouet,
Solaque que fugiunt perituraque coniuga curans,
20   Moribus infesta federa feda probat, | 1ᵛ |
Nec vitam virtute volet sibi federe iuncta
    Sic solidare suam, quo sit in orbe valens.
Pectus et os socianda sibi confedere firmo
    Distrahit et variat censor vtrimque rudis;
25 Quin potius sensatus homo coniungere fido
    ffedere pergat ea consociata sibi;
ffederet ergo simul duo sic sociale ligamen,
    Quo bene conveniant pectus et oris opus.

[1.] Uix ego quidem talia fine predestinato precluderam, cum
30 consors meus sua pro consuetudine secum cepit submurmurare
Philippus, tandemque tales prorupit in sermones, velut per verba

---

[1] Helie Rubei Tripolawensis Serium Senectutis Incipit S. *Above the incipit S writes:* Assit principio Sancta Maria meo <amen>.

[2] Argiona S

[3] Rhetis S

Elias Rubeus of Thriplow
GRAVE THOUGHTS IN OLD AGE

The scholar who alters the sacred union of man and wife
    Often fails to achieve a joyful union
And loquaciously betrays the mysteries of gods and men;
    A bond to be honored in marriage to the limits of faith
Unites Juno with Jove, the lame craftsman
    With the Cyprian, couples Abderite and Coan,
Joins Argiona to Janus, while striving
    To mate Philology and Mercury by Jove's judgment,
And Thetis is joined to Peleus by just Jove,
    But man often willingly hinders the match:
He will not want to hesitate about mating
    His Alcestis to Admetus by divine assistance,
Nor does a man refrain from marrying a daughter who deserves
    Such a wealthy husband to Dis, who lusts after all;
Quick to sin, man rejoices during his lifetime in seeking
    Marital connections by all possible means.
Likewise, his wife decides to put her own interests first,
    And often entertains desires harmful to him;
Caring only for goods which flee and perish,
    Behaving hostilely, his wife puts a foul union to the test,
Nor, joined to him by contract, will she wish
    To strengthen his life so he flourishes on earth.
A crude critic of both estranges and separates
    Breast and mouth, which he should unite by firm covenant,
But the sensible man will conjoin in faithful union
    Those things which he should ally with each other;
Thus, a conjugal bond should ally the two,
    So breast and mouth act in concord.

[1.] I had indeed scarce brought these matters to their preordained conclusion when, as is his wont, my companion Philip started muttering to himself and at length burst into speech as if

taliter effusa foret opido consternatus: Numquid,[1] Helia, repetitis
tot annorum iam reuolucionibus, mentis talem tam cito deduceris
ad inanicionem quod eciam dormitando nasove vigilanti stertendo
35   pergas allucinatum? Profecto cum iam canus decuriatus sis haut
intempestiuis computacionibus, ut censeas[2] lustrales annorum
repeticiones tue frontis facieique riuulis, talibus tamque vanis
temperare de hinc de racione deberes a deliramentis, solique dare
locum seueritati solisque semper et ex proposito seriis. Presertim
40   cum res ridiculosissima sit senes interesse scurrilitatibus, iocarive
iuueniliter in thalamis, vanitatibusue vacare veneriis, verbaue tot et
tam sepe vana matrimonia- | 2ʳ | libus varie de contractibus, nupcia-
libusque tam frequenter fando de federibus, adeo frequentes facere
repeticiones epithalamicis de carminibus ymeneicisque de cantilenis.
45   Profecto cum vox animi proles fore perhibeatur et filia, te senem
naturalis vrget pungitque petulancia, legittimaue mouet intempestiue concupiscentia. Triuialis enim consuetudinis est et invecerate
quod aurum quod opido desiderat opido loquitur auarus, mendacesque frequencius fundos falsasque fatur fortunas ostentator
50   meritissime ridiculosus, mollique molles memorat mollis eciam
sermone mulieres feminasue veneriis vir deditus uel luxuriosus. Et,
vt sit ad vnum dicere, quod suo cuiuis[3] optatiue diducitur in animo
sua sibi sepius ligua repetit, volensque crebrius voluit in vdo.

Metrum Secundum[4]

55   Omne quod in mente silet[5] est vox filia mentis
      Prompta referre palam quod fuit estve latens;
Detegit omne iacens animi sub tegmine tandem
      lligua loquax, animo clausa referre procax.

Prosa Secunda[6]

60   [2.] Talibus itaque suis sermonibus non minus quam prius ille
meis ad iram post incitatus, sic e uestigio subiunxi: Profecto, frater,
si prefata (quibus citra causam moueri videris) diligencius discre-
tiusque diiudicasses, haut adeo procaciter eis michiue propterea

---

[1] Nuquid *S*
[2] ut censeas] eciam *S*
[3] cuius *S*
[4] Metrum Secundum *R*
[5] silex *S*
[6] Prosa Secunda *R*

greatly perplexed by what I had said: Is it possible, Elias, that after all these years you have been reduced to such mental vacuity that you continue to babble even when asleep and snoring with wakeful nose? Indeed, when you have achieved the dignity of an elder statesman by scarce unseasonable reckonings, and measure the quinquennial progression of the years by the wrinkles on face and brow, you should by reason refrain from such absurdities and find time for nothing but earnest austerity. Nothing is more absurd than an old man who occupies himself with scurrilities, childishly cracks bedroom jokes, finds time for venereal vacuities, or frequently repeats epithalamic songs and hymeneal ditties with inane lyrics about matrimonial contracts and nuptial unions. Indeed, since speech is said to be the mind's offspring or daughter, we may deduce that either innate lasciviousness pricks you on, old man, or lawful concupiscence moves you out of season. It is a well-known fact that the avaricious man talks constantly about the gold he covets, that the absurd poseur boasts of non-existent estates and imaginary wealth, and that the effeminate man who is a wanton prisoner of sex lisps of amorous wives and mistresses. And, in general, a man's tongue often speaks of that which his mind ponders, and what he wants is on his lips.

Second Meter

Man's voice, daughter of mind, is quick to report openly
    What is silent or lies hidden in the mind;
The loquacious tongue, eager to report the mind's secrets,
    Uncovers at last all that the mind conceals.

Second Prose

[2.] No less roused to anger by his words than he had been by mine, I immediately replied: Indeed, brother, if you were to weigh with more discernment the statements which disturbed you for no good reason, you would scarce presume to disparage or vilify me

derogare uel verbaliter aduersari presumpsisses. Reuera, |2ᵛ| vix
aliquid (quod si sensatum saperes predidicisse debuisses) fuit
ordinarium quod perproperum fuerit vel precipitatum. Sic igitur tu
tibi tuis, ut auguror, in agendis minus ordinarie prouidisti dum tam
precipitanter in preassertis assertorem reprobare non erubuisti,
presertim cum veritatis sinceritati bellissime sint accomoda, sintque
falsitatis feditati funditus inpermixta, sed et indifferenter vniuersis
sub sole spirantibus medianis efficacissime sint expedientissima.

[3.] Copulari reuera matrimonialiterque coniungi Iouem Iunoni
est expedientissimum, quo tempestiue suas veniant ad maturitates
que pernecessaria sunt eis ad vsum. Tantoque viuis est expedienci-
us in sub lodice gerendis sua sociari cum Venere Wlcanum, quanto
salubrior est et efficacior ad genituram coitus, calor ad effectum.
Nec minus vtile sublunaribus est ad modumque fructuosum quod
contubernali sua cum Cibele legittimum sene senex Saturnus socie-
tur ad colludium, quo sua sic operetur morosus in muliere maritus,
ut sibi sociatam brumalis algor Saturni sub exicio constringat, Iouis
eam ver sub risu laxare pergat, estas illam Wlcani sub vertice
desiccet, quo tempestiue temporaliterque tandem Iunonis sub
vberibus |3ʳ| eandem autumpnus¹ progenitorum maturitate venus-
tet. Sed et ad vtilitatem iam facit Ianique² Argioneque coniugium,
repetita (quam crebro miramur) temporum pro nouitate medianorum.

[4.] De cetero, certe conveniens est et commendabilis, vniuersitati-
que subsolarium satis expediens est et vtilis, Philologie cursilisque
Cilenii societas matrimonialis. Admeto quidem, Phicii non minus
fauore quam Tirincii subsidiato, suam sibi socialiter adlaterari sane
sensatus Alcestem vix aliquid humanitatis accedere negaret ad
vtilitatem, quo dissidentibus feris ad currum coniunctis, coniugali
sorciatur in sodalicio salubrem sibi satis animositatem. Non minus
eciam vel honestatis contemplacione communis communiter conueniens hominibus est et appetibilis contractus in medio matrimonialis, quo pocius quam spuria nothaue prole, probabili medianus
habundet orbis legittimaque. Verumptamen parem non omnibus ad
vtilitatem vel honestatis non inficior ad effectum pari matrimonialia
cedunt in omine.

[5.] Non autem medianis reor raciocinantibus animi ligueque
coniugium ceteris est vtile minus expediensue matrimonialibus.
Atqui talium tamque conveniencium coniugalis confederacio duo-

---

¹ autumpnus *ed.*
² Ianique *ed.*

and what I said. In fact, as you would have learned already if you had any sense, few things done in haste prove well-ordered in the long run. According to my judgment, you showed insufficient care for your position when you hastily reproved me for what I said, especially since it is consonant with the integrity of truth, and is not only unalloyed with the filth of falsehood, but is, without exception, expedient for all who draw their breath on earth.

[3.] It is expedient to couple in matrimony Jove and Juno, so those things most necessary for the living come to harvest in good time. The more efficacious and conducive intercourse is to procreation, as warmth is to conception, the more expedient it is for the living to mate Vulcan with Venus by frolicking between the sheets. Nor is it less fruitful for sublunar beings that old man Saturn mate lawfully with his aged spouse Cybele (a morose husband frolicking with his wife), so the winter cold binds the earth, its mate, at the passing of Saturn, the Spring loosens her under Jove's smile, Summer parches her under Vulcan's ascendant, and Autumn finally beautifies her with ripe offspring under the breasts of Juno. And the marriage of Janus and Argiona is also useful for the continual renewal of the earthly seasons we so admire.

[4.] Furthermore, the matrimonial partnership of Philology and swift Cillenius is fitting and expedient for all who live under the sun. Any sensible person will agree that it is in man's best interest to join his Alcestis in marriage to Admetus, aided by the goodwill of Apollo and Hercules, so that once the antithetical lion and boar are yoked to the chariot, he will be granted a healthy ardor in the discharge of his conjugal duty. Likewise, a public marriage contract is fitting and desirable for the sake of common decency, so that the earth might abound with legitimate offspring rather than illegitimate bastards. However, I will not deny that marriage under equal auspices does not prove equally useful or conducive to honor for all.

[5.] But I reckon that for any rational man the marriage of mind and tongue is no less useful and expedient than any other marriage. What is more, the conjugal confederation of such a well-matched

rum supremi via recta rectoris ad tabernaculum celsitudinis et
incircumuenibilis infinitiuum ducit ad habitaculum. Nempe (quo
105 sane nota, salubriterque triuialia, sed et in vdo consue- |3ᵛ| tudina-
liter existencia loquamur sollempniter et trita) philosophus eum qui
suis non dumtaxat in labiis verum preconceptam corde veritatem
suo fatur in animo, licentis et arbitrarii regis habitaculum quia
promeruerit ingressurum censet ecclesiasticus, dum tamen viuens in
110 innocentia iusticiam cooperetur vt iustus, eiusque longius amandetur a ligua dolus, suus nec ab eo dampnificetur perperamue
ledatur proximus. Nec sua sordeat in munere manus, fedoue feteat
in fenore forulus, sibique semper sit in uditate vilitatibus involutus;
sitque sibi quiuis sane Deum timens vir vera virtute gloriosus.

115   [6.] hhiis itaque coniunctim disiunctimve diligenter investigatis,
sane sensato cuilibet de facili manifestum fiet quod in modico
secernibilis sit a derisibiliter delirante uel infatuato quisquis seria de
contractibus quos premencionauimus copulisue nupcialibus facientem fore censet verba vituperabilem. Sed de postremo precipue
120 quidem, presertim cum philosophus idem—mera vir in veritate
gloriosus—omnem potestatis arbitrio precellentis et absolute peritu-
rum fore perhibeat mendose loquentem, doloseve iurantem, falsaue
fallaciter inficiantem, veraue solo non in vero sed peruerse secus
asserentem; quo talium (si libeat) verborum subtilis sumere pergat
125 indagator ex scemate, quod falsorum non omnis assertor semper sit
et indistincte mendax, situe quiuis in veritate enunciator passim
simpliciterue verax. Sed hiis omnem citra¹ distinctionem considera-
tis,² qui contra mentem fatur |4ʳ| est mendax; qui vero verum
loquitur in corde, quauis amandata longius excepcione, vere videbi-
130 tur bellissimeque censebitur esse verax.

    [7.] Sed et eodem tam pertinaci quam theologice philosophico
veritatis astipulatore³ manifestius asserente, quiuis in vita videre
dies velle videtur vituperabiles, qui sponte supersederit a malo
prohibere liguam, quiue labia sic circumcidere sua renuerit ut non
135 loquantur dolum. Iam dictis itaque sano diligentique scrutinio
discussis, sane sensato patebit quod vel viuentibus pernitiosum non
sit enormiter dampnificari, fatoue functis dampnosum non sit
penalitatis perhennitate puniri, uel perutile saluberrimumque
spirantibus est animum cum ligua matrimoniali federe firmissimo
140 maritari, falsitatumque lenocinia longius a labiis mendaciaque cum

---

¹ circa S
² consideratis *ed.*
³ a stipulatore S

couple leads by a direct route to the tabernacle of the supreme Governor and the infinite dwelling of incircumscribable Celsitude. Certainly (to speak in well-known commonplaces which are traditionally on the tip of our tongue), the Church philosopher David asserts that he who speaks the truth conceived by his heart not only with his lips but in his mind will merit entry into the dwelling of the unconstrained and judicious King, as long as he concerns himself with justice, lives in innocence as a just man, banishes trickery far from his tongue, and does not wrong or injure his neighbor. Neither shall his hand be soiled by gifts, or his coffer reek of vile usury; nor shall he be enveloped in vice by drink. Any man who truly fears God is indeed glorious in true virtue.

[6.] Once these matters have been carefully weighed together or severally, it becomes clear that anyone who imagines that the author of the serious contracts or nuptial bonds we have just mentioned is worthy of censure, is himself barely distinguishable from a raving lunatic. This is particularly true of what David says, since that same philosopher—a man glorying in unalloyed truth—holds that all who speak falsely, swear fraudulently, insinuate falsehoods, or twist the truth to their own perverse ends, will perish by the judgment of the preeminent and absolute Authority. A subtle investigator might, if he wished, gather from the drift of these words that not everyone who makes false assertions is always and without further examination mendacious; nor does anyone always speak the whole truth. But, all things considered, he who speaks contrary to his own mind is inevitably mendacious; he who without reservation speaks the truth from a true heart will rightly be reckoned veracious.

[7.] According to the more explicit assertions of the same theologically philosophical adherent of the truth, anyone who willfully refuses to prohibit his tongue from speaking evil or to circumcise his lips so they do not speak trickery seems to want to have a blameworthy life. Now that we have completed a sensible and diligent analysis of my statements, it will be clear to any sensible person that either it is not inordinately pernicious to the living to be damned, and ruinous to the dead to suffer an eternity of punishment, or it is useful and healthy for men who still draw breath to marry mind with tongue in a firm union and to banish the enticements of falsehood far from their lips and deceiving lies far from

dolis a corde remocius amandari.

LLIBER SECUNDUS

Solus iners viciisque volens vir vilificatus
    Distrahit ad varias os animumque vices;
Vix ea vir volet invalidus sociare loquendo:
    Solus enim valide copulat illa loquens.
5 Vera quidem quiuis ex corde loquendo locutor
    Solus in effuso famine falsa fugit.
Non equidem vir vera loquens vitauerit omnis
    ffalsidici vicium veraque fando dolum:
Vera loquens etenim labiis, animoque dolosi,
10   ffalsidicique modis derogat ore viri; |4ᵛ|
Nec sua se per falsa facit vir famina semper
    Mendacem, quia mens est sibi sepe fauens,[1]
Arbitrio quia falsa loquens et mentis et oris
    Solus erit mendax famine factus iners.
15 lligua loquens igitur par est animusque loquentis:
    Sint sociata sibi conueniantque simul.

[1.] Sed ad talia michi meus sic cepit adeo familiaris aduersarius:
Numquid, Helia, de te tam delire tamque subsannabiliter videri non
verecundaris velle, tamque contumaciter presumere, quod consuetu-
20 dinum sane commendabilium, moraliumve commendabiliter et
ordinarie maritandorum te solum supine scium censeas et antonomasice gnarum, quo commenticias recenterque non minus quam
cachinnabiliter excogitatas animum presumas applicare uel cogitatus legittimarum nupciales ad concupiscenciarum sollempnitates,
25 verasue verba (uel in superficie sola) matrimoniales ad copulas,
personarum congruas quaslibet citra comparaciones, ordinumque
competentes et ordinarias maritandorum citra consideraciones?
[2.] Reuera, frater, et si secus suspicari supine videaris, tam rudis
michi fibra non est vel adeo cornea, fluidave vel vacillans memoria;
30 quin eorum que predidici meminisse michi facillimum sit uel
reminisci, quod scilicet infinibilis et arbitrarius vniuersitatis auctor
Deus et examinator absolutus infinitos infinibiliter desti- |5ʳ| naue-
rit ad tormenta ligue mendaciorumque pro fedamentis, orisque feda
male mencientis ob fermenta, transgressionumque non minus ob

---

[1] fauens] S ad. uel comes in marg.

their hearts.

BOOK TWO

Only a torpid man, debased and eager to sin,
  Directs mouth and mind towards different goals;
A weak man scarce wishes to pair them while speaking;
  Indeed, only the man who speaks firmly couples them.
Only by speaking the truth from his heart can any speaker
  Avoid falsehood in the words he pours forth;
However, not every man who speaks the truth avoids
  The sin of false-speaking or trickery,
For he who speaks the truth with his lips, but with
  The mind and mouth of a liar, sets aside due measure;
Nor does a man make himself mendacious
  By speaking a falsehood which he thinks is correct;
Only the man who speaks falsely by judgment of mind
  And mouth is made idly mendacious by his speech;
Thus a speaking tongue and the speaker's mind are equals:
  They should be paired with each other and agree as one.

[1.] In response to this my familiar adversary addressed me as follows: Elias, are you really not embarrassed by the ridiculous contumacy of your presumption that you alone are all-knowing, the wise man *par excellence*, concerning those good habits or moral qualities which are to be married to each other in the conduct of one's life? You presume to apply your thoughts to the newly and equally laughably invented nuptial solemnities of legitimate desires, and your words (superficially, at least) to true matrimonial bonds, without any balanced comparison of persons or any suitable consideration of the social positions of those to be married.

[2.] In fact, brother, my feelings are not so crude or so bony, my memory so fluid or wavering, even if you abjectly suspect otherwise; rather, it is quite easy for me to remember what I have learned, namely that God, infinite and discretionary Maker and absolute Judge of the universe, has destined endless numbers of people to unending torment on account of the obscenities and fermentations of their lying mouths, and on account of their mad

35 deliramenta, quod eciam deorum derisibilibus antiquitas (uel in hoc
sane subsannabilis) olym laguens sub pluralitatibus, ridiculosis
eciam cachynnabiliter et ymaginariis insaniaque comitatis sub
enormitatibus, suos sepissime deos memoret offensos fataliter
penaliterque puniuisse quamplures propter mendacia, preuaricacio-
40 numque non minus peccaminumque propter contagia. Licet et in
hoc manifeste suam (salua tamen semper ut decet antiquitatis
reuerencia) detexisse visa fuerit impericiam, quod ligna lapidesue
uel metalla credere potuerit moueri per iracundiam.

[3.] Notum profecto satis et in vdo sane sentientibus (nec id, ut
45 auguror, inficiari volueris) quod spiritualis ille soliloquus ecclesias-
ticusque philosophus plano non minus quam sincero sermonum
scemate suis inserere seriis dignum ducit assercionibus, incircumue-
nibilem summumque summi licentis et imperii moderatorem quemuis exterminaturum fore supervacue mencientem, perperamque
50 quemlibet male liguosum sua dum viuit in vita directurum. Non
autem multomagis communi reor est a cognicione remotum quod
idem veritatis mere dumtaxat astipulator et asserit et astipulatur
quod vanos hominum filios mendacesque suis medianos in stateris,
superficialibus iusticie videlicet vanisque libraminibus, quo facilius
55 per inania solaque per superficialia fallant et efficacius— |5ᵛ| uel in
stateris mendaces (suis scilicet in mensuris uel ponderibus) que, si
duplicia fuerint ad fallendum uel dampnificandum circumuenien-
dumue dolosa, summum semper penes arbitrium solis indifferencia
sunt abhominacionibus—summa destinet deitatis sapiencia penalita-
60 tibus.

[4.] Unde post tales talium reprobaciones de facto taliter in
factoue menciencium, domino se semel Deo loquente subsequenter
professus est audisse quod Dei (scilicet, licentis absolutique mode-
ratoris) vlciscendi iudicandiue sit potentia licens,[1] potestas et arbi-
65 traria, quodque socialiter ad expediens vniuersale predictis coambu-
let misericordia, secundum suas cuilibet operaciones uel opera
meritum mercedemue rectissime redditura, subintelligendum[2]
bellissime relinquens quod meritis cruciatuum[3] sic mencientes sit
amaritudinibus male tandem molestatura. Verum ne cuiusquam
70 cauillatoris improbitas contrarietatis ad inconcinnitates trahere
nitatur vel vicium, semel loquente Deo quod audiens audierit
exaudieritue domino. Profecto licet hominum censura multis homi-

---

[1] licensque S
[2] sub in intelligendum S
[3] cruciatiuum S

transgressions. I also know that Antiquity (which at least in this respect clearly deserved to be ridiculed), languishing under ludicrous multitudes of deranged gods and their absurd fictional exploits, frequently mentions that its gods, once offended, fatally punished men for lies as well as transgressions and sins. Saving (as behooves us) Antiquity's reverence, the ancients betrayed their ignorance in this affair, by showing themselves capable of believing that pieces of wood, stone, or metal were moved by wrath.

[3.] What that spiritual soliloquizer and ecclesiastical philosopher, with his simple but sincere style of speech, considered worth inserting among his serious assertions is well-known and often remarked by sensible men, nor (as I reckon) would you wish to deny it: the unsurpassable and supreme Ruler of highest authority and dominion shall banish from His realm anyone who lies unnecessarily, and He shall lead astray anyone who chatters wrongfully while alive. Nor do I reckon much more remote from common knowledge the testimony of that same adherent of unalloyed truth that the highest wisdom of the Deity will destine to punishment those vain sons of men who are liars in the balances, namely in their superficial and vain weighing of justice, employing vanities to deceive others more easily and efficaciously. Or, who are liars in the balances, namely in their weights and measures, which, if they are fraudulently rigged to deceive or circumvent others, are always indistinguishable from simple abominations at the Last Judgment.

[4.] After reproving those who lie in thought or deed, David confesses to having heard from the mouth of the Lord that the potential of God, the free and absolute Governor, to judge or avenge shall be free, and His power judicial, and that to expedite the process mercy shall accompany justice as partner, rendering to each his due reward according to his actions. He fittingly leaves us to understand that mercy will afflict those who lie in this manner with the anguish of merited torment, lest some dishonest quibbler turn the truth of what the lord God once said into the dissonance of contrariety or vice. Indeed, although God may seem to men to

nibus loquatur loquiue videatur modis Deus, aput se tamen est
elocutus. Unicum nempe, per quod sancta dispositaque simul
75 vniuersa, genuit Deus ipse verbum, de Deo Deum, sicque Deo sic
semel ab eloquente domino sunt audita taliter exaudiente.

[5.] Triuiale quidem non minus est quod virtutis pertinacissimus
assertor veritatisque veracissimus astipulator asserit idem, quod
iustus omnino verbi gratia iudexque non iniurians Deus sui suos
80 |6ʳ| ore dumtaxat amatores loquelaliterque superficiales, liguaque
sibi sua male subsannabiliterque mencientes, cor eciam corruptibile
suum rectitudinis a sinceritate viaue diouolariter diuaricantes, quo
non minus in obseruacione mandatorum custodiaue testamentali
quam custodie probabili seruacionis in stabilitate¹ pacti funditus
85 invenirentur infideles, + arcusque facile remissibilis in prauitatem se
sua sponte conuertentes, + iustissime spernat, pridemque spreuerit
et ad nichilum valde redigat retroque redegerit; talium tradat tam²
virtutem quam pulchritudinem si qua fuerit in manus inimici,
pridemque tradiderit. Sed et adeo delire delinquencium³ suos
90 vlcionis ad exaggeracionem tempestiuamue meritorum retribucio-
nem, solis sibi defectiuos diducit dies in vanitatibus vitamque
vilificantibus, commenticie vanis et in inuencionibus, suosque solius
de racione destinandos utilitatis ad effectus annos pernicibus trans-
currere iubet in festinacionibus, cum possent, si sensate sapuissent,
95 veraci corde credentes ad iusticiam, sinceroque ore liguaue confiten-
tes ad salutem, solis suos in vtilitatibus temporumque⁴ prosperis in
produccionibus continuare dies annuosque transcursus vanitatum-
que vanis omnino sine vilitatibus.

[6.] Ulcionis eciam diuine quamplura variaque quampluribus
100 patent exempla commenticiis omnino falsitatibus impermixta. Nota
satis est viri proletariique prolis Egipciaci mulieris et Israelitis
Israelite cum viro castris in Israelitis infauste sibi non minus quam
fataliter |6ᵛ| habita iurgacio, qua delire Dei Deum blasphemare
nomen non erubuit maledicendo. Quam Moysis ante presenciam
105 carceris ab ergastulo productam, Moyses, summa sensatissime vir
a sapiencia preinstructus, suaque iudex extra castra lapidari iussit in
iurisdiccione iustissimus. Nempe sano soloque sic et adeo seuere
sentenciauit summe sincero deitatis ex imperio. Sic itaque notha
proles sobolesque satis infausta generali non minus quam seuero

---

¹ in stabilitate] instabilitate S
² tam *ed.*
³ delinquenciumque S
⁴ -que *ed.*

speak His censure of men in many different ways, nevertheless He spoke to Himself. For God himself engendered the Word, God of God, through which alone the universe was at once ordered and sanctified; and the unique statements of the lord God were heard by One who understands them in this manner.

[5.] It is equally well known that this same determined defender of virtue and honest adherent of truth asserts that by virtue of the Word God is wholly just, a judge who does no wrong. But He rightfully spurns, long since has spurned, and will, indeed has, utterly reduced to nothing those who only say they love Him, ridiculously lying to themselves with their tongue, even promiscuously separating their perishable hearts from the way of rectitude, until they are found fundamentally unfaithful to their pledge to observe and keep the commandments with steady purpose and have turned the bow easily unbent on themselves by their depravity. He will, and long since has handed over the virtue and beauty of such liars to the enemy. But so as to intensify the timely vengeance and merited retribution for such mad sinners, He squanders their defective days in nothing but vanities and lies which debase life, and He commands them to pass their years, which should by reason be spent in the performance of useful actions, in a hasty rush. But they could, if they understood properly (believing in justice with true heart and confessing salvation with unblemished mouth and tongue), pass their days in useful activities altogether without the empty meanness of vanities.

[6.] Many different examples of divine vengeance, all utterly untainted by the falsehood of fiction, are available to all. Everyone knows about the conflict in the Israelite camp between an Israelite and the son of an Egyptian worker and an Israelite woman. Its outcome was not merely unfavorable but fatal to the latter, inasmuch as he madly dared to blaspheme against the name of God. When he was led from prison into the presence of Moses, Moses—a man most sensibly informed by the highest wisdom, and a judge most just in his rulings—ordered him stoned outside the camp. Certainly he passed such a severe sentence only by unambiguous command of the supreme Deity. This unfortunate bastard was cause

110 temporaliterque duraturo causam dedit edicto quod suo scilicet quicumque condicionisque cuiusque Deo maledicere presumpserit homo, verboue nomen Dei vano blasphemare vel stultiloquio, federe fatalitati destinatus fato fungatur lapidacionis in supplicio, penasque pendat amare mortis in improperio.

115 [7.] Verumptamen, quo tamen salua summi numinis semper labiorum laxentur habene reuerencia, michi (fortassis in hoc exfronter infrunito non minus quam subsannabiliter infatuato[1]) satis ad ammirabile cedit et ad admirandum quod summa sinceraque bonitas et absoluta, misericordieque fons indeficiens et origo iugis 120 antonomasiceque maiestatiua, tam faciles et perfunctorias tamque transitorias et vanas verbales cruciatibus adeo grauibus et exquisitis vlciscendas esse serio censuerit iniurias, tamque speciales et inexorabiles per penas edictaliter puniri preceperit expiariue per penalitates. Presertim cum genialiter leuem | 7ʳ | ligue labiorumue lubricita 125 tem facile mobilis eciam sublunaris homo promereri rarissime censeat penam, parereue puniendi quemquam penaliter occasionem, quo verbales imperatoris imperii temporaliter licentis humaniterque deficientis ad id in argumentum sumantur asserciones non minus quam benignitatis in coniectura commendabiles.

130 [8.] Ait enim: Si quis modestie nescius pudoris et ignarus improbo petulantique maledicto nomina nostra crediderit lacescenda, temulenciaue turbulentus obtrectator ipsorum fuerit, eum pene volumus subiacere neque durum quid nec asperum sustinere. Quoniam si lenitatis id ex facilitate processerit, contempnendum; si 135 uero furoris ex impetu, miseracione dignissimum; siquidem contigerit ex iniuria, benigne remittendum. Verumptamen omnibus integris ad nostram scientiam rem referri iubemus, ut ex personis hominum dicta pensemus et an pretermitti debeat an exequi censeamus.

[9.] Sic itaque, me iudice, perperam forte veritatis a via deviante, 140 non est omnino verisimile sinceritatiue racionis adlaterabile quod iniurie tam facilis tamque contemptibilis ulcio verbalis, sentenciaque tam preceps edictaliterque tam precisa tamque crudelis et inconcinna, summe sincereque pietatis iugis et misericordie scaturiginum, fontis et inexhauste miseracionis et infinibilis, patrono processerit et 145 examinatore, presertim cum demonis sit non deitatis humani gaudere vel delectari de saguinis effusione.

[10.] De cetero, quasi wlgarem venit eciam quampluribus ad cognicionem populare | 7ᵛ | murmur subsequensque vindicta murmuris a monte Synai trium via dierum comproficiscencium continuatique

---

[1] infatuato] infatuat<e> S, infatuata Sᶜ

for the severe and long-standing edict that any man of whatever condition who presumes to abuse his God or blaspheme against His name with vain or stupid speech should be consigned to death by the covenant and suffer his fate by stoning, paying the penalty for his abuse with the bitter reproach of death.

[7.] Nevertheless, to give our lips full rein even while preserving unimpaired our reverence for the highest Divinity, it astonishes me (although in this matter I may be shamelessly stupid and foolish) that the highest, pure, and absolute Goodness, the unfailing and antonomastically majestic Spring and Source of mercy, should seriously deem such perfunctory, passing, and insubstantial verbal abuse punishable by cruel and unusual torment, and issue an edict that those guilty of it be sentenced to such unique and inexorable punishments, especially since even earthbound man seldom deems the genial levity of an easily inconstant tongue or lips worthy of punishment or subject to penal correction. We may use as proof the equitable words of an emperor with only human powers and temporal sway.

[8.] He says: "If anyone should be so immodest and ignorant of shame as to imagine that our names may be challenged by reprobate and insolent slander, or should disparage them when muddle-headed with wine, we scarce wish him to be subject to any oppressive or harsh suffering. For such behavior is to be despised if it proceeds from facile ease; if, in fact, from a burst of rage, it is most worthy of compassion; if it results from unlawful behavior, it should be remitted with a good will. Even so, we order that the case be made known to us as an open issue, so that we might weigh the words according to the nature of the speaker and judge whether they should be passed over or pursued."

[9.] According to my judgment (perhaps wrongly deviating from the path of truth), it is not altogether consistent with the integrity of reason that vengeance upon such slight and contemptible verbal abuse and such cruel and inept summary judgment should be credited to the Patron and Judge of the springs of highest and purest pity and unending mercy, and the inexhaustible and infinite fountain of commiseration, especially since it belongs to a demon rather than the Deity to delight in shedding human blood.

[10.] To continue, it is common knowledge that after they had travelled for three days from Mt. Sinai, the Israelite people were

150   pro sudoris difficultate murmurancium, quod deitatis absoluta
potestas et incircumuenibilis ad iram licenter incitata festina non
minus est vlcione quam terribili prosecuta, dum castrorum pars est
extrema terribiliter ab igne diuino deuorata.

    [11.] Terribilius et aliud eciam murmur ulcioneque[1] terribiliori
155   populare vis diuinitatis est ulta + quo recordata. + Dentibus, ut fit,
ipsis[2] saliua mercuriali madentibus carnium, pisciumque, cucume-
rum peponumque simul, et cepe, necnon et alliorum quibus gratis
in solo saciebantur Egipciorum, populi pariter et plebis vniuersitas
wlgique promiscui summe summam murmurare non abhorruit con-
160   tra deitatis excellenciam, dum sibi suam causaretur animam man
male fastidiens arefactam, dumque sedens miserabiliter et flens sese
solam subsannabiliter inclinaret ad concupiscenciam, dumque
pertritas[3] et in olla subiecta[4] decoctas saporis fastidiret panis oleati
que preplacuere tortulas.[5] Sed eo mota bonitas summa deitasque
165   benigna non vno uel altero die sed ad mensem dierum carnis non
cuiuscumque sed delicatissime sic adhabundans dedit eis sic sibi
male murmurantibus edulium, quo per nares exiret vorantibus et ad
nauseam veniret,[6] volantibus in aere conturnicibus et quasi capi
volentibus cubitis dumtaxat a terra duobus. Sed delictum diuinitas
170   vix aliquod derelinquens impunitum (mastigancibus adhuc in
carnium sufficienciis a concupiscencia sic infatuatis), velud |8ʳ| ira
vel furore foret in populo concitata, plaga percussit eum fatalitate-
que peremptoria.

    [12.] Non autem suam solummodo sed et suorum, sicut asseritur,
175   in murmurantibus sibiue vel suis verbaliter detrahentibus diuina
Dei potencia penaliter est iniuriam prosecuta. Nempe nota libros
legentibus voluminaque perscrutantibus satis est seria sui fratris ex
relacione contra Moysen murmurantis Marie lepra repente candens
et temperaria, sed et eius extra castra separacio penitentialis et
180   purgatoria.

    [13.] Non equidem minus, ut auguror, est in legendi studio
pertinacibus cognicio familiaris et mansueta contemplatorum terre
promissionis a Moyse transmissorum fatalitatis ad effectum, suo
moti per eos ad murmurandum populi pro murmure, Dei prorsus
185   inexorabilis pronunciacio penalis et execucio fatalisque sentencie,

---

[1] ulcionique S
[2] ipsius S
[3] percritas S
[4] sub S
[5] tortulas *Vulgate*, turculas S
[6] veniret S, vertatur *Vulgate*

punished for murmuring about the hardship of their unending toils. The absolute and unavoidable power of the Deity, which they had willfully incited to wrath, pursued them with swift and terrible vengeance, devouring the outermost part of the camp with divine fire.

[11.] As a reminder, the power of Divinity exacted even more terrible vengeance upon these people for later muttering. Their very teeth dripping with quicksilver salivation for the meats and fish, cucumbers and melons, onions and garlic by which they had been satiated in Egypt, all the Israelites, both commoners and indiscriminate mob, did not hesitate to murmur against the highest excellence of the supreme Deity. Foolishly scorning the manna, they complained of their dried-out souls and, sitting and weeping pathetically, ridiculously inclined themselves to concupiscence, rejecting the rolls, ground finely and fried in pans, with a taste like oiled bread, which had once pleased them. Moved by their unjust complaints, the highest Goodness and benign Deity gave them as abundant food not any flesh, but the great delicacy of quails flying through the air only two cubits off the ground and seemingly wishing to be caught, and not for only one or two days, but for a month of days, until it came out through the noses of those who devoured it and nauseated them. But the Deity, who rarely leaves an offense unpunished, was moved to wrathful fury against this people and struck them with a deadly plague while they were still chewing like concupiscent fools on the ample supplies of meat.

[12.] The divine power of God has inflicted punishment not just on those who murmur against Him, but on those who verbally abuse His followers. Those who read books and study tomes are well acquainted, from the sober account of her brother, with the sudden and fitting leprosy of Miriam, who murmured against Moses, not to mention her penitential isolation outside the camp.

[13.] Nor, according to my judgment, are those who persevere in their scholarly reading any less familiar with the scouts of the Promised Land, sent by Moses to fulfill destiny, with the Israelites who were moved to murmuring by their discouraging report, and with God's inexorable verdict and execution of His fatal sentence.

dum filius Nun Josue, Calephque filius Iephone, qui cum ceteris et
ipsi precontemplati fuere terram, vestimentorum per cissuras
multitudinisque murmurum popularis per mitificaciones incircumuenibilis eciam arbitrarii iudicis absoluteque licentis gratiam pro-
190 meruere, tantaque tante gratia gratie perhenniter permanentis
viuere visuri terram vitamque diuine promissionis perpetualiterque
duraturam, pulchramque non minus quam pollucibiliter fructuosam
superne planiciem pollicitacionis. Suntque ceteri terre contemplato-
res ad castra reuersi voluntariique detractores eiusdem viles et
195 mendacissimi; sentenciam Dei seriam secundum seriem, presenten-
ciantisque secundum scema sermonis vniuersi, sunt in solitudine
sepulti. Sic itaque meritissime dampnificati suis pro multiloquiis
|8ᵛ| mendaciorumque tot tantisque profluuiis, desiderabili diuine
promissionis a participacione sunt longe semoti, sed et omni sunt
200 eius omnino porcione destituti. Non bene gnari quod miserabile
non minus quam subsannabile sit exercicium perhennem sibi procurare iacturam sola commenticiorum vanaque superfluitate mendaciorum sibi nil omnino nisi dumtaxat vt officiant collatiuorum.

[14.] Triuiale quidem tritumque pridem fuit et adhuc est in udo
205 prouerbium quod esculento frui poculentoue quiuis est indignissi-
mus quod verbis presumpserit preuituperare commenticiis, seriisue
non erubuerit preculpare sermonibus, wltuue uel verbo prefastidire
uel gestibus. Eo quidem quiuis ipso quod apposita sibi victualia
vituperat wltuue fastidit, eius et ab usu se sic et ab esu subsannabi-
210 liter excludit. Par igitur esse videtur equitatique conveniens mani-
festissime quod commenticia promissionis in vituperacione se
commentatores tam temerarii fructuose funditus excluserint tam
preciosa tam preciosi promissoris a promissione, quo iudicis adeo
sensati sentencia racionis equitatisque podio statuque stabili stet
215 coniecturaliter eciam subpodiata. Uerumptamen adeo licentis
examinatoris in tribunali vel iudicio coniecture locus non est, pre-
sumpcioniue, uel allegacionis nitori uel subsidio, sed nec racionis
extrinsice nec equitatis aduenticie subpodiacioni,[1] nec iniuriarum
contumeliarumue uel fauorum lenocinio, refutacionisue uel appel-
220 lacionis remedio, licet in eo sepe locum sorciatur sincera, supplex et
intenta sup-|9ʳ|plicacio.

[15.] Litterarum preterea studiis pertinaciter invigilantibus et
Chore, Dathanque, necnon et Hon et Abyron, ducentorumque

---

[1] subpodiacioni] subpoditario S, subpodiatorio Sᶜ

At the same time, Joshua, son of Nun, and Caleph, son of Iephone, who had scouted the land with the others, earned the grace of the free and absolutely unconstrained Judge by rending their garments and mollifying the murmurs of the populace. By virtue of such perennial grace they lived to see the life without end of the Promised Land, and the beautiful and fruitful plain which the Lord had promised. Because the other scouts felt free to disparage the Promised Land with vile falsehoods when they returned to camp, they were buried in the desert, fulfilling their sentence according to God's purpose and the spoken judgment of all. Unaware that it is pathetically ridiculous for any army to earn itself eternal loss solely by telling superfluous lies which redound to its own harm, they were rightfully damned for their garrulity and great discharge of lies, excluded from their longed for share of the divine promise, and deprived of any part in it.

[14.] According to a proverb long since trivial and trite but still on everyone's lips, anyone who presumes to invent criticism of some food or drink, or does not blush to censure it in all seriousness, or disdain it with countenance or gesture, is unworthy to enjoy it. Indeed, by the very act of criticizing or making faces at the food placed before him, he ridiculously debars himself from its use or consumption. It seems manifestly equitable that by their false vituperation of God's bountiful promise, these rash liars should have wholly excluded themselves from the precious promise of such a precious Promiser. Thus, the sentence of this sensible judge is also, according to my conjecture, supported by a stable base of reason and equity. Nevertheless, there is no place for conjecture in the tribunal of the altogether free Judge, nor for presumption or corollary allegation, nor for extrinsic logic or adventitious equity, nor the pimping of injustices, contumelies or favors, nor the remedies of refutation or appeal, albeit pure, humble, and earnest supplication finds a place there.

[15.] The terrible execution of divine vengeance upon the heretical and seditious confederation of Chore, Dathan, Hon, and Abyron

quinquaginta[1] virorum procerumque synagoge prenominatorum
225   detestabilis enormitas erroris, fedaque confederacio sedicionis,
necnon et[2] execucio diuina murmuris contra Moysen Aaronque
moti facta terribiliter ulcionis legendi per assiduitatem nota satis est
et opido familiaris. Quibus adeo presumptuose derisibiliterque
delirantibus, et in deliramenti protelacione murmuris et in conti-
230   nuacione tam cenosi sceleris et in enormitate pertinacissime perse-
uerantibus, vir Moyses mitissimus, ut mitem decuit, sanctissime
tunc est elocutus (quamuis ad ultimum) quod quemuis eciam de
iure iudicem decet bellissime ordinarie morigeratum; ius ulcionis in
fine iudex in iudicando rigidissime circumspectus terribiliter est
235   executus ordinarium, penaliter et inexorabiliter tandem puniendo
peccata tam presumptuosorum.

[16.] Moyses itaque, multitudinis murmure motus, sic inquit:
Audite[3] filii prolesque sacerdotalis Leui. Num parum vobis est
quod Deus ab omni populo vos separauerit, sibique sic separatos
240   specialiter adlaterauerit ut in cultu tabernaculi seruientes eique
coram frequencia populi ministrantes staretis? Numquid ad se sic
accersiuit ut vobis eciam sacerdocium vendicaretis globatimque
contra dominum staretis? Demumque Moyses, vocatis Dathan et
Abiron, eius et ad presenciam venire stolide contumaciterque
245   detrectantibus, dixit ad Chore: Tu totaque cognacio tua state coram
domino, stet et Aaron |9ᵛ| separatim die crastino. Sit et tuorum
quisque congregatorum suo, suoque sit et Aaron compotitus turibu-
lo, quo super inposito subsequenter incenso, compromptificati sitis
thurificare domino. Tandemque ceteris a tam presumptuosorum
250   cetu suasu Moysaico separatis remociusque semotis, suo Moyse
more consueto multitudinis humiliter ad vniuersitatem sermocinan-
te, terra dehiscens presumptuosorum sub pedibus dirupta velut os
aperiens tam contumaces et ad eos pertinencia deglutiuit vniuersa.
Ducentos uero quinquagintaque viros suis egressus ignis absumpsit
255   diuinus thuribulis compotitos, dum Chore, Dathan, Hon et Abyron
terra vorax viuos vorauit inexorabiliter dampnificatos.

[17.] Atqui non multum[4] remissior miciorue Chore post interitum
sibique tam temerarie consenciencium multitudinis murmur sequenti die contra Moysen et Aaron motum diuinitatis est ulcio subsecu-
260   ta. Popularis nempe conueniens luce multitudo causari murmuran-

---

[1] quinquaginta *Vulgate*, quadraginta S (*Cf. 2.254 below.*)
[2] necnon et *ed.*
[3] Auditi S
[4] multos S

with the two hundred and fifty leading men of the synagogue, and the murmuring they stirred up against Moses and Aaron, are exceedingly familiar from their assiduous reading to those who persistently burn the midnight oil in the study of letters. Moses, the mildest of men, most blessedly (as befits the mild) said what by right befits any reasonably indulgent judge to these presumptuous and delirious conspirators, obstinately persevering in their pro- longed delusion, their filthy murmuring, and enormous sin; but in the end, as a judge strictly prudent in passing judgment, he execut- ed the harsh established law of retribution to punish the sins of these presumptuous conspirators.

[16.] Moved by the murmuring of the multitude, Moses said: "Listen, sons and offspring of the priest Levi. Is it not enough for you that God set you apart from an entire people and took you to His side to serve Him in the worship of the tabernacle and to minister to Him before the concourse of the people? Did He sum- mon you to Him that you might claim the priesthood as your own and stand united against the Lord?" Then Moses, having called Dathan and Abyron, who defiantly refused to come into his pres- ence, said to Chore: "Tomorrow you and all your kin shall stand before the Lord; likewise, Aaron will stand apart. And like Aaron, each member of your group shall hold his censer, and after incense has been placed upon it, you will all be ready to offer incense to the Lord." At Moses' urging, the conspirators had been sequestered apart from the rest of the populace, and as Moses spoke in his accustomed humble manner to the entire multitude, the sundered earth yawned beneath the feet of the presumptuous and contuma- cious conspirators, swallowing them and all their belongings. The divine flame issuing from their censers consumed the two hundred and fifty men who held them, while the hungry earth devoured Chore, Dathan, Hon, and Abyron, all inexorably damned.

[17.] Even on the day following the death of Chore and those who rashly favored his cause, divine vengeance was no more slack or indulgent about tracking down the multitude's murmuring against Moses and Aaron. For the multitudinous populace, assem-

do non formidat quod Moyses et Aaron populum ordinarie dimi-
nuerint inmeritaque de medio fatalitate deleuerint. Sed ubi Moyses
et Aaron improbius impetiti sediciones et murmura tumultusque
vehemencius increbrescere contemplarentur minusque moderatum
265   populi concursum, sibi consulendo per fugam fugere festinauere
federis ad tabernaculum. Sed adeo derisorie delirantem diuina Dei
deleuit potencia peremptorium[1] populi multitudinem subitumque
per incendium, donec Aaron orantis sanoque[2] Moysis ex iniuncto
thuribulum[3] tenentis ad oracionem, plage Deus inmensitatem
270   cessare |10[r]| precepit vlcionis quoque penalitatem.

[18.] Profecto, licet in variis euentibus et multis misericors et
mitissimus homo Moyses esse videretur iudexque rigidus commendabiliterque circumspectus et laudabiliter ordinarius, precipuam[4]
tamen (ut michi videre videor) causam commendacionis et occasio-
275   nem tam contemplacione pietatis et misericordie quam seueritatis
iurisdiccionisque rigidissime sua meruit in iniciali iurisdiccione.
Nempe cum sua populus in absencia suus subsannabilissime depra-
uatus erroris in abhominacionem decidisset tamque detestabilis in
adinuencionis enormitatem, quod aurum vituline speciei non minus
280   artificialiter quam reprobabiliter in formam transfiguratum summe
deitatis excellencie detestabiliter deliratus preponere non erubuit
geniculariter adoratum (quo talium talis adoracio tamque terribilis
auaricie diuturnioris aurique sitis future sordidioris efficax et
competentissimum sumi possit in argumentum presagiiue verisi-
285   milis in probamentum), mitis misericorsque vir Moyses, caduceator-
que clemens et humanissimus, iudicansque iustissime, iudex et
mansuetissimus, licet ira tante prauitatis opido pro prauitate motus,
adeo peruersis adeoque proteruiter[5] in peruersitate pertinacibus
efficaciter orare perseuerauit pro preuaricatoribus.

290   [19.] Nichilominus, ut iudex sensatissime circumspectus iurisdiccionis et in exercicio prouidissime pertinax et prudentissime veges,
ordinariam tam detestabilis se promptificare transgressionis promptificauit vlcionis ad execucionem, iudiciali cognicione tribunaliter
usus, dum proiectis quas |10[v]| manu gestabat confractis tabulis,
295   trium vigintique milium vitali cruoris effusione tantarum purgari
populum procurauit a prauitate preuaricacionum. Non ignarus

---

[1] peremptoriam S
[2] canoque S
[3] thuribulo S
[4] precipuum S
[5] proteruiter] prudenter S

bling at dawn, was not afraid to murmur accusations that Moses
and Aaron were systematically destroying their people, achieving
genocide through gratuitous killings. When Moses and Aaron, who
deserved no such attack, saw sedition, murmurs, and tumult sprea-
ding rapidly, and the populace growing less temperate, they took
thought for their safety and fled to the tabernacle of the covenant.
But God's divine power devastated this delirious multitude with a
sudden and deadly conflagration, until at the prayer of Aaron, who
prayed and raised a censer according to the sensible precept of
Moses, God commanded the avenging plague to cease its devasta-
tion.

[18.] Although on a number of different occasions Moses showed
himself to be a mercifully mild man, and a strict but circumspect
and systematic judge, nevertheless it seems to me that from the
outset he laid an outstanding claim to praise as much by his pity
and mercy as by his severe and firm execution of justice. In his
absence, his depraved people so lapsed into the abomination of
heresy and religious innovation that they did not blush to prefer
bending the knee before gold transfigured disgracefully, albeit
skillfully, into the likeness of a calf to worshipping the excellence of
the supreme Deity. Indeed, their frightening worship might be
taken as valid evidence or an apposite symbol foreboding more
permanent avarice and a sordid thirst for gold in the future. Even
though swayed to anger by the utter depravity of such great wickedness, Moses, mild and merciful as a man, lenient and humane as
a leader, just and gentle as a judge, continued to pray effectively for
the renegades who were so obstinate in their self-destructive perversity.

[19.] Nevertheless, as a circumspect judge, full of foresight and
prudent vigor in the exercise of his jurisdiction, he used his legal
knowledge to execute swift vengeance on this detestable transgression. Having thrown down and smashed the tablets of the law he
carried in his hands, he was able to purge the depravity of such a
great betrayal from the populace by spilling the life blood of

quod delinquentibus impunitas perniciosa delicti parere perniciosum sepe consueuit incentiuum redelinquendi, quodque prosperitatis euentus (delinquenti consuetudinaliter comes familiariterque
300   coambulus) impunite delinquentem frequencius ad delinquendum
dampnosius, peccandumve pernicius ambulare consuescat et per-
seuerancius.

[20.] Sic itaque ciuilium conuenienter ad instar iurisdiccionum,
Moyses luculencia quasi morum melioratus ordinariorum, suis se
305   sibi subiectis (sicut omnem ciuiliter institutum bellissime decet,
pridemque decuit) ordinarie vindicem[1] facilem prebere mansueuit
ad adeundum, contumaciaque remocius amandata commendabiliter
humanum se cuilibet exibere studuit ad alloquendum, sane sibi
cauendo tamen ne familiaritatis vlteriorem subditorum sibi per
310   admissionem cachynnabilem caderet, ut fit, turpiter in contemptum.
fforte non ignarus quod conuersatio par et indifferentialis, cohabita-
cioque consuetudinaliter indifferens et equalis, contempciones
parere prompta sit semper et parata, deprecaciones dignitatum,
diuitum derogaciones et honoratorum. Sensatissime gnarus eciam
315   forte quod commendabiliter circumspectum ciuiliterque non minus
institutum quemuis conuenientissime deceat, decentissimeque
decorum iurisdiccionis exercitorem, quod precipitanter excandescere
non consuescat in eos quos, mendaci presumpcione sola fallaciue
coniectura motus, male mo-|11ʳ| rigeratos esse suspicetur perpe-
320   ramue peruersos, quodque calamitosorum[2] precibus illacrimari prepropere proclinatum se non exibeat.

[21.] Id enim recti constantisque[3] iudicis non est et iusti quod
eius animi proditor custosque wltus affectum defacili precipitante-
rue detegat, cum iudicis sit sane cuiuslibet sencientis ut sic sensate
325   sumatimque ius reddere pergat, ut industria sua iudicialis auctorita-
tem dignitatis augere mansuescat, ut et iudiciali suo sic sane nego-
ciari studeat in officio, legisticique tramitis sic proficisci perseueret
in directorio, neue remissius seueriusve iudicando sentenciandoue
constituere presumat aliud quam quod litis instancia uel instans
330   causa deposcat. Nempe sedenti sentenciantique[4] quouis est in
iudice pernix et obliteranda subsannabilisque seueritatis ambicio
semper nimietatisque clemencie,[5] presertim cum de iure iudex

---

[1] vindicum S
[2] calamosorum S
[3] constantique S
[4] sentenciandique S
[5] clemencie S, demencie Sᶜ

twenty-three thousand. He was not unaware that the pernicious failure to punish a wrong often creates a deadly incentive for wrongdoers to sin again, and that a prosperous outcome (the wrongdoer's customary companion and familiar consort) ordinarily habituates the unpunished wrongdoer to doing more serious wrong, or sinning sooner and more persistently.

[20.] Thus, as a model for civil judges, Moses, as if bettered by the distinction of systematic morals, became accustomed (as properly befits anyone holding public office) to offering himself to his subjects as an easily approachable avenger, and setting aside his pride, he showed himself eager to hear what any of his followers might say or ask. But he wisely took care lest (as often happens) he should fall into the shameful ignominy of excessive familiarity by admitting into his presence too many of those under him. Perhaps he was not unaware that intimate contact based on equality rather than social hierarchy is always ready and able to spawn contempt or grumbling against people in high places, the wealthy, and the honored. He was also aware that it befits any circumspect civil official, or any decent administrator, that in the exercise of his jurisdiction he not become accustomed to flaring up suddenly against those whom he wrongly surmises to be evildoers or morally perverse, and that he not be too quick to weep at the prayers of the wretched.

[21.] A resolute and upstanding judge will not allow his face, keeper or betrayer of his mind, to reveal his disposition prematurely. Any judge must dispense justice quickly and sensibly, augmenting the authority of his station by his diligence and performing his duties according to the guiding path of the law, lest he presume to decree a sentence more lax or harsh than what the case at hand or any relevant point of law demands. A sitting judge should avoid the mistake of striving after either ridiculous severity or excessive leniency, especially since the law requires that every judge decree

indifferenter omnis perpenso subtilitate iudicio, libratoque uel
subtilius uel pragmatice diduccionis examine, quod in iudicium
335 deducta res expostulauerit statuere teneatur sollerter et examinare.
Verumptamen in leuioribus causis procliuiores ad leuitatem iuris
iustiorem benignitas et iudicat et iubet iudices esse debere. Non
minus et in penis grauioribus seueritatem legum cum temperamen-
to benignitatis aliquo sentencialiter exercere,[1] quamuis ex ordine
340 regulari iure facti questio iudicantis voluntario persepe[2] fit in
iudicio. Pena vero uel penalis execucio sanccite legis attribuatur
arbitrio.

　　[22.] Talia sicut auguror ordinaria, subtili |11ᵛ| sanaque suppo-
diata racione, perscrutanti studio subtiliter et inspicienti Moysaice
345 cuilibet invenire fas est et facultas iurisdiccionis in execucione. Sed
et ad summam, me iudice, singula que superius iam posita verbaliter tam peruerse preuaricanti tamque pertinaciter exasperanti[3] de
populo sunt exempla consternacionis attonite sane, sicut opinor,
sensatis opido sunt incitatiua. Sunț et admiracionis infinitiue sano
350 sensateque cerebrato, sicut auguror, cuilibet excitatiua, si que
contigere tam peruersis adeo varie mirabiliterque singula contigisse
perhiberentur eis in figura futurorum figuratiue non minus quam
quasi preambulatorie predesignatiua. Nemo nempe natus sub sole,
reor, adeo peruersum uel in procacitate preuaricacionis adeo perti-
355 nacem posse nasci credere potuisset in medio populum, diuinitate [4]
post tantorum gratuitas beneficiorum tot exibiciones, preuarica-
cionumque tam terribiles vlcionalesque punicionum post penalitates, adeo pertinaciter ingratum tamque subsannabiliter induratum
tamque bestialiter infrunitum, si tamen vniuersa (quod quamuis
360 admirans admodum spontaneus admitto) sint omnino vera que tam
peruerso dicta sunt dicunturque de populo pertinacique suo tam
derisibiliter in deliramento.

LIBER TERCIUS[5]

Uix validam que sponte mouet quis dicere plebem
　　Vir uolet usque suum desipiendo Deum;

---

[1] extitere S
[2] presepe S
[3] ex asperanti S
[4] diuinitatiue S
[5] R repeats liber tercius in marg.

what the case before the court demands by a carefully weighed exercise of judgment and a subtle or pragmatic examination of the conduct of the case. However, in cases of less serious import, the law's benevolence asks that judges be inclined to a just leniency. Likewise, in more serious cases it asks that the sentence display the severity of the law with an admixture of benevolence, even though in the normal course of events a question of fact almost always pertains by law to the discretionary power of the judge. Indeed, a penalty or punishment should be assigned by the authority of statutory law.

[22.] I reckon it proper for any zealous investigator to find such directives, supported by subtle and sober logic, in Moses' administration of justice. But the several examples mentioned above of a people so perversely prevaricating and obstinate in speech are, in my opinion, more than enough to arouse astonished consternation on the part of any sober observer. And they will amaze any sensible person, since the various events which so miraculously befell this perverse nation did so as figures of things to come. No one born under the sun could believe that after so many unsolicited displays of divine favor and such terrible vengeance on their apostasy, these people could remain so perversely obstinate in the wanton betrayal of their faith, so ungrateful, hard-hearted, and bestially stupid, if, as I quite freely admit despite my amazement, everything which has been said about this perversely deluded nation is absolutely true.

BOOK THREE

By trifling with God a man wholly desires that
   Which one man deliberately provoked a feeble race to say;

Iudicis offensi veniens reus ultro uel errans,
    Actor ad arbitrium querere dampna venit.
5 Ultro dei quecumque[1] sui gens excitat iram
    Desipit offensum sponte colendo deum; |12ʳ|
Seruit ut insipiens sua sponte stipendia perdens,
    Dum domini motum mentis acerbat iners.
Vix eciam sibi verna veges dominum bene gratum
10   Senciet, offensum fraudibus usque suis;
Solus enim bene grata suo seruicia seruus
    Prestabit domino fidus amansque fidem;
Sponte sui vix verna valens exasperat heri
    Bilem per sordes, dum sibi seruit inops.
15 Gens igitur delira Deo prepucia dampnans
    Et seruiuit egens cessit et ultro dolis;
Murmurat ut fatuus et munera sumit inepte,
    A domino famulus murmure factus iners.
Sponte sua se quisque facit fatuus male dignum
20   Munere munifici murmure verna suo;
Quisque sagax igitur dum seruit ab ore releget
    Murmuris officium longius omne libens.

[1.] Antiquitas[2] eciam deorum pridem sub pluralitate tam temeraria modoque tam subsannabili commenticia, numinumque sub
25 multitudine (cui coambulum vix esse uel a propinquo subsecutiuum
quid consueuit honestum uel honestati socialiter adlateratum[3]) tam
cachynnabiliter erronea suos asserit ultores mendaciorum non
minus atroces quam promptos et inexorabiles extitisse deos detesta-
biliumque delictorum. Triuialis profecto[4] satis est et in udo, triuiali-
30 terque trita, lippisque non minus quam luscis lumine cecucientibus
nota suo Bati mendacis[5] pro mendacio prompto procurata |12ᵛ|
commendabiliter a Mercurio meritissima mutacio. Verumtamen id,
ut michi videre videor, Maiugene[6] demeritam magni modice[7] facit
ad commendacionem laudisue gloriam. Nempe cum Phicium
35 dispari fistula septemque cannis alternatimque se positis, rutroque
pastorali uel baculo, pelleque pastoria penulaue pastoraliter compo-

---

¹ quicumque S
² S ad. prosa in marg.
³ adlateratum S, adlateraturi Sᶜ
⁴ profectio S
⁵ suo ... mendacis] sua ... mendaces S
⁶ Manigene S
⁷ modicum S

Appearing before an offended judge, the guilty perpetrator
  Sins willingly by coming to court to seek compensation.
Any nation that willingly excites the wrath of its god
  Raves in freely worshipping an offended god;
It serves like a fool who willfully loses his pay
  When he slothfully embitters his master's mind.
A thriving house slave will not find the master he has
  Offended by his deceits well-disposed towards him;
Indeed, only a faithful servant who loves honor
  Will offer services wholly pleasing to his master;
An ineffective servant willfully raises his master's bile
  By his poor and niggardly service.
So this deranged race consigned its foreskins to God,
  But served poorly and yielded willingly to treachery,
Murmured like an idiot, and foolishly received gifts—
  A servant useless to his master because of his murmuring.
Of his own volition, a foolish servant makes himself
  Unworthy of a bountiful reward by his murmuring;
Thus a man of discernment should willingly banish every murmur
  Of discontent from his mouth while he serves.

[1.] Even Antiquity—living under a plurality of gods as ill-considered then as it is ridiculously untrue now, and under a multitude of laughably heretical deities who were never associated with anything honest or even close to honesty—claimed that its savage gods were prompt and inexorable avengers of lies and misdeeds. Certainly, Mercury's laudable transformation of the deserving Battus on account of his ready lie is a piece of trivia on everyone's lips, a worn-out commonplace known to the bleary-eyed no less than those blind in one eye. But as I see it, this scarcely works to the credit or fame of Maia's great son. For when Pythian Apollo posed as a herdsman with an unequal pipe of seven reeds, a spade or staff, and a herdsman's skin or cloak, Mercury cheated this god

titum, iuris adeo peritum, prenoscicatoremque medicinalem tam
circumspectum futurorumque tam sapientem precircumuenerit
specialemque presagum,[1] dum boues eius subtiliter preabactas sibi
40   subtraxit vmbrosa silue sub obscuritate sensate satis sagaciterque
preabsconditas.

[2.] Atqui qui tam scium tamque cautum sua cauillator arte
cauillatoria deum circumueniendo predampnificauerit enormiter
adeoque diuinum nil glorie laudisue rustici ruraliter ruris morigera-
45   ti, rusticaliterque poronati,[2] uel aratoris lege sub agraria professionaliter instituti promereri potuit in circumuencione; fallere reuera
fallacem cauillatoris bellissime facit ad commendacionem bene
circumspecti cauillatorem. Commendabilem uel in hoc tamen
opidoque sensatum Maie censerem[3] fore filium quod sibi uel in
50   duricia ruralitatis belle conuenientis mendacem penalitate puniuit
adeo rudem, tamque procacem,[4] contumacemque proditorem, quo
ceteris rusticitatis in duricia sibi similibus ligue mendacis orisque
plus iusto procacis lapis appareat ad castigacionem diuciusque
duraturum castigacionis ad argumentum.

55   [3.] Sed vereor ne tam pertinaci rusticitatis in duricia[5] tam continue professionaliterque perseuerantis, adeoque pertinaciter vniuer-
salis,[6] quodlibet argumencale castigacionis ligue mendacis orisue
procacitatis inane sit et inefficax abanimatiuum. |13ʳ| Rarissime
quidem presumpcionali cuiquam fas fuit uel facultas castigacione,
60   verbaliue uel commenticia, vicium funditus obliterare temporali
diuturnitate consuetudinatum. Tali profecto vix in casu consumatos
habere consueuerunt effectus laudabiles eciam mores[7] allegacionum.

[4.] Uerumptamen ad summam talem se suasque sic iniurias
65   ulciscentem deum dicere non dubitarem derisibiliter delirum, quod
proditorem rusticum suas[8] suo examine sibi nequiter illatas ulcis-
cendo penaliter iniurias in inmutando lapidis in substanciam, fecisse
non animaduertit se sibi consubstancialem. Suos etenim deos, in
duricia conuenientes vniuersos, lapideis in soliditatibus fecit adora-
70   biles antiquitatis subsannabile deliramentum uel, si forte vehementi-

---

[1] presagium S
[2] rusticaliterque morigerati poronati S
[3] Maie censerem] Maiecense/rem S
[4] prophacem S
[5] in duricia] induricia S
[6] vniuersitatis S
[7] mores S, m[er]itores Sᶜ
[8] suos S

so learned in law, so circumspect as a medical prognosticator and so skilled at predicting things to come. Having stealthily rustled his cattle, Mercury led them away and cleverly hid them for himself in the shady darkness of a wood.

[2.] But the quibbler, who had already used his outrageous skill to harm so knowing and cautious a god, could earn no praise or glory by circumventing a bumpkin who had rustic manners, wore clodhoppers, and worked for a living under the agrarian law of the plowman; in fact, it is fit praise of the circumspect quibbler that he deceived such a fallible quibbler. However, I reckon we should commend the intelligence of Maia's son, inasmuch as he punished this lying, crude, impudent, and proud traitor with a penalty quite appropriate to his hardened rusticity, so the stone might serve both to castigate his lying and impudent mouth and as long enduring proof of his punishment for others equally hardened in their boorishness.

[3.] But I am afraid that in dealing with obtuse rustics, so ubiquitous and persistent in their obstinacy, any attempt to castigate a lying tongue or impudent mouth will be worthless and inefficacious. Indeed, hardly anyone can completely efface a vice become habitual with the passage of time merely by issuing a presumptuous spoken or fictional reprimand. Indeed, in such cases even the best method, direct accusation, rarely achieves the desired result.

[4.] However, I cannot help but laugh at the delirium of a god who avenges his injuries in this manner, since in punishing the injustices, which (according to his own inquest) were wrongfully inflicted upon him, by transforming the rustic traitor into a rock, he did not reflect that he was making him consubstantial with himself. Indeed, Antiquity was so ridiculously deluded as to worship its gods, all of whom were alike in their hardness, in solid rock; or if

ore ducerentur errore, deorum uel reuerencia deliraque dileccione,
metallica venerabantur eos in soliditate, numinumque multitudines
fecere sic adorabiles omnino supervacuaneorum. Ridiculosissime
reuera suo suas in seruiente paterfamilias quiuis ulciscitur iniurias,
75 qui delinquentem suo sibi qualifacit in gaudio substanciaue parifica-
bilem. Bene meritorum nempe satis est ad remuneracionem vernaliter ancillancium quod eis ingredi facultas sui concedatur dominatoris in gaudium.

[5.] Detestabilium quoque non minus suos procaces deos memo-
80 rat antiquitas ultores extitisse delictorum, sed et illatarum sibi
contumaciter iniuriarum, debitasue sibi circa religiones negligencia-
rum. Penthei profecto triuialis est, oris et in udo populica, festorum
temeraria Tionei contemptoris impericia penaliter a Tioneo punita.
Sed et punicionis deitatis anomale maneries platealiter est puplicata
85 triuialiterque trita; |13^v| sed nec lippos latet, luscosue nec tonsores
vlcionis vinaliter diuine modus uel forma. Uix autem cuiusquam
superficialiter eciam litterati memorie subducit obliuio uel agnicioni
qualiter Agaue,[1] facilis ad fatuitatem Lenei viribus infatuata vinosis
et instigata, propriam Pentheum prophana mater interfecerit pro-
90 lem, religionis in amore pertinacissimum. Qualiterue genialis consi-
tor uue[2] magisterque Bromius, ignigenaque Bachus, macescens
sponte sua, temporaliterque transfiguratus, maris et in litore reper-
tus, et in naui quam diu sibi libero libuit quasi captiualiter retentus,
suas vlciscendo numinaliter iniurias, presumptuosos temerarieque
95 violentos in pisces marinos mutauerit retentores, udosque per
vinolenciam, madidosque per temulenciam perpetuos fecit in vdo
natatores.

[6.] Non minus nota, ut auguror, est artificialium commenticio-
rumque supremi deorum commenticieque precipui suarum sibi
100 Iouis illatarum grauis vlcio sequens iniuriarum. Nempe cum quidam Procarti[3] cuiusdam negociatoris filius, Allexander appellatus,
ab Egipciorum rege Tholomeo fuisset in Syriam transmissus, Antiocho rege suis cum Syris Parthorum viribus interempto, qui com-
menticio iure successionis non minus quam bellis sibi regnum pete-
105 ret et armis, omne citra bellum pacienter admissus est a Syris. A
Tholomeo namque precomposita venit Allexander ad fallendum Syros
fallaciter fabula quod uiuo videlicet ab Antiocho per adopcionem rege
|14^r| regiam receptus artificio legali fuisset Allexander in familiam.

---

[1] aga ue S
[2] uuebi S
[3] Procarti S, Protarci Justin

perchance it was led by more violent heresy or insane reverence for the gods, it venerated them in solid metal, and made and worshipped multitudes of wholly redundant gods. Any master who avenged his injuries on a servant by making the offender equal to himself in his joy or wealth would seem absurd. In fact, it is sufficient reward for the merits of those who serve well that they be allowed to enter into the joy of their master.

[5.] Antiquity also speaks of its gods as unabashed avengers of abominable offenses or the injuries inflicted on them by proud men who neglected their proper worship. Indeed, the rash ignorance of Pentheus, who was punished by Dionysus for scoffing at his festival, is a commonplace on the lips of everyone. The unusual method of punishment chosen by the god is also a trite commonplace known on every street corner; nor is the mode of drunkenly divine vengeance hidden from the bleary-eyed, one-eyed, or barbers. Indeed, forgetfulness will not have erased from the memory of anyone who is even superficially literate how Pentheus, unswerving in his love of religion, was killed by his own foolish and impious mother Agave, besotted and urged on to folly by the drunken power of Leneus. They will also remember how Bromius, or fireborn Bacchus, sower and father of the jolly grape, souring of his own will, was temporarily transformed into a child and discovered on the seashore. He was held a seeming captive on shipboard as long as he acquiesced, then avenged his injuries by turning his overbold and violent captors into salt water fish, and leaving those who were already sodden with drink to swim the deep forever.

[6.] The heavy vengeance which Jove, first and foremost of fictitious, man-made gods, exacted for injuries he suffered is, according to my judgment, no less well-known. After King Antiochus and his Syrians had been wiped out by the Parthians, a certain Alexander, son of a wholesaler named Procartus, was sent to Syria by the Egyptian king Ptolemy to seek that kingdom for himself by a fictional succession as well as by arms and conquest. Alexander was received patiently and without a fight by the Syrians, for he came ready to deceive them with a stratagem devised by Ptolemy, namely that he had, according to the fictive justification, been accepted into the royal family by King Antiochus while the latter was still alive.

[7.] Verum quia vilis vilitatisque consuetudinaliter est esseque
110 retro consueuit vilis in vicium cadere leuiter ingratitudinis, eciam
Tholomeum (cuius commenticiis consiliisque non minus et auxiliis
Syrie fuit in regnum subornatus), rerum successu temerarie tumens,
aspernari cepit insolenciaque superbe contumaciterque contempnere. Verum Tholomeus, consiliorum subtilitatibus commentorumue
115 profectibus haut adhuc omnino destitutus, Allexandrum regno quod
sua non minus subtilitate quam suffragiis acquisierat destituere
summis instituit opibus cautelisque sompniculosis. Transmittit
igitur illac Gripum nepotem suum summis ingentibusque cum
copiis, eique suam sibi filiam verbis pollicetur patenter expressis
120 matrimonialiter indiuidualiterque sociandam, quo Syrie sic populos
in auxilium nepotis belli non tantum societate sollicitet, sua sed
affinitate saguinis eciam coniuncta cum propinquitate. Nec sua sic
preconcepta congruo coniectura finis fuit effectu denique frustrata.
Namque cum Gripum Syri taliter omnes instructum tantis Egipti
125 viribus viderent, paulatim sua sibi sponte consulentes ab Allexan-
dro consensu quasi confederato communi defecere. Fit inter invisos
tamen reges tandem prelium; quo victus, vilemque versus Allexander in fugam, profugit Antiochiam.

[8.] Sed inops ibi tempestiue sibi minus effectus pecunie, cum
130 debita castrorum de more | 14ᵛ | moraretur stipendia male molesta-
tus inedia, castraliumque remuneraciones laborum turbulencia-
rumue (quod cuilibet est duci supreme perniciosum) ducis per indi-
genciam deessent, a templo Iouis ex auro solidum victorie signum
tolli precepit; vafreciis iocorumque faceciis, temeraria tyranni pro
135 consuetudine Syracusani, sacrilegium circumscribere non formidauit. Victoriam nempe dicebat a Ioue sibi fuisse commendatam, non
bene gnarus quod sibi sic laciuiendo fatalem properauerit[1] sibi
procurare confusionem fatale funditus per factum, Iouialisque
ridiculam tante commendacionis per iactanciam. Paucis nempe
140 postea diebus interiectis, cum Iouis illud aureum ponderis infiniti
simulachrum tacite precepisset auelli, deprehensus et in sacrilegio
popularis concursu multitudinis fuisset infinito, vilem vilissimus in
fugam versus et a suis ignominiosissime desertus, magnaque subsequenter vi tempestatis oppressus, Iouisque diuino numine perpe-
145 trati procuranti sacrelegii penalis potenter ulcionis inmanitatem,
denique captus est a latronibus et ad Gripum perductus, attrociter
et interfectus. Sic fatali fatuus in euentu didicit quod ingratitudinis
in vicio quiuis viliter errare presumat ingratus, quod et hominis

---

[1] perperauerit S

[7.] But since it is, and always has been, the vice of the base-born to fall easy prey to ingratitude, Alexander, swelling rashly with pride because of the successful outcome of events, began in his insolence to spurn and insult even Ptolemy, through whose feigning counsels and military support he had been dressed up as king of Syria. But Ptolemy, still not altogether lacking in subtlety of counsel or fictional stratagems, set out with all his resources and imaginative stratagems to deprive Alexander of the kingship which he had helped him to acquire with his brains and might. So he sent his grandson Grypos to Syria with a massive army, and publicly promised him his daughter in marriage, so as to win the people of Syria over to his grandson's aid not only by military alliance but by affinity of blood and close kinship. Nor did his plot, thus conceived, fail of a suitable outcome. For when all the Syrians saw Grypos supplied with so many Egyptian troops, they gradually gave thought to their safety and defected from Alexander as if by common consent. The two rival kings met in battle; Alexander was defeated and departed from Antioch in base flight.

[8.] Lacking the ready money he needed and suffering badly from hunger, Alexander withheld the wages due his troops, and his soldiers lacked remuneration for their labors because of their leader's indigence—a ruinous situation for any leader. So he ordered the removal of a solid gold victory standard from Jove's temple. Nor was he afraid to embellish the sacrilege with clever jokes in the rash style of a Syracusan tyrant. He said that victory had been entrusted to him by Jove, not aware that his suicidal action and absurd boast of Jove's favor had hastened the approach of his own demise. A few days later he secretly ordered his men to pull down the immensely heavy gold likeness of Jove, but he was caught in the act of sacrilege by an infinite multitude of people. Turned in flight and ignominiously deserted by his people, this base man was subsequently overwhelmed by a great storm, and with the divine godhead of Jove exacting this savage vengeance as punishment for the sacrilege Alexander had committed, he was finally captured by thieves, brought before Grypos, and put to death. The fool learned from his fatal end that anyone who basely presumes to embrace the vice of ingratitude is hateful to all, and that it is typical of the fool

infatuatissimi sit et solius ad fatale compendiario viaue recta peri-
150   culum properantis inhumaniter hominibus viuere contumaciterue
numinibus.

[9.] Cambisis eciam criminis adeo cachynnabilis reuerende[1]
memorat vetustatis (in deorum pluralitate delirantis) auctoritas
Hamonis in iniuriam | 15[r] | commissi mote diuinitatis per iniurias
155   ulcionem. Cambises enim, fataliter cum sui, ut fit,[2] elati patris heres
iure[3] successorio relictus, Egiptum viriliter paterno subiecisset
imperio, velut offensus superfluis Egipciorum supersticionibus,
Isidisque, Apisque, Mercurii necnon et Appollinis, et Esculapii,
ceterorumque templa deorum ridiculo[4] religioni derisibiliter ritu
160   tunc pontificali dedicata destrui diruique precepit ut omnino vana
funditusque prophana. Sed et ad Hamonis uiribus sacrilegisque
violenciis expugnandum dirimendumque nobile templum Libies
arentis, arisque centum pluribusue famosissimum transmittit exercitum. Uerum suas,[5] ut (in tali casu sponte circumscribilis et erra-
165   bunda) coniectabat antiquitas, arbitrio numinis ulciscente Iouialis
iniurias, temeritate sacrilega sic transmissus vi tempestatis totus
arenarum molibus letaliter oppressus obiter interiit exercitus.

[10.] Nec talibus[6] Hamon arenosus auctori pepercit offensus[7]
tam temerarie transmissionis. Nempe cum per quietem nocturnam
170   fratrem suum, nomine Mergum, post se regnaturum vidisset (hec
Hamone, sicut vana vetustatis opinabatur facillitas, preostenso
procurante), vehementer vehementissime consternatus non formidauit, eciam post perpetratum spei destinacione sacrilegium, re simul
et facto committere paricidium, protinusque magum[8] quendam
175   fratrem suum transmisit ad perimendum. Sed interim sibi tam
perniciosus transmissor ipse, paricidas Hamone manus incitante,
gladio furialiter euaginato suo se sua sponte letaliter wlnerauit in
femore, fratrique commoritur sic cum commoriente, penasque sic
tempestiuissime | 15[v] | pendit seu preimperati tam crudelis parisci-
180   dii, seu preperpetrati tam detestabilis sacrilegii.

[11.] De rarissime siquidem contingentibus et est et esse consue-

---

[1] reuertende S
[2] sit S
[3] S ad. sui *before* successorio
[4] ridicule S
[5] suo suas S
[6] talis S
[7] S ad. auctor *before* tam
[8] magum *Justin, om.* S

who chooses the direct route or shortcut to fatal peril to live inhumanely among men and defiantly before the gods.

[9.] Venerable Antiquity, raving about a plurality of gods, also mentions how his injuries roused Hammon to seek vengeance on a laughable crime against his godhead. When Cambyses was left heir to his deceased father by the law of succession, and had subjugated Egypt to the paternal empire, he was so offended by the superfluous superstitions of the Egyptians that he ordered the temples of Isis, Apis, Mercury, Apollo, Aesculapius, and the other gods, at that time dedicated by pontifical rite to an absurd religion, pulled down as fundamentally worthless and profane. And he sent a military force to plunder with sacrilegious violence the renowned temple of Hammon in parched Libya, famous for its hundred or more altars. But as Antiquity (which was willfully limited and misguided in such matters) reckoned, Jove's avenging godhead caused the entire military force sent out with such sacrilegious rashness to perish *en route* in a tempest, buried by the lethal expanses of sand.

[10.] Nor, offended by such actions, did sandy Hammon spare the instigator of such a rash expedition. According to the inane fickleness of old times, Hammon caused Cambyses to dream during the calm of the night that his brother Mergis was to reign after him. This disturbed him so violently that, even after the earlier sacrilege he had perpetrated at the urging of hope, he was not afraid to commit parricide, so he immediately sent a certain magician to murder his brother. But meanwhile, the self-destructive sender, with Hammon urging on his parricidal hands, unsheathed his own sword in a frenzy and fatally wounded himself in the thigh. Thus he died with his brother and paid in good time the penalty for both the parricide he had commanded and the sacrilege he had committed.

[11.] It has always been among the rarest of occurrences that a

uit quod scilicet is sit[1] commendabiliter parsurus qui diuiciarum
fuerit superfluitate fermentatus, vicioue crudelitatis inhumane
deterioratus, suosue fuerit aduersus deos numinaque contumaci
185 deliramento subsannabilique grassatus. Sero quis victurus humaniter est homini qui viuere Deo contumaciter non erubuerit religio-
nisue sinceritati. Profecto defacili fuerit omnis aspernator confortunalium sibi genialiterque consimilium, qui numinum reuerenciam
non verecundatur aspernari, potenciamue supernarum fastu fatui-
190 tatis contempnere potestatum.

[12.] De cetero, quo fatuitatis adhuc antiquitatis laciuire liceat in
latifundiis, Xerse Persarum principe nota satis est diouolariterque
wlgaris iniuriarum sibi destinatarum Delfici numinis exquisita
seueritas ulcionis. Xerses enim bellum cum Grecis prius a Dario
195 patre suo ceptum perseuerauit instruere[2] per quinquennium. Tandemque suo septingenta milia rex armatorum de regno, suis et ex
auxiliis extrinsecis ccc milia cateruauerat certo preliaturus ex proposito, sed et naues perhibetur coadunasse iii[3] milia numero, quo non
inmerito sit scripto paginaque perpetuatum[4] fuisse flumina Xersis
200 ab exercitu funditus exsiccata, totamque Greciam totum capere
tanti[5] vix potuisse regis exercitum. Tanto tamen exercitui dux
defuit ad expediens animosus, ut qui consuetudinaliter primus ad
fugam, ad pugnam postremus, animi vilitate remissi foret insti-
gatus: in periculis timore prepropero[6] consternatus; |16ʳ| inflatus,
205 superbiaque tumens in prosperitatibus. Uerumptamen bellicos ante
congressus, virium fiducia uel opulenciarum velut ipsius nature
domitor uel dominus, et montes in planiciem nonnullos deduxit
valliumque connexa non nulla complanauit. Maria quedam ponci-
um preignara pontibus strauit, nauigacionis et ad commodum non
210 nulla deduxit, artificialium longe pertinacior ad contignaciones
quam controuersiarum bellicarum dubias et duras ad congressiones.
Unde sicut eius ingressus Grecis admodum terribilis fuit et aduentus abhominabilis, sic eiusdem fuit eisdem denique discessus
summe subsannabilis, fugaque fetens et feda, derisibiliterque turpis.
215 [13.] Nempe cum Spartanorum rex Leonida, milibus militum
solummodo quatuor comitatus, angustias quas crebrius preinuesti-

[1] S ad. qui before commendabiliter
[2] bellum cum Grecis ... perseuerauit instruere] bellum ... aduersus Graeciam
... instruxit Justin, cum bellum ... perseuerasset instruere S
[3] ccc S
[4] perpetuatim S
[5] tantum S
[6] pre properero S

man corrupted by excessive wealth, debased by inhuman cruelty, or enraged against his gods by proud delusion, should show any self-restraint worth praising. Anyone who does not blush to live in defiance of God and the integrity of religion will be slow to live humanely among men. Any arrogant fool who is not afraid to spurn the reverence of the gods or the potency of the heavenly powers will easily reject his relatives and those who share his fate.

[12.] Since it is still permissible to frolic in the broad domains of ancient foolery, the studied severity of the Delphic godhead's vengeance upon the harm intended him by Xerxes, King of Persia, is well known and meretriciously commonplace. Xerxes spent five years preparing to continue the war with the Greeks begun by his father. Wholly resolved on battle, the king at length assembled 700,000 soldiers from his own realm and 300,000 from his foreign auxiliaries, not to mention the 3,000 ships he is said to have brought together. Pen and page have rightly immortalized the rivers drunk dry by Xerxes's forces, an army so large that all of Greece could scarcely contain it. But this huge army lacked a leader with the courage to succeed in battle, since Xerxes, impelled by the baseness of a lazy spirit, was habitually last in battle and first in flight, dismayed by precipitate fear in peril and puffed up with pride in prosperity. Trusting in his forces and wealth as if he were the lord or conqueror of nature herself, he reduced not a few mountains to plains and levelled many passes between valleys before doing battle. Far more assiduous in framing artifices than in braving the doubtful and harsh shocks of battle, he spanned seas which had not previously known bridges and diverted others for ease of navigation. But just as his approach and arrival were terrifying to the Greeks, his shameful departure in flight was supremely worthy of their ridicule.

[13.] For when the Spartan king Leonidas, accompanied by only 4,000 soldiers, took up the defensive position he had already scout-

gauerat ut indigena occupasset,[1] contemptu paucitatis eos rex
Xerses quorum cognati pridem prehabita perempti fuerant in pugna
capescere pugnam precepit. Quidam[2] suos ulcisci prepropere pa-
220 rant et bellice sibi cladis et confusionis peremptorie precipicium
primiciare procurant. Succedenteque magna subsequenter et utili
minus inordinataque turba, maior succedit cedes mestiorque ruina.
Tribus illis diebus in angustiis Persarum cum detrimento, dolore
necnon et indignacione dimicatum fuit et diminucione. Leonida
225 profecto Spartanorum rex angustias ideo preoccupauerat ut si
casurus certaret, citeriori detrimento caderet, si vero victurus pug-
naret, gloria cum paucis eleganciore triumpharet. Sed maiori suo-
rum |16ᵛ| parti tandem sociorum, plus patrie quam proprie[3] vite
contemplans utilitatem, se redditu conseruare vite securiorem
230 persuadere nisus est ad statum, quo patrie tempora se reseruarent
ad meliora. Sicque cognita voluntate regia persuasionibus declarata,
solis secum remanentibus Spartanis, ceterorum caterua rediit vniuersa.

[14.] Dimissis itaque rex animosis[4] quos sibi presociauerat maiori
235 pro parte sua sponte sodalibus, hortari retentos sibi socios aggredi-
tur Spartanos, hostiumque contemplando multitudines innumeras,
eis conconsiderare suadet suis se qualitercumque preliantibus
cedendum[5] fore tandem tam numerosis hostibus. Eisque non minus
totis cauendum fore conatibus bellissime subinfert, ne sociorum
240 libencius ad instar in futurum redisse forciusue remansisse quam
dimicasse videantur. Nec ut ab hostibus circumuenirentur subintulit
expectandum, sed dum tempestiuam nox intempesta causam presta-
ret et occasionem securis et nil tale suspicantibus superueniendum,[6] presertim cum nusquam preliantes animosi commendabilius
245 quam mediis hostium sint in castris honestiusue perituri.

[15.] Sed magnanimis iamque paratis efficaciter persuasis mori
nichil impossibile fuit difficileue persuaderi. Protinus igitur omnes,
omni remocius amandata deliberacione, viriliter ad arma concur-
runt, dum longe plura patrie quam vite deberi laudabiliter in animo
250 condiducunt. Sexcentique viri |17ʳ| dumtaxat in castra quingento-
rum milium citra timorem perniciter irrumpunt. Nempe rex in
bellum profecturus suos ad idem comprofecturos ita preconfirma-

---

[1] occupasset *Justin, om. S*
[2] Quidam *S*, Qui dum *Justin*
[3] propriam *S*
[4] animosis *S*, animosus *Sᶜ*
[5] cedendum *S*, cadendum *Justin*
[6] superueniendum *Justin*, superuenientibus *S*

ed in the pass at Thermopylae, King Xerxes, out of contempt for the Greeks' scarcity, ordered into battle those of his soldiers whose kinsmen had died at Marathon. They prepared in haste to avenge their relatives and initiate the battle's headlong shock of carnage and confusion. With the huge, disorganized, and useless rabble moving up in reserve, greater slaughter followed and more grievous ruin. The battle in the pass continued for three days, with suffering, indignation, and loss falling to the lot of the Persians. Leonidas had occupied the pass with the intention of falling with fewer losses if he were destined to fail in battle, or triumphing with greater glory if he were destined to achieve victory. But caring more for the good of the country than his own life, he persuaded the greater part of his allies to preserve their lives by retreat and to reserve themselves for their country's better times. And so, when they knew the king's express will, only the Spartans remained with him, and all the other forces fell back.

[14.] Having sent away these courageous allies, most of whom had joined him of their own volition, the king exhorted the Spartans who remained with him, and glancing at the innumerable multitude of enemy soldiers, he urged them to consider with him that no matter how they and their fellow soldiers might fight, they must yield in the end to such numerous foes. He added that in what was to come they should take care lest they seem more willing to stand fast or retreat like their allies than to fight. Nor, he added, should they wait to be surrounded by their foes; instead, they should take advantage of the nighttime darkness to mount a surprise attack on their confident and unsuspecting enemy, especially since courageous fighters cannot die more honorably than in the camp of their foes.

[15.] But he would have had no difficulty persuading these brave men, who were fully prepared to die, to do anything he asked. Laudably deciding that they owed more to their country than their own lives, they set aside all deliberation and stood manfully to arms. Numbering only 600 men, they burst without fear into the camp of 500,000 soldiers. Before they went into battle, the king had so reassured those who went with him, that they did not hesitate to

90   SERIUM SENECTUTIS

uerat ut se proficisci paratis ad moriendum non hesitarent animis
animorumque propositis, sicque suis prandia predederat ad prelian-
255 dum profecturis quasi forent apud inferos nusquamue cenaturi.
Simul itaque subsequenter vnanimiter regis ad tentorium ruunt
principaleue pretorium, quo cum rege si prospere pugnauerint, aut
in eius potissimum sede ruituri, si minus optate forent preliaturi;
totis[1] inconcinnus e uestigio tumultus in castris exoritur. Statimque
260 Spartani, rege non invento, spe frustrati uel in hoc et desiderio, per
omnia castra victores vagantur, validique castrensium peremptores
cedunt, sternuntque sibi quelibet indifferenter obuia. Non secus
quam qui se scirent non spe victorie sed sue pocius necis in ulcionem tot hostibus hostiliter obuiare. ffere noctis a principio prelium
265 subsequentis est in partem diei maiorem protractum. Sunt et ad
postremum Spartani non superati sed superando sic fatigati quod
inter ingentes hostium cateruas[2] tam strenue stratorum cedibus
occiderunt exinaniti.

[16.] Sed rex Xerses, duobus terrestri prelio wlneribus exceptis in
270 terris aliquatenus iam confusus, terrestribus et in euentibus varians
et timore consternatus, marinis experiri fortunam statuit in congres-
sionibus, pusillanimorum more stolidorumque, quorum semper esse
proprium quis-|17ᵛ|quis veracissime dixerit alio corpus et alio
mentem diducere, distrahique varios in animi motus corporisque
275 gestus in diuersos. Unde prius quam naualis ineat prelii congressiones, dum dampnosas sibi timidorum pro consuetudine querit odio
belli dilaciones, armatorum quatuor milia misit Delphos ad Appollinis templum sacrilege diruendum manubialiterque spoliandum,
quasi minus sibi sufficere parumue videretur bellice solis cum
280 Grecis contendere nisi dis inmortalibus eciam bella presumeret
inequaliter inferre. Sed eo manus vniuersitasque tota, debitas dei
destinacione sacrilegis penas preinfligente, fulminibus imbriumque
fluoribus vlcionaliter invndantibus sic est extincta, quod nisi desipe-
ret suis exicialem per expertum rex intelligere posset quam nulla sit,
285 ut et ait antiquitas, aduersus inmortales contendendi pugnandiue
deos hominum sub sole uis viriumue facultas.

[17.] Non autem deus, ut sepe delusa diuinauit antiquitas, Appol-
lo talibus in finibus solis sue finem posuit ulcionis, sed eo Xersi
peruersos pertinaciter euentus preprocurante, postquam timiditate
290 Xersis et ignauia remissioris et animi torpente subsannabiliter
inercia numinis Appollonei propositum promouente, perniciter est

---

[1] totis *Justin*, totus *S*
[2] cateruas *Justin, om. S*

set out with a courageous resolve to die. He also gave his soldiers a meal before they entered battle, as if they were to dine next in the otherworld or nowhere. Then they all rushed with one spirit to the tent housing the headquarters of the Persian king, meaning to fall with him if they fought auspiciously or at least near his dwelling if they met with less success. A harsh tumult arose suddenly throughout the camp. But the Spartans, frustrated of their hope by their inability to find the Persian king, roamed victoriously through the entire camp, manfully slaying the camp's occupants and laying low everything in their path, like those who know they are attacking so many foes not in hope of victory, but to avenge their own death. The battle was drawn out from the beginning of the night through the greater part of the following day. In the end, the Spartans were not defeated, but so drained by the effort of slaying their many foes that they collapsed in exhaustion among the huge piles of the dead.

[16.] Dismayed by the two wounds he had received at Thermopylae and hesitant to risk another land battle for fear of its outcome, King Xerxes resolved to try his fortunes in a sea engagement. But he did so in the manner of the fainthearted and stupid, who (as someone has rightly said) by their nature direct their body one way and their mind another, and so dissociate the various movements of body and soul. Too timid and unwarlike to risk immediate engagement in a naval battle and eager for delays that only harmed his own cause, he sacrilegiously sent 4,000 soldiers to Delphi to despoil the temple of Apollo, as if doing battle with the Greeks alone was not enough for him unless he should presume to wage unequal war even upon the immortal gods. But when they arrived there, according to the purpose of the god, who inflicted in advance the due penalty for sacrilege, the entire force was obliterated by lightning and torrents of rain. It poured with such a vengeance that, had he not been hopelessly obtuse, the king might have understood from the fatal attempt how nonexistent, as even Antiquity admits, is earthbound man's power to contend with the immortal gods.

[17.] However, as deluded Antiquity divined, Apollo did not restrict his vengeance to the storm alone. With the Apollonian godhead procuring an outcome unfavorable to Xerxes in advance, and with Xerxes's faintheartedness and ridiculously unspirited inertia furthering the god's purpose, Xerxes soon fought an ill-

a Xerse nauali prelio perperamque pungnatum, sibi suo facillimis
est (ut id opido timoris instinctu desideranti) suasionibus a quodam
familiari persuasum, quatinus eo cum trecentis milibus armatorum[1]
295 in Grecia dimisso, suum sibi sane consulendo per reditum se |18^r|
recipere pergat in regnum. Racionesque suasor subiunxit ad persuadendum tales: primo, ne quis sediciones in regno moueat, aduersi
recepta belli per famam fama. Secundo subintulit aut se tam breui
manu non sine magna Persarum gloria Greciam perdomiturum, vel
300 si secus sequens euenerit euentus se sine regis hostibus absentis
infamia cessurum. Probatis igitur probato racionibus consilio,
quemlibet timore citra pudorem punctus attonito, quia uel in ea
fuerat admodum parte facilis et frugi, raptim cum tocius exercitus
parte recedendo sibi perplacite parat cedere persuasioni.
305 [18.] Sed audita Greci regis adeo temeraria tam timidi fuga,
pontis inire pergunt interrumpendi consilium quem suo contumax
in ingressu primo quasi tunc maris hominumque victor Abido rex
instruxerat, verum cum bellissime discretus id quidam pertinaciter
dissuaderet, sensatissime timens ne sic hostes interclusi desperacio-
310 nem de salute secus suspicantes in animositatem verterent, ut fit, et
in virtutem, sed et iter animose quod aliter non pateret ferro ferien-
do pararent, satis eciam multos hostes in Grecia remanere subdicti-
tans, hostium nec augeri numerum retinendo sic invitos oportere
laudabiliter allegans. Sed cum suo sic allegando more vincere
315 ceteros non potuisset, subtilitate vir veges et consilio, suam que sibi
sic non valuit alia via salutarem reuersus ad subtilitatem, seruum
sagacissime subornatum, quem facillimo predidicerat terrore con-
sternabilem, transmisit ad regem timore satis iam consternatum,
suoque facit consilio consternaciorem, dum fuga suadet ei pontis
320 occupare citissima |18^v| transitum.
[19.] Protinus ille suo more consternacione percussus, traditis
exercituum ducibus ut eos perducerent militibus, trepidus cum
paucis ignominiose contendit[2] Abidum, scaphamque qua transue-
heretur tremens est ingressus piscatoriam. Talis reuera res et euen-
325 tus speciali tunc fuit spectaculo perdignus et estimacione sortis
humane rerum per varietates admirandus, in paruo principem
videre nauigio latitantem quem paulo vix ante maris equor omne
capiebat exercitus in infinitate gloriantem. Quolibet eciam seruorum
ministerio tam cito tamque derisibiliter destitutum cuius exercitus
330 terris eciam graues erant multitudinis propter infinitatem.

---

[1] armatorum *Justin, om.* S
[2] contendit *Justin,* conscendit S

conceived naval battle. Afterwards, he was persuaded by the prompting of his own fear and the deft arguments of his advisor Mardonius to take thought for his safety by fleeing to his kingdom, leaving only Mardonius with 300,000 troops in Greece. Mardonius
urged that he do so lest anyone instigate a rebellion against his rule
upon hearing rumors of his defeat. He added that with such a small
force he would either subjugate Greece to the great glory of the
Persians or, if things should turn out otherwise, he would fall to
their foe without disgracing the departed king. Urged by frenzied
and shameless fear to assent to this reasoning, the king willingly
yielded to persuasion (proving that in this respect he was altogether
complaisant and cautious) and retreated immediately with the
greater part of his army.

[18.] But the Greeks, when they heard about the timid king's
hasty flight, took counsel whether to sever the bridge which he had
constructed at Abydos when he first entered Europe, as if he were
victor over sea and men. The prudent Themistocles argued against
doing so, suspecting that the enemy troops, if made to fear for their
lives by being bottled up in this manner, would (as often happens)
turn desperation into valor and bravely cut a path to safety by
laying on with their swords. He added that as things stood many of
the enemy remained in Greece, and pleaded that it made no sense
to increase the numbers of their foe by restraining them against
their will. But when he could not prevail upon the others by his
pleading in council, this man, flourishing in good counsel, reverted
to his redeeming subtlety and cleverly sent a suborned servant,
whom he already knew to be prone to confusion at the slightest
alarm, to Xerxes. He found him confounded by fear, and confounded him further by counseling him to cross the bridge in the swiftest
possible flight.

[19.] Struck senseless by confusion, as was his wont, Xerxes
entrusted the leaders of his several armies with the task of leading
his soldiers home. Fearful and with few followers, Xerxes hastened
to Abydos, trembling as he entered the fishing skiff which was to
carry him across the Hellespont. This outcome of events deserves
close inspection as an admirable intimation of how man's lot varies
according to the vicissitudes of life. Behold the prince, whom a
short time before the entire expanse of the sea had scarcely held
glorying in the infinite vastness of his army, hiding in a small craft.
See the man whose troops weighed down the earth on account of
their infinite multitude so soon without any assistance from servants.

[20.] Sed nec pedestribus militaribusue copiis quas preassignaue-
rat ad perducendum ducibus fuit iter felicius. Siquidem cotidianis
laboribus addictos (rara nempe consueuit esse quies continue
metuentibus) edulitatis austeritas famis et improperium male
335 molestabat, dierumque deinde fami casualiter incidens et habundancia cibariorum, panisque potuumque copia, fatalem plus iusto
voracibus pestem perniciter ingerebat. Tantaque deficiencium
fatalitas succedebat quod et vias ex cadauerum multitudinibus
contracta caries putredinisque pestilencia perniciosissime corrumpe-
340 bat. Auiumque multitudines eciam rapaciumque bestiarum multitudo moriencium cadauerumque sufficiencia superhabundans sollici-
tabat.

[21.] Et ad summam, quo consumatum suam prosequeretur
iniuriam delictis[1] ad finem, cum suam Xerses Persarum rex, terra-
345 rumque terror antea, bello tam miserabiliter tamque perniciter in
Grecia gesto, patriam fuisset non minus infeliciter ingressus, suis
eciam contemptui cepit esse sicut et eis quibus se contumaciter
preposuerat numinibus. Unde deficienti tam remisse cotidie |19ʳ|
regis maiestate, prefectus[2] eius in spem regni redeductus,[3] regiam
350 face suprema cum vii filiis quos habebat robustis est ingressus.
Nempe diutini[4] iure federis amicicie regie sibi patebat ad libitum
semper introitus. Sicque licite regem trucidauit adeo uilibus finem
prefigendo superfluisque consternacionibus.

[22.] Non autem multos, ut auguror, studiis officiose litteralibus
355 latet assiduatos qua seueritate suas in Metapontinis, Sybaritanis[5] et
Crotoniensibus, ceteros ab Italia Grecos expellere pridem concer-
tantibus, illatas ulta sibi fuerit Minerua iniurias. Nempe cum suo
conferuentes in proposito ciuitatem Syrim[6] expugnassent primum,
ciuitatis eius in expugnacione quinquaginta iuuenes qui velut ad
360 asilum Minerue confugerant, ut fit, ad templum, dee symulachrum
reuerenter eciam coamplexos, ipsiusque sacerdotem vestibus et
ornamentis velatum vestitumque diuinis ipsa trucidauerunt inter
altaria. Sed eos dea, delusa sicut asserit antiquitas et ad vanitates
tunc inclinatiua, tale propter sacrilegium scelusque facti locique
365 contemplacione satis enormiter perperamque perpetratum, letalibus
turbauit adeo contumaces pestilenciis, tumultuosisque sedicionibus

---

[1] delicis S

[2] prefectus Justin, profectus S

[3] redeductus S, deductus Sᶜ

[4] diutim S

[5] Sybaritanis Justin, Eubaritanis S

[6] Syrim] Sirim Justin, Syrimed S

[20.] Nor were the hordes of soldiers whom Xerxes had consigned to the leadership of his generals more fortunate in their passage. Doomed as they were to daily struggle (indeed, rest is rare for those in constant fear), short rations and hunger harmed them severely. Then, when abundant provisions and an excess of food and drink put an end to the famine, they afflicted those who devoured too much with a fatal plague. So many of the stricken died that the pestilence contracted from the heaps of rotting bodies fatally infected the roads, and the vast multitudes of the dead and dying attracted masses of birds and beasts of prey.

[21.] His injustice was crowned by one final misdeed. When Xerxes, king of Persia and once scourge of the world, reentered his native land after having waged such a miserable and ruinous war in Greece, he found himself held in contempt by his own people as well as by the gods to whom he had contumaciously preferred himself. As a result, his prefect, led to hope for the kingship by the daily waning of the king's feeble dignity, entered the royal palace at dusk with his seven robust sons. The palace entrance stood open for him to enter at will by reason of the long-standing friendship of Xerxes. He rightfully slaughtered the king and so put an end to his base and unwarranted dismay.

[22.] Nor are many scholars who pursue their literary studies with zeal unaware of what severe vengeance Minerva exacted for the injuries which the Metapontines, Sybaritans, and Crotonians inflicted on her when they banded together to drive the other Greeks from Italy. All alike fired by their objective, they began by storming the city of Heraclea and slaughtering fifty youths who, as the city was being stormed, had fled for sanctuary to the temple of Minerva and (as often happens) had reverently embraced the goddess's likeness. They even slaughtered her priest, clothed in the divine vestments and insignia, at the altar itself. But on account of this sacrilegious crime, which was quite outrageous in light of where it took place, the goddess (as Antiquity, deluded and inclined to vanities, claims) confounded these contumacious men with a fatal pestilence and buffeted them with turbulent discord. But

vexauit et diminutionibus. Uerumtamen quia tyrannorum truculen-
tissimorum, ne dum commenticiarum[1] seueritates commenticie
diuinitatum supplicacionibus frequentissime mitigantur, voluntariis-
370   que delictorum confessionibus obliterantur, Crotoniensibus Delphis
prius et humiliter aditis oraculum petentibus, est ut fabulatores
aiunt ab Appolline responsum finem mali fore venturum si Minerue
numen violatum manesque placassent interfectorum. |19ᵛ| Itaque
cum statuas iuste magnitudinis iuuenibus et sacerdoti trucidatis,
375   sed in primis Minerue, fabricare cepissent Crotoniate, Metapontani,
tunc oraculo dei cognito, deorum preoccupandam gratiam deeque
rati beniuolenciam, iuuenibus modica lapideaque cito ponunt
simulachra, deamque panificiis[2] placant. Sicque pestis est utrobique
sedata, cum Crotoniate magnificencia, Metapontani celeritate certas-
380   sent.

[23.] Hercules eciam detracte religioni[3] sue grauem manifes-
tamque perhibetur exegisse penam. Nempe cum Poticii[4] sacrorum
dei ritum deo diucius exibitum, quem pro dono genti Poticiorum
specialiter ab ipso preassignatum velut hereditarium preoptinue-
385   rant, ad humile seruorum ministerium transtulissent, omnes qui
supra viginti[5] numero puberes fuerant annui temporis[6] intra spa-
cium fuere specialiter elati. Nomenque Poticianum[7] duodecim solas
inter familias diuisum prope prorsus interiit ut exanimatum. Censor
et Apius luminibus est captus.

390   [24.] Procax etiam satis et acerbus sui numinis vindex fuisse
perhibetur Apollo qui, Cartagine victoribus a Romanis viriliter
oppugnata veste viduatus manubialiter aurea, dicitur id egisse quod
fracte vestis ipsius inter fragmenta manus sacrilege reperirentur
abscise. Sua sibi sane plus iusto cara Phebo videtur fuisse vestis,
395   cuius subtractionem manuum compensare manubiatoris cum graui-
tate sustinuit abscisionis, presertim cum nec eius indigus fuerit uel
alterius ut ab omni frigoris infestacione semper securus.

[25.] Appollinis filius ulcionis in atrocitate procaciter patrissare
videtur Esculapius qui, cum sibi suoque consecratum templo

---

[1] commenticiorum S
[2] panificiis *Justin*, panificis S
[3] religioni S, religionis *Valerius*
[4] Poticii] Potitii *Valerius*, Pocii S
[5] viginti S, xxx *Valerius*
[6] annui temporis] annuitemporis S
[7] Poncianum S

since the harsh decrees of the most ferocious tyrants or fictitious divinities are frequently mitigated by supplication and effaced by voluntary confession, the Crotonians humbly sought an oracle from the sanctuary at Delphi. According to the writers of fable, Apollo responded that they could put an end to the evil by placating Minerva's violated godhead and the spirits of those they had murdered. So the Crotonians undertook to fashion on the proper scale statues of the slain youths, the priest, and first of all, Minerva. When the Metapontines learned about the oracle of the god, they decided to preempt the goodwill of the gods. So, trusting in the goddess's benevolence, they swiftly erected modest stone likenesses of the youths and placated the goddess with cakes. Thus the plague was calmed in both places, because the Crotonians vied in magnificence and the Metapontines in speed.

[23.] Hercules as well is said to have exacted a conspicuously heavy penalty for slighting his religion. When the Potitian *gens* transferred the long-honored observance of his rites, which they had obtained from the god as a hereditary gift, to the humble ministry of slaves, all the Potitii who were grown men, more than twenty in number, were buried one by one within the space of a year. And the name of the Potitii, divided among only twelve families, almost completely perished. The censor Appius went blind.

[24.] Apollo is also said to have avenged his godhead harshly. When the Romans who had manfully sacked Carthage despoiled his statue of a gold garment, he brought it about that the hands of those who had perpetrated the sacrilege were found amputated among the fragments of the shattered garment. His cruel willingness to compensate for the removal of his garment by cutting off the despoilers' hands makes it clear that the garment was dearer than it should have been to Phoebus, inasmuch as he did not need it or any other clothing to preserve him from a chill.

[25.] Apollo's son Aesculapius took after his father in exacting savage vengeance. When Antony's prefect Turullius cut down most

400 lucum[1] |20[r]| Cirillius[2] Antonii prefectus ad naues Antonio fabri-
candas magna pro parte succidisset, eumque sic Esculapius succi-
sum doleret, Antonii devictis inter opus ipsum sacrilegii nefarium
partibus, imperio Cesaris fatalitati destinatum manifestis Cyrillium
numinis sui viribus in eum quem violauerat locum traxit id et
405 effecit ut ibi potissimum Cesaris a militibus occisus occumberet, quo
meritas arboribus de succisis penas penderet, superstitibusque suam
quam penes[3] accolas maximam semper habuerant[4] veneracionem
redintegraret.

[26.] Notum[5] satis est eciam qualiter illatas sibi per periurium
410 Iupiter in rege Macedonum Tolomeo pridem fuerit ultus iniurias.
Ptolomeus enim, Macedonum regno dolis et machinacionibus sibi
confirmato, necnon et externo metu sompniculosis nequiciarum
scrutiniis obliterato, facinorosum non formidauit ad domestica
conuertere scelera vir sceleratissimus animum. Nempe sorori sue,
415 scilicet Arsinoe,[6] parare peremptorias non erubuit affectiuasque
fatalitatis insidias, quibus et sororem sororisque filios, quos elato
iam tunc marito suo progenuerat regi Lisimaco, vita priuaret,
Cassandrie simul et urbis possessione. Primus ei fuit inicialisque
dolus quod simulato sororis amore sororem sibi petere sociari
420 procaciter pararet in matrimonium, quia non aliter ad sororis filios,
quorum preoccupauerat regnum, nisi simulata cum sorore concordia poterat (quod opido desiderabat) peruenire perimendos. Sed
quia precognitam coniectauit sue[7] tam sceleratam sorori mentis
voluntatisque maliciam, sorori suum sibi male |20[v]| credenti
425 mandat[8] per nuncium uelle se suis cum filiis[9] sui consorcium
coniungere regni, cum quibus non ideo se (sicut asserebat) armis
contendisse quod eis sibi saguinis proximitate tam coniunctis
eripere regnum proposuisset, sed quod eos id sui titulo muneris
possidere uoluisset. Mittere de hinc illam iurisiurandi rogat arbi-
430 trum,[10] quo presente patrios aput deos se quibus vellet obsecracionibus obligaret.

---

[1] S ad. quem *before* Cirillius
[2] Cirillius S, Turullius *Valerius*
[3] penes] penas S, apud *Valerius*
[4] habuerat S
[5] Motum S
[6] Arsinoe] Arsinoae *Justin*, Arsione S (*Cf. 3.432 and passim.*)
[7] se S
[8] mandat *Justin*, mandare S
[9] filis S
[10] arbitrum *Justin*, arbitrium S

of a grove consecrated to Aesculapius and his temple to make ships for Antony, the god mourned his loss. So after Antony's followers were defeated in the very act of sacrilege, Aesculapius employed the manifest powers of his godhead to drag Turullius, who was destined to death by order of Caesar, to the grove he had violated, and caused him to meet an appropriate death there at the hands of Caesar's soldiers. Thus Turullius suffered the due punishment for cutting down the trees, and Aesculapius restored for the remaining trees the great veneration they had always enjoyed among those who dwelt nearby.

[26.] How Jupiter avenged on Ptolemy, king of Macedonia, the injuries he suffered as a result of the king's perjury has also been mooted frequently. Having consolidated his rule over the Macedonians by deceit and machination, and having eliminated all external threats by inexhaustible villainy, Ptolemy, the most criminal of men, was not afraid to turn his wicked mind to domestic crimes. He did not blush to prepare a deadly trap for his sister Arsinoe, by which he deprived her and her sons, whom she had borne to her deceased husband King Lysimachus, of both their lives and the city of Cassandria. Since he could not bring about the death of his sister's sons, whose kingdom he had already seized, except by dissimulated concord with his sister, his initial deceit was a wanton resolve to feign a loving desire to seek his sister in marriage. But as he guessed that his innate malice was already known to her, he announced by messenger to his sister, who scarce believed him, that he wished to share his realm with her sons. He claimed that he had contended in arms with them not because he proposed to snatch the realm from those so closely conjoined to him by blood relation, but because he wanted them to possess it by right of his gift. He then asked her to send someone as witness to an oath, in whose presence he would bind himself before their ancestral gods by whatever prayers she might wish.

[27.] Incerta quid ageret Arsinoe satis est et perplexa: timebat enim si mitteret peruersi periurio circumueniri. Si uero mittere supersederet, fraterne rabiem crudelitatis per hoc ad malignandum verebatur exacerbari. Suis itaque longe magis metuens liberis quam sibi, suis ex amicis sibi familiarissimis vnum sanius denique ducit ad fratrem transmitti. Quo producto, proditor frater Iouis in templum religionis antiquissime ritu summe verendum, suas in manus amplexusque sumptis altaribus, contingens et simulachra puluinariaque deorum, sibi conceptissime mandatis ultimis necnon et horrendis dictuque diris execracionibus, iurat sororis fide sincera pecere matrimonium, seque reginam citra fraudes eam fideque bona nuncupaturum, nec eius in contumeliam se secundam uel aliam sibi coniugem superinducturum, nec alios quam filios eius sibi liberos habiturum.

[28.] Sic igitur Arsinoe, postquam certa sicut verisimillime coniectabat spe[1] confirmata fuerat omnique metu suspicioneque soluta, beniuolum fratris venit in colloquium. Cuius cum wltus oculique[2] blandientes fidem non minorem quam prestitum promitterent iusiurandum, fratris se letabunda copulari patitur in matrimonium. Nupciis magnis apparatibus[3] omniumque leticiis |21ʳ| indifferenter celebratis,[4] ad concionemque convocato sicut consuetudinis erat exercitu, capiti dyadema sororis a fratre sollempniter imponitur; a fratre regina soror appellatur.

[29.] Quo nomine mox in leticias Arsynoe largas infusa, quia quod morte mariti Lisimachi prioris amiserat suo iam iudicio recuperasset, ultro virum mulier in urbem suam Cassandriam gaudens invitat, cuius urbis cupiditate fraus adeo sordens et inhumana prestructa fuerat. Preingressa de hinc urbem virum, ferias indicit[5] urbi diemque festiuum[6] viri noui propter aduentum. De more templa ceteraque iubet exornari singula,[7] sed et aras hostiasque disponi; filios eciam suos (Lisymacum sedecim tunc annos natum, Philippumque triennio minorem), forma satis insignes, venienti iubet occurrere coronatos. Quos Ptolomeus, ad obnubilandam fraudis malignitatem, cupide nimis et ultra modum sincere

---

[1] spe *Justin*, sepe *S*

[2] wltus oculique] vultus et . . . oculi *Justin*, wltum oculosque *S*

[3] apparatibus] apparibus *S*, apparatu *Justin*

[4] Nupcie . . . indifferentibus celebrantibus *S*

[5] indicit *Justin*, inducit *S*, indecit *S*ᶜ

[6] festiuumque *S*

[7] templa ceteraque . . . singula] templa ceteraque . . . omnia *Justin*, templaque cetera . . . singula *S*

[27.] Arsinoe was perplexed and uncertain what to do: she was afraid that if she sent someone she would be circumvented by her brother's perjury. If, on the other hand, she were to refuse to send anyone, she was afraid that she would rouse the fury of her cruel brother to her own harm. Fearing more for her sons than for herself, she at length chose one of her closest friends to send to her brother. When he arrived, her traitorous brother, embracing the altar and touching the likenesses and couches of the gods, swore formally in Jove's temple (which was to be held in highest awe according to the rites of the most ancient religion), with extreme and terrible promises and curses dreadful to hear, that he sought to marry his sister in good faith, and that he would name her queen without deceit, nor would he harm her by taking a second wife or accepting any children other than hers as his rightful offspring.

[28.] Arsinoe, once she imagined herself confirmed in certain hope and released from all fear or suspicion, entered into friendly contact with her brother. And since his face and fawning eyes promised no less good faith than his tendered oath, she gladly allowed herself to be united with her brother in matrimony. Their nuptials were celebrated by all with great pomp and joy, and the army was called to the assembly according to custom. Ptolemy solemnly placed the diadem on his sister's head; Arsinoe was called queen by her brother.

[29.] Revelling in the great joy of that name, and judging that she had recovered what she lost at the death of her first husband Lysimachus, Arsinoe gladly invited her husband into her city Cassandria, for the sake of which he had contrived his vile and inhuman stratagem. Entering the city before her husband, she proclaimed a holiday festival throughout the city on account of her new husband's arrival. She commanded that the temples and other buildings be adorned according to custom, and that altars and victims be set out. She commanded her sons Lysimachus (who was sixteen) and Philip (who was three years younger)—both remarkably handsome—to meet the approaching king wearing their crowns. In order to obscure his malignant deception, Ptolemy

dileccionis amplexibus et osculis diu fatigauit.

[30.] Sed ubi ventum ciuitatis est ad portam, protinus occupari iubet arcem puerorumque maturari iubet fatali ferro fatalitatem. Qui, cum suam miseri ad matrem confugissent, in gremio genitricis
470   inter ipsa lamentantis oscula trucidantur, proclamante miserabiliter Arsynoe quod tantum nubendo nefas contraxisset aut post nupcias. Crebro se pro filiis libens obicere promptificauit persecutoribus[1]; puerorum frequencius suo corpore corpora protexit, ea maternaliter amplexata, letaliaque que suis intendebantur liberis conabatur
475   excipere wlnera. Sed et ad ultimum filiorum funeribus filiis abho- minabiliter viduata, duobus dumtaxat comitata |21ᵛ| seruulis est ab urbe violenter eiecta, Samotraciamque[2] miserabiliter abiit, exilio penitus inexorabili destituta, solo dumtaxat eo miserabilissima quod ei suis mori non licuit cum filiis, quod sibi summo fuisset suis tunc
480   talibus in suspiriis pro solacio.

[31.] Non autem Ptolomeo tot ipsis eciam summis abhominacioni- bus abhominabilia scelera fuere diucius inpunita, Ioue tot periuria, tamque cruenta per fraudes perpetrata dolosque paricidia, denique digna prosequi parante vindicta. Nempe cum Galli multitudine
485   superhabundanti sua sic superhabundarent in patria, quotque genuerat non caperet eos terra, ccc milia suorum nouas (apum velut ad instar) ad sedes emisere sibi querendas. Ex quibus, ut fertur, in Ytalia pars quedam consedit, que Romam suis expugnatam viribus incendit; pars autem sinus Ylliricos, auguriis iter eis auium pre-
490   monstrantibus (pre ceteris[3] enim Galli studiis augurizando perhi- bentur esse precipui), barbarorum per strages penetrauit et in Pannonia consedit: gens audax et aspera, sagax et opido bellicosa. Que quidem prima post Herculem, cui res eadem virtutis admiraci- ones inmortalitatisque fidem fecit laudisque procurauit perpetui-
495   tates, glaciales Alpium scrupulositates iugaque iugibus transcendit, frigoribus exasperata niuiumque concrecionibus ineuitabiliter obsita. Pannoniis itaque perdomitis, annos per quamplures aduersus sibi finitimos bella gerere perseuerarunt. Uerum felicibus id sibi denique suggerentibus crebrisque successibus, prediuisis agminibus, alii
500   Greciam, quidam uero Macedoniam singula ferro prosternentes adiere.

[32.] Tantus tunc terror Gallici nominis emersit ut et non lacessiti reges patriarumque |22ʳ| principes ultro sibi pacem peccunia

---

[1] percussoribus *Justin*
[2] Samo traciamque *S*
[3] pre ceteris] preceteris *S*

wearied them with long embraces and kisses too eager to be within the bounds of sincere affection.

[30.] But when he arrived at the city gate, he suddenly ordered his soldiers to occupy the citadel and hasten the destiny of the boys with fatal steel. They fled in misery to their lamenting mother but were slain in her lap amidst her kisses, while Arsinoe miserably proclaimed that she had incurred such a horror by her marriage or its aftermath. She repeatedly tried to expose herself to the lethal blows intended for her sons by their persecutors; holding her sons in a maternal embrace, she often shielded their bodies with her own. But finally, made destitute by the abominable deaths of her sons, she was expelled by force from the city, accompanied only by two young slaves, and went in misery to Samothrace, abandoned to inexorable exile. Her greatest misery was that she was unable to die with her sons, which would have been the supreme solace to her sighs.

[31.] Ptolemy's abominable crimes, including these supreme abominations, did not remain unpunished: at long last Jove pursued so many perjuries, such bloody parricides achieved through fraud and guile, with fit vengeance. When the Gauls in their superabundant multitude became too numerous for their homeland, and the land could not contain all those it gave birth to, they sent 300,000 of their people off like bees to seek new settlements for themselves. According to tradition, one group of them settled in Italy, sacking and burning Rome. But another group, with avian auguries showing it the way (for the Gauls are said to excel more in the practice of augury than in any other study), penetrated the Illyrian gulf, slaughtering barbarians along the way, and settled in Pannonia. They were a daring and tough people, wise and extremely bellicose, who were the first men after Hercules (for whom the same feat won perpetual praise, admiration for his virtue, and faith in his immortality) to cross the icy cliffs and many ridges of the Alps, afflicted by the cold and enveloped in packed snow. Having pacified the Pannonians, they waged war for many years against their immediate neighbors. Their frequent and great success suggested that they should divide their troops: some went to Greece, others to Macedonia, overthrowing everything with the sword.

[32.] The Gauls aroused such fear that even kings and princes of nations not under attack sought to purchase peace for themselves

precibus eciam multa conditis redimere procurarent, dum solus
505   Macedoniorum rex, proditor et paricida, Ptolomeus, infortuniis pro
uelle Iouis fedeque fatalitati destinatus, Gallorum prestolatur aduentus[1] et audiit intrepidus, forte suis sibi spem ponens adhuc in
prodicionibus. Ille quidem cum paucis et ad preliandum pene
incompositis, quasi prelia non difficilius periculosiusue patrarentur
510   quam prodiciones et paricidia, paricidiorum forte furiis exagitatus,
occurrere presumit aduenientibus. Sed ad detectiorem sue fatuitatis
inmensitatem, Dardanorum delirus offerencium sibi viginti milia
subsidiatorum superbo spreuit fastu legacionem, superadditis eciam
sic stolidissime contumeliis: Actum de Macedoniis[2] ait iam nunc
515   videtur esse totum, si cum[3] pridem suis orientem solummodo
viribus domuissent vniuersum, suorum nunc in defensione finium
Dardaneorum denique supplementis subsidiorum et adiectionibus
indigerent. Milites se subiecit habere filios eorum qui sub Alexan-
dro, tocius orbis terrarum domitore, demerita meruere stipendia.
520   Sed ubi tam temeraria Dardano regi talia Ptolomei dicta fuere
nunciata, Macedonum[4] tam nobile regnum tam male maturi iuuenis in breui temeritate simul et insolencia dixit esse ruiturum.

[33.] Non autem male coniectauit verbaue vir prudens taliter
effusa fudit in irritum. Truces[5] et enim Galli, bellissimeque bellicis
525   in accionibus sagaces, quo Macedonum pretemptarent et animo-
sitates et audaciam, legatos ad Ptolomeum transmittunt, ipsi pacem
si redimere voluerit offerentes venalem. Sed Ptholomeus, inter suos
belli metu pacem petere Gallos (gallorum | 22ᵛ | more suis in ster-
quiliniis supreme gloriancium) gloriatus, non minus minaciter se
530   Gallorum coram legatis quam suos inter sibi familiares iactare non
supersedit eis se non aliter pacem daturum nisi suos sibi principes
armaque resignauerint. Non enim se fidem superbe dicebat eis nisi
nudis et inermibus habiturum. Relatum sibi tam stolide superbientis
Galli risere responsum, dedignantes conclamauerunt an sibi consu-
535   lentes an ipsi pacem preoptulerint in breui sensurum.

[34.] Diebus itaque non multis subsequenter interiectis, horrisonis
(ut fit) vltro citroque concursibus, bellum conseritur; victi Macedo-
nes miserrime ceduntur; Ptolomeus, nuper adeo contumax et super-
bus, quam plurimis preexceptis capitur wlneribus; caput eius, Ioue

---

[1] aduentus S, aduentum *Justin*
[2] Macedoniis] Lacedemoniis S, Macedonia *Justin*
[3] si cum *Justin*, suum S
[4] Macedonum] Macedorum S, Macedoniae *Justin*
[5] Truces] Traces S, *om. Justin*

by freely sweetening their entreaties with large amounts of money. Only the Macedonian king Ptolemy, traitor and parricide, destined for misfortunes and a horrible death by the will of Jove, awaited the coming of the Gauls without fear, perhaps placing all his hope in his skill at betrayal. Driven perhaps by the furies of the relatives he had slain, he confronted the approaching Gauls with a few disorderly followers, as if victory in battle could be achieved with as little peril or difficulty as betrayals and parricides. But to make the extent of his stupidity more apparent, he was so madly arrogant as to reject an embassy of Illyrians offering him 20,000 auxiliaries, and even to add some foolish insults. "It is all over for the Macedonians," he said, "if having once conquered the entire Orient with their own forces, they should now require Illyrian reinforcements and auxiliaries for the defense of their own borders." He added that he had soldiers who were the sons of those who earned their pay under Alexander, the conqueror of the entire world. But when Ptolemy's ill-considered words were announced to the Illyrian king, he said that the noble kingdom of Macedonia would be destroyed by the impetuous arrogance of such an immature youth.

[33.] This prudent man did not forecast wrongly, nor did he speak in vain. Experienced in the conduct of battle, the savage Gauls decided to test the spirits and bravery of the Macedonians by sending envoys to Ptolemy offering him a venal peace if he were willing to pay their asking price. Having bragged to his followers that the Gauls, like roosters glorying in their dungheaps, sought peace from fear of war, Ptolemy could not refrain from boasting to the Gallic envoys, as he had to his familiars, that he would not grant them peace unless they resigned their leaders and arms to him. He proudly claimed that he could only trust Gauls who were naked and unarmed. The Gauls laughed at the response of a fool so proud of himself, scornfully shouting that it would soon be known whether they consulted their own good or the Macedonians' in offering peace.

[34.] After the lapse of a few days, battle was joined with noisy shocks back and forth. The Macedonians were defeated with horrible slaughter, and Ptolemy, just now so defiant and proud, was captured with numerous wounds. As Jove at last exacted the penal-

540 demeritas sero tamen periuriorumque simul et prodicionum penas
exigente, crudeliter amputatum totam circumfertur aciei per vniuersitatem communiter subsannatum lancea preinfixum, quo fuit
efficax horroris incentiuum. Lentis profecto sepius diuina passibus
procedere consueuit ulcio, suam tamen denique tarditatem pensare
545 penalitatis solet acerbe cum supplicio.

[35.] Non nullis eciam familiaris est et optime nota satis enormes
exacerbati per iniurias Appollinis ad iram iurisdictio,[1] subsequentis
illatas ob iniurias acerbitate penalitatis specialissima, qua[2] Gallorum ducem Brennium derisibilis deduci procurauit delecionis ad
550 improperium, fede consumatum fatalitatis ad infortunium. Dux
enim Gallorum Brennius,[3] postquam nemine prohibente Macedonie
tocius agros[4] et ciuitates manubialiter extenuerat, quasi terrestria
sibi iam spolia sorderent et subsolaria, sacra sui[5] male sibi sorden-
tis |23ʳ| animi voracitates vertere deorum non formidauit ad
555 templa. Suumque tam subsannabile propositum scurilitate prosequi
non dubitauit sic ystrionaliter iocosa. Locupletatos ait sibique
superuacua possidentes largiri deos hominibus oportere, statimque
tam temerarium quam sibi perniciosum Delfos uersus iter vertit,
predamque reuerencie religionis, et aurum deorum preferens
560 offense, deorumque numinibus et maliuolencie, quos eciam nullis
indigere dicebat opulenciis, ut qui solis eas hominibus largiri sole-
ant constanter subridendo tamen allegabat.

[36.] Est autem, sicut (qui magna de magnis fari consueuere)
perhibent poete, templum Delfis Parnasii montis in rupe situm sic
565 Appollinis. Rupes vndique concurrentes in eo saxo conueniunt; sic
templum ciuitatemque non muri manualiter facti sed precipicia, non
artificialia sed naturalia, murorum vices supplendo, pro muris ciues
et templum ciuitatemque defendunt, quo sit uel esse videatur
prorsum incertum munimentumue loci maiestasue potestatiua Delii
570 maioris sibi fit admiracionis excitatiuum. Media quidem saxi rupes
in theatri similitudinem formamque cedit,[6] quo fit ut et hominum
clamor (et si quando solus acciderit aduenticius, compersonantibus
inter se conresonantibusque rupibus audiri videatur multiplicatus)
amplior quam sicut editur resonare senciatur. Que res terrorem
575 maiestatis multo maiorem rei racionem perfunctorie considerantibus

---

[1] iuridicta S
[2] S ad. Gallos before Gallorum
[3] Brennius S, Brennus Justin
[4] agros Justin, om. S
[5] sua S
[6] cedit S, recessit Justin

ty for perjury and betrayal, the Gauls savagely amputated his head
and, as a means of horrifying the Macedonians, carried it about
fixed on a lance to the ridicule of the entire army. Without question,
divine vengeance proceeds by slow steps, but it normally compen-
sates for its slowness by inflicting a harsh punishment.

[35.] The justice of Apollo when roused to wrath by egregious
injuries is well known and familiar to many. It was unique on
account of the harsh punishment for his injuries which he inflicted
on Brennus, leader of the Gauls, who was led away to a ridiculous
and ignominious death, the crowning misfortune of a foul destiny.
For after Brennus and his Gauls had despoiled the cities and countryside of all Macedonia without opposition, he was not afraid to
turn his foul and ravenous spirit towards the sacred temples of the
gods, as if earthly and subsolar spoils were no longer enough for
him. He did not hesitate to carry out his ridiculous plan with the
scurrilous humor of an actor, saying that the rich gods, possessing
more than they need, should lavish their goods on men. He suddenly turned his reckless and self-destructive steps towards Delphi,
preferring booty to religious reverence and gold to the animosity of
the gods, their power and malevolence. He said they would lack no
wealth, as is natural for those who lavish it only on humans, he
constantly added with a smile.

[36.] As the poets (who are accustomed to saying great things
about great events) claim, there is at Delphi a temple of Apollo,
placed in the cliff of Mt. Parnassus. The cliffs which extend in every
direction converge on that rock: natural precipices rather than walls
made by hand defended temple and city, so that it was uncertain
whether the fortification of the place or the potent majesty of the
Delian excited greater admiration. The central cliff of the range is
recessed in the form of a theater, so that the clamor of humans
resonates more loudly than it sounded originally, and when a lone
wanderer comes within hearing it sounds as if he has been multi-
plied by the cliffs echoing and resounding between themselves. This
often instills great fear of the god's majesty in those who do not

admiracionemque[1] frequencius incutere solet insolencia consternatis.

[37.] In eo rupis (theatri videlicet in formam cedentis) anfractu,
media ferme montis in altitudine, planicies esse fertur exigua
580 foraminis in profunditate cuiusdam cernentibus a cunctis consternabiliter admirata. Quod adeo profundum terre foramen in oraculis
patere perhibetur. Ex quo frigidus quasi venti flatus in sublime
velud expulsus |23ᵛ| vatum vertere mentes in vecordiam solet,
impletasque deo[2] responsa consulentibus dare cogi dicuntur. Sic
585 igitur ibi multa principum populorumque donaria visuntur opulen-
ta muneraque pro donatorum varietate varietatibus diuersificata,
que magnificencia sui gratam donatorum detegere mansuescunt et
manus et animi munificenciam, deique[3] suis prodere videntur in
responsis maiestatis veritatisque sinceritatem.

590 [38.] Uerum Brennius, ut ad eum reuertamur, Appollinis de
deitate nil omnino curans uel de responsis, ducibusque quos in
societatem prede sibi preiunxerat duobus, dum prorsus inparati
forent hostes et aduentus insolencia terroreque recentis hostium
consternati, moras suadentibus euestigio longius amandari, raptim
595 prorumpere properat ad arma. Sed iam Gallorum wlgus, inopiis
affectum retro fatigacionibusque diutinis, ubi primum vino ceterisque que vite sunt ad vsum rura summas ad habundancias invenit
affatimque referta, non minus habundancia quam victoria letum,
per agros, per villas et rura se sparserant, desertisque signis simul
600 et ordinibus, ad occupanda que reperire poterant vniuersa quasi
victores vagique discurrebant. Qui discursus, dum Delphis dat
dilacionem, Brennio sodalibusque[4] suis duobus admodum perniciosus fuit et infructuosus. Namque dum Gallorum wlgus, vini
voracitatibus esculentorum[5] non minus quam[6] poculentorum
605 superfluitatibus indulgens, pergit protrahere moras sepe morosas
meri per superhabundancias |24ʳ| aliquam diu protelatas, Delfi,
finitimorum viribus et auxiliis sibi socialiter adlateratis sagaciter
aucti, suam simul in primis vrbem tutam quatenus possent munire
pergunt ad tuicionem, dum Galli, vino velut prede manubiorumue
610 dulcedinibus incumbentes,[7] vix ad signa, morosoque mero fatigati

---

[1] -que *ed.*
[2] deo *Justin, om. S*
[3] deique *S*, deorum *Justin*
[4] -que *ed.*
[5] esculentorumque *S¹*
[6] quam *ed.*
[7] incumbentes *S*, incubantes *Justin*

consider its cause carefully, and admiration in those confounded by the novelty.

[37.] In this bend of the cliff, receding in the form of a theater, there is said to be a small patch of level ground roughly halfway up the mountain admired with wonder by all onlookers because of the depth of a certain cleft in the earth. This deep cleft is said to give vent to oracles. A cold gust of wind expelled from below turns the minds of seers to frenzy, and their minds filled with the compelling god, they are said to give responses to those who consult them. There were many opulent votive offerings of princes and peoples on display there, and gifts varied in kind according to the variety of givers; by their magnificence they revealed their donors' bounty of hand and spirit and affirmed the god's majesty and the truth of his responses.

[38.] But to return to Brennus: caring absolutely nothing for Apollo's godhead or responses, and with the two leaders who were his partners in spoils urging him to put aside all delay while their foes were unprepared and confounded by the surprise and terror of their recent coming, Brennus tried to rush his troops to arms. But when they first discovered that the countryside was bursting with wine and a great abundance of the other things necessary for life, the Gallic rabble, which had been afflicted by lack of provisions and extended exertions, scattered through fields, villages, and countryside, rejoicing in abundance as in victory, and deserting their standards to scramble like conquerors scavenging for whatever they could seize. This scramble afforded the people of Delphi a delay but was fruitless and ruinous for Brennus and his two associates. For while the Gallic rabble, indulging their appetite for wine with excesses of food and drink, prolonged already considerable delays because of the abundance of sluggish wine, the people of Delphi, reinforced by the troops and auxiliaries of allied neighbors, improved the defensive fortifications of their city as much as possible. Meanwhile, the Gauls, devoting themselves to wine as if it were the sweets of plunder, slowly returned to their standards, worn out by

morose reuertuntur.

[39.] Habebat autem Brennius exercitus ex vniuersitate peditum quinquaginta[1] quinque milia. Delforum uero suorumque consociatorum non nisi milia militum quatuor erant, quorum contemptu
615 Brennius ad acuendos suorum loquelaliter, ut fit, animos in primis omnibus ad prelium preparatis prede tot et tantas vbertates ostendit, statuas scilicet cum quadrigis quarum copias verpo demonstrabat directo vix numerabiles solido dumtaxat ex auro fusas. Subsequenter in pondere prede multo plus fore quam foret adeo splendenti
620 dicebat in superficie. Talibus igitur incitati tamque verisimilibus Galli communiter assercionibus, simul et hesterno mero manetenus continuato satis et ad habundans adhuc inundati, periculorum quemlibet citra respectum cateruatim ruunt omnes in prelium. Uerum deo suo Delfi plus fidentes in Delio quam suis in viribus
625 consubsidianciumve sibi numero, non sine derisu contemptuque sibi coaduersancium, sua pro possibilitate conatu resistere pertinacissimo perseuerant. Ruentes Gallos prerupti montis a vertice summo sequenti partim saxo, fatali partim ferro vite subsolari subducere festinant.

630   [40.] In eo sic concertancium[2] primo certamine, templorum repente (sicut[3] peribetur[4]) vniuersorum simul antistites necnon et ipse vates sparsis[5] crinibus, |24ᵛ| insignibusque pariter et infulis compotitis,[6] pauidi necnon et vecordes primam conpugnancium procurrunt in aciem. Deum clarius advenisse conclamant eumque se
635 vidisse desilientem[7] per aperta culminis in templum fastigia, dumque quasi consensu confederato communi Delfici numinis opem suppliciter implorarent vniuersi, iuuenem cernunt humanum preuilegio supra modum pulchritudinis insignitum, duas eciam comites ei virgines videlicet armatas ex propinquis edibus, Minerue scilicet
640 et Dyane, duabus occurrere. Nec oculis talia tantum (si vacillantis in via veritatis verbo fides est habenda vetustatis) inspexere sed et arcuum stridores armorumque strepitus audiere. Proinde talibus incitati ne vana viderentur desperacione cunctari, cum iam per deos quasi pro signis ad prelium procedentes se cernerent animari,
645 viriliter hostes cedere seque deorum victorie vegecius adiungere

---

[1] quinquaginta S, sexaginta *Justin*
[2] constertancium S
[3] sicut *ed.*
[4] peribentur S
[5] sparsis *Justin*, sparsi S
[6] compotiti S
[7] desilientem *Justin*, desiliente S

sluggish wine.

[39.] Brennus had 55,000 foot soldiers from his full army; the people of Delphi and their allies had only 4,000 soldiers. Scorning his enemy's forces, Brennus sharpened the spirits of his followers by reminding those ready for battle of the great store of spoils at the shrine, pointing out with his finger the innumerable quantity of statues and chariots cast from solid gold. He added that the resplendent exterior of the booty was nothing compared to its great weight. Inspired by such claims, and at the same time still inebriated after a nightlong bout of drinking, the Gauls rushed into battle as a mob without any thought for danger. But the people of Delphi, trusting more in the Delian than in their own forces or the number of their allies, put up a stiff fight, not without contemptuous scorn for their opponents. Rushing down headlong, they overwhelmed the Gauls, in part by dropping rocks from the extreme summit of the precipitous mountain, in part with fatal steel.

[40.] At the first encounter of the rival armies, the high priests of all the temples and the seer himself, hair dishevelled and wearing emblems and headbands, are said to have suddenly run, fearful and frenzied, to the front lines of the two armies. They shouted that the god had come, and that they had seen him leaping down into the temple through the open peak of its roof. While they all joined in imploring the aid of the Delphic godhead, they saw a youth endowed with more than human beauty, and his companions, two armed virgins, come running to him from the neighboring shrines of Minerva and Diana. Not only did they see this with their eyes, but (if one can have faith in the words of Antiquity, which wavered in the way of truth) they also heard the hissing of bows and the din of arms. Incited by this vision, they urgently entreated the people of Delphi not to hesitate in vain desperation when they saw the gods advancing before them into battle as standard-bearers, but to slay their foes manfully and actively associate themselves with the gods in victory.

summis obsecracionibus pertinacissime pergunt coadmonere.

[41.] Talibus sicque admonicionibus incensi, properanter in prelium certatimque ruunt vniuersi, deique protinus presenciam senciunt sibi saluberrime propicii. Terribili[1] namque Gallisque
650 grauissimo motu Parnasii porcio montis abrupta Gallorum strauit exercitum, cuneosque confertissimos discussit non sine wlnerum fatali molestia letiferorum. Dux ipse Brennius, dum tali casu tunc exceptorum wlnerum pati non valuisset angustias difficultatesque molestiarum, serium suis imposuit[2] finem molestiis per pugionem.
655 Duobus alter |25^r| ex conducibus ad prelium presubstitutis autoribus agmine citato recedit[3] a Grecia solis sauciorum cum x milibus.

[42.] Sed sibi sic per fugam consulentes omine non minus infelici fortunaue Delficus est vigor persecutus quam remanentes. Siquidem pauidis atra nox est omnis tectorum sine solaciis, nullus omnino
660 dies actus summis sine sudoribus continuacionibusue periculorum pernicissime peremptoriis. Sed et ymbres assidui, concretaque nix et gelu, famisque pernicies, et lassitudo suas suppleuere vices in molestiarum superhabundanciis. Infelicis eciam tam miseras[4] belli remanencium reliquias uix intermissarum sompniculose prote-
665 laciones pervigiliarum molestare consumatum mansuescunt ad interitum. Gentes eciam nacionesque quibus non nisi suo commorabantur enormi periculo, dum fame fatigatos palantesque[5] speculantur et vagos, se velut ad predam prorsus impune confederant eos ire direptum. Sic itaque tandem res talem,[6] Delio procurante,
670 tamque specialem devenit ad finem quod exercitu de tam numeroso, qui suarum fiducia virium nuper etiam contra deos contumaciter et homines contendere non hesitabant, uel ad memoriam tante cladis nec vnus super esset homo.

[43.] Junonis eciam wlgata satis est et triuialis vniuersaliterque
675 nota penalis ob iniurias a Fuluio censore sibi contumaciter illatas ulcio, grauisque sequens in predelinquentem[7] vindicta. Censor enim sua Fuluius in censura,[8] cum tegulas ex Iunonis Lacinie[9] templo marmoreas in Equestris edem Fortune, quam Rome temera-

---

[1] Terribili S, terrae Justin
[2] imponere S
[3] recedit] recidit S, excedit Justin
[4] miseras Justin, miseros S
[5] palantesque] pallantesque S, palantes Justin
[6] tale S
[7] predelinquente S
[8] in censura] incensura S
[9] Lacinie] Laciniae Valerius, Latine S

[41.] Fired by these admonitions, the people of Delphi rushed emulously into battle and immediately sensed the propitious presence of the god who was their greatest benefactor. For a portion of Mt. Parnassus, broken off by a shock both frightening and harmful to the Gauls, levelled the Gallic army and shattered their tightly-formed wedges with death-dealing wounds. Their commander Brennus, unable after such an outcome to endure the anguish of the wounds he had received in the fray, put an end to his pains with a dagger. One of the two co-commanders who led the troops in battle retreated from Greece in a rapid column with 10,000 wounded.

[42.] Apollo pursued with an unpropitious fate those who fled as well as those who remained. For the fearful Gauls each dark night was without the solace of a roof over their heads; no day went by without great exertions or dangers prolonged to the point of imminent death. Constant rains, snow and ice, hunger and exhaustion all caused their share of overabundant distress. The wearying length of nightlong vigils drove the miserable remnants of those who had survived defeat in battle to the brink of the grave. Then, when the nations among whom they sojourned at their enormous peril saw the Gauls worn out and scattered by famine, they banded together to plunder them with utter impunity. Thus, by the Delian's doing, the matter came to such an end that of this large army, which shortly before did not hesitate to contend proudly against gods and men, confiding in its strength, not even one man remained as a reminder of such great slaughter.

[43.] Juno's vengeance on the injuries the Censor Fulvius caused her, and her grave punishment of the offender, have circulated widely and are commonly known. Contumacious in his contempt for Juno's religion, deranged in his wrongdoing, Fulvius, while censor, was not afraid to transfer marble tiles from the temple of Lacinian Juno to the shrine of Equestrian Fortune which he was

1

14   SERIUM SENECTUTIS

rius edificator inaniterque |25ᵛ| sollicitus edificabat, transferre non
680 formidaret, Iunonie religionis in contemptu contumax et delirus et
in culpa, mitis est postea factus aliquatenusque sapiens subsequenter in pena. Nempe numquam tale post facinus uel enorme factum
belle sui compos fuisse uel sibi sane postquam peribetur constitisse.
Quin eciam per summam sue mentis animiue valitudinem dicitur
685 expirasse cum filiis suis quos habebat ex duobus tunc in Yllirico
militantibus alterum defecisse recepisset. Cuius rei per causam,
senatus infortunii per euentum motus tegulas ad Locros vnde
translate fuerant reportandas curauit, decretique circumspectissima
sic subtilitate¹ tam presumptuosum censoris opus obliterare procu-
690 rauit. Uerum Fuluii pro filiis anxietatem plus peccati talis contulisse
crederem reatus et adeo leuis ad punicionem quam lapidee potestatem Iunonis uel eree lapidum propter amocionem.

[44.] Verumptamen eandem (tam commenticie diuinitatis in
vanitatibus sepe plus iusto sompniculosa) refert antiquitas Iunonem
695 iuste satis et alias ultam fuisse penaliter iniurias. Nempe cum sue
rex Epirotarum Pirrus vite violentas adeoque sordidas inter vilitates,
Locrensibus ab eo vi coactis et iniuria, consecrato Iunoni Iunonis ex
thesauro Locrenses ei (licet invitos) peccunie magnam coegisset
numerare quantitatem, dum preda compotitus nefaria, predo nefari-
700 us in alto nauigaret et onustus, subite vi tempestatis et tempestiue
vicinis dee tota cum classe littoribus est illisus. Est et in hiis peccu-
nia totaliter incolumis inventa Iunoniique custodie thezauri restitu-
ta. Sed et hic |26ʳ| violentis ventorum censetur² in varietatibus
multomagis imputandam quam ventose Iunonis varietati vanitatis
705 uel potencie talem peccunie restitucionem.

[45.] Tales profecto diuinis decentissime litteris adnotatas veri
viuique Dei numinisque vere diuini bene noui, nostique non minus
mi consors et tu, norunt et infiniti mendaciorum mendaciis crebro
coambulas crebroque subsecutiuas vlcionum penalitates ceterorum-
710 que criminum puniciones, suarumque deorum non minus commenticiorum commenticias iniuriarum mendaciorumque ceterarumque
transgressionum vindictas ulcionumve varietates. Uerumptamen,
me quali quali iudice, terrorum suis censende non sunt incussionibus tante vel talis efficacie quod loquendi modos peruertere valeant,
715 contumaciterve radant raciones³ racionis analogistice, varientue
fandi regularis vsus consuetudinis diucius et approbate, resue rebus

---

¹ subtilitate *S*, sanctitate *Valerius*
² censere *S*
³ raciones *ed.*

building in Rome with rash and senseless efforts. But he was tamed and made wiser by his subsequent punishment. For it is said that after this outrageous misdeed he was never in his right mind or fully in command of his faculties. He is said to have breathed his last because of the great infirmity of spirit which resulted from learning that one of his sons had died fighting in Illyria. Moved by the censor's unfortunate end, the Senate undertook to return the tiles to Locri, whence they came, and with subtle circumspection effaced the censor's presumptuous work by decree. But I would prefer to believe that Fulvius's anxiety for his son contributed more to the punishment of this insignificant sin than the rage of a Juno made from stone or brass on account of some missing stones.

[44.] Often overly fanciful concerning the vanities of such feigned divinities, Antiquity reports that the same Juno avenged other injustices with appropriate penalties. Among the many violent and sordid villainies of his life, Pyrrhus, King of Epirus, unjustly coerced the unwilling Locrians to disburse to him a large quantity of money from the consecrated treasury of Juno. When this unprincipled pirate took possession of his vile spoils and set sail under load on the deep, a sudden and timely tempest dashed him and his entire fleet on a shore near the temple. The money was found intact and returned to the possession of Juno's treasury. But here as well, we might attribute such restitution more to the violent vicissitudes of the winds than to the breezy fickleness of Juno or the power of a nonentity.

[45.] You, my friend, are as familiar from Holy Scripture as I or anyone else with the true and living God and truly divine Godhead's punishments for lies and the other crimes accomplished through lies, as well as the feigned retribution and varied vengeance of the feigned gods upon their injuries, as well as lies and other transgressions. But if I am any sort of judge, these punishments are not so intimidating as to pervert one's manner of speech, erase the laws of analogical reason, vary the regular and approved

omnino sibi contrariis coniungere, dissonisue sibi funditus addicere
perperam minusque conuenienter officiis. Reuera suam quiuis
subsannabiliter satis detegere pergit impericiam morumque uel
720 animi peruersitatem, qui, cum recti sane saluo sermonis scemate,
cursuique consuetudini[1] vniuersali competenter accomodo suadere
possit apposite uel serio dicere quod tenet in proposito persuadere-
ue proponit, ambagibus inconsuetis verborumque vafreciis remotis
a partibus externisque derisibiliter arcersitis declarare mawlt detege-
725 reue[2] quod intendit.

[46.] Atqui cuiusuis iudicio sensati iudicis, derisibiliter videtur in
via delirare discrecionis qui, cum suos publice possit strate milita-
risve medio[3] vel vicinalis in planicie uel plano[4] |26ᵛ| itinerarias[5]
citra difficultates dirigere gressus, diuerticulorum confragosos pre-
730 elegerit iter agere per anfractus. Sed que nam subsannabilior oro
dicas uel racionis a sinceritate semocior rerum iunctura, coniugacio-
ve uel copula sodalitatis[6] maxime matrimonialis in forma, quam
ligue animique[7] nupcialis et anomale conueniens adlateracio funditus et inconcinna. Quid itaque solius eciam sola sonantis in pronun-
735 ciacione sermonis inconsonancius quam vota liguam migrare uel
animum velle conuencionaliter ad matrimonialia? Conueniens
profecto fuerit quid cuiquam rarissime rei sine se competenter
eidem conuenienti. Sic igitur nec ligua nec animus votis poterit ad
bene conueniens congruere matrimonialibus, cum se semper (eis
740 etsi reniti niterentur) oppositissimos omninoque dissidentes sint
exibituri. Reuera vix contrariorum uel inexorabiliter oppositorum
suis contrariis uel prorsus oppositis conueniencie stabilitatis est
aliquid inueniri.

[47.] Talibus igitur tamque temerariis, frater, in friuolis adeo
745 feruens adeoque pertinax in impericiis, supersedere pergas a scurrilitatibus, vsuumque loquendi viuendive consuetudinariorum desistere non segnificeris a derogacionibus. Et si pungitiuo moueris, ut
mores habent diutina pro consuetudine, punctus ad scribendum uel
aliquid incitatiuo, ne laguente tuo manus plus iusto pauset et
750 animus agresti calamo, nugulis ab animo manuque longius amandatis, aliquid uel ad delectacionis conuenienciam, ludicrum uel

---

[1] consuetudinis S
[2] -ue ed.
[3] me S
[4] S ad. suos before it[in]erarias
[5] iterarias S
[6] sodalicis S
[7] animique ed.

usages of speech, conjoin contraries, or perversely assign things to functions for which they are fundamentally unsuited. Anyone who prefers to declare his intent with unusual circumlocutions and verbal ingenuities fetched from ridiculously remote foreign realms, when he is capable of saying appositely what he intends to argue in accord with proper speech and universal custom, reveals his ridiculous ignorance and moral or intellectual perversity.

[46.] Any sensible judge will agree that one who chooses to make his way along the twists and turns of byways when he might instead step smartly down the middle of a public or military street or the level plain of a local path deviates derisibly from the way of discretion. But pray tell what yoking of things, conjunction or bond, especially in the form of matrimonial sodality, is more ridiculously remote from the integrity of reason than the ill-joined and fundamentally awkward nuptial association of tongue and mind? What could be more inconsistent, even in the very utterance of the spoken word, than for the tongue and mind to turn in unison to marital desires? Indeed, it only rarely happens that one thing is suited to another without the converse being true. Neither tongue nor mind could fittingly agree to matrimonial vows, since they always show themselves utterly opposed and in total disagreement, even if they both struggle to resist marriage vows. It is almost impossible to find an example of stable agreement between contraries (or things inexorably opposed) and their antitheses (or rather opposites).

[47.] Fired by such rash frivolities and obstinate in your ignorance, brother, you should abstain from scurrilities and stop slandering the customary usages of speaking or living. And if, according to long custom, a sharp pang moves you to write something, you should respond by banishing all trifles from mind and hand, lest hand and mind pause more than they should over your languishing and boorish pen, and write with apposite pen something

magis expediens vtilitatis calamo scribere competenti potius inciteris
ad incitatiuum. Uetustatis profecto semper et de iuris exigencia
venerande studiorum |27ʳ| sompniculosis addicti sudoribus poete,
755 quo sibi fame perpetuitates[1] laudisque promererentur inmortalitates, pungitiuorumque dulces premiorum percepciones, aut delectacionis excitatiuas aut vtilitatis effectiuas scribendo solas nitebatur
perpetuare paginas.

LIBER QUARTUS

Qui quod agunt agit in simili similes sibi plures
    Officio paucis ridiculosus erit:
Si sibi dissimilis simili velit esse sodali,
    Pluribus in vili viuere vilis erit.
5 Quisquis in arte sua similes sibi vel meliorum
    Spernit in arte modos vix bene doctus erit;
Precipuos vir quisque sagax sectatur amator
    Artis in arte sua ni male fidus amet.
Ergo tuas procul ambages[2] et verba releges
10   Dissona consuetis vsibus atque modis;
Nempe nouos quicumque modos sibi sumit et vsus
    Soli vix cuiquam vix bene lautus erit.

[1.] Porro, postquam talia sermonum scemate tam diffuso meus
sic sodalis effuderat verba, quasi de rixe uel contencionis forma
15 plurimum referencia uel iurgio, verba sic cepi non minus acerba
repositurus velud ex aduerso: Reuera mi meum comes omne citra
commodum modi metas michi consuetas excedentis est admiracionis excitatiuum quod temeritatis in proteruitate sis adeo pertinax
perseueranciaque deliramentorum; delirare quidem uel aliquando
20 sub sole spirantem non est insolencie vel consternacionis incitatiuum. Nempe nichil humanis in invencionibus est inveniri condicio-
nibusve uel[3] vix |27ᵛ| aliquid ex omni parte perfeccionaliterque
consumatum. Sed id profecto summe meo sapienti cuilibet est
admiracionis ingens causa[4] iudicio quod se sua sponte suarum non
25 interpolate stolidus involuere pergit in volutabro temeritatum.

---

[1] perpetuitatis *S*
[2] ambiges *S*
[3] uel *ed.*
[4] causa *ed.*

consistent with delight or rather a sport conducive to profit. In Antiquity, which is always to be revered by rightful necessity, the poets, devoted to unwearied studies, sought to perpetuate their pages by writing only what caused delight or profit, so that they might obtain for themselves perpetual fame, immortal praise, and the sweet increase of poignant rewards.

BOOK FOUR

He who does what many others like him do
   In similar situations will seem absurd to few;
If he wishes to be dissimilar to a fellow like himself,
   He will be contemptible to many for living the low life.
Anyone who spurns the methods of those like him
   Or better at his craft is hardly well taught;
Any wise man who loves his calling follows the best
   In his field unless he loves it in bad faith.
So banish your circumlocutions and words
   Inconsistent with customary usage and measure;
For whoever chooses new measure and usage for himself
   Will seem respectable to almost no one.

[1.] After my companion had poured forth these words at such length, as if he were party to some conflict or dispute, I chose to pay him back with equally harsh terms of disagreement: Truly, my friend, it astonishes me beyond the bounds of customary measure that you should act so obstinately rash and deluded. That a mortal should sometimes be deluded is no cause for surprise or consternation, for there is nothing, or practically nothing, to be found in human inventions or affairs which is perfectly achieved in all its parts. But I imagine it will utterly astonish any wise person that a fool of his own volition constantly seeks to wallow in the slough of his impetuosity.

[2.] Sapiens, ut auguror, profecto frater, te tue temeritatis in detectione tam pertinacem sane nemo censeret esse sensatum. Certe si sane cerebratum saperes meminisse debuisses, presertim quia retro memores oportuerit sed et oporteat nunc esse mendaces, quod
30 oracionis inter inicia tue tam diffusa, nec minus invtiliter subsannabiliterque confusa,[1] verbis supine iactaueris contumacibus et expressis adeo rudem tibi non fore fibram uel adeo fluidam corneamue memoriam, quin facillimum tibi foret eorum meminisse uel reminisci que predidiceris. Subsequenter et subiunxisti te predidi-
35 cisse memoriterque tenuisse quod arbiter vniuersorum Deus interminabilis infinibiles infinitis perhennauerit penalitates propter mendacia, non minus et enormia propter delicta; commenticios eciam censeri commenticie non erubuisti dicere deos ad consimilia pronos,[2] quod quidem non multum tamen veritatis abhorret a via.
40 Sed et oracionis in fine tandem, quasi conclusionis ad instar, eadem repetere non erubuisti uel omnino pene consimilia.

[3.] Uerumptamen quo tue tam temerariam satis exfronter impericie properares ad deteccionem, ligue plus iusto liguosus et animi copule non es verecundatus detrahere matrimoniali. Sed et eorum
45 de coniunctione nupciali sermonem facere ridiculum iudicare, ridiculis et addicere verbis non hesitasti scurrilitatisve vanitati, forte scur- |28ʳ| riliter ignarus vel voluntarie nescius quod perpetuata coniunctione duorum tam terribiliter punibilium vite vitetur feditas et inmundicia mendaciorum, quod eciam si bene memini retro
50 manifestius est sermonumque serio scemate conceptissimoque declaratum. Derisibiliter igitur ea mendax esse detegeris in assercione, qua cachynnabile prorsus et invtile consorcium fere conari videris innuere predictorum quasi matrimonialiter contubernale.

[4.] Nec aliter[3] ridicule non minus assercionis presumptuosa
55 fatuitate[4] tue detegis et errores et derisibilitates impericie, dum subsannabilissimam racionis et a sinceritate semotissimam ligue non erubueris et animi iuncturam matrimonialemve coniunctionis asserere conuenienciam, dumque nil inconueniencius sola solius eciam sonantis in pronunciacione sermonis fore non formidaueris
60 affirmare quam desideria liguam transire uel animum velle consorciaque[5] concupiscibiliter ad contubernalia, stolidamque tibi tuam

---

[1] confuse S
[2] pronos ed.
[3] alterius S
[4] presumptuose fatuitatis S
[5] -que ed.

[2.] I cannot imagine that any wise man would consider your obstinate urge to reveal your impetuosity sensible. If you possessed any intelligence you should have remembered (especially since it suited us to be mindful then, but now suits us to dissemble) that among the diffuse beginnings of your ridiculously confused oration you complacently boasted in so many words that your feelings were not so crude or your memory so fluid or bony as to prevent you from remembering what you learned previously. Then you added that you had learned that God, unending Judge of all things, established unending penalties for lies and major offenses for an infinite number of sinners. You did not blush to say that even the feigned gods are credited by fiction with similar actions, which is indeed not far removed from the way of truth. Finally, you did not blush to conclude your oration by repeating the same thing, or something remarkably similar.

[3.] In order to disclose your brazen ignorance, you have not shown any scruples about disparaging with your idle chatter the matrimonial bond of tongue and mind. You did not hesitate to judge a speech on their nuptial conjunction absurd, or to add absurd words and vain scurrilities, perhaps scurrilously ignorant or willfully unaware that a repulsive life and dirty lies can be avoided by the uninterrupted conjunction of these two faculties so terribly subject to punishment. This, if I remember rightly, was stated explicitly at an earlier point in the formal scheme of my earnest discourse. Your assertion intimating that the partnership of tongue and mind in marital intimacy is utterly laughable and useless shows your derisible mendacity.

[4.] Likewise, you did not blush to reveal the error and folly of your ignorance by your absurdly presumptuous assertion that the conjunction of tongue and mind is altogether remote from pure reason, and your affirmation that nothing could be more discordant, even in the very utterance of the spoken word, than for the tongue or mind to wish to move on lustfully to objects of desire and intimate associations. You did not cease to substitute your stupid

subnectere non supersederis pro racione deliracionem, quod scilicet
uel nil cuiquam sine se bono bonum, sic nichil alicui sine se congruo congruum. Tandem subinferre non verecundaris animum non
65 minus quam liguam[1] nexibus ab indiuiduis funditus abhorrere
matrimonialium. Talique tandem racione tales sermones[2] eciam
solis adicere matrimonialibus turpe non minus esse censueris quam
temerarium, loquendique consuetudinariis vsibus omnino scurrili-
terque derogatiuum.

70   [5.] Uerum si sompniculosis te studiorum sudoribus discipline-
que[3] sollicitudine salubri preeximiauisses, scrutiniisque litteralium[4]
te scienciarum |28^v| salubribus presolidare studuisses, tua longe
laudabilior in censura tuaque multo citerior procacitatis in pertinacia[5] fuisses, saniusque satis mitiusque[6] reprobabilem citra delira-
75 cionem tali de talibus in casu fortassis examinasses, presertim cum
cuilibet eciam citra longa sompniculosave scrutinia studenti sermonum posiciones obviam sua sponte veniant et de consimilibus et
consimiles: sanctorum sanctis non solum sapientumque seriis in
sinceritate veritatis in assercionibus, sed et in ethnicis eciam crebro
80 commenticiis in supersticionibus.[7] Atqui non incompetenter, examine meo, superius positorum reprobando iuncturas exfronter igno-
ranterue verborum, non tantum theologorum litterarum pericia
supreme preditorum[8] verba virorum reprobare videris per consequenciam, sed et in philosophia precipue priuilegiatorum.

85   [6.] Salutarem profecto summa Salomonis in sapientia spirituali-
que solidati loquendi modum iuncturamve verborum vituperare
non verecundari videris, consideracione non minus obliterabili
contemplacioneve uel causa nullatenus absimili. Reuera sicut iam
tuis manifeste satis verbalibus sumi potest ex deliramentis, vix
90 aliquid inconsonancius absurdiusve uel inconueniencius fore (motu
facillimo contumaciterque presumeres examinare) quam suo sponsam cum sponso socialiter ecclesiam copulari matrimonialiter et
agno, talisque talem sponsi sponsam desiderare solaciari suauiter
oris in osculo, dulcique delectari dulciter in colloquio. Nec te talibus
95 tue parsurum reor in elocucionibus theologo cuiquam temerario

---

[1] S ad. e *before* nexibus
[2] sermonibus S
[3] disciplinaque S
[4] litterarum S
[5] in censura ... in pertinacia] incensura ... inpertinacia S
[6] minusque S
[7] supersticiis S
[8] predictorum S

raving for reason, claiming for example that as nothing can be good to something which is not of itself good, so nothing can be in harmony with something which is out of harmony with itself. You were not even afraid to add that the mind no less than the tongue recoils from the indivisible bonds of matrimony. Finally, you conclude that it is disgraceful and rash even to apply such language to matrimony, and that it scurrilously detracts from the customary usages of speech.

[5.] But if you had distinguished yourself beforehand by unwearied study and the healthy solicitude of discipline and had concentrated on strengthening yourself by the redeeming scrutiny of literary knowledge, you would have been far more laudable in your censure and much milder in your obstinate effrontery. Perhaps if that had been the case, you would have examined these matters more sanely, without your blameworthy raving, especially since even without long or unwearied search any student will be able to think of similar discussions of similar topics. This is frequently true not only of the holy assertions of the saints and those wise in the integrity of truth, but also of the pagans and their feigned superstitions. By rashly and ignorantly reproving the metaphors I properly employed, you implicitly reprove not only the words of theologians—men rich in the knowledge of letters—but also of men especially privileged in philosophy.

[6.] You seem unafraid, on account of an equally forgettable reason or cause, to vituperate the salutary metaphorical language of Solomon, who was confirmed in the highest spiritual wisdom. Indeed, as can be inferred plainly from your vocal raving, scarce anything could be more absurd or discordant (since you proudly presume to judge with inconstant mind) than for the Bride to be coupled in marriage with the Groom, and the Church married to the Lamb, or for the Bride to long to be solaced by the kiss of her spouse's mouth and to take pleasure in his sweet conversation. Nor do I imagine that in the hasty effrontery of your judgment you will

procacitatis in iudicio, sed | 29ʳ | nec eciam suo Salomoni sapientia
condito Salomonis in eloquio, quin contumaciter et euestigio iudi-
caturus fores quod talium iuncturas dissonancia uel inconcinnitas
iret impeditum deterioraretue verborum, uel quod coniunctorum
100   coniungendorumve convenienciam contrarietatis inexorabilitas
impediret uel inconsciliabilis opposicio.

[7.] Contempta tamen tui tam temeraria procacitate iudicii remocius et amandata uel omnino pocius obliterata, potencie spiritualis
et sapiencie vir Salomon agni stantis in monte, sponsi sepius sui sibi
105   prepromissi, non veretur ecclesiam fateri luculenciis et asserere
verbalibus expressis oris osculum desiderare, quo coniunctionis
dulcedine conuenienciaque contactus adeoque salutaris sponsus,
vtraque faciens vnum, pacis interuenire faceret et oris osculum. Nec
talibus vir adeo preditus[1] idem, tue cancella tutus[2] satis efficaciter
110   sentencie uel iudicii, talia talium circa matrimonialium federalia
sensatissime fandi substitit in finibus. Sed et sponse sponsi salutaris
osculum desiderantis presencie sic subsequenter supponit verba,
causali quadam quasi contemplacione, subiunctiua: Quia vino
meliora sunt vbera sunt et vnguentis optimis fragranciora. Sic
115   itaque sui sponsa sponsi fore patenter innuit asseritque verbaliter
ubera, que non marum sed sua solummodo mulierum sane censen-
tur esse muliebria. Uerumptamen taliter enunciatum, tuo licet
examine temerario sit inconueniens et inconcinnum, figurate sinceri-
tatique racionis non inconcinne significacionis est innuitiuum, quo
120   uel elocucione tali carminis in inicio figurata[3] se figurate sub- | 29ᵛ |
sequenter esse declarat[4] locuturum.

[8.] Non autem sic solus sapiencie Salomon sinceritate priuilegiatus tue suis pertinaciam temeritatis et inercie confundit assercionibus, sed et alii supreme sanctitatis sciencia fluenti[5] sobrie non
125   minus quam salubriter inebriati tuo seriis errori derogare mansuescunt expressisque sermocinacionibus.[6] Unde quidam sapiencie
fontis indeficienti scaturigine crapulatus sensati sic ait, Salomonis
velut alludens assercionibus: Ciuitatem sanctam vidi Ierusalem
descendentem sicut sponsam viro suo monilibus ornatam. Sed et
130   aliis quasi suis alludens eisdem sic inquit in elocucionibus ad
eandem de celo sic adeoque sollempniter descendentem, sui suum

---

[1] predius S
[2] tuus S
[3] figuratum S
[4] declarate S
[5] sciencie fluentis S
[6] sermocinantibus S

spare any theologian for such pronouncements, not even Solomon, with the wisdom of Solomon in his occult utterance. Instead, you will immediately judge that his metaphors are vitiated by dissonance or clumsiness, or that inexorable contrariety or irreconcilable opposition prevents harmony between the things he linked in metaphor.

[7.] But leaving aside, or rather wholly obliterating the hasty effrontery of your judgment, Solomon, a man of spiritual power and wisdom, was not afraid to make the extravagant assertion that the Church desired the kiss of the mouth of the spouse who had often been promised her, the Lamb standing on the mount, so that touched by the sweetness and harmony of the conjunction and moreover salvific, the spouse, conjoining the two, would create a kiss of peace and of the mouth. Nor did that same man, so rich in ideas and completely safe from your censure, stop at the limits of sober speech in discussing this matrimonial alliance. Instead, he adds the words of the Bride desiring the kiss of the Groom of saving presence, subordinated as if according to some causal notion: "Because your breasts are better than wine and more fragrant than the best unguents." Thus the Bride plainly hints, even asserts in so many words, that her groom has breasts, which are surely reckoned to be the private parts not of men but only of women. But such a disclosure, although discordant or awkward according to your rash judgment, hints at an elegant figurative meaning in accord with the purity of reason, so that by using this figurative expression in the beginning of the song he testifies that he will speak figuratively afterwards.

[8.] Privileged by the purity of his wisdom, Solomon is not alone in confounding your obstinate rashness and sloth with his assertions. Others as well, soberly as well as profitably drunk on the overflowing knowledge of supreme sanctity, are accustomed to dismiss your error with serious and express discourse. Hence one man drunk on the unfailing spring of the fountain of wisdom said, as if alluding to the wise assertions of Solomon: "I saw the holy city Jerusalem descending, as a bride adorned with necklaces for her husband." Alluding to other statements as though they were his own, he spoke to the Bride in the same terms as she solemnly

quasi nomine sponsi dirigendo sermonem: Sponsus ego sponsabo te michi meam tuus in veritate iusticiaque.

[9.] Pretereaque sensatissime soliloquus theologiceque philoso-
135 phus te tuis temerarium fore psalmista detegit in procacitatibus licitorumque ludicris in reprobacionibus. Sua nempe sano sub silencio presolidata faustaque sic fatur inter seria, de gloriante sermonem fando faciens in malicia: Tota die cogitauit iniusticiam ligua tua, nouaculaque sicut acuta fecisti dolum. Sed et alias is idem
140 salubrem sensate citraque iactanciam sic inquit faciendo sermonem: Ligua mea tota die meditabitur iusticiam. Nec incircumspeccius sic et alias: Os iusti meditabitur sapienciam. Nec inconueniencius iterum: Protector meus et cornu salutis mee. Nec incompetencius et iterum: Deus precinxit me virtute. Nec insubtilius et alibi: Beatus
145 qui tenebit suos et allidet ad petram |30^r| paruulos. Et alibi: Ligna campi et cedri Libani saturabuntur quas plantauit. Atqui talia talibusque similia fas est et facile scrutatoribus invenire sompniculosis infinita, sed et obuiam velut in vestibulo veniunt lupanaliterve velut prostituta.

150 [10.] Uerumtamen tu, talibus taliumque similibus (licet licite litteralitatisque modo uel analogice conuenientibus) sic enunciatis, aure delira uel auditu male discreto conceptis, te prorimareris[1] ad garriendum stolidiusue promptificares ad submurmurandum, non bene gnarus quod dum talia frequencius figurate fundendo sane
155 sensati laudabiliterque literati sic sermocinanter[2] verbaliterque sibi non bene conveniencia coniungunt,[3] loquendi liberas sibi laxant[4] sic habenas. Loqui mansuescunt famina sic per effusa figurate, uel aliquid subintelligi posse uel eciam debere bellissime relinquunt. Sic[5] quoque tibi tueque vel ex habundanti satisfacere per expres-
160 sum procacitatis in aliquo saltem pergam pertinacitati, tuas ad audiendum tam truces arrigere[6] si libet auriculas.

[11.] Ait enim spiritualis ille soliloquus: Tota die cogitauit, et cetera. Ligue quidem, licet absonissime, cogitatus attribui videatur; sic dictum taliterque tamen absoluit a vicio quod relinquitur sane
165 subintelligendum, quo scilicet sermone tali sane relinquatur debere subintelligi verbaliterve vituperari mentis leuitas elocuciove preceps

---

[1] prorimis S
[2] sermonicinanter S
[3] coniungendo S
[4] laxando S
[5] Sic *ed.*
[6] arrige S

descended from heaven, directing his speech to her in the name of her groom: "Your husband, I shall marry you to myself in my truth and justice."

[9.] That sensible soliloquizer and theological philosopher the Psalmist reveals how hasty you are in your rude and histrionic censure of perfectly acceptable statements. Speaking of those who boast of their evil, he says in the midst of a serious discourse strengthened by sensible silence: "All the day long thy tongue hath devised injustice: as a sharp razor, thou hast wrought deceit." Another time, speaking sensibly and without boasting, this same man says: "My tongue shall meditate justice all the day." Nor does he say with less circumspection at another time: "The mouth of the just shall meditate wisdom." Nor, again, less appositely: "My protector and the horn of my salvation." Nor less suitably yet again: "God hath girt me with strength." Nor less subtly elsewhere: "Blessed is he that shall take and dash his little ones against the rock." And elsewhere: "The trees of the field shall be filled, and the cedars of Lebanus which he hath planted." Indeed, it is permissible, even easy, for unwearying investigators to find any number of these and similar things, and they stand out at first approach like common prostitutes.

[10.] But having with deluded ear or indiscreet hearing misconstrued statements of this sort, which make acceptable sense either literally or by analogy, you would have sought matter to chatter about or murmur against, unaware that the soberly sensible and laudably literate loosen the reins of free speech when they utter such frequent metaphors, using language to conjoin things not harmonious by nature. Those who are accustomed to speaking freely in metaphor implicitly leave something that can or even must be understood beneath the verbal surface. So I will in some measure satisfy you and, what is more, your obstinate effrontery if you care to perk up your ferocious little ears and listen.

[11.] The spiritual soliloquizer says: "All the day long thy tongue hath devised injustice." He seems, quite discordantly, to attribute the power of thought to the tongue; however, what he leaves us to understand absolves the expression from fault. He leaves us to understand that this statement vituperates the mental vacuity or

perperam circumspecti, cuiusuis[1] examine sana longius a discreci-
one uel constancia semoti, qui non antequam[2] loqui pronuncian-
dum pergit meditacione preexaminatum.[3] Ligue vel oris officium
170   sanissime censetur esse ridiculum pre cogitatu diiudicari, |30ᵛ| quo
sua sapienti spontaneus astipulator assurgat in assercione Salomoni,
quod suo cor stulti sit in ore commendabiliter non minus quam
figuraliter asserenti.

[12.] Talium profecto tamque reprobabiliter et inordinate labia
175   laxancium fore proprium sane peribetur uel consuetudinarium quod
si procedere non valuerint ad effectum vel verbaliter venire nitantur
ad malum, quod eciam si peruenire nequeant loquelaliter ad nequi-
ciam uel cogitatu se contaminari procurent nequicie per mendam,
quo si quando mali quid abest a manu, non absit a corde uel cogita-
180   tu. Quid uero sua pro possibilitate talis exequatur per subsequencia
decentissime declaratur: Sicut nouacula acuta fecisti dolum, sic
scilicet expedite sicut nouacula radit acuta prompcius et in facilitate.
Sequitur: Et ligua mea meditabitur iusticiam tuam, tota die laudem
tuam. Talibus itaque ligue videretur incompetenter attribuere quod
185   cordis est animive, nisi sicut autenticis antonomasiceque sacris
legitur in scripturis, approbatumque invenitur in paginis, quod vox
ita vociferantis Christi sic consonare perhibeatur cordi (quod id
quod est cordis attribuatur ori) cuius ligua iusticiam dicitur esse
meditata Dei salutaris in predicacione nouique testamenti.

190   [13.] Subinde subponitur: Os iusti meditabitur sapienciam. Sensate premeditatam, scilicet, ad aliorum sane loquitur instruccionem,
quo sanum talemque per intellectum sermonis, quod mentis est ori
superficialiter attribuentis, obliteretur quod apparere videtur in
superficie vicium. Subicitur et illud: Protector meus et cornu salutis
195   mee. Cel- |31ʳ| situdo scilicet salutis mee solida, quo tali sub
intelligencia cornute[4] salutis inconueniencia remocius sit amandata.
Subsequitur: Uirtute precinxit me Deus ad bellum. Carnis videlicet
ne fluencia dissolutave desideria me committenda valide contra
vicia prepedirent in pungna, quo tam competenter verborum conue-
200   niencia plus iusto procacibus suspecta, virtutis velut inconueniens
et absona, cinguli cancilletur subpuncteturve subcinctura[5] sane
minus et ad expediens et intellecta.

---

[1] cuius S
[2] ante quam S
[3] *I transpose* qui ... preexaminatum, *which S places before* quo (4.170).
[4] cornu te S
[5] sub cinctura S

hasty speech of one who is lacking in circumspection and, as anyone would agree, is far removed from sensible discretion or constancy, who says things he has not thought out beforehand. He
clearly reckons that without forethought the operation of tongue or
mouth is very sensibly decreed to be judged to be absurd. Thus he
agrees with Solomon, who claims in a commendable metaphor that
the fool's heart is in his mouth.

[12.] Furthermore, it is typical of those who loosen their lips so
inordinately that if they are unable to achieve the outcome they
desire, they still speak evil, and even if they are unable to speak
evil, they manage to contaminate their thoughts with depravity, so
that even when nothing evil is at hand, it is not absent from heart
or mind. In what follows, he announces what such a person pur-
sues to the best of his ability: "As a sharp razor thou hast wrought
deceit," that is, swiftly, as a sharp razor shaves quickly and with
ease. Then follows: "And my tongue shall meditate thy justice, thy
praise all the day long." Here he would seem to attribute inappositely to the tongue the abilities of heart or mind, were it not that
(as we read in preeminently Sacred Scripture and find approved by
the Sacred Page) the voice of a man speaking in this manner accords so well with the heart of Christ that the abilities of the heart
may be attributed to the mouth. His tongue is said to have meditated justice in preaching a saving God and the New Testament.

[13.] He adds: "The mouth of the just shall meditate wisdom";
that is, it articulates sensibly premeditated instruction for the good
of others. Such a sensible understanding of this statement, which
superficially attributes the mind's properties to the mouth, effaces
what seemed a flaw in the superficial sense. This comes later: "My
protector and the horn of my salvation"; that is, unyielding height
of my salvation. This interpretation banishes the discord of a
horned salvation. Next follows: "God hath girt me with strength for
battle," lest the flesh's shifting or dissolute desires impede me in
the hard-fought battle against the vices. The buckling of a useless
and incomprehensible belt is fitly canceled or expunctuated by the
harmony of these words held suspect more than was just by the
rash, as if discordant or inconsistent with virtue.

[14.] Subinde supponitur: Beatus qui tenebit suos et allidet paruulos ad petram. Reuera viuens homo qui viuis bellissime censetur
205 esse beatus, qui prauos ex carne nascentes animi primosque motus (paruulos Babilonis videlicet natos ex filia filiolos), ne perniciosam procedant ad crescenciam libereque luxurientur ad perniciem, tenet et ad petram que Christus est allidit,[1] quo confracti maturacioneque tempestiua preuenti dispereant, citraque crescenciam maturita-
210 temue[2] medullitus intereant. Babilonis profecto filia fore caro competentissime dicitur et alumpna. Nempe viciorum confusiones ingerere mansuescit sompniculosa vigilque virtutis ut aduersaria, cui compensacio dignissima dari tunc sensatissime censetur cum sicut incitare pergit ad illicita, sic acerbissime repressa virtutibus
215 subiecta seruiliter ancilletur. Cuius filioli dum male nati parentes eciam proprios parent suffocare peccaminibus excrescenciisque suis, eciam deprauare nitantur erroribus, tali dignissime tales sunt remuneracione preueniendi, quo dum parui sunt et |31ᵛ| inbecilles interueniente veri vera cognicione Dei priusquam virile viriumque
220 veniant ad robur, ad petram difficultatem citra periculosam letaliter allidantur. Sed et si maiorem forte perniciter ad etatem peruenerint et ad virilitatem, licet interuenire videantur, tunc difficultatis impedimento[3] nichilominus interimantur. Talis itaque tam sincera racionis intellectusve contemplacione, beatitudinis propriorum[4] perempp-
225 cione paruulorum rudis et anomale procacitatis examine friuola funditus et irregularis inconueniencia, conueniencie competenti solidetur in apparencia.

[15.] Sequitur eciam subsequenter: Ligna campi cedri Libani saturabuntur quas plantauit. Sed ne protinus ad talia tua pro con-
230 suetudine contumaci proteruire presumas, cachinnatorque preproperus[5] et procax proteruiter[6] aggarrire non verecunderis quasi lignorum saturacio cedrorumve sacietas ridicula sit inconueniensve et absurda, racionique consuetudinarioque fandi modo funditus sit inconcinna, quo tua temperancius in temeritate voluteris et sic sane
235 positis[7] in superficie sola tuo uel aliquatenus examine reris[8] in inconueniencia; notabilibus aliquid sensate subintelligendum relin-

---

[1] tenet . . . allidit] tenent . . . allidunt S
[2] maturianamue S
[3] impedimentum S
[4] propriorum] improperiorum S
[5] preproperiis S
[6] proteruus S
[7] sic sane positis et S
[8] reor S

[14.] He soon adds: "Blessed is he that shall take and dash his little ones against the rock." In fact, the man whom others will consider blessed is the man who, lest they grow ruinously and flourish to the point of danger, takes and dashes upon the rock, which is Christ, those first motions of the spirit born depraved from the flesh (namely the tiny sons born from the Daughter of Babylon), so that broken and forestalled by timely haste, they might perish inwardly before achieving maturity. Indeed, the flesh is rightly said to be the daughter and nursling of Babylon. For as the unwearied and vigilant adversary of virtue, she is accustomed to lavish the anarchy of the vices upon man. As she incites man to pursue forbidden goods, her fit recompense is to be constrained to serve humbly, subject to the virtues. Her children, because they are base-born and try to strangle their own parents in sin and excess, even struggle to pervert them with their errors, are best forestalled by such remuneration. While they are still small and helpless, before they come to the virile strength of men, a recognition of the true God fatally dashes them on the rock without endangering the good man. But if they should chance to grow swiftly to manhood, though they seem a hindrance, even then let them perish on the obstacle of resistance. In the pure light of such an explanation, what seems by the test of rude and anomalous effrontery the silly and irregular incompatibility of beatitude with the slaughter of one's own children is established in the apposite appearance of concord.

[15.] Next follows: "The trees of the field, the cedars of Libanus shall be filled which he hath planted." Lest you immediately presume to rage contumaciously at this or jabber shamelessly like a hasty and impudent mocker, as if the filling of trees or satiety of cedars were senselessly absurd and fundamentally out of harmony with logic or ordinary speech, and so that you might wallow more temperately in your temerity and consider such plain expressions only superficially in disharmony (as you would have it), do not

qui non dubites in sermonibus. Atqui veram vere virtutis per potenciam pane vinoque de terra productis et oleo saturabuntur, eisque saciantur ligna campi cedrique Libani non quelibet sed
240 quas[1] numinis in fide plantauit potencia diuini. Saturabuntur eis, inquam, ligna campi (plebes videlicet humilesque) prius, cedrique (potentes in seculo scilicet) posterius. Nempe prius ignobiles a Deo sunt electi seculariterque contemptibiles quam seculo sapientes nobilitateve vana contumaces. Cedri quidem |32ʳ| saturabuntur
245 Libani, videlicet in fide candidati. Nempe Libanus candidacio peribetur interpretari. Sic igitur in hiis sicut et in predictis sensate uel aliquid est adiciendum subintelligendumve, quo subintelligencia competenti redigatur ad conueniens quod superficie tenus abhorrere videtur a convenienci.
250   [16.] Plurimorum preterea quamplures eciam, sicut et superius paucis est pretaxatum, digne non minus quam commendabiliter in philosophia preditorum denigrare[2] non verecundaris asserciones, autenticasque non minus locucionum luculencias, autenticosque sermocinandi modos ethnicorum. Circa[3] matrimonialia quidem mas
255 maturissime meditatus sic ait Marcianus, ad Hymeneum bellissime suum dirigendo sermonem: Namque elementa ligas vicibus mundumque maritas. Atqui si tua more tuo pertinax in temeritate persisteres, retractis in rugas ad talia naribus e uestigio nauseares, taliave fastidientis ad instar nausealiter aspernari non erubesceres,
260 presertim quia ligamina ligancium vicibus attribuere vicium fore[4] contumaciter examinares. Nec minus elementa vicibus quibusuisve ligari ligaminibus uel maritari pertinaciter abhorrere non formidares, dum stolide solam considerare contemplarique superficiem sic enunciatorum perseuerares.
265   [17.] Verum si sanum saperes et sensatum, uel aliquid ad vicium superficialiter[5] submouendum laute preinvestigandum subintelligendumve censeres. Hymeneus quidem, rerum scilicet omnium naturalis[6] effectus uel amor, concordia uel vigor nature quo creaturarum subsistit vniuersitas, elementaque subsistunt |32ᵛ| vniuersa,
270 vicibus (id est, per vices et alternatim) ligare dicitur elementa, quod apparet in hyeme[7] quando terra (videlicet germinibus) clauditur,

---

[1] quos S
[2] denigrare ed.
[3] Citra S
[4] vicium fore] vicium non fore S
[5] superficiale S
[6] naturales S
[7] humo S

doubt that noteworthy speeches sensibly leave something for us to understand. Indeed, the power of true virtue will fill them with bread, wine, and oil produced by the earth. But not all the trees of the field and cedars of Libanus will be filled, only those which the power of the divine godhead planted in faith. First, the trees of the field will be filled, that is, the common people and the low-born; then the cedars, that is, those mighty in this world. For the ignoble and contemptible of this world were chosen by God before those wise in worldly things or proud of their empty nobility. Indeed, the cedars of Libanus will be filled, that is, those purified in faith, since *Libanus* is said to be translated as 'whiteness.' Thus, we are to supply or understand a suitable hidden sense in these quotations, as in those preceding, which reduces to harmony what appears superficially incompatible.

[16.] I have already criticized your shamelessness in impugning numerous assertions by worthy men commendably endowed in philosophy, not to mention the pagans' authoritative linguistic splendors and approved figures of speech. Martianus Capella, a man who had thought maturely about marriage, addresses himself to Hymen, saying: "For you bind the elements reciprocally and fecundate the earth." But if, as is your way, you remained obstinately reckless, you would wrinkle up your nose and become nauseated on the spot, or would not blush to scorn such things squeamishly, especially since you would proudly judge it a solecism to explain bonds by the reciprocity of the bonding agents. Nor would you fear recoiling from the notion that the elements are bound or married by reciprocal bonds, as long as you stupidly insisted upon considering only the surface of statements of this kind.

[17.] If you could think clearly and sensibly, you would consider worth investigating finely beforehand or understanding in a hidden sense anything which superficially ought to be removed as a flaw. Hymen, the natural affection or love of all things, the concord and vitality of nature by which all creatures and all elements exist, is said to bind the elements reciprocally, that is, alternately or by turns, as he does in the winter, when the earth is closed to seeds

nascendique vigor obtunditur. Mundumque maritat, id est fecundat, vernali videlicet in tempore cum terre germina producuntur: mariti germinantis ad instar inpregnat. Sed et elementa per vices alternat
275 dum Wlcani[1] sub vertice progenita decoquit et maturat, dum sub Iunonis vberibus matura desiccat, dum grauibus Saturnum brume sub turbulenciis exicat.[2] Sana sic subintelligencia superficiales sermonum sepe salebrositates consonantis amenitati consciencie consciliat.

280 [18.] Sed et hoc, ut auguror, quod eleganter asserit idem cachynnator ut indiscretus de facili fores ridere promptificatus. Asserit enim quod seminudum, clamideque paruula penulaliter indutum, sed et invelatum[3] cetera cacumen humerorum dumtaxat obnubilatum, gene iam pubescentes magno Cipridis risus[4] sine cachynno
285 non paciebantur incedere Cillenium. Nempe prompcius, ut coniecto, procaciter causari non supersederes humeris haut bene prima facie conveniencia quod dicitur humerorum cacumina, presertim quia moncium, locorumque nec non arduorum, rerumve summitatibus solis videntur esse accomoda. Sed nec sinere, pative uel sustinere
290 genis esse uel obnubere clamidi iudicares attribuenda. Uerum rudi frequencius et absona sermonum sub superficie, corticisve cruda verbalis sub ruditate, dulcedo latet interius rustici[5] dure detegenda corticis erasione. Profecto per humerorum cacumina nil aliud dat intelligi quam quas in humeris humerorum fas est et facile reperire
295 summitates.

[19.] Atqui te dictorum tam procacem |33ʳ| tamque pertinacem sermonumque reprobatorem, Mercurialis officii uel in deitatis dignitate ministerii sic ignarum fore non crederem, quin eloquencie Cillenium scias esse prelatum, discussorem deorum consuetudinali-
300 ter exercitum ministerialiter et expeditum, sic eum seminudum paruaque clamide militaliter, palestraliterve, uel scurriliter amictum, quo talibus sermonis allusio celeritati[6] superficialiter adeo ridiculis fiat attribucionibus. Vnde tam pruinose tamque succincte clamidati genarum, perque consequenciam nacium pilescencie iam pubes-
305 centis Mercurii detectarum sic incedentis, talia contemplantem Veneris excitauere risum, quo sensate subintelligendum relinquat quod nudus (sapiencie videlicet expers et viduatus), licet eloquens

---

[1] Wlcanum S
[2] exiciat S
[3] in velatum S
[4] risus] vsus S, risu *Martianus*
[5] interius rustici] interrusci S
[6] celebritati S

and their power to be born is blunted. And he fecundates, that is, makes fertile, the world in the spring when the earth's buds come forth: he impregnates the earth like a husband inseminating his wife. And he causes the elements to alternate by turns when he smelts and matures what has come into being in Vulcan's smithy, when he dries what is mature under the breasts of Juno, when he castrates Saturn during the turbulence of winter. Thus a sober hidden sense often reconciles the superficial irregularity of a statement with the comfort of a conscience in harmony with itself.

[18.] I imagine that like an indiscreet mocker you would deride what the same author elegantly asserts. He claims that his newly bearded cheeks would not allow Cillenius to go about half-naked, wearing a tiny cape as a hood, with everything else uncovered except for the clouded peak of his shoulders, without a great guffaw from the laughing Cyprian. I guess you would find it hard to refrain from a hasty objection that at first glance it does not seem suitable to say "peak of his shoulders," especially since "peak" seems suitable only to the summit of a mountain or other lofty places. You will also judge that cheeks cannot be said to allow, endure, or withstand, or a cape be said to cloud over. But under the rough and jarring surface of language, or under the crude roughness of the verbal bark, frequently hides an inner sweetness to be laboriously uncovered by the removal of the coarse bark. Certainly by "peak of his shoulders" he means nothing other than the tops of the shoulders, which are easy to locate on the human body.

[19.] But I cannot believe that you are so obstinate or in such haste to condemn what others say or write, or that you are so ignorant about Mercury's office and the dignity of his function. On the contrary, you know Cillenius is the lord of eloquence, always busy as investigator of the gods, and skilled in his line of work. That he is half-naked and clad like a soldier or wrestler, or just scurrilously, in a small cape, which seems so absurd on the surface, becomes an allusion to the swiftness of speech. Hence, the hairiness of the adolescent Mercury's cheeks and uncovered buttocks excited the laughter of Venus as she watched him arrive so frostily and scantily clad. Martianus clearly leaves us to understand that a naked man (that is, one devoid of wisdom), although he be elo-

136   SERIUM SENECTUTIS

fuerit et facundus, a Cipride deridetur, id est ab illo qui sapiencia
preditus et eloquencia, suppodiatus et est utraque. Puerorum reuera
310 risui nuda non sunt genitalia Veneri, scilicet in quibus nondum
viget moueturve pruritus.

[20.] Sed nec illud, ut coniecto, sua quod inter seria ponit idem de
facili[1] pertransires irreprobatum, quod scilicet Mercurius, Phebum
feliciter suggestu Virtutis aditurus, volatilem Virtuti virgam permi-
315 serit, ut secum mundi penita permeare recessus et ethereos irrum-
pere parili posset celeritate, dum suis ipse talaria nectere pedibus
pergit argentea,[2] petasum videlicet alatumve calciamentum. Profecto protinus, ut michi videre videor, ad hec aggarires virge perperam
volatilitatem calciamentoque non minus inconuenientem[3] alatilita-
320 tem, consueto tuam tue vicio procacitatis incontinenti detegendo
subsannabiliter impericiam, dum |33ᵛ| solam te derisibiliter con-
templari promptificares sic enunciatorum superficiem, contemplandamque subtilius delire contempneres totam sane subintelligendam.
Volatilem profecto virgam geminisque serpentibus annexam peribe-
325 tur habere Cillenius, qui[4] sermonis et eloquencie censetur a cecis et
a deitatis indignitate cecucientibus esse deus, commenticiaque
quadam deificacione deificatus, quam virgam Virtuti (licet et id
absonum tibi videtur) suo de more peribetur commisisse, quo
sensate subintelligi debere reliquatur quod facundie sermo, licet
330 ornatus per se uel ex se sepe sit et clarus, nisi sapiencie tamen
modo moderetur et virtute vagus deprehendatur,[5] vilis et in vani-
tate quamuis et omnino carens utilitate. Uirgam reuera videtur
habere Maiugena[6] quam Virtuti committere crebro mansuescit
volatilem. Nempe nisi sermo facundie recto procedat oracionis
335 tramite, prompto pronunciacionis pronuncietur officio, vis allegacionis ad persuadendum non perueniet apposite. Volatilis eciam
Mercurii dicitur esse virga, sed et eius calciamentum fore perhibetur
alatum, talaribusque petasinis eum fore velocificatum, quo uel eius
sane subintelligas sideris celeritatem, sermonisve uel eloquencie
340 velocitatem.

[21.] Sed et eiusdem volatilis eadem virga geminis fore fertur
serpentibus annexa, quo verba rethorum sepe venenosa rethorisue
facundiam sensate contempleris pungitiuam frequencius et acutam.

---

[1] de facile S
[2] argentea S, aurea *Martianus*
[3] inconuenienter S
[4] cui S
[5] deprehendetur S
[6] Manigena S

quent and articulate, is derided by the Cyprian, that is, by the man who is endowed with sustaining wisdom and eloquence. For the naked genitals of boys in whom the sexual urge is not yet actively flourishing do not deserve Venus's laughter.

[20.] Nor, as I imagine, would you easily pass over without reproof the same author's claim, made in all seriousness, that Mercury, before successfully approaching Phoebus at the suggestion of Virtue, granted his flying wand to Virtue so she might traverse the remotest parts of the world with him and penetrate the ethereal recesses with equal swiftness, while he proceeded to bind silver sandals (that is, a *petasus* or winged footwear) on his own feet. Moreover, it seems to me that you would immediately chatter about the wrong-headedness of the wand's ability to fly and the shoe's ill-fitting wings, thus revealing your ignorance by your unrestrained effrontery. For you are in a ridiculous hurry to consider only the surface of statements and madly disregard their hidden meaning, which should be considered with more subtlety. Cillenius is considered god of speech and eloquence even by the blind and those dazzled by the outrageousness of the deity, who was after all deified by some feigned deification. He is said to have a flying wand entwined with two snakes, and although it seems in bad taste to you, he is said to have entrusted this wand to Virtue according to habit. Martianus asks that we understand that eloquent speech, although it is often ornate and brilliant in and of itself, is worthless, vain, and without use if it is not also moderated by the rule of wisdom and brought back to the fold by virtue when it errs. Maia's son has a flying wand which he is accustomed to entrust to Virtue. Indeed, unless eloquent speech follows the path of proper utterance and is pronounced with fluent diction, it will not persuade us to accept its argument. It is said that Mercury's wand is capable of flight, that his footwear has wings, and that he is sped on his way by those winged sandals: by this you may understand the swiftness of his star or the rapidity of eloquent speech.

[21.] His flying wand is said to be entwined by two snakes, in order that you might contemplate the oft poisonous words of rhetoricians, or their prickly and pointed eloquence. As to the wand

Sed et talibus uirge taliter innexe, per quam rethorici subintelligere
345 rectitudinem sermonis iusticieque rigorem fas est et inflexibilitatem,
summitas fore fertur aurea, media uero pars glaucea, finalis autem
pars |34ʳ| picea. Rethorum nempe sermo pulcher apparet in princi-
pio, subsequenter exasperatur in medio, nigrescit tandem condemp-
nacionis in vltimo. Sic quoque variatam Maiugene[1] volatilem vir-
350 gam dici dicunt non sine causa caduceum: sermo nempe sepe facit
et eloquencia cadere lites turbulenciasque iurgiorum. Uocantur
namque caduceatores per quos pace consolidata rixe cadunt et con-
tenciones, que singula sermonis effectiue fieri contingit et eloquencie gratia.
355 [22.] Non autem remissius, ut existimo, te tui petulancia splenis
intempestiuum prompcius anomalumque[2] moueret ad cachynnum
quod idem de Philologia loquens ad superos ascensura, bellissime
sic scribit post alia quod inmortalis iam facta, virgo Philologia
primitus Athanasie matrique sue subsequenter Apotheosi supplica-
360 uerit, multaque litacione gratiam persoluerit eoque quod ad inmortalitatem transiens nec Vedium viderit, nec vsserit eam Vedius
igne,[3] nec lympha subluerit, anime nec eius[4] simulachrum Syri
cuiusdam pro dogmate verberauerit, nec Phasi senis pro ritu Charontis involutam manibus inmortalitatem mortis auspicio consecra-
365 uerit. Atqui nisi tuis sepissime de temeritatibus sumpte coniecturali-
terue crebrius prenotata me fallant (que raro me fefellerunt) pre-
sumpciones uel argumenta, more tuo statim tu tales fatue fastidien-
do sermocinaciones horripilaliter inhorreres, dum superficiales
solito solas more tuo rituque detestabili perseuerares sic enunciato-
370 rum contemplari crudelitates, dumque causari pertinaciter non
erubesceres Inmortalitatis propria iam virginis ex acerra[5] litacio-
nes,[6] addicteque iam non minus inmortalitati |34ᵛ| vel ignis exus-
siones uel limphe subluciones, nec non et anime simulachrum
simulachrive vanas ridiculasque verberaciones, sed et involutam
375 Charontis in manibus citra mortis auspicium uel auspicio mortis
inmortalitatem.

---

[1] Nauigene S
[2] anamolumque S
[3] nec Vedium ... Vedius igne S, nec Vedium cum uxore conspexerit, sicut
suadebat Etruria, nec Eumenidas, ut Chaldaea miracula, formidarit, nec igne usserit
Martianus (Cf. 4.403–12 below.)
[4] eam S
[5] ex acerra] exacerra S
[6] licitaciones S

entwined by these snakes, by which we may understand the rectitude of rhetoric and the rigor and inflexibility of justice, the top is
said to be gold, the middle grayish, and the bottom pitch black. The
speech of rhetoricians appears attractive at the outset, grows rough-
er in the middle, and darkens in final condemnation. They also say
Mercury's flying wand is called the caduceus for a reason: eloquent
speech often causes disputes and quarrels to cease. For those who
effectively use their eloquence to make brawls and conflicts end in
confirmed peace are called bearers of the caduceus, or heralds.

[22.] Nor would your impudent spleen fail to move you to an
untimely and anomalous guffaw at what the same author writes
about Philology when she is about to ascend to the gods. He says
that having been made immortal, the virgin Philology petitioned
Athanasia and her mother Apotheosis, rendering thanks to them
with much sacrifice, so that in passing over to immortality she did
not see Vedius, nor did Vedius burn her with fire or bathe her in
water, nor scourge the likeness of her soul according to the doctrine
of some Syrian, nor by the rite of old Colchis consecrate her immortality under the auspices of death, concealed in the hands of Charon. But unless presuppositions based on your impetuosity deceive
me, which has rarely been the case, you would suddenly bristle and
fatuously turn up your nose at such dialogue, because (according to
your customary and detestable practice) you would insist on considering only the superficial cruelties. You would obstinately object
to the virgin's offerings to Immortality from her own incense box,
the scorching fire and baths appointed for immortality, not to
mention the likeness of the soul and the vain and absurd scourging
of that likeness, and immortality concealed in the hands of Charon
without, or under, the auspices of death.

[23.] Reuera reor tua funditus in contumacia[1] uel fatuitatis obstinate non[2] fuisses[3] in pertinaciis infatuatus, si sic sermocinancium
racionem contemplari mansueuisses intrinsecam. Talis Philologia
380 profecto uel Philosophia (racionis amor videlicet uel sapiencie
solidus sanaque contemplacionis subsistencia consumatus) vbi
sublunaria (mediana scilicet) sane transcenderit et sensate salubriterque studia, talia sic transcendentem libens Athanasia, dum sua
sibi subsidium supplet Apotheosis mater et alumpna, transferri
385 procurat inmortalitatis ad infinibilia. Nempe purgacio, deificaciove,
uel consecracio mater est et[4] causa conuenienter inmortalitatis
effectiua. Non est igitur sane sensatis convenienterve cerebratis
magne motiuum uel admiracionis, excitatiuumve rudis et temerarie
reprobacionis quod inmortalis facta purgacionis, deificacionisque,
390 uel consecracionis gratia feliciter Philosophia, supplici[5] sinceraque
subsidiatricibus litacione gratias persoluisse perhibeatur honestis-
sime deuota, quo sicut et subsidiatrices et subsidium, sic et litacio-
nis gratias sola contemplari pergas in figura.

[24.] De cetero, pecualiter perperamque causari presumeres
395 inmortalitate beatificatis uel ignis vssiones uel limphe subluciones
innuitiue verbali vel expressione (tuo quo tam | 35ʳ | temere deduce-
ris examine) prorsus incompetenter attribuere. Sed si sic sermoci-
nantis mentem, racionisve, uel intencionis tibi libuisset, licuissetque
(semota procacitatis tue pertinacia) preperscrutari sinceritatem, tui
400 forsan mitificasses melioratusve mutasses in melius examinis acerbitatem. Talia profecto taliter enuncians, se serium non exibet in
talibus assertorem, sed assercionis voluntarium vetustatis erronee
retractatorem. Uetustas enim, deorum derisorie delirans ridiculis in
adinuencionibus commenticiorum, Vedium (Plutonem videlicet uel
405 Orcum[6]) sua cum coniuge Proserpina uel Allecto seductis[7] a corporibus exeuncium, necis et ulterius a condicione sentencialiter
absolutarum, forte fingebat insidiatores animarum, quo noua nouiter (ut fit) in condicione de facili consternabilibus terrores incuterent
perturbacionesque formidinum. Sed Eumenides est (furias puta plu-
410 tuniales) nouarum commenta cruciatrices animarum. Suoque fingebat igne nouicias vrere, suaque subluere limpha penaliter animas

---

[1] in tua funditus contumacia S, S¹ ad. in *before* contumacia
[2] non *ed.*
[3] fueris S
[4] et *ed.*
[5] supplicibus S
[6] Ortum S
[7] sedudos S

[23.] But such obdurate and stubborn pride would not have caused you to act foolishly if you had been accustomed to considering the inner logic of discourses in this manner. When Philology or Philosophy (that is, the firm love of reason or wisdom perfected by contemplation) has transcended sublunar (earthly, that is) studies, Athanasia willingly transports the transcendent one to unending immortality, while Apotheosis, her mother and nurse, lends her assistance. For purgation, deification, or consecration is rightly mother and efficient cause of immortality. Therefore, among those who are clear-headed or reasonably intelligent, it is not a great cause for astonishment or crude and hasty condemnation that, having been made immortal by purgation and deification or consecration, Philosophy rendered thanks to her benefactresses by humble and pure sacrifice, most honorably devout. So you may consider the sacrifice of thanksgiving, like benefactresses and benefaction, as only figures.

[24.] To continue, your rash prejudice would lead you to the brutish presumption of objecting either implicitly or explicitly that it is wrong-headed to attribute either scorching by fire or bathing in water to those blessed by immortality. But had you been willing and able to set aside your obstinate effrontery and examine beforehand the mind of the speaker or the integrity of his logic or intention, perhaps you would have softened your harsh judgment or, as a result of your own amelioration, changed it for the better. In speaking of such matters, Martianus did not seek to assert their truth, but to rework the false assertions of Antiquity to his own ends. For Antiquity, deranged to the point of absurdly inventing feigned gods, chanced to imagine that Vedius (Pluto, that is, or Orcus) and his wife Proserpina or Allecto ambushed souls as they departed from their now distant bodies, absolved by judgment from the condition of further death, so that once again god and goddess struck terror and perturbation into those who were easily flustered by their new condition. Antiquity also feigned that the Eumenides, that is, the infernal furies, tortured new souls. And it feigned that Vedius burned the new-made souls with his fire and washed them

purgatiua Vedium. Simulachrumque quoddam fore dogmatizabat
anime quod, animas iniciales suas reuertentes condicionaliter ad
origines, eis obuiam veniendo veniebat verberatum.

415   [25.] Sic itaque que commenticie cachinnabiliterque preexcogitata
doctrinaliter predisseminauerat, tria purgacionum genera retractat.
Animas enim predogmatizauerat uel igne purgari, uel aqua, verbe-
ribusve. Senis et Phasi, quem convenienter ibidem retractat idem,
doctrine modus[1] dogmatizandique ritus tibi reuera reor risus in-
420   tempestiui |35ᵛ| mouerent[2] intempestiuos defacili rictus. Phasi
profecto senis in philosophia fauste fauorabiliterque famosi dogma
fuit ritusque docendi posse nullum nisi per mortem venire viuens
ad inmortalitatem. Sicque sensatus per consequenciam subtilisque
senex inmortalitatis inuolutam dogmatizare non detrectabat Pormee
425   uel Charontis in manibus fore felicitatem. Pullus enim, Pormea,
Charonve fore nauta fertur inferorum cymba Stigem transportans
animas ultra paludem. Sic itaque commendabiliter, et si tu secus (ut
auguror) exfronter examinares, suo solam iudicio fatalem vite per
finalitatem viuendi peruenitur ad infinibilitatem. Tu vero in consue-
430   tis, perperamque tollerabilibus, procacitatisue pertinaciis insistere[3]
de nouo non[4] renueris morumque proteruitatibus; per oppositum
proteruus e uestigio proclamares opposti posse perueniri serius ad
effectum, non bene gnarus quod effectum crebrius ex opposito
sanum[5] non minus quam salubre sumere[6] soleat opposti remedi-
435   um.

[26.] Talibus itaque que scrutatori studioso cuilibet sponte primis
obuiam veniunt in luminibus infinita coniunctim diuisimque diligenter inspectis, subtiliterque non minus et non in superficie sola
sed intrinsecus investigatis, temperare pertinaciam tue procacitatis
440   pergas tam temerarie et non minus intempestiue quam ridicule
prorsus et inconcinne garrulitatis tue, quo plus iusto fluidum ligue
loquacitatisue lubricum tui pergas oris opitulare uel aliquando
cachynnum. Non enim, licet ut arbiter arbitrari non verecundaris
preproperus[7] et loquax, loquelaliterque leuis, verbaliter et errabun-
445   dus, in |36ʳ| animi contractis[8] et ligue matrimonialibus premen-

---

[1] modos S
[2] moueret S
[3] ingerere S
[4] non ed.
[5] sanum ed.
[6] sumi S
[7] preproperiis S
[8] contractus S

punitively with his purifying water. And it held as dogma that there was a certain likeness of the soul that, when souls reverted conditionally to their first origins, came before them already scourged.

[25.] Thus he reworks the three kinds of purgation which Antiquity had already invented and disseminated as false doctrine. For it had dogmatized that souls are purified by flame, water, or lashes. I reckon that the doctrine and dogma of aged Phasus, whom he fittingly recalls in the same place, would easily move you to untimely laughter. Certainly, it was the dogma and teaching of aged Phasus, fortunately famous in philosophy, that the living cannot achieve immortality except through death. As a result, that sensible and subtle old man did not recoil from dogmatizing that the blessing of immortality is hidden in the hands of Pormea or Charon. For Pullus, Pormea, or Charon is said to have been the seaman of the underworld, transporting souls beyond the Stygian marsh in a skiff. Thus, even if (as I expect) you shamelessly judge otherwise, one is, according to his account, rightly brought to infinite life only through the fated termination of earthly life. In fact, you may not refrain from insisting anew on your intolerable obstinacy and wanton boldness; suddenly impudent, you might proclaim it impossible to achieve a state through its antithesis, not aware that an effective remedy often draws its salutary effect from its antithesis.

[26.] Having diligently inspected together and severally the many things which occur at first glance to any hard working investigator, and having subtly investigated them intrinsically and not just on the surface, you should set about tempering your effrontery and your absurdly untimely and unfitting garrulity. In this manner, you might remedy your volatile and inconsistent guffawing and loquacity, at least sometimes. While you are not ashamed to cast judgment as a hasty and loquacious judge, a flighty conversationalist unable to stick to the point, in the case of the marriage contracted between

cionata commendacione solam sum seriis[1] in assercionibus sermocinacionis acerbitatem superficiei contemplatus uel inconcinnitatem,
sed et intrinsece considerandam censui longe licencius multoque
commendabilius subintelligencie sinceritatem.

450 [27.] Non enim tale talium sermonibus sic seriis procommendaui
matrimonialis sodalicii contractum quod nocturnis genialiter in
occultis[2] sub lodice gerendis[3] matrimonialiter talium convenien-
tissime coniunctorum venereum contemplarer aliquod sic fando
futurum fore feditatisve colludium. Nec adhuc adeo cornei quidem
455 sum sensus, ebetisve memorie, uel facillantis ingenii, quin ipsorum
bellissime non minus quam competenter et expedientissime coniunctorum prorsus incompetentes ad talia presertim funditus fore
non minus quam fuisse fuerim copulatiuas quaslibet uel in superficie contemplatus attentissime coniunctiones. Non tamen eam quam
460 retro libens eorum meoque laudabiliter examine precommendaui,
nec minus et opido nunc hylariterque commendo, maxime matrimonialem reprobare uel ullatenus impedire me uel velle uel posse pati
possum[4] perpetuoque duraturam confederacionem. Reuera non alia
racione feci facereve presumpsi tam coniungibilium matrimonialita-
465 tis mencionem nisi quod coniunctorum necessariam coniunctionis
innuerem matrimonialis ad instar federis fore perpetuitatem, con-
tractique non minus ad modum similitudinemque matrimonii, vite
viuendique perpetuam consuetudinis indiuiduitatem, dum diuorcii
diuiduitatisue qualibet eciam causa remocius amandetur omnis
470 euentus, ad perpetuandam confederacionis adeo felicis et fauste
fauorabilisque firmitatem.

[28.] Tua uel nunc |36ᵛ| temperare meo, Philippe, si sanum
sapere sensatumve curas, consilio parens a procacitate, ne me tam
temere tamque proteruiter arguendo, precipuos in sciencia litterali
475 per consequenciam quamplures arguere videaris contradictoriisque
retro iudiciis autenticatos. Aut saltem si splenis vicio plus iusto
petulantis a garrulitate superflua paruiloquioue desistere non possis
uel a cachynno, manu tota tuum uel digito compesce labellum, quo
sic arte uel artificio viribusue uel violencia garrulitatis intactus
480 euadas[5] adeo vile vituperium, procacitatisque tam vitabile vilita-
tisue vicium. Liberius et ego licenciusque tam belle conveniencium,

---

[1] sum seriis] sumseriis *S*
[2] oculis *S*
[3] *S ad.* quod *before* matrimonialiter
[4] non possum *S*
[5] intactus euadas] nitatus vadas *S*

mind and tongue by the recommendation of Virtue, I have not seized upon the harsh dissonance of the discourse's superficial sense, but have decided that the purity of the implied sense within should be pondered more freely and to greater purpose.

[27.] I did not employ such serious terms to commend this particular marriage contract because I had in mind any sexual activity or obscene sport which was to occur in the still of the night while these partners so well suited in marriage lay between the sheets. I am not yet a man of such horned understanding, dull memory, or wavering ingenuity; rather, even on a superficial view, I consider the copulative conjunction of a couple so fitly and usefully conjoined to be, as it always has been, utterly unsuited to such an end. However, I am neither willing nor able to reprove or in any way hinder their union in everlasting marriage, which I have already praised freely and, according to my analysis, rightly, and now commend with exceeding joy. In fact, I presumed to mention the marriage of such eligible partners for no other reason than because I meant to suggest that the conjunction of mind and tongue demands a permanence equal to that of the matrimonial bond. Likewise, they should live together perpetually conjoined in the manner and likeness of the partners joined in the marriage bond, since every cause of divorce or separation should be excluded from the lasting stability of a league so happy, fortunate, and favorable.

[28.] Now, Philip, if you care to think clearly and sensibly, submit to my counsel and refrain from your effrontery, lest in your haste to criticize me you implicitly criticize many men confirmed as preeminent in literary knowledge by many judgments contrary to your own. Or if, because of your excessively unruly spleen, you are unable to refrain from needless disparagement or guffaws, stifle your lip with your finger or entire hand, so that by art or artifice, fear or violence, you escape unscathed the vile reproach of garrulity and the easily avoided vice of effrontery. And, setting aside all murmuring and persiflage, I will freely and unreservedly describe

tamque salubriter expediens, et ad vniuersis indifferenter vtile sub
sole spirantibus consociandorum, remocius amandato murmure
quouis et aggaricione, paupercula rudique pergam prosequi penna
485   matrimoniale consorcium.

LIBER QUINTUS[1]

Qvisque scius, qui[2] scire sapit, cui mens sana sanum
    Viuere dat, liguam temperet usque suam:
Ligua procax, leuiterque loquens os, labraque loris
    Indiga vix validos instituere viros.
5   Verbosus vir sero suos bene diriget actus;
    Sepe suum stolide precipitabit opus;
Ligua sua se sibi sepe nocens odiosum
    Et sibi conviuis lubrica ligua facit.
Ligua supervacue stolidi sua sepe loquaci
10   Est et ad interitum causa maligna mali:
Hec Zambri bene nouit arans in coniuge stulta,
    Stultus et in ludo ludicra leta luens, |37^r|
Dum probus insequitur stolidum perimitque petulcum
    Vir Phinees legem zelotipando suam,
15   Dumque sua speciale sibi probitate perhennat
    Nomen et eternat perpetuale decus.
Idque Dathan Abyronque simul sensere superbi,
    Dum stolide cupiunt thurificare Deo.
Sensit idem Maria procax in murmure moto,
20   In Moysen Moysis haut bene mota soror,
Dum male muscantem liuens lepra prodit, et albor
    Arguit errantem detegit atque nefas.
Excitus his, vicium validus vir garrulitatis
    Nisibus intensis arceat omne procul.

25   [1.] Porro postquam talia scemate sermocinacionis tam[3] diffuso
tamque moroso mei procacitate sodalis ad id incitatus proteruiter
effuderam, mea velut improbitate foret emendacior, solitoque uel
aliquatenus temperacior effectus, sic consequenter est elocutus:
Profecto, frater, tua tuo que tibi libuerit de proposito libens verba

---

[1] Explicit liber quartus Incipit Quintus S
[2] cui S
[3] iam S

with poor and rude pen the matrimonial association of such well-suited partners, without exception salutary, expedient, and useful to all who breathe under the sun.

BOOK FIVE

Anyone bright enough to know how to think, whose sober mind
    Lets him live sanely, should constantly temper his tongue:
An importunate tongue, glib mouth, and unrestrained lips
    Scarcely create a man of character.
A wordy man is slow to direct his affairs aright;
    Often he foolishly forestalls his own undertakings;
He often harms himself with his tongue, and his slippery tongue
    Makes him odious to himself and to his companions.
For the excessively loquacious, the tongue is often
    A harmful cause of senseless evil, even death:
Zambri learned this, plowing a stupid spouse,
    And stupidly atoning for his joyful follies in his sport,
When upright Phinees, because of his zeal for the law,
    Followed the fool and killed the wanton goat;
By his probity Phinees perpetuated a special name
    For himself and earned himself unending glory.
Together proud Dathan and Abyron sensed the same,
    When they stupidly desired to burn incense to God.
Moses' sister Miriam sensed the same, impudent in the murmur
    She started against her brother Moses:
Livid leprosy betrayed this disfigured woman, and the pallor
    Which proved the erring one guilty revealed her sacrilege.
Inspired by these examples, a forceful man should struggle hard
    To banish the vice of garrulity far from him.

[1.] After my fellow's importunity had incited me to utter such a recklessly diffuse and protracted discourse, he spoke as follows, as if my audacity had caused him to mend his ways and become somewhat more moderate than usual: Undoubtedly, brother, I should, with ears readily attentive in expectant silence, strive to

30 facientem et auribus attento sub silencio non minus attentis quam
voluntariis excipere nitar, et exaudire curiosius, et intelligere sermones et proposita. Nec eciam, licet michi tuis quid displicuit perperamue sederit seriis, dico tamen dumtaxat in elocucionibus, contencionaliter quicquid reponere pergam, controuersionalibusue de
35 repositionibus, verbalibusue contencionum de dictionibus. Non
enim sermonum diduccionibus quasi contencionaliter alternatis, ver-
borumue conferenciis corrixatiue vicissitudinaliterque variatis, fami-
nibusue fari libet vlterius alternatim quasi corrixatiue diuersificatis,
quo quidem |37ᵛ| quod tibi libuerit omne fari pergas, omni ces-
40 sante contradiccionis acerbitate, dum tamen in loquendi modo
modum non excedas omnem falsitatis mendaciorumue per inconuenienciam, ridiculamve possibilitatis per transgressionem. Non enim
sane silenti cedere consueuit ad vituperium quod sensate sermoci-
nantem sana pacienter audit libens et exaudit omnes omnino citra
45 reposiciones contradiccionum, rixarum sepe non minus excitatiuas
inconcinnarum quam conamine quouis a sapiente continuo fugien-
darum continuatiuas inimiciciarum.

[2.] Reuera sicut pugnam probe committi serissime contingit, ibi
pulsante dumtaxat impetitore,[1] solus subsannabiliter vapulat impe-
50 titus, sic quoque rixam tardissime continget interuenire dum duorum dumtaxat alter simul socialiterque considencium labia laxare
licitis pergat in sermocinacionibus. Sed nec litem fieri controuersia-
lemve verborum diduccionem contingere consueuit ordinaria de
facilitate uel conueniencia cum confabulancium familiariter vnus
55 quasi ferias agit in silencio, reliquus[2] vero famine fatur quod sibi
sederit ore licito, voluntarioue quod sibi placuerit eloquio. Reuera
serissime controuersiales sermocinantibus serioue conloquentibus
incidere consueuerunt acerbitates ubi, moderacione melleoque
mansuetudinis dulcore melioratus, omnino nichil est acerbitatis
60 inutilitatisue repositurus. Uniuersalem si libet igitur contencionis[3]
citra legem tuo tibi quod libeat pro velle liceat ponendo loquelaliter
effari, meaque michi pro voluntate libera fas sit et facultas licencie
renunciando sermocinali, solo quia sic libet silencio luxuriari.

---

[1] imperitore S
[2] reliquis S
[3] contencionalis S

understand what you intend and pay careful attention to comprehend the sense of your words. Even though you may have said
something which displeased or sat wrong with me (I refer only to
your means of expression), I will not continue the argument by
making a contentious reply or using hostile language. It no longer
appeals to me to take turns stating and restating our arguments,
varying our wording or modifying our positions as we go. So you
are free to say whatever pleases you, without fear of any harsh
contradiction, provided that you do not exceed all measure in your
discourse through disharmonious falsehood or lies, or through
some absurd violation of probability. It is not normally a cause for
reproach that a man should listen in silence to someone speaking
good sense and not utter any contradictory replies, which are often
the cause of disharmonious squabbles and protract such hostilities
as are to be constantly avoided by any wise man.

[2.] One cannot say that battle is rightfully joined when only the
victim is thrashed by an ignorant assailant who delivers all the
blows; likewise, a squabble is unlikely to develop when only one of
a pair of companions is permitted to loosen his lips in discourse.
Nor does a dispute or an acrimonious exchange of words normally
result from ordinary good nature when one of the conversationalists
takes a vacation in silence, so to speak, and the other is permitted
to say whatever is on his lips or whatever he wishes to articulate
freely. In fact, acrimonious controversy will normally be slow to
occur between those who discuss serious matters when one, bettered by moderation and honeyed mildness, says nothing harsh or
useless in reply. You are entitled to speak out, taking your pleasure
for your guide without regard for the universal law of dispute; I
can and will renounce the license of speech by my free will, since I
choose to luxuriate in pure silence.

LIBER SEXTUS[1] |38ʳ|

Fvndere que libeant liceat tibi famina soli[2];
    Oris ab eloquio sit michi ligua vacans:
Vocis et officio mea ligua vacet viduata,
    Dum tua quod libeat proferat omne loquens.
5 Nil ego prolata tibi post tua verba reponam,
    Quo tua sit soli libera ligua tibi;
Tu tamen attente caueas tibi ne tua tutos
    Turpiter excedat lubrica ligua modos,
Ne nimium tua si laxes tibi lora loquendi,
10   Ledere compellar lesus et ipse modum.
Sepe quidem fatue fans quod sibi sederit omne
    Audit ab inuito verba molesta sibi.

[1.] Ergo[3] michi care mi consors, canicie iam tempestiua segnifi-
cato senioque iam silicerniali confecto, sensati quod iter agentes
15 facere mansuescunt, vegecius est agendum qui, quo tardius iter
arrepturi surrexerint, morosam[4] velocitate vegetique segniciem
promptificacione pensare pergunt. Epithalamicis igitur quia michi
iam nunc sic sedet carminibus, hymeneicisque cantilenis, concenti-
busue corealiter tripudialibus,[5] paranimphalibusque conclama-
20 cionibus remocius amandatis, sermonumque sepius subsannabiles
citra sesquipedalitates, succincte nitar simpliciterque prosequi quod
admodum iam diucius ire prosecutum mee possibilitatis pro parti-
cularitate desideraui. Nupcialibus igitur relictis omnino pene post
tergum sollempnitatibus, stilo rudi simplicique penna uel calamo
25 satis et agresti que mente concepi stilo satis in ydemptitate ruditatis
producere nitar in lucem conrudescenti.
    [2.] Reuera modicum uel (ut sit ad vnum dicere) ferme |38ᵛ|
nichilum largitatis sponsalicie contractus de specialitate dotisue, uel
propter nupcias de donacionis insinuacione paucula curaturus, uel
30 ea pene prorsus per omnia perfunctorie preteriturus, sed et vix
aliquid in mente mecum meditatiue sub silencio, liguave loquelaliter in aperto superflue prosecuturus, omnino nichil[6] ad id dico
quod ex proposito iam nunc exequi procuro curans, quod noua

---

[1] Explicit liber quartus Incipit Quintus *R, S corr. to* Quintus ... Sextus
[2] *R ad.* Metrum *in marg.*
[3] *R ad.* prosa hec Responsus *in marg.*
[4] moram *S*
[5] tripudialiter *S*
[6] *S ad.* quod *before* ad

Book Six

You alone are entitled to utter any words you please;
  My tongue will refrain from spoken eloquence:
My widowed tongue will refrain from the voice's duty,
  While yours says whatever it wants to.
I will make no reply to the words you produce,
  So your tongue shall be free for you alone;
You, however, should pay careful attention to yourself,
  Lest your slippery tongue shamefully exceed safe limits;
If you yourself loosen the reins of speech too much,
  I will be compelled by injury to exceed the same limit.
Indeed, he who foolishly says whatever occurs to him
  Often fears hostile words from his opponent.

[1.] So, my dear colleague, slowed now by timely gray and consumed by funereal old age, we must move more quickly, like intelligent travellers who, because they arise later before starting their journey, compensate for their tardy inertia by rapidity and lively haste. Now it pleases me to set aside epithalamic hymns, hymeneal ditties or harmonies in dance measures, acclamations by attendants, and ridiculous sesquipedalities of speech, and to the best of my ability to pursue briefly and simply some thoughts I have wanted to develop for a long time. So turning my back on all nuptial solemnities, with crude stylus and simple quill or rural reed, I will strive to bring into the light what I have conceived in my mind, my stylus braying with equal ignorance.

[2.] In fact, I will pay little or (what amounts to the same thing) almost no attention to the specifics of the marriage contract's largesse or dowry and very little to reporting the marriage gift; at worst, I will pass over them all perfunctorily without delay. I will not pursue anything superfluous, either meditated to myself in my mind's silence or openly verbalized with my tongue. I will not in any way embellish what I now propose to pursue: that since the

noui iuris ex promulgacione pridem fuerit et adhuc sit eo decursum
35 quod sponsalicia largitas (donacio videlicet propter nupcias) specialis sit contractus subsecucione nullius insinuacionis indigus, licet ab
alio nomine uiri fiat hoc pacto quod maritus velut ipse dederit
conscribat.

[3.] Nempe generali iuris ex institucione, futuras et si donacionis
40 ante propterue nupcias, uel dotis instrumenta, pompaue defuerit,
aliave nupciarum celebritas fuerit omissa, nullus ob id estimare
debet alias inito recte matrimonio solidam firmitatis deficere stabili-
tatem, uel liberis ex eo natis legittimorum iura talem posse per
occasionem cautelas auferri per cauillatorias. Honestate, profecto,
45 pares inter personas, nulla lege prepediente consorcium quod
ipsorum consensu concorditer et animorum fide fuerit firmatum, de
condicione matrimoniali perpetualiter est,[1] eritque duraturum,
condicione qualibet et die remocius amandatis a perpetuitate nup-
ciali matrimonialiter coniunctorum. Iuris et enim racio vix variabilis
50 temporaliterve perfunctoria solidis actuum condiciones non minus
quam dies longius abigere perseuerat a perseueranciis legittimorum.
Diei nempe sero consueuerunt actus associabiles esse uel condicioni.
Triuialiter enim propositorum pridem fuit et adhuc est et in appro-
bacione solidatorum, legittimos actus | 39[r] | vniuersaliter et dies non
55 minus quam condiciones et aspernari contumacius et amandare
remocius, adeo quidem quod in totum vicientur temporis adiectione
uel condicionis. Non nunquam tamen, ut iuris asserit consultus, ea
supra scripta[2] tacite recipiunt actus que vicium detegere mansuescunt comprehensa detectius.

60 [4.] Nempe si presencialiter accepto feratur ei qui sub condicione
tenetur quia sub condicione promisit, ita demum quid egisse facta
videbitur sic acceptilacio, si precedentis extiterit obligacionis condi-
cio que (si nominatim comprehendatur) accepto ferentis nullius
momenti faciet effectus intencionis. Ad idem satis a propinquo
65 satisfacere videtur quod alias aliunde[3] ait iurisperitus. Sic itaque
scribit: Illi, si volet, Sticum do; condicionale sic factum tale censetur
esse legatum, non aliter ad heredem transitiuum quam si legatarius
voluerit, quamuis alias quod sine tali (scilicet si volet) adiectione
legatum fuerit ad heredem legatarii transmittitur. Aliud enim iuris
70 est si quid tacite contineatur, aliud si verbis apercius exprimatur.

[5.] Atqui nichil omnino talibus in personis quodam quasi iure

---

[1] esse S
[2] scripte S
[3] aliuds S

promulgation of the new law it has been a point of recourse that the marriage due (that is, a gift on account of nuptials) is a special contract which requires no report as follow-up, although it be from another man in the groom's name, provided that the husband signs for it as if he had given it.

[3.] According to the general practice of the law, even if the documents concerning a gift or dowry for an upcoming wedding are lacking, or the banquet or any other ceremony is omitted, no one may conclude from this that an otherwise correctly celebrated marriage lacks a firm foundation, or that for such a reason the laws governing free men can be speciously denied the children born from it. Indeed, as long as no law presents an obstacle to the harmonious partnership established in moral rectitude by their consent and the faith of their souls, that partnership will always remain in accord with the marriage contract, and no condition or stipulated time will be able to affect the perpetual nuptials of those joined in marriage. The rule of law, which is hardly variable or a plaything of time, does not allow conditions and stipulated times to affect the solid persistence of legitimate marriage contracts. Indeed, contracts are hardly to be limited by a day or condition. It was and is a regular confirmation of an established purpose that legitimate contracts boldly exclude all stipulated times and conditions, so much so that they are utterly vitiated by any stipulation of time or condition. However, as the jurist says, those principles which customarily expose a defect when understood more openly sometimes tacitly allow exceptions for certain forms of behavior.

[4.] For if a man who is bound by a contract is immediately released from it because he agreed conditionally, such a release will seem to stipulate something only if there is a condition of prior obligation which, if explicitly provided for, would make the result of the donor's intention worthless to the recipient. What the jurist says elsewhere at another time seems to suffice nearly enough for this matter. He writes: "I give him Stichus if he wishes: such a bequest, made in this manner, is reckoned to be conditional and is not transferable to an heir unless the legatee so wishes, even though otherwise what was bequeathed without such an addition is transferred to the legatee's heir." For in law it is one thing if something is contained tacitly, another if it is stated explicitly in words.

[5.] But as regards those faculties which are to be coupled in

matrimoniali perpetualiter coniungendis matrimonialiterque copu-
landis, ficticio nupciarum de deo non minus quam superficiei
contemplacione subsannabili satis et ridiculo curare curo quid
75 Hymeneo, uel instrumentis de dotalibus, rebusue parafernalibus.
Sed nec floreis luminum quid curo de sertis, vnificisue coronis, nec
Hymenei genitore de Genio, sed nec aliquid eiusdem venereo
genitricis de gremio, talibus[1] nec non meo remocius amandatis a
commento ioculis inani sub lodice gerendis Hermofroditi voluptaria
80 genitrice.[2]

[6.] Sic igitur, nupciis analogice wlgaribus vniuersaliterque non
minus quam genialiter generalibus |39ᵛ| nostro presencialiter
instanti prorsus a proposito longius eliminatis,[3] matrimoniale
duorum tam bene tamque salubriter conueniencium mea prosequi
85 pergam pro possibilitate sodalicium, nupciasque quasi quadam sana
satis sub irregularitate regulares, omnium communis in affectu
virilitatis specialissimas. Omnino nichil de voluntarie semper per-
niciusque prompta paratisque propicia suffragare connubiale curaturus de Iunone nupciale non minus[4] preside putatiua quam com-
90 menticie pronuba. Remocius omnes eciam funditus amandare pergo
Musarum melicas suis cum concentibus, solicanisve cum melifica-
cionibus modulaciones, armonicosque tibiarum[5] tinnitus vdrauli-
cosque, fidium consonantesque sonitus.

LIBER SEPTIMUS

Seria ridiculis sensatus, ut auguror, omnis
Vix volet et vanis depingere vir sua ludis;
Ludicra ludenti iuueni sua sunt sibi menti,
Seria sola senis sunt conueniencia cordi:
5 fforma quidem fuit in ludis odiosa senilis,
Est et adhuc res in thalamis odiosa senectus.
Sic igitur segnis quia segnificare senectus
Me venit, omne pigra prauum procul arceat etas,
Vtilibusque paret se promptificare recentem,
10 Vt uiuat virtutis opus, viciisque valenter

---

[1] tali S
[2] Hermofroditis voluptario genitricis S
[3] S ad. quali *before* matrimoniale
[4] minus *ed.*
[5] tibiarum *Martianus,* ubrarum S

perpetual matrimony as if by a certain matrimonial law, I do not at all wish to concern myself with Hymen, the absurdly fictitious god of nuptials (according to the superficial sense), or with dotal documents or a married woman's property. Nor do I care at all about floral garlands of lights or unifying wreaths, nor about Genius, father of Hymen, nor about the venereal lap of his mother, and set aside from my commentary such sports as are performed between idle sheets by the pleasure-loving mother of Hermaphrodite.

[6.] Having swiftly eliminated from immediate consideration analogies with commonplace marriages, which are ubiquitous by nature, I will to the best of my ability consider the matrimonial partnership of two who are so thoroughly and salubriously compatible, and nuptials which are according to rule, so to speak, despite a certain quite sensible irregularity, and most unique in the power they can confer upon all. I will pay no heed to connubial Juno, always favorably inclined to give prompt aid to those willing to accept it, the putative nuptial guardian and feigned *pronuba*. I will altogether banish from my lips the Muses' melodious modulations, their harmonies or solo modulations, and the harmonious jangling of flutes, water organs, and harmonious lyres.

Book Seven

No sensible man, I imagine, wants to embroider
His serious concerns with absurd and fatuous games;
Such amusements suit a young man's playful mind,
Only serious concerns befit an old man's heart;
An old body at sport has always been a distasteful spectacle,
And old age remains hateful to the marriage bed.
So, since decrepitude has begun to slow me down,
My torpid age shall banish all depravity
And prepare itself anew for useful things:
To live a life of virtue, war stoutly against the vices,

Bella paret, viresque valens virtute vigoret,
Et moueat veges intensas cum corpore rixas,
Stans ope virtutis leuis in certamine victrix,
Et uiuat virtute sacri certaminis auctrix,
15   Dormiat et viciis, uiuat virtutibus, ut sic
Transigat in melius vitalia tempora viuus.

[1.] Sic igitur in eo quod in presenti pergere prosequi pro[1] posse
procuro, solam quasi maris et |40^r| femine conuenienciam consue-
tudinis et consensus perpetuitate quasi matrimonialiter solidatam,
20   in eo vite consuetudinem contemplor hoc proposito. Satis circumspectus[2] uel in hoc gnarus eciam quod libere mulieris virginisue
matrimoniale contubernium,[3] personis ad invicem sana condicionis
in inspectione comparatis, non concubinatus esse censeatur sed
matrimonium, presertim cum tabule non efficiant, sed affectio
25   conueniens et adprobata, matrimoniale commercium. Variis itaque
triuialiterque tritis ad id inductiuissime racionibus subsolaribus[4]
argumentalibusque presumpcionibus talium talem[5] tam sane con-
iunctiuorum coniunctionis matrimonialis[6] nitor ad indiuiduitatem,
quo continue conviuant honestatis in indifferenti continuacione,
30   perpetuaque penalitatis sane viuentes[7] proficiant in euitacione.
[2.] Reuera venerande vetustatis varia sumere fas est ex assercionibus argumenta quod mendacium subsecutiue sint fuerintve
mendaciorum punitiue penalitates et tormenta. Non tamen omnia
passim vetustatis asserta veritatis in sinceritate fateor omnino pura,
35   sed ad restringendas mendaciorum laxitatis habenas vel superficialiter argumentatiua.
[3.] Notum satis, ut auguror, est rudibus eciam rusticis rustico
vetustate iam diu diucius autenticatum triuiale figmentum sibi male
mencienti de Bato. Batus itaque (quo triuialiter trita vel aliquanto[8]
40   loquelaliter ludendo prosequi pergamus), dum rurali rusticus
aratorque peronatus rustice vagaretur in agro, Maiugene veniret
obuius latrocinanti diuino, dum fur fraudulenter abaccas furaretur
boues tunc derisibiliter desidenti Herecintio. Manifesto tandem

---

[1] pro *ed.*
[2] circumspecte S
[3] contuberniumque S
[4] subsolaris S
[5] tale S
[6] matrimonialem S
[7] viuenti S
[8] aliquando S

Reinvigorate its powers, flourishing in virtue,
And wage battle strenuously with the body,
Proving an easy victor by means of virtue,
And live virtuously, a paragon of holy conflict,
Asleep to vices, awake to virtues, so that
It brings its time on earth to a good end.

[1.] I have examined marital life because I am trying, to the best of my ability, to define a unique harmony like that established by the unbroken intimacy and concord between a married man and his wife. I know for a fact that marital cohabitation with a free-born woman or girl should, in the case of people who are equal in social status, be considered matrimony rather than concubinage, especially since legitimate marital intercourse arises from mutual affection, not documents. So I have relied on some relevant rational common-places and logical presuppositions to establish the indivisibility here on earth of the marital bond between such well-matched partners, in order that they might live together always in unending honor, and successfully avoid all cause for punishment.

[2.] In fact, we may properly adduce from revered Antiquity various proofs that liars have and will be afflicted with just punishments for their mendacity. However, I do not claim that everything the ancients said is the unalloyed truth, only that they offer at least superficially practical arguments for reining in casual lies.

[3.] I imagine that the worn-out fable (now long since confirmed by Antiquity) of rustic Battus, who lied to his own harm, is well known even to crude rustics. To retell for pleasure a well-worn story, as the plowman Battus wandered through a field in his clodhoppers, he came upon Maia's son Mercury, the god of thieves, who was rustling cattle he had stolen while Apollo foolishly trifled with love. But in the end Battus was tricked by Mercury's promise

|40^v| suo satis enormiter dampnificatus pro mendacio, sed et
45 enormiter[1] eciam denique duplicato delusus in premio, dum nequi-
ret, eidem prodere pergit eundem viliter involuto,[2] manifesto non
erubescens in falsiloquio, sed id adeo delire non egit mendose
liguosus ruricola perniciterque circumuentus penalitatis abhominande sine subsecutiuo. Mercurius enim (quo fas in via verbis autentice
50 detur antiquitatis) in menciendo tam delire procacem perpetuo
silenciarium transfigurauit in silicem. Mendacitatis et in eo bene
premeritum sic imposuit finem. Sed et in elegancioris vite viros
suas exercuere vires punitiue mendaciorum penalitates.

[4.] Nota satis, ut auguror, est triuialiterque trita de transmissis a
55 Moyse terram promissionis ad explorandam preinstructis adeo
commendabiliter exploratoribus historia, nec minus exploratorum[3]
subsequenter (licet non omnium) voluntarie menciencium puniciones mendaciorum. Moyses quidem vir bellissime morigeratus,
mitisque non minus et paciens, commendabiliterque circumspectus,
60 ad eam sagaciter explorandam duodecim viros (quo populariter
publicata loquar) promissionis transmisit ad terram: de tribu videlicet Effraym, Josue filium Nun; de tribu Jude, Caleph filium Iepho-
ue; reliquosque x suis[4] de singulis tribubus designatos[5] de nomine.
Sed omnes preter Josue, quasi consensu preconfederato communi,
65 de terre statu necnon et situ conuentuque populari patenter et
exfrontissime sunt mentiti, mendaciter asserere non abhorrentes non
posse tam fortes a tam debilibus expugnari, tot innumerabiles a tam
paucis subpeditari; |41^r| ciuitatumque numerositates, murorum
prorsus et inexpugnabilium, virorum virtuosorum multitudines et
70 inexsuperabilium sunt mendosissime commentiti.[6] Sed et inhabitato-
rum terram deuoratricem suorum fore mendaci[7] sunt et elata fronte
professi. Verum non inpune tandem sunt adeo mendaci[8] sic mencientes[9] ore locuti. Nempe dominus omnes quos promissionis
terram Moyses transmiserat ad explorandam, duobus dumtaxat
75 (Iosue videlicet et Caleb) exceptis, summi scilicet numinis vis et
potestas penaliter percussit summa semper et insuperabilis.

---

[1] enormis S
[2] involuti S
[3] exploratoribus S
[4] suos S
[5] designatis S
[6] commenti S
[7] mendati S
[8] mendati S
[9] S *ad.* sunt *before* ore

of a double reward and punished brutally for his lie. Even though he did not blush at his own manifest falsehood, Battus was unable to betray Mercury to the god himself in disguise; indeed, the fast-talking rustic was quickly outwitted and suffered the punishment consequent upon such mad behavior. If we are for the moment to give proper credence to the words of Antiquity, Mercury permanently metamorphosed the madly audacious liar into silent flint. Thus he put a well-deserved end to Battus's mendacity. But even men of higher station have suffered the brunt of punishment for lies.

[4.] An equally familiar and well-worn commonplace, I imagine, is the history of the explorers sent by Moses' command to explore the Promised Land, and the punishment of most (but not all) for their gratuitous lies about that land. Indeed, to repeat a matter of common knowledge, Moses—a man of high morals, but at the same time mild, patient, and circumspect—wisely sent twelve men to explore the Promised Land: from the tribe of Ephraim, Joshua the son of Nun; from the tribe of Juda, Caleb the son of Jephone; and the remaining ten named according to their several tribes. But all except Joshua, as if leagued together by prior consent, lied openly and without shame about the land's condition, geography, and popular assembly; nor did they recoil from the false claim that such a powerful nation could not be overcome by such a feeble one, or so many be subdued by so few. They lied about an abundance of cities with impregnable walls and multitudes of valiant and invincible men. And they published the barefaced lie that the land devoured its inhabitants. But in the end they did not speak such utter falsehoods with impunity, for the Lord—the supreme and invincible might of the highest godhead—struck with punishment all those whom Moses had sent to explore the Promised Land, with the exception of Joshua and Caleb.

[5.] Sed et alia quidem quamplura mendaciorum penaliter punito-
rum primo veniunt a limite querentibus eciam tepide satis et invitis
exempla. Sed iam nunc, quia sic placet, dumtaxat vnum punicionis
80   mendaciorum ponere sufficiat exemplum quasi compitaliter quidem
satis diouolariterve diuulgatum. Notum[1] satis est, ut opinor, tam
lippis eciam quam tonsoribus, populariterque publicatum, sacer-
dotum crimen ipsis eciam facinoribus abhominabile Babilonicorum
diuine viribus virtutis tandem pernicissime punitum, qui iustam
85   Ioachym iusti coniugem petulancia puncti petulanter exarserunt in
Susannam, mulierem non minus castam quam decoram, suumque
sibi salubriter Deum sana dilectionis in soliditate metuentem.
Nempe sacerdotes illi dierumque malorum populi iudices inveterati
(quo uel ex habundanti, quia iam nunc sic libet, sub breuitate
90   succincta prosequi pergam veraci vetustate venustata wlgariterque
diwlgata), dum consuetudinaliter meridionalis sub intemperie
temporis sola suo sicut estimabat se Suzanna solaretur deambulans
in pomerio, |41^v| male felices et infausti sacerdotes illi petulanciis-
que funditus infatuati, suis in quibus se preabsconderant prosilien-
95   tes a latebris (quia suos sibi petulancia semper habet impetus,
suasque libido vires), tremulis ei sermonibus primo supplicare
pergunt ut eos libidinis in adiectiones adinvitat;[2] sed ubi suam sue
castitatis nullatenus posse frangi coniectauere pertinaciam, male
mencientes inmeritam deferre pergunt adulterii ream quod se
100   vidisse constanter asserent eam suo cum coadulterante coadulteran-
tem, quo sic contra fas et pium, testium simul, accusatorum nec non
et officio fungerentur examinatorum.
[6.] Uerum Deus, iustorum iustissimus, arbiter et incircumuenibilis, semper excelsus et sublimis et habitans eternitatem, summus et
105   vniuersitatis opifex, voluntariusque magister, fidusque dispensator,
pervigilque minister, minus iuste sic impetite satis effectiue preuidit
noua preuisionis in spiritualitate, dum prorsus innocentis ad libera-
cionem Danielis spiritum suscitaret adolescentis et intelligenciam,
fecundaretque subtilitatem, dum iuuenis eos condempnabiles esse
110   comprobaret et mendaces per diiudicacionem. Sicque peremptoriam
sustinuere tandem mendaciorum pro mendaciis meritissime penali-
tatem, dum popularem populus eos tam commendabiliter de mendaciis conuictos sublunari cedere coegit de medio per lapidacionem,
male feliciter in perpetuum morituros infamie per perpetuitatem,
115   vel pocius eternales eternaliter sibi perperam victuros penalitatis

---

[1] Motum S
[2] adinvitant S

[5.] Many other examples of lies duly punished will occur even to those who seek only halfheartedly in the most obvious places. But for our present purpose it will suffice to give but one example, which is to be heard on any street corner or in any brothel, of the punishment for lying. The power of divine virtue punished in the end the abominable crime of the Babylonian priests who, spurred on by wantonness, burned for Susanna, the righteous wife of Ioachim—a woman as chaste as she was beautiful, who feared her God with the sober firmness of love. The story is, I imagine, well known even to barbers and the bleary eyed. Furthermore, to indulge ourselves briefly with matters made famous by true Antiquity, one day, when Susanna was relaxing according to her custom by strolling alone (as she thought) in her orchard during the midday heat, these priests and judges, grown old in evil days and reduced to utter foolishness by their lust, leapt from the hiding place in which they had concealed themselves, for lust will indulge its impulses and wantonness exert its force. At first they begged her meekly to entertain their swelling lust, but when they realized that it would be impossible to prevail upon her resolute chastity, they proceeded to accuse her unjustly, claiming repeatedly that they had seen her commit adultery with her lover. Thus, contrary to right and justice, they would perform the office of both witnesses and prosecutors, not to mention judges.

[6.] But God—most just of the just and a judge impossible to circumvent, always on high and dwelling in eternity, supreme artificer, unconstrained master, unfailing administrator and ever-vigilant minister of the universe—provided for the unjustly accused by rousing the spiritual power of foresight in Daniel and enriching the youth's intelligence with subtlety sufficient to free the innocent victim, for the youth proved the priests guilty by trying them separately. So in the end they rightly endured the fatal punishment for their falsehoods: after they had condemned themselves by their own lies, they were forced by public stoning to quit this sublunar realm, to die forever unfortunate in unending infamy, or rather to live eternally to their own harm in perpetual punishment.

perpetue per infinibilitatem.

[7.] Sunt et alia quidem quam plurima primis et in luminibus obuiam voluntarie |42ʳ| veniencia meritissime punitiua semper vilis, admodumque semper abhominande mendositatis exempla.
120 Sed et id maxime mendaciorum facit abhominacionem quod satis autenticis et in uirtutis apice solidatis (fit ut et succincta sub breuitate pretaxauimus) asseritur a viris, quod videlicet os quod mentitur mencientis occidit animam, summumque Deum delirissime mouet ad iram perniciter et impellit offensionis ad amaritudinem; sed et
125 eternaliter durature quietatis eternitate se dampnabiliter defraudare suam nec animaduertit male menciens homo, nec animaduertere dignatur animam.

LIBER OCTAUUS

Uir sibi sensatus male per mendacia mendax
    Se sua confundens tendit ad interitum;[1]
Ad miserum trahit interitum per famina mendax
    Os hominem morum mortificando modos;
5 Os anime parat accessus ad limina[2] mendax
    Mortis, et ad mortem pena perhennat eam.
Ligua loquax sua liguosi male dirigit actus,
    Dum parit interitum ligua maligna sibi;
Liguosum male ligua leuis sua sepe molestum
10   Esse facit validis per sua verba viris.
Occurrent mala mendoso sua tempore mortis,
    Interitusque sibi denique durus erit;
Ergo suum bene sensatus vir quisque labellum
    Vel digito temptet segnificare libens.

15 [1.] Sed euestigio consors meus, paulo prius adeo silenciarius admodumque paciens commendabiliterque pacificus, velud ad talia fuisset adprime motus, wltu solito satis in deterius |42ᵛ| mutato, taliter est exorsus: Numquid, Helya, tuas reinfatuatus consuetudines redire paras ad erroneas, ut inter animalium tot animas, hominis
20 animam dumtaxat esse credas inmortalem? Reuera quiuis, me iudice, se satis fore fatetur infatuatum qui prescise quid asserere

---

[1] interitus S
[2] lumina S

[7.] There are, of course, many other examples of punishments for base and abhorrent mendacity which will strike one at first glance. But, as we have already touched upon briefly, men confirmed by faith at the apex of virtue have themselves defined what makes lies most abominable, namely that a lying mouth slays the liar's soul, moves God Almighty to wrath, and quickly compels Him to take bitter offense. The man who lies wrongfully does not deign to consider that he is damnably defrauding his soul of rest for all eternity.

BOOK EIGHT

The liar who lacks self-knowledge destroys himself
    With his lies and heads for ruin;
The words from a lying mouth drag a man
    To miserable ruin by destroying moral bounds;
A lying mouth prepares the soul's approach to the threshold
    Of death, where it lives in unending torment.
His talkative tongue misdirects the loudmouth's actions,
    While a spiteful tongue causes his ruin;
His light tongue often causes the unfortunate loudmouth
    To harm valiant men with his words.
His misdeeds will confront the liar at his death,
    And death will be hard on him;
So any sensible man will at least be glad
    To try slowing his lips with his finger.

[1.] Immediately my companion, who just a moment earlier had been patiently silent and at peace, changed his expression for the worse and began to speak out, as if he were powerfully moved: Don't tell me, Elias, that you are once again so thoroughly deluded as to return to your habitual error of believing that among the souls of so many animals only the soul of man is immortal? In my judgment, anyone who presumes to assert categorically a proposition

verbali stoliditate presumit cuius assercio[1] omnem subsistit contra
racionem probacionisque citra subsidium, presertim dum quod
assertiue pronunciando ponere pergit anxioma non sit artisue
25 principium, locumue uel vices sorciatur preambularum[2] quauis in
arte peticionum. Qui quidem conatur astruere quod tot inter spiran-
cia dumtaxat hominis anima sit inmortalitate priuilegiata, quodque
Deus omnium sit vnus arbitraria solus potestate priuilegiatus, et ad
ea cuiusuis citra racionis inspeccionem motu voluntario motus
30 volens ad asserendum venit assertor velud exfrontissime pertinax,
experimentaliterque certus omninoque sciens et indubius, subsannabiliter suos cachynnabiliterque delirando detegere pergit erratus,
presertim cum nulla racione fundamentaliter firma, superficialiterue
probabili, verisimiliterue sana superficiali sua sit in assercione
35 subpodiatus.

[2.] Atqui diuersis diuersorum philosophicis[3] in exerciciis philosophorum precipuorum sunt satis note et a discretis adhuc triuialiter satis, compitaliterue trite diuersitates opinionum, varietatesque
sentenciarum circa diffiniciones anime uel descripciones humane
40 varia diducencium, sibique scienter in anime substancia uel descrip-
cione dissidencium. Sic itaque sibi scienter aduersancium falsitatis
commenticie uel mendacitatis cedit in argumentum, presumpciona-
lisue venit erroris ad innuitiuum.[4] Sic igitur, quo sola subponere
pergam diouolaliter nota remociusque meis nitar in assercionibus
45 amandare |43ʳ| mendacia, diuersorum diuersas philosophorum
sentencias anime de situ uel existencia ponere pergam, variaque
contencionum corrixacionumque seminaria. Rarissime reuera verum
fore reperietur cognicionaliterue certum quod antinomias[5] parit
materiasque mouet altercacionum. Sic itaque, cum viri veteres
50 philozophaliterque sensati nullatenus in anime diffinicione uel
existencia geniali, uel in conueniencie[6] luculencia sibi convenire
potuissent, ut omnes a se remotius antinomias[7] contradiccionum-
que diductiones amandarent, vix est quod modernorum tam supine
simplicitates et ignorancie diffinicionis anime genialisve cognicionis
55 ad existencie perfeccionem pertingere possint. Excipias igitur auten-

---

[1] assercionis S
[2] preambularumque S
[3] diuersis ... philosophicis] diuersa ... philosophus S
[4] inuitiuum S
[5] antimonias S
[6] in conueniencie] inconueniencie S
[7] antimonias S

contrary to all reason and unsupported by proof betrays his utter foolishness, especially when what he tries to establish by verbal fiat is not an axiom or premise of a discipline, or does not serve as a preliminary postulate to any body of knowledge. Indeed, the man who tries to assert that among so many living organisms only the soul of man is endowed with immortality, and that of all things only God is endowed with unconstrained power, and who more-over makes these assertions willfully without considering any reason, like a brash partisan, certain from experience, all-knowing and without doubts, manages only to reveal his own faults by his ridiculous raving, especially since he is not supported by any reason which is fundamentally sound, superficially probable, or even plausible.

[2.] By now, the learned are familiar with, even bored by, the divergent opinions and various thoughts concerning the definition or description of the human soul in the writings of eminent philoso-phers, who differ in their deductions and disagree knowingly with each other about the soul's substance. All this suggests falsehood or mendacity and implies an error of presumption in those who willingly oppose each other. So, in order to assume only common knowledge and avoid any false assertion, I will state the opinions of the various philosophers concerning the location or existence of the soul, and the various causes which have nursed contention and strife. In fact, claims which give rise to antinomies and supply matter for disputes are rarely found to be true or epistemologically certain. The ancients, men who were philosophically sophisticated, were wholly unable to agree among themselves in splendid harmo-ny either on the definition or innate composition of the soul, and so set aside all antinomies and contradictory deductions. So it is scarcely to be hoped that the moderns' supine simplicity and igno-rance should be able to achieve a perfect definition or innate cogni-zance of the soul. You might consider, if you like, the various

ticorum, ni displiceat, virorum varias circa[1] diffiniciones anime uel descripciones humane sentencias.

[3.] Uenerande vetustatis a tempore primitiuo precipuus in philosophia, plurimumque placens Plato sentencialiter animam fore
60   dicebat essenciam sese mouentem. Sed Aristotiles animam fore dicebat endelichiam, perfectam scilicet formam. Pitagoras quidem, sibique consenciens Philolaus, animam fore dixerunt armoniam, concordiam scilicet uel consonanciam. Pollodonius[2] ydeam, visionem videlicet; Asclepiades animam fore dicebat exercicium quinque
65   sensuum sibi consonum. Sed Ypocrates animam fore dicebat tenuem spiritum per corpus omne dispersum. Phisicus aiebat Heraclitus[3] animam stellaris essencie scintillam. Sed Heraclitus[4] philosophus animam dicebat lucem. Zenon aiebat animam concretum fore corporis spiritum. Spiritum Democritus athomis aiebat insertum,
70   sua sic facilitate motum quod illi corpus omne sic pervium. Critholaus vero perypatecus animam de quinta constare dicebat essencia. Sed |43ᵛ| Yparcus animam dicebat ignem, sed Axiemenes aerem, Cricias et Empedocles saguinem. Parmenides ex terra simul et igne constare dicebat animam, Xenofantes ex terra simul et aqua, Boetes
75   ex aere simul et igne. Sed Epicurus ex igne speciem simul et aere spirituque mixtam dicebat animam. Uirgilius uero, poetarum peritissimus, anime naturam commendabiliter insinuans sic ait: Igneus est illi vigor et celestis ymago. Sic et Yparco necnon et utrique simul Heraclito, Platoni necnon et Pitagore sane videtur inspicienti con-
80   sentire.

[4.] Verumptamen quod admiracionis magne michi mouet incitatiuum, consternacionisque non minus coacerbat excitatiuum, simul omnes anime quasi confederaliter inmortalitate necnon et incorporeitate dissensionum qua<s>que citra turbulencias philosophi
85   consenciunt, quo quidem iustissime remocius philosofice dignitatis ab appellacione sue sibi speciales vite vitalitates Phariseos amandent. Id autem michi magne pridem fuit et adhuc est admiracionis sepissime repetitiuum quod humanam dumtaxat homines indifferenter animam simul omnes opinantur, ymmo certissime credunt,
90   sed et scire citra dubitacionem profitentur in inmortalitate priuilegiatam, cum ceterorum spiritus et animas animalium suis vna cum

---

[1] citra S
[2] Pollodonius S, Posidonius *Macrobius*
[3] Phisicus ... Heraclitus] Phisicus ... Heraclius S, Heraclides (Heraclitus *var.*) Ponticus *Macrobius* (*Cf. 8.79 below.*)
[4] Heraclitus *Macrobius*, Heraclius S

opinions of authoritative men concerning the definition or description of the human soul.

[3.] Plato, preeminent in philosophy from the early days of venerable Antiquity, held the pleasing opinion that the soul is a self-moving essence. But Aristotle said the soul is an entelechy, that is, a perfected form. Pythagoras, and Philolaus who agreed with him, said the soul is harmony, that is, concord or consonance; Posidonius, idea, that is, a mental image; and Asclepiades said the soul is the harmonious exercise of the five senses. But Hippocrates said the soul is a tenuous spirit diffused through the entire body. Heraclides the natural philosopher said the soul is a spark of the starry essence. But the philosopher Heraclides called the soul light. Zeno said the soul is the solidified spirit of the body. Democritus said it is a spirit inserted in atoms and so moved by its nature that any body is open to it. Critolaus the Peripatetic said the soul is a quintessence. But Hipparchus called the soul fire, while Anaximenes called it air, Critias and Empedocles blood. Parmenides said the soul consists of both earth and fire, Xenophantes of both earth and water, Boethos of both air and fire. But Epicurus called the soul an image concocted from fire, air, and breath. Vergil, the most learned of poets, commendably hinted at the soul's nature in saying: "Its vigor is fiery and its image heavenly." Thus he seems to a sensible investigator to agree with Hipparchus, either Heraclides, Plato, and also Pythagoras.

[4.] It greatly amazes me and at the same time exacerbates my dismay that all the philosophers have leagued together to agree without any turbulent dissent on the immortality and the incorporeality of the soul, with the result that the unique vigor of their own lives justly excludes these Pharisees from any claim to philosophic dignity. But it has never ceased to amaze me that all men without exception suppose, indeed claim to know beyond a doubt as certain knowledge, that only the human soul is endowed with immortality, while not doubting that the spirits and souls of other animals are

corporibus mortis indubias per asserciones deduci[1] communem
non dubitent ad interitum, presertim cum nec potestas suprema nec
Ramnusie beniuolencia (fatorum perseuerancia de qua gloriamur)
95 humanam specialiter in nullo spirantibus pre ceteris[2] priuilegiauerit
animalitatem, sed sibi suum speciale donum ceteris habere concessit
ut animalibus vniuersis; reuera nec id inficiari sano cuiquam fas est.

[5.] Sagacitatis in exercicio sub sole spirantibus est homo |44ʳ|
meritissime preferendus ut inter subsolares sensatissimus, animal
100 leo rugiens in audatia primitiuum, viuencium viuens animal animalium fortis elephans fortissimum, velocium tigris animal velocissi-
mum, visu perspicacium linx animal perspicacissimum, canis in
odoratu precellentissimum, phenix in pulchritudine prestantissi-
mum; cuiuslibet eciam gratiarum tam varie distinctarum gradus
105 peruenitur ad summum per varie distinctos. Astutus quidem (quo
uel aliquatenus labiis laxentur habene) sane iudicatur esse canis,
astucior homo pene symia nature degenerantis, homo quidem
sanissime censetur astutissimus. Equus fortis, forcior camelus,
elephans[3] fortissimus; consimiliterque procedas in ceteris ne per
110 singula superflue discurramus.

[6.] Subtilius itaque discutere pergat subtilitas humanitatis qua
racione summo concessori teneatur homo, pro concessa sibi subtilis
astucie gratia, gratias[4] ad exibendas, plus quam[5] tam speciali
tamque miranda sua fortis elephans pro fortitudine, linx luminum
115 pro perspicacitate, quamque cetera gratis sibi concessis animalia pro
graciis. Hoc eciam subtilius subtilitas considerare deberet humanitatis quod in hoc Deus insensate preferre videtur hominibus animalia,
quod congruis et indeficientibus (homine nuditatis improperio
naturaliter dampnificato sue) nuditatis preuidit eis vetustatis omnes
120 citra violencias duraturis ad expediens in indumentis. Gratuitas
eciam beneficiorum per collaciones brutis bellissime prodigus est et
elegantissime gratificatus animalibus, quo quelibet consuetudinaliter
(hominibus dumtaxat exceptis) animalia[6] beantur euexie rarius
interpolata continuacione, diutinaque per tempora vite viuunt in
125 equalitate. Quodque multo mirabilius est, senectutis omnem citra
nouercacionem pulchriora temporis efficiuntur |44ᵛ| ex diuturnita-

---

[1] deducero S
[2] pre ceteris] preceteris S
[3] elephas S
[4] S ad. teneatur *before* ad
[5] plus quam] quam pro S
[6] est ... animalia] est elegantissime gratificatus, qui quelibet homine quique
consuetudinaliter (hominibus dumtaxat exceptis) animalibus animalia S

led away by death to share extinction with their bodies, especially since neither the supreme Power nor the benevolence of Nemesis (the perseverance of the fates in which we glory) privileged man's animal nature beyond other living creatures. Instead, they allowed him to have his own unique gift like all other animals, a fact which it is impossible for any sensible person to deny.

[5.] Man is rightly to be preferred as the most astute among earthly creatures in the exercise of intellect; the roaring lion is the animal foremost in boldness; the powerful elephant is the strongest of all living animals; the tiger is the swiftest; the lynx the most sharp-sighted; the dog preeminent in sense of smell; the phoenix outstanding for beauty: the acme of any of these attributes is reached by a series of distinct steps. To loosen the lips' reins somewhat, a dog is astute; an ape is more astute, almost a man of degenerate nature; man, indeed, is most astute. A horse is strong, a camel stronger, an elephant strongest: you may do the same with other attributes to save us the trouble of superfluous enumeration.

[6.] We must discuss with greater subtlety why man is obliged to render more thanks to the supreme Giver for the gift of subtle intellect than the elephant is for his unique and remarkable strength, the lynx for the visual acuity of his eyes, or the other animals for the favors freely granted them. We should consider this matter more subtly, since God seems irrationally to prefer animals to man: whereas man is naturally condemned to the reproach of nudity, He usefully provided for animals to persevere in well-chosen and permanent clothing without suffering any indignities from naked old age. He has been extremely generous in giving unsolicited advantages to brute animals, with the result that all animals except for man are habitually blessed by uniform good health and live their long lives in harmony. What is more remarkable still, they are made more beautiful by the passage of time, without becoming

te. Sed et inter animalia soli minimas subsistunt homines citra
delectaciones: dum uero uolucres cum libuerit in solido deambu-
lant, et in aridis delectantur et in aquosis, pro passis eleuantur in
130 aera pennis, reuera lentis homo gradibus graditur in solo dumtaxat
et in solido segnis.

[7.] Sed nec sibi, si sanum sapiat, stolide blandiatur homo uel
congaudeat, superciliumve fragilitas humanitatis stolide superbiens
extollat quod sub sole sola racionis in priuilegio sit excellenciata.
135 Reuera pocius eciam subtiles aiunt archigenes id humani reuer-
tendum[1] corporis est ad formam, racionisque simul et discipline
perceptibilem capitis ad disposicionem quam sit ad anime vim
genialem genialiter ab aliorum brutis animis[2] animalium per racio-
nalitatem differentialiter semotam: probabile satis ab animalibus ad
140 hominis similitudinem uel aliquatenus accedentibus, si libet, sumere
licet et efficax argumentum. Reuera quanto magis humanam quid-
uis animal accedit ad ymaginem, tanto magis, ut et alias scripsi,
gestus exprimit humanos imitaturque sagacitates; assercionis huius
in[3] summa testis assurgit elegans et fidelissimus.

145   [8.] Sed et ut nos quasi bestialiter proripere pergamus, si vas illud
in quo[4] subsistit[5] anima, quam quasi confederaliter asserunt esse
racionalitatis autricem uel causam, summam summe deitatis per
potenciam, nature violencia uel valitudine videlicet aduersa, vel
lesionis euentu forte fuerit in deterius adactum[6] (frenesi puta,
150 wlnereue, uel euentu quolibet[7] alio capud hominis euenerit esse
deprauatum), qui prius animi compos et discrecionis fuit, homo
protinus abibit in vicia deliramentorum. Corporis igitur humani
verisimillimum fore videtur quod vas racionalitatis causa, solum
velut ad id abile sic formatum, |45ʳ| sit instrumentum quod eciam
155 que corpus elephantinum tam grande uel bubalinum vegetat anima,
si figure fuisset hominis infusa tam parue, tam nobilis instrumenti
gratia frueretur bellissimeque gauderet racionalitatis prerogatiua.
Reuera neruus, fidisue, uel corda sonoro concorditer resonat instru-
mento que raucum redderet murmur in obtuso. Sic igitur sane
160 sencientibus videri dignissime debet esse ludibrium subsannabiliterque friuolum de solius hominis anime uel spiritus inmortalitate
vanum diducere cogitatum uel ad diducciones venire verbalitatum.

---

[1] reuerendum *S*
[2] animalibus *S*
[3] in *ed.*
[4] quod *S*
[5] subsistit *ed.*
[6] in deterius adactum] indeterius ad actum *S*
[7] quodlibet *S*

stepchildren to old age. But among animals only men remain without the slightest delights: birds can stroll upon solid ground when they please, delight in land and sea, and lift themselves into the air with outstretched wings; man, on the other hand, makes his way only on solid ground with slow and weary steps.

[7.] A sensible man should not foolishly flatter himself, nor should human frailty be so stupidly proud as to raise an eyebrow and rejoice, because man alone beneath the sun is distinguished by the privilege of reason. In fact, even subtle doctors say it is to be imputed more to the form of the human body and the disposition of the head, which is capable of accommodating reason and instruction, than to the genial vigor of a soul different in nature from the brute souls of other animals because it possesses reason. It is possible to draw a probable and valid proof from animals in the likeness, or (if you prefer) approaching the likeness, of man. In fact, as I have written elsewhere, the more an animal resembles the human image, the more it reproduces human gestures and imitates human intelligence; in short, I possess an elegant and trustworthy authority for my assertion.

[8.] But to rush forward like beasts (so to speak), if the vessel that contains the soul, which they have all leagued together to assert is the creator or cause of rationality, should be impaired by the power of the supreme Deity, either by natural violence (this is, bad health) or perhaps by the effect of an injury—if, for example, a man's head is deformed by frenzy, a wound or any other occurrence—the man who was previously of sound mind and discretion will immediately fall prey to delusions. Thus it seems to be true of the human body that the vessel which causes rationality is an instrument so uniquely suited to its task that even if the soul which invigorates the huge body of an elephant or ox were infused into the tiny figure of man, it would, on account of such a noble instrument, be blessed with and fittingly rejoice in the prerogative of rationality. In fact, a lyre string which resonates harmoniously on a well-tuned instrument will yield only a raucous drone on one that is out of tune. Thus, all sensible people will think it a frivolous joke to develop vain notions about the unique immortality of the human soul or spirit or to deliver speeches on the subject.

LIBER NONUS

Uana satis fuit, est, et erit diducere vanum
    ffamina de vanis uel variare vices;
Vana quidem sapiens arcere procul volet omnis,
    Dum sua sensato seria sola placent;
5 Dum stolido libet in vanis consumere tempus
    Omne suum, sapiens vir sapienter agit.
Vix validus volet in viciis vir viuere vanis,
    Et valido mors est viuere more malo;
Solus enim virtutis amor virtute valentem
10   Abstrahit a viciis, spernere vana facit;
Sic vanum virtute valens vir vitat ut omne
    Longius a curis arceat usque suis.

[1.] De cetero propositorum progredi pergamus ad secundum:
Deum fore sed et vnum precipue solum constanter cuilibet sensato
15 sane videtur videriue debet adprime mirum, presertim cum venera-
bilis antiquitas, cui summe sanccita pridem fuit et adhuc esse debet
reuerencie perpetuitas, deorum pluralitates |45ᵛ| fere sibi constitue-
rit deuociusque coluerit innumeras; ymmo phisicorum sapientissi-
morum non nulli licitis subsistere licenter in dubiis Dei deorumue
20 circa substancias. Unde quidam phisicus Euandau, vir inter primos
pridem serio sic ait precipuus: Si Deus est, sit ut est; si non est,
michi sit ut nunc est. Reliquit itaque sic condicionaliter per enunciatum se summe[1] de deitatis existencia minus fuisse consciencialiter
indubium.
25 [2.] Verumptamen vetustas opido semper est reuerenda, cui
reuerencia de iure pridem fuit et adhuc est velut edictali perpetuitate sanccita; diis suis fere funditus innumerabilibus summam summe
studuit exibere reuerenciam, sed eis precipue quibus uti se lectis
specialem non minus quam secretam veneracionis consancciuere pre-
30 rogatiuam, perfunctorie tunc, ut auguror, curantes considerantesue
quod multitudo superhabundans rarissime mansuescat adlaterareue
consuescat ad honesta. Minus eciam forte secum tunc aduertentes
quod multorum sepissime parilitas compossessorum perniciosissima
consueuerit excicatrix esse corrixacionum.

---

[1] summa S

Book Nine

It always has been and will be quite vain to produce
    Empty talk or ring the changes on senseless topics;
Any wise man will want to put vanities well aside,
    Since only serious thoughts please a sensible man;
While it pleases a fool to waste all his time
    On vanities, a wise man acts wisely.
A weak man will want to live in senseless vices,
    And living badly is death to the robust man;
Only the love of virtue frees a man flourishing
    In virtue from vices and makes him spurn vanities;
Thus a man strong in virtue avoids vanity
    And banishes it utterly from all his concerns.

[1.] Let us proceed to the second topic: it ought to seem remarkable to any sensible person that there should be one and only one God, especially since venerable Antiquity, for which supreme reverence was long since decreed in perpetuity, established for itself and devoutly worshipped innumerable multitudes of gods; on the other hand, not a few of the wisest natural philosophers remained in legitimate doubt concerning the substances of God or gods. So a certain natural philosopher Ibn Dāūd, a man who was once preeminent among the best, could say in earnest: "If God exists, let Him be; if He does not exist, let me be." By speaking conditionally, he made it clear that he was less than perfectly certain about the existence of the supreme Deity.

[2.] Antiquity is always to be revered greatly: reverence was and is legally decreed for it as if by perpetual edict. The ancients strove to show the highest reverence for their innumerable gods, but they especially consecrated the secret spiritual prerogative of veneration to their chosen gods, little caring (as far as I can tell) that an overabundant multitude is rarely in the habit of accommodating itself to virtue. Perhaps they also failed to take heed of how frequently the parity of numerous joint possessors incites ruinous squabbles.

35   [3.] Sed et Israelite, qui sibi Deum dumtaxat preelegerant vnanimiterque selegerant vnum, deorum veneratores mutati, pluralitates
concoluere deorum. Sed et antiquissimorum quidam sciencialiter
preditissimorum de diis velut artificialiter inuenticiis serio sic est et
excellenter elocutus: Deus et pater quiue summus est precipuusve
40   deus sicut effector est deorum celestium, sic effector est homo qui
coluntur in templis deorum, condicionis humane spontanea proximitate contentorum, qui suis scilicet reuerentissime coluntur in
abditis sacrariisque templorum, qui non solum suis illuminantur a
cultoribus, sed et suos quasi retransitiue cultores prosecuntur |46ʳ|
45 veneracionibus illuminacionum.

    [4.] Sed et idem sic subsequenter supponit: Species profecto
deorum quas conformat humanitas suam sumit ex vtraque natura
formam, videlicet ex diuina que prior et longe diuinior est, et ex ea
que viuit et versatur inter homines estque materialiter fabricata, non
50 solum capitibus solis sed et membris omnibus totoque figurata
corpore. Sic igitur humanitas, sue semper nature memor et originis,
illa perseuerat in imitacione religionis, quo sicut Deus vniuersorum
pater, vniuersalisque dominus deos ut sibi similes essent fecit
eternos, sic suos homo deos in sui wltus similitudine figurauit
55 temperarios. Supponit et idem subsequenter vir elegantissime
sensatus et indubitanter asserit statuas[1] non solum sensu spirituque
fore plenas, sed anima vegetatas, futurorumque prescias, et inbecil-
litates hominibus inferentes,[2] curacionumque remedia subicientes.
Idemque post pauca sic supponit: Terrenis facile quidem diis atque
60 mundanis irasci sicut qui sunt ab hominibus ex utraque natura
compositi, videlicet ex demone uel angelo uocaliter euocato, necnon
et simulachro.

    [5.] Non solum profecto suis in diis faciendis hominum similitu-
dines imitari dignum duxere venerandi venerabilesque viri veteres,
65 sed brutorum formas animalium sibi fecere pro diis adorabiles.
Atqui populus (quo nota loquar) Israeliticus[3] onerosa mirabiliter
seruitute liberatus Egipciata, dum laboribus ab Egipto fugientes in
deserto vexarentur itinerariis, aureum pronus adorare pro deo non
dubitauerunt conflatilemque vitulum: deo gens dignissima tam rudi
70 tunc et bouino, nisi deum fore talem pronius adorandum, quod
semper admodum desiderabat solum propter aurum, solo crederet
et in auro. Dignissima |46ᵛ| quidem vox tam viliter agentis est

---

[1] statuas *Asclepius, om. S*
[2] inferentes *S*, facientes *Asclepius*
[3] Israeliticus *ed.*

[3.] Even the Israelites, who had once elected and unanimously chosen for themselves only one God, became worshippers of the gods and venerated a plurality of gods. One of the best endowed ancient intellectuals spoke in full earnest about these gods who seem like literary fictions: "As the God and father, who is the highest or preeminent god, is the creator of the celestial gods, so man is the creator of those gods who are worshipped in temples, content with the willing proximity of the human condition. I mean those gods who are reverently worshipped in the recesses and shrines of their temples, and who are not only illuminated by their worshippers, but also return the favor by rewarding their worshippers with illuminations."

[4.] The same author adds later: "The image of the gods which humanity created took its form from either nature, that is, from the divine, which is prior and far more divine, and from that which lives and moves among men and is made from matter, fashioned not only with heads but with members and entire bodies. Thus humanity, always mindful of its nature and origin, persists in this imitation of religion, so that as God, father of all things and universal lord, made gods that were eternal so they would be like him, in the same way man fashioned his transitory gods in the likeness of his visage." This same eloquently sensible man later makes the confident assertion that these statues are not only imbued with sense and spirit but animated by a soul and prescient of future events; they inflict infirmities on men and furnish their remedies in turn. He adds soon afterwards: "It is easy for terrestrial and earthly gods to become wrathful, as they are compounded by men from either nature, that is, from a demon or angel conjured by name, and from a statue."

[5.] Not only did the revered men of earlier times consider it worth their while to imitate the likenesses of men in making their gods, but they also made for themselves images of brute animals to be adored as gods. To give an obvious example, the people of Israel, when they were liberated miraculously from onerous servitude in Egypt but afflicted by the difficulties of fleeing through the desert, did not hesitate to prostrate themselves and worship a calf forged from gold as a god—a people worthy of such a crude and bovine god, unless such a god was to be worshipped with bended knee on account of the gold, which they always desired greatly, and unless they believed only in gold. The voice of people who acted so

populi bouem sibi fore deum profiteri, cum se sic tam subsannabiliter profitendo boue multum deteriorem multoque citeriorem cense-
75 re videatur per consequenciam debere censeri.

[6.] Nemo nempe commendabiliter scius deo se suo profiteri
debet plus equilibriterue, sed in sciencia[1] presertim, potenciave, uel
sagacitate priuilegiari. Reuera vere minimum differt ab insanienti,
si tamen michi fides est habenda sic examinanti, qui rei pro deo sibi
80 suppliciter ad supplicandum potest inclinari se longe simul et in
potencia scientiaque citeriori. Non autem semel tantum gens adeo
tunc nobilis adeoque suo sepius a Deo mirabiliter subsidialiterque
solaciata bouinam pro deo vitulinamve formam reuerenter est
geniculariterque venerata, sacrificiis eciam simul et supplicantibus
85 diuinis et exibicionibus est prosecuta, dum duos populi deo suo sibi
tam propiciato tam subsannabiliter ingratificati supplicacionibus et
votis boues uel vitulos (vnum videlicet in Dan, in Bethel alterum
positos), homini longe licencius satisfaciendo quam sibi spiritualissi-
me pregratificato numero, voluntarie sunt prosecuti.

90 [7.] Sed et eorundem tam cachinnabiliter infatuatorum sensatissimus Salomon simul et opulentissimus est adeo tandem vanas
opulenciarum per superfluitates infatuatus, quod spiritu[2] qui sibi
pregratificatus fuerat, ut dicitur, Deo contumaciterque relicto, diis
artificialibus sacrificandum fore constituerit, sibique sacrificiis eos et
95 supplicacionibus propiciare non erubuerit, amore mulierum (quo[3]
nichil efficacius ad circumueniendum) circumuentus, dum fallacibus
fidem femineis habere verbis, ut asseritur, fatuissime preelegerit,
quo tam sapientis ab errore tam supino sanum satis et |47ʳ| effica-
cissimum sumatur argumentum quod de nemine dum sublunari
100 spirat uel viuit in lumine sic indubitanter presumendum, nec de
viuente quam sua diu[4] viuit in sanitate sit omnino desperandum.

[8.] Ciuitas eciam Romana, que mundum sibi sublunarem viribus
et sagacitate subiecit vniuersum, suoque domuit sub imperio,
suaque tenuit sub dicione quasi seruiliter indifferenterque sibi
105 subiugatum, sibi suos non solum deos effigiauit artificiales manuali-
terque[5] figuratos, sed eciam beluas humanitati genialiter abhorren-
das sibi constituit[6] pro diis adorabiles letaliterque venenosas, sub

---

[1] in sciencia] insciencia S
[2] spirito S
[3] qua S
[4] dum S
[5] manubialiterque S
[6] constituere S

basely worthily avows that an ox is its god, since by avowing themselves inferior to an ox they seem in consequence to be judged by their own judgment.

[6.] Certainly no knowledgeable person should avow himself to be better endowed than his god with knowledge, power, or mental acuity. In fact, if you put any faith in my account, the man who is capable of bowing down and humbly supplicating a god far inferior to himself in both power and knowledge hardly differs from a madman. Nor was it only once that this people, so noble and so often consoled by the miraculous assistance of their God, reverently bent the knee to god in the form of an ox or calf and honored it with sacrifices of supplication and divine worship. These people, so ridiculously ungrateful to the God who had been well disposed towards them, freely honored with supplications and vows two oxen or calves, one in Dan and the other in Bethel—a number which pleased man more than it benefited him spiritually.

[7.] Solomon, who was the most intelligent and the wealthiest of this laughably deluded race, was at length so utterly deluded by an empty excess of wealth that, proudly abandoning the spirit which is said to have previously shown him favor as well as God, he decreed sacrifices to fictive gods whom he did not blush to propitiate with sacrifices and prayers. He was circumvented by the love of women (which surpasses everything in its power to circumvent) because, as the story goes, he fatuously chose to put his faith in women's words. We may draw from the supine error of such a wise man a clear and effective proof that no one should be taken utterly for granted as long as they live and breathe in the sublunar light, nor should one utterly despair of any living person as long as he retains his sanity.

[8.] Even the city of Rome, which conquered the entire sublunar world by shrewdness and force and subdued and held it in servile subjugation, not only shaped by hand fictive gods for itself, but also established monsters naturally abhorrent to humanity as gods at once worthy of worship and fatally poisonous. Under them the

quibus Romana res publica viuentibus ad invidiam iure[1] domina-
cionis dicionisque fimbrias summe felicitatis continuacione comitata
110 dilatauit. Nota satis est,[2] ut auguror, quod dumtaxat vnum tangere
pergamus hic exemplum diffusius alias explanatum, compitaliter-
que[3] diwlgata deorum tam propensa tamque propicia pridem
ciuitati Rome beniuolencia. Deus pridem precipue reuerendus fertur
abhominabilis in specie serpentis ab Epidauro Mercurius nauigio
115 Romam reuerentissime transportatus, qui fatalem diucius in ciuitate
peruagantem salubri numinis obliterauit presencia pestilenciam, qui
temporibus in illis eciam pro deo Rome reuera reuerentissime
postea diucius Esculapii sub appellacione fuit autenticatus, et a
Romanis thure et sacrificiis, sollempnibus et uotis deitatis in reue-
120 rencia deuotissime placatus.

[9.] Non autem multominus, ut michi videre videor, diouolaliter
est diwlgatum qualiter Egipcii tam subsannabiliter (ut non nullis
videbatur, utque sicut coniecto iam nunc videtur) fuerint infatuati
quod Apem, taurum videlicet in humero dextro lunari signo corni-
125 culari candido patentissime signatum, sed et a flumine consuetudinaliter egressum, diuinis honoribus suumque fuerint deuotissime
sicut deum prosecuti; dumque confluentes ad eum quasi confederaliter omnes, omnique musicorum genere psallentes, in susum
starent aspicientes, in aere leuabatur et super eos tamquam saliens
130 ferebatur et admotus, |47ᵛ| vel staciones ipsius ipsi mouebantur
uel stabant, eademque die post euanescebant.

[10.] Sic itaque diuersi deorum numinisue diuini sub sectis, de
deitatis vnitate nichil omnino curantes, sua sub prosperitatis indif-
ferentia diutissime tempora transegerunt. Pergas igitur et de tue si
135 libet liberrime iactites animeue uel spiritus prorsus inaniter inmortalitate,[4] perhenniterque duratura[5] de vitalitate, uel diffidas in[6] racionibus argumentalibusue subsidiis, uel si quas ad manus habes
probacionibus tuam subpodiare firmiusue subsequenter solidare
racionem[7] procures.

---

[1] iura S
[2] est ed.
[3] -que ed.
[4] inmortalitates S
[5] ducatura S
[6] diffidas in] indiffidas S
[7] racionem ed.

Roman republic enlarged its borders by the law of conquest and grew in happiness to become the envy of those living now. The benevolence of the gods who were once so partial to the city of Rome is sufficiently well known as a topic of street talk that we will touch here on only one example expounded elsewhere at greater length. The god Mercury, once greatly worshipped, is said to have been reverently transported by ship from Epidaurus to Rome in the shape of an abominable snake. The salutary presence of his godhead eliminated a deadly pestilence which had long ravaged the city. He was reverently established as a god at Rome under the name of Aesculapius and was for a long time afterwards devoutly placated by the Romans with incense and sacrifices, solemnities and vows, in reverence of his godhead.

[9.] It seems to me a meretricious commonplace that the Egyptians were so ridiculously deluded (a point on which many people would agree) that they devoutly honored as a god Apis, a bull customarily shown emerging from a river, marked prominently on his right shoulder with the horned sign of the white moon. They all converged towards him of one accord and hymned him with every sort of music, and while they stood looking upwards, he was lifted into the air and carried above them; or his guards were themselves moved, or stood still and then disappeared later on the same day.

[10.] Divided thus among various sects of the gods or the divine *numen*, caring absolutely nothing for the unity of the godhead, the various ancients passed their time in long and unbroken prosperity. Go right ahead then, if you want to, and boast in vain about the immortality of your soul and the life essence which will endure forever, and either despair of logic or proof, or if you have any at hand, you should use them to shore up your argument when your time comes.

LIBER DECIMUS

Uir merito quiuis censendus erit sua vilis
Si racionis egens fuerit per verba verendus;
Is sua sensate quiuis fans famina fundit
Si sua ligua libens racionis opem sibi curat
5 Associare loquens, mens et mendacia uitet;
Si renuat sibi conuiuis conuiuere concors,
In medio medianus, agatque vices sibi vanas,
Communis odiosa suis erit hiis sibi vita.
Conciliare solent humiles consorcia mores;
10 Dissociant modi socialia vincula morum.
Tu tamen ad libitum, tibi si fuerint raciones,
Affer eas solidesque tuos racionibus apte
Sermones, quos fronte retro firma solidasti,
Quo tua sint asserta tibi solidata decenter.

15   [1.] Atqui, frater, exfrontissime factus es, ut michi videtur, iterato
contradictorius verbaliterque de nouo longe magis solito superfluus.
Verumptamen racionis non minus es veritatisue citra[1] sinceritatem
segnissime circumspectus dum tam temerarie tamque pertinaciter
hominis inter animalia solius anime sanccitam specialiter inficiari
20 non erubescis inmortalitatem, presertim cum soli concessam non
neges homini racionalitatis inter |48ʳ| animalia prerogatiuam. Nec
inficiari, sicut auguror, audeas nisi delirum uel insanientem ridiculosissime sapias, quin summis hominem[2] numinibus uel angelis
assimilari uel aliquatenus adlaterare sola faciat sine precio preciosa
25 res racionalitas.
    [2.] Atqui, frater, quo tuis satisfacere pergam pro posse dictis et
voluntati, placite tamen et abhorribilis omne citra scrupulum cor-
rixacionis, humane raciones inmortalitatis anime uel aliquas suppo-
nere nitar quas[3] predidici. Triuialiter igitur, ni displiceat, in primis
30 tritum diouolaliterque diwlgatum ponere pergamus hominis anime
diuturnitatis exemplum uel verisimile pocius inmortalitatis argumentum. Reuera certissimam iam nunc est hominum pridemque
fuit diducta res ad noticiam frequens satis et consuetudinaliter
vsitatum per experimentum. Certe, quo vera wlgataque fans funde-

---

[1] circa S
[2] hominum S
[3] que S

BOOK TEN

Any man will rightly be valued but slightly
If he is feared on account of his irrational words;
A speaker utters his speech sensibly
If his speaking tongue desires to join with it
The power of reason, and his mind avoids lies;
If he refuses to live together in concord with his fellows,
One among many, and behaves himself senselessly,
His life in commons will become odious to his fellows.
Humble manners normally cement close ties;
Marginal behavior sunders social bonds.
But if you have proofs, you should adduce them
At your pleasure to serve as apt support
For the statements you made earlier with a serious face,
So you suitably support your assertions.

[1.] It seems to me, Brother, I replied, that your contradictory statements have made you far more brazenly superfluous than usual. Lacking the purity of logic or truth, you are no less tardily circumspect when you do not blush to deny the immortality of man's soul, unique among animals, even though you grant that the prerogative of rationality is granted to man alone among the animals. Nor can I imagine that you would dare to deny it, were it not that you absurdly affect delirious or insane notions; instead, reason alone, a precious thing without price, causes man to become like, or in some measure equal, the highest spirits or angels.

[2.] Brother, in order that I might, to the best of my ability, attend to your words and intent, graciously and without any fear of abhorrent squabbling, I will try to put forward at least some of the arguments which I have learned for the immortality of the human soul. If you are willing, we will begin by adducing a trivial and meretriciously commonplace example of the durability of man's soul, even an apparent proof of its immortality. In fact, the matter has long been known to men through a frequent and familiar experience. To speak of a true commonplace, when anyone who has

35 re vadam, siquis ut inferatur[1] recenter occisus, uel eciam post
aliquatenus protensum tempus iaceat uel in solo, si perempti forte
casualiter uel ex proposito[2] cadaueri peremptor apropinquauerit ab
aliquatenus remotis eciam, sonitu statim cum tumultuoso saguinem
rutilabit cadauer, eciam si iam fuerit (ut fit) infrigidatum, quod
40 tamen, ut et commentantur et sompniare parant fabulatores vitrei
philosophique phisicales, quadam racione quam fingunt contingere
profitentur et asserunt. Aiunt enim, sed tamen ut michi frequenter
videre[3] videor non ineleganter, quod homine perempto zinzugia
quedam (spiritus, scilicet, qui contraria duo uel pocius opposita sine
45 medio male coniungibilia coniungit[4]) positum quid contrahens ex
utroque sit medium sine medio—quidem stabile raro reperitur inter
opposita sodalicium—quod ex affectu perempto remanens adhuc
cum corpore saguinem, qui semper amicissimus ei fuit, velud
indignacione uel ire motu motum mouet, talique racione subsequen-
50 ter motus emanat.

[3.] Sic ergo sicut mediatorum (corruptibile videlicet corpus)
alterum remanet et corrumpitur ut temporarium, sic alterum (vege-
tans videlicet et viuens anima) necis est citra timorem uel iniuriam
duratura feliciterque victura si bene meruerit in perpetuum. Quia
55 nichil proprie iuris habet in re mors |48ᵛ| incorporea sibi genialiter
a Genio genitore concessum, presertim cum mors ex sui natura
nullo peruenire modo possit ad incorporeum. Reuera quod anime
sit animal homo sub sole solum velud inter animalia specialiter
inmortalitate priuilegiatum, veritatis accedit ad soliditatem fere per
60 infinitates argumentorum, non nisi per improbitates inficiacionum
de facto dumtaxat irritabilium. Profecto fidei uel secte qualibet in
vniuersitate frequens est et quasi diouolaliter vsuale tritumque:
dubitacionibus omnino longius eliminatis, anime perpetuitatis et
inmortalitatis humane diutina sinceritate religionis approbata,
65 primis eciam veniunt in luminibus obuiam racionibus crebro comitata verisimillimis argumenta.

[4.] Sic igitur in primis, quia sic libet,[5] progredi pergamus ad
antiquiora que viris a venerabilibus et in vetustate fidelitatis et in
constancia reuerenciaque venustatis asserantur serio de prelibatis, ut
70 et ab eis actualiter expertis et in sinceritate veritatis firmitate funda-

---

[1] inferetur S
[2] ex proposito] exproposito S
[3] videre S, vider[i] Sᶜ
[4] coniungit ed.
[5] S ad. quo before progredi

recently died and been buried or been lying stretched out in the ground for some time is approached accidentally or on purpose by that person's slayer, even at a distance, blood will suddenly flow from the corpse with a loud noise, even if that corpse is already, as is often the case, cold. Transparent storytellers and natural philosophers claim that this occurs because of a certain reason they feign according to their lies and dreams. They say (not inelegantly, as it seems to me) that when a man is slain, a certain syzygy (which is to say a spirit that conjoins two contraries, or rather opposites, difficult to conjoin without a mean), drawing a disposition from either, becomes a mean without a middle (indeed, a stable partnership between opposites is rare) which, remaining with the murdered corpse out of affection, is roused by indignation or an access of wrath to stir the blood which was always friendly to it, and for this reason the blood pours forth.

[3.] Thus one of the mediated parties (namely the corruptible body) stays behind and decomposes because it is transitory, while the other (the animating and vital soul) will, if it so deserved, live in perpetual bliss without fearing any injury from death. For father Genius has not granted death any proper jurisdiction over incorporeal things, especially since death cannot, of its own nature, reach as far as the incorporeal. In fact, we can establish the fact that man is the only animal under the sun privileged with an immortal soul as a certain truth by an infinite number of proofs, even by the unscrupulous denials of irritable critics. Indeed, it is almost meretriciously usual and trite that in any sect or community of faith, once all doubts are set aside, proofs of the permanence and immortality of the human soul appear at first glance, confirmed by the well-tried integrity of religion and frequently accompanied by plausible explanations.

[4.] To begin then at our pleasure, we will proceed to ancient opinions which were seriously asserted about the topics we have sampled by venerable men adorned by ancient faith and constant reverence. This will enable us to publicize certain events according to the accounts of those who actually experienced them, men whose

mentali bellissime solidatis in medium proponere procuremus,
patribus videlicet Israeliticis. Atqui, me quali iudice, quibuslibet ad
inmortalitatis[1] anime probamentum debet esse satis humane quod
post hominis interitum uiuentis eciam per hominem, corpus anima
75   redit ad preinanimatum violenciaque reuegetat[2] fatalitatis exinani-
tum.

[5.] Quo quidem nota loquar populariterque publicata, vir Helias
viuus compassibilisque viuentibus, hospes ab hospite tenui tenuis
et vidua tandem satis humaniter est exceptus in Sarepta dum fame
80   fatigatus et siti, dumque paululum sibi supplicaret aque dari panisque uel paucula refocillari buccella, sua nec exaudiretur in primis in
peticione tam paruula. Verumptamen cum lignula legentis in olei
lechitus indefectu spem solidauit et ydrie cum farinula, libens est in
utroque tandem tam nobili famelico sicientique tam beniuolo vidua
85   fidens et ad exaudiendum facilis gratificata, nec se suspicari femina
falli curauit adeo famelica, |49r| licet in eo quod sibi prius subcine-
ricium fieri supplicauerit de tam paucula panem farina, verisimillime presumi posset quod circumuencio subesset uel fallacia, sed
commendabilis et honesta fidei tante facilitati subfuit causa, quia
90   fidus et innocens omni verbo de facili fidem facit et habet, sua
facillime securificatus in innocentia. Nec sua fuit in securitate
circumuenta, quia nec olei lechitus nec farinula defecit in ydria
donec salubris et habundancie prenuncia pluuie veniret habundancia.

95   [6.] Non autem solis Helias hiis beneficiorum vidue substitit in
collacionibus, ymmo longe laudabilius est ei suis subsequenter in
beneficiis gratificatus. Nempe dum sic tantus in inquilinatu cum
vidua nausitaret inquilinus, fatalitate functus est vidue filius, quo
progredi paremus ad quod intencionem premencionauimus. Ast
100 mater, ut moris est incontinenti, velut furiis ex inprouiso foret
exagitata, limphatice discurrendo clamorem quod potest extollit ad
superiora, tandemque suum satis inmeritum doloris eam mouet in
contubernalem vehemencia. Quid tibi michique vir Dei, velud
insaniens exclamat et ut efferata. Numquid ut ad indignam vir ad
105 me sanctus sic es ingressus ut tecum cohabitando peccatrix pecca-
rem sic ut meus extigueretur filius?

[7.] Verum vir Dei vidue[3] mulieris subtilius nimis, ut fit, in
perturbacione molestatus, Tuum da michi filium, suppliciter ait.

---

[1] inmortalitates S
[2] reuegetati S
[3] videns S

true integrity was based on a firm foundation: to wit, the patriarchs of Israel. According to my judgment, anyone should find it sufficient proof of the immortality of the human soul that when a living man has been killed by another man, the soul returns to revivify the body which it previously animated, even after it has been despoiled by the violence of death.

[5.] To speak of things that are public knowledge, Elijah, a man who was alive with compassion for the living, was received quite humanely as a humble guest by the lowly widow of Sarepta when he was wearied by hunger and thirst. He begged her to give him a pittance of water and bread or revive him with a tiny morsel, but she did not at first heed his slight request. However, after the cruse, with its unfailing supply of oil, and the meal in the jar strengthened the faith of the woman as she gathered wood, this faithful and complaisant widow was at length glad to oblige this noble and benevolent man's hunger and thirst. Nor did this woman, who was herself suffering from hunger, care to suspect fraud, albeit that since he first asked her to make him a hearth cake from so little meal, it would have been quite reasonable to assume some underlying trickery or deceit. Instead, there was a praiseworthy and honorable cause underlying such ready faith, since the innocently faithful man or woman easily gives and keeps faith in every word, utterly secure in his or her innocence. Nor was she deceived in her assurance, since neither the cruse of oil nor the pot of meal failed until an abundance of rain came as harbinger of abundant food.

[6.] Nor did Elijah limit his assistance to the widow to these gifts; instead, he laudably showed her far greater favor with his kindnesses. For when this great tenant had drawn out his sojourn with the widow, the widow's son died. (In this manner we may proceed to our stated purpose.) But his intemperate mother ran about with her thoughts in a frenzy, as if she were driven by furies, and raised a clamor to the heavens. At length, the vehemence of her grief caused her to turn upon her undeserving house guest: "What have I to do with thee, thou man of God," she exclaimed as if driven insane, "Are you not come to me, holy man, as to one who is unworthy, so that by living with you as a sinner I should so sin that my son should perish?"

[7.] But the man of God, subtly worried (as often happens) by the widowed woman's distress, said in humble entreaty: "Give me thy

Suamque suum sic ad Deum oracionem subsequenter fudit: Reuer-
110 tatur huius anima pueri sua, domine precor, in viscera.

[8.] Quod factum protinus est ita, qui sicut a peritis puer perhibetur postea Ionas fuit propheta, quo dignis dignior factus digne
dicatur a dignissimo suscitatus. Atqui suis sic supplicantis sermoni-
bus ex predictis efficax inmortalitatis anime sumi |49^v| posse
115 videtur argumentum, dum pueri precatur animam reuerti corpus in
exanimatum sueque supplicacionis adeo laudabilem venit ad effectum: Dei tunc in tali casu vir tantus exauditu[1] dignissimus, cuius et
adhuc a veridicis perhibetur viuere virtutibus.

[9.] Sed iam nunc adeo dignum, si libet, Helie discipulum venia-
120 mus ad Helyseum velut a tanto tantum dignissime denominatum.
Postquam uero subleuatus ab eo suum suo duplicauerat Helyas in
Heliseo spiritum, suum quod habuit in Samaria reuersus est Heliseus in domicilium, qui, postquam plurima fecisset in nomine Dei sui
magnaque mirabilia suamque venisset in ciuitatem, mulieris cuius-
125 dam sicut hospes oblatus domicilium quo cibum sumeret est ingressus, humiliter et ab ea mores ut habent commendabiles est exceptus.
Idque cum[2] sepius tum propter cultus edicularum[3] tum propter
honestarum domesticas domus honestates consuetudinum facere
consueuisset, sui mulier contemplans hospitis sibi sepius sic oblati
130 mores, morumque modos secum quam maxime commendans
consuetudinarios, tanti non tantum probauit viri tantam conuersa-
cionem, sed et suo cum sibi liberet in domicilio licenter et pro libito
concessit habere cohabitacionem. Nec hiis femina tam fortis sue
finem gratificacionis posuit in finibus, verum viro commendabili
135 motu suo suasit tandemque feminea pertinacitate continuata persua-
sit, ut in partem suus sibi seorsum vir ediculam faceret, stratumque
sibi sterneret, mensulamque simul et sellam, candelabrumque
poneret, quia summe virum virtutis eum caritatis sinceritate comitatum coniectabat, sed et in veritate credebat esse mancipium, sibique
140 subsequenter subministrarent que cotidianum forent ad vsum
frugalitate parcimoniaque comitatum (videlicet ad esculentum
poculentumque), talibusque taliter ordinatis, suum cum veniret solo
cum seruiente Giezi secure diuerteret Heliseus in cenaculum. |50^r|

[10.] Verum quia quiuis vir sane sensatus se uel naturaliter teneri
145 continue memor est ad antidota, suam uel in aliquo cupiens Heliseus antidotizare tam sane familiarem, siquid a se sibi femina tam

---

[1] ex auditu *S*
[2] cum *ed.*
[3] ediculorum *S*

son." And he uttered this prayer to his God: "Let the soul of this child, I beseech thee Lord, return into his body."

[8.] The boy revived immediately, as he had asked, and according to the learned became the prophet Jonah, so that having been made more worthy than the worthy, he might worthily be revived later by the most Worthy. Thus it seems possible to draw an effective proof of the soul's immortality from the suppliant's own words, since he achieved the laudable aim of his prayer that the soul return to the boy's dead body. He was a great man, worthy in such a case of a favorable hearing from God, in Whose virtues he is said by the prophets to live still.

[9.] Now, if we may, let us turn to Elijah's worthy pupil Elisha, who was it seems worthy to be named after his great teacher. After Elijah had duplicated his spirit in Elisha and was lifted up from him, Elisha returned to his dwelling in Samaria and performed many great wonders in the name of his God. Coming into his city, he was (according to good manners) humbly received by a certain woman as a chance guest and entered her dwelling to receive food. Once he was in the habit of doing this often, because the house was well cared for and the behavior of its inhabitants was honorable, the woman, pondering the manners of this guest who often visited her, and commending the habitual moderation of his behavior towards her, not only approved of the great man's frequent sojourns but allowed him to reside freely in her dwelling according to his pleasure. Nor did this forceful woman limit herself to this kindness. Urging a praiseworthy thought home with unrelenting female obstinacy, she persuaded her husband to make a little room apart for Elisha, spread a bed for him, and place there a table, stool, and candlestick, because she conjectured that this man of great virtue was accompanied by pure charity, but she believed he was in fact a servant. At her suggestion, they supplied him with the food and drink necessary for the daily sustenance of one accompanied by frugality and restraint. Once things were established on this basis, Elisha dwelt apart in his garret without misgivings when he came with his servant Giezi.

[10.] Either because any sensible man is always mindful of the favors he has received, or because Elisha was eager to recompense his sensible hostess in some measure, he saw to it that Giezi asked

frugi quasi nomine remuneracionis desierauerit meritissime fieri procurauit a Giezi reuerenter inquiri. Tandemque transmissi mota mulier tam belle munifica persuasionibus internuncii, quia sua fuit,

150 ut fit, in sterilitate confusa sicut estimabat in futurum prole caritura, presertim cum suus iam vir ageret in senectute matura, sibi non dubitauit ab eo petere prolem. Cui sic subsequenter ait Heliseus: Hoc in eodem spacio anni[1] reuoluto filium fueris tuo partura viro. Nec suo vir feminam sic fando subsequenti sic fefellit in promisso,

155 sed eodem tempore, momentoue, uel hora prole nata letabatur et filio; deindeque magis in eunte delectabatur, et in ablactato, et in discussore pater, et in coambulo.

[11.] Uerum pro prole noua nouiter conceptam fatalitas in breui discussit hylaritatem; febri namque tenellus facillime puer defatiga-

160 tus, subsolari[2] cessit vniuerso fatali vita facilitate functus. Sed tunc maxime mater, more femineo quasi furialiter efferata, tanti doloris inuenire solacium studet insolabiliter pene confusa. Sed et ad vltimum sagaciter eum parat habere prolis in amissione suffraga-torem quem gratum sobolis habuit in carencia subsidiatorem. Parat

165 et eum mesta mater adire familias in Monte Carmeli residentem; reclusoque prius elati cadauere pueri latenter in Helisei cenaculo, suum quem sperauit habere propicium properauit ad solaciatorem. Nec sua spes eam fefellit sensatissime sperantem: libens enim cum sua supplicatrice simpliciter descendit, suumque sibi rediuiuum

170 reddit filium post fatalitatem.

[12.] Sed quod longe mirabilius, ut auguror, |50ᵛ| quilibet sane censeret esse sensatus, recenter elatum tempore prius aliquantulo miraculosissime resuscitauit elatus, eodem videlicet quo mortuus est anno. Nempe cum quidam de filiis Israel Samaritani mortuum

175 deferrent ut eum supremo sicut sit officio mandarent, cum latruncu-los ob iter cernerent in Israel irruentes Israelitarum predam sagui-nemque predonum pro rapacitate sicientes, insolencia rei timorisque turbulencia perculsi, verentes ulterius progredi cadauer elati, quo celerius fugerent et expedicius, in sepulchro posuerunt Helisei. Sed

180 ubi sacra tetigit ossa corpus exanimatum vnius uirtute uel viribus reuixit recessitque prius intumulati. Sic mortui virtute diuina reui-goratus animaque quam preeffuderat reuegetatus, tumuli claustrum vegeto discessu passibusque citatis hilariter incedens est aspernatus dum se reuiuus reconuiuis reconuiuere est recongratulatus.

185 [13.] Hec itaque sincere uetustatis veneranda vetustas inmortalita-

---

[1] annui S
[2] sub solari S

whether this worthy woman desired for herself anything that he could worthily accomplish in the name of repayment. Moved at length by the persuasion of the messenger sent to her, the generous woman did not hesitate to ask him for offspring of her own, because (as often happens) she was afflicted by sterility and reckoned that she would always lack offspring, especially since her husband had already reached a ripe old age. Elisha said to her: "At this time next year you will have born a son to your husband." Nor, as it turned out, did he deceive her by making such a promise, but at that exact time and day she was delighted by the birth of a son; from then on her husband was greatly delighted by their son as he started to crawl, was weaned, began to ask questions, and walk.

[11.] But death soon dispelled her newly conceived joy in her recent offspring, for the delicate boy was easily exhausted by a fever and departed from this sublunar world, relinquishing life with fatal ease. Then this mother, inconsolably dismayed and raving wildly as women will, sought to find solace for her sorrow. She finally sought as intercessor for her lost offspring the man whose aid she had welcomed in the absence of progeny. The mournful matron prepared to visit him as he resided on Mount Carmel; privately shutting the body of the departed boy in Elisha's garret, she hastened towards the man who she hoped would console her. Nor did her sensible hope deceive her: he willingly and without reserve came down with his supplicant and restored her son to her from death.

[12.] But I imagine any sensible person would consider it far more miraculous that, having himself been buried a short time before, Elisha miraculously revived a man who died in the year of Elisha's own death. For some Samaritans were carrying a dead man from among the sons of Israel in order to consign him to his last rites, when they saw in their path roving brigands attacking Israel, thirsting rapaciously for spoils and the blood of the Israelites. Stricken with unsettling fear by this unusual event and reluctant to go any further, they put the body of the dead man in Elisha's sepulchre, so as to flee swiftly and without encumbrance. But when the dead body touched those holy bones, it came to life and walked away by the powerful virtue of one already buried. Reinvigorated by the divine power of the dead man and revivified by the soul which he had previously discharged, he spurned the prison of the grave and walked away in delight with a lively gait, congratulating himself on being alive again to carouse with his companions.

[13.] That Antiquity which is truly venerable advanced and

tis anime memorat reuerenter et autenticat argumenta, quo firma
semper et indubitata sit[1] inter[2] inmortales hominum brutorumque
cum corpore morituras animas differencia. Nec minus quo quos
eciam brutis viuos secreuit[3] ab animalibus racionalitas anime secer-
190   nat racionalis et elatos inmortalitas.

[14.] Sed iam nunc serias animarum citra vitalitates humanarum
uel inmortalitates, veniamus ad asserciones ethnicorum si libet et ad
argumenta[4] vetustissimorum. Non quo uerbis eorum seriis eciam
uel assercionalibus habendam fidem funditus indubiam uel indubi-
195   tanter credam, uel per omnia simpliciter existimem sicut predictorum, sed quasi pro veritate si cui libuerit verisimiliterue receptibili-
um contemplacione, presertim venerande vetustatis virorum tot
retrotemporum transcursionibus autenticatorum.

[15.] Quo Platonis igitur in primis viri virtutibus et sciencia
200   precipue placentis serias citra predicta ponere |51ʳ| pergamus
asserciones et verba, Plato sic scribit, vir inter primos precipuus in
philosophia, viros inter quamplures sicut fit in prelio peremptos,
quidam nomine Pamphilus x diebus verissime dicitur iacuisse
peremptus, biduoque postquam sublatus inde fuisset impositus[5]
205   rogo, reuixisse miraque quedam mortis tempore visa retulisse. Sed
et non minus indubitate reuerenda refert antiquitas Her militem,[6]
suis cum commilitonibus in prelio commilitantem, suis ab impetito-
ribus in bellico conflictu peremptum, dies post quamplures rediuiuum milites inter cooccisos inuentum.

210   [16.] Sunt eciam quamplura uel aliquatenus verisimilia poetarum
commenta vetustatisue semper admodumque reuerende serie satis
asserciones et figmenta vitalitatis anime uel inmortalitatis humane
de perseuerancia uel superficialiter argumentatiua. Notum satis est
eciam subsannabiliter ydiotis vetus illud et poeticum tam graui de
215   gigante machia figmentum, qua Bachus proletaria[7] Iouis magni
proles et filius est—Ioue paternaliter Euchi proclamante—membratim discerptus, giganteis et viribus omnino letaliterque dilaceratus,
et in vanno fatali frustratim collocatus, et in crastino viuus et inte-
ger inuentus. Verumptamen si cui forte veritatem libuisset interitus
220   inspicere latitantem, libens omnem longius amandare pergeret

---

[1] sic S
[2] inter ed.
[3] secreuit] fecerint S
[4] argumento S
[5] impositum S
[6] Her militem] Hermilitem S
[7] proletarii S

reverently confirmed these arguments for the immortality of the soul, so that the difference between the immortal souls of men and those of beasts, which will die with the body, might remain firm and undoubted, and likewise, so that those who are distinguished from brute animals in life by a rational soul might be distinguished in death by reason's immortality.

[14.] Now, setting aside the important life essence of souls or man's immortality, let us approach the assertions of the pagans, if you please, and the proofs of the ancients, not because I believe that we should uncritically put our faith in their serious or tendentious statements, or because I always value those statements without question like the stories I have just told, but (so to speak) as truths subject to approval in light of their seeming acceptability, especially those confirmed by the perusal of so many men of times past in venerable Antiquity.

[15.] We will begin by exempting from our strictures the important assertions of Plato, a preeminent philosopher pleasing for his virtue and knowledge, who writes that among the many men slain (as always) in battle, one by the name of Pamphilius was said to have lain slain for ten days. After two more days he was carried away and placed on a pyre but revived to relate various marvelous visions from the time of his death. Revered Antiquity reports with equal certainty that the soldier Er was slain by opponents while fighting alongside his fellow soldiers but was found revivified some days later among the soldiers killed with him.

[16.] There are many other plausible fictions of the poets, or important assertions or inventions of Antiquity (which is always to be revered greatly), which at least superficially prove the continued vitality or immortality of the human soul. Even those who are ridiculously unlearned are familiar with that old poetic figment about the fierce *gigantomachia*, in which Bacchus, the lowly son of mighty Jove, was torn limb from limb while his father Jove cried out "Euhe." Having been utterly ripped to pieces by the powerful giants, Bacchus was assembled piecemeal in a fatal winnowing-basket and discovered alive and whole the next day. Anyone who cares to examine the hidden truth of Bacchus's death should will-

admiracionem. Nichilominus ex talibus inmortalitatis anime qualem
sumere fas[1] fuit, et adhuc fortassis est[2] presumpcionem verisimi-
litudinisue superficiem, presertim cum satis admissibile sit uel esse
videatur meram per minus eciam verisimilia conari commendabili-
225 ter astruere veritatem.

[17.] Preter hec quo per antiquissimorum verba, sentenciasve, uel
asserciones expressas adhuc uel aliquatenus alludere pergamus ad
predicta, Trimegistus quidem |51ᵛ| qui uel Hermes eciam dicitur
uel Mercurius, cum suo sermonem faciens satisue socialiter habens
230 Esculapio, sic ait: Auus o mi care consors tuus Esculapi, qui pro
sole deus est inuentor medicine primus, cui templum circa litus
cocodrillorum Libies et in monte consecratum quo[3] mundanus
homo iacet, eius videlicet corpus (reliquus uero uel pocius totus,
cum sit homo totus in sensu vite, melior in celum remeauit), omnia
235 viuis eciam nunc hominibus numine prestans infirmis que sua
solebat arte patrare viuus.[4] Apertissime quidem talia se sua sic
loquens intellexisse reliquit intelligendum per verba quod anima
specialiter humana sit inmortalitate priuilegiata.

[18.] Satis ad idem Senece, viri summe subtilitatis et sciencie,
240 prioris Affricani de bonitate Scipionis diligencius habita faciunt
asserta. Scribit enim vir viro tam commendabilis de tam commen-
dando; suo sic scribit sua pro consuetudine Lucillo: Iacens in ipsa
Cipionis Affricani villa tibi talia scribo, manibus adoratis et ara,
quam tanti fore viri sepulchrum suspicor. Animum[5] quidem tan-
245 tum viri viuentis ex quo venerat[6] in celum redisse persuadeo michi,
non quia magnos exercitus duxit (hos enim Cambises furiosus
suoque furore feliciter usus habuit), sed ob egregiam moderacionem
pietatemque, quam magis admiror in illo cum suam reliquit patriam
quam cum defendit. Aut enim deesse Scipio Rome debebat, aut
250 Roma libertati. Sed et hic vir tantus viro de tanto tam confidenter
loquens manifeste dedit intelligi se corporibus infusas humanis
animas fore non dubitasse solas specialiter inmortalitate priuilegia-
tas.

[19.] Ad ultimum uero quia iam nunc sic sedet in instanti propo-
255 sito, quas ad anime fidei Catholice fideles in-|52ʳ| mortalitates
humane professores indubie iam veritatis in sinceritate solidatas

---

[1] S ad. est before fuit
[2] S ad. sumere before presumpcionem
[3] consecratum quo S, consecratum est, in quo Asclepius
[4] viuis S
[5] Animum Seneca, An vnum S
[6] venerat S, erat Seneca

ingly set aside his astonishment. Nevertheless, it was and perhaps still is permissible to derive from such stories some hint or appearance of truth for the immortality of the soul, especially since we may be permitted to construe the unalloyed truth by means of less certain truths.

[17.] Furthermore, to discover further allusions to this matter in the opinions or explicit assertions of the most ancient writers, Trismegistus, who is also called Hermes or Mercury, says while talking familiarly with his Aesculapius: "My dear companion Aesculapius, your ancestor, who in the guise of the sun is the first inventor of medicine, to whom a temple is consecrated on the shore of crocodiles and on the mountain of Libya where the earthly man lies, that is, his body (the rest, or rather all, since the whole man consists in the sense of life, returned more fortunate to the sky), even now by his godhead furnishes everything to sick humans which he was accustomed to accomplish with his art when alive." He openly leaves us to understand from his words that the human soul is especially privileged with immortality.

[18.] The strongly espoused assertions of Seneca, a man of supreme subtlety and knowledge, concerning the excellence of the first Scipio Africanus tend toward the same end. As was his custom, this praiseworthy author writes about a man so worthy of commendation in a letter to his friend Lucilius: "I write these things to you resting in the very villa of Scipio Africanus, having worshipped the ashes and altar which I suspect to be the sepulchre of so great a man. I am convinced that the great soul of the living man returned to the sky whence it came, not because he led great armies, for the madman Cambyses commanded them successfully in his madness, but because of his exceptional moderation and sense of duty, which I admire in him more when he left his country than when he defended it. Either Scipio had to forgo Rome or Rome liberty." Here a great man speaking confidently of another great man clearly leaves us to understand that he had no doubt that only those souls infused in human bodies are privileged with immortality.

[19.] Since it concerns the present topic, let us from among innumerable arguments repeat in some measure the arguments and proofs already adduced in public and confirmed in the undoubted

raciones inducant et argumenta, de tot et tantis ymmo fere funditus innumerabilibus in publicum pridem producta reproducere procuremus uel aliqua, que quidem (quia placita sui sunt in natura) plus
260   placebunt eciam sepissime repetita. Sic itaque summi summo mediatoris ab opere subsolariter in medio spirantis nostre nostrum presencialiter instantis inicium sumere pergamus intencionis. Nec me quis precor causari velit ut presumptuosum, uel velut os suum ponere presumentem contumaciter in celum, dum sumere presumo
265   meum factis a tam sublimibus hoc in instanti verbale principium.

[20.] Deus et Dei filius homo Iesus iudex arbitrarius et potencialiter infinitus Marie Lazarum Martheque germanum, partibus in sub sole meridionali fataliter frequentissime feruentibus fetidum, quatuor et ut in sepulchro post inhumationem dies habentem, viuum
270   vocauit de sepulchro vitalitatique restituit, quo sanum sanissime sumatur in argumentum vices humana non habere uel vires in anima modos condicionesue mortalitatum, quo tam specialem spiritus animalis per restitucionem fuisse subintelligas corpus exanimatum virtuosam Dei vere viuentis anime per reuocacionem[1]
275   resuscitatum. Non quod nouam si sibi libuisset animam creare deitatis absolute potestati non licuisset, sed quo quali sumpto supplicis ex Helisei verbis in casu consimili vel superficialiter argumento satis probabili, quod anima suum vidue (filii videlicet elati) reuerteretur in corpus supplicantis violente satis sumere liceat
280   in presidium presumpcionis.

[21.] Sed et elata principis filia potenciaque subsequenter diuine virtutis vite restituta verisimilia venit vitalitatis anime |52ᵛ| non deficientis ad argumenta. Nempe cum principaliter potens incircumscribilisque phisicus exorantis fidei[2] firmitate motus resuscitandam
285   voluntarie veniret ad filiam, libens et facile mobilis ad exauditum,[3] sane supplicantis non defuit effectui peticionis, licet[4] fatua fuisset a turba ciuium derisus fatuissime dum non mortuam sed dormientem fore veraciter asserendo ridiculosos[5] coegit ad recessus. Manu manum mortue tenens suis viuam viuis restituit sibi conviuentibus,
290   anima fatalitate funditus insuperabili consuetos habitaculi reuocata potencialiter ad vsus, quo si libeat ad animum reuocare non supersedeas quoniam supplex casu consimili summo (de quo fari presu-

---

[1] S ad. fuisse subintelligas *before* resuscitatum
[2] fide S
[3] exauditus S
[4] S ad. a *before* fatua
[5] ridiculosus S

integrity of truth which faithful believers of the Catholic faith might use to argue the immortality of the human soul. Since they are pleasing by nature, they please even more when often repeated. We will begin with the supreme work of the supreme Mediator during His public ministry on earth. I ask that no one confront me with the rebuke that I have contumaciously presumed to set my face against heaven by beginning my argument here from such sublime actions.

[20.] The man Jesus, God and son of God, an unconstrained judge of infinite power, called Lazarus, the brother of Mary and Martha, back to life from the grave and restored him to vitality after he had been buried in his sepulchre for four days and stank under the lethally hot southern sun. This can be taken as clear proof that the condition of mortality has no power over the human soul. You may implicitly understand from this special restitution of his animal spirit that Lazarus's dead body was revivified by the living God's powerful recall of his soul. Not because the absolute power of the Deity would not have been permitted to create a new soul if it pleased Him, but so we might draw from the suppliant words of Elisha in a similar case the defense of the extreme presumption of the suppliant widow that the soul of her dead son returned to its body.

[21.] The prince's daughter, who died and was restored to life by the power of divine virtue, serves as plausible proof of the unfailing vitality of the soul. For when the preeminently powerful and unlimited physician, who was easily swayed to lend an ear, was moved by the firm faith of the suppliant prince to approach his daughter for the purpose of reviving her, clearly he did not fail to achieve the outcome sought by the prince, although he was derided by a foolish mob of citizens whom he forced to move back by asserting the truth that she was not dead. Holding the dead girl's hand in His, He recalled her soul from unconquerable mortality to the accustomed possession of its dwelling and restored her to her living companions. So if you please, you should keep in mind that in a similar

mimus in presenti) suscitatori supplicauerit omnino medianus
suscitator Heliseus.

295   [22.] Non autem crederem veri suscitatoris terciam vita functi
resuscitacionem, crebra repeticione retractacionis adeo dignam,
nostro quod instat proposito[1] nostre nunc elocucionis in profluuio
rudi sub silencio transeundam. Cum vero Iesus, sub sole spirancium saluator specialis et summus, iudexque licens, arbiterque
300   licenter arbitrarius, suis ciuitatem Naym cum discipulis turbisque
populorum copiosis ingrederetur, salutaris tunc itinerarius, vnicus
vidue cuiusdam filius efferebatur elatus turba populari plurima
comitatus. Sed cum viduam vidisset pius potensque prelatus fleti-
bus, ut fit, lamentacionibusque maternaliter madidatam, misericor-
305   dia motus ait eiulanti: Femina, flere noli. Subsequenter et ad elatum
venit loculumque tetigit, subsistentibusque latoribus, elato sic
subsequenter subintulit: Adolescens, tibi dico, surge. Statimque se
qui mortuus fuerat erexit farique cepit, sueque viuum matri iam
non merenti reddit. Indifferenter et vniuersos tam speciale factum
310   tamque mirandum summi summum timoris et admiracionis impulit
in incentiuum. Tantis et in tantorum factis mirabiliumque |53ʳ|
nouitatibus semper admirabilem glorificabant deuotissime Deum.

[23.] Reuera tam specialis et hec anime corpus in exanimatum
reuocacio satis effectiuum sumi potest inmortalitatis anime subtiliter
315   ab inspicientibus in argumentum, que reuocabilis ita remansit post
corpus omni vitalitatis omnino vegetacione destitutum. Non autem
sibi tantam soli tamque specialem Deus et homo Christus[2] anime
corpus in exanimatum retinuit in reuocacione potestatem, sed et
aliis in eius nomine quampluribus eundem consimilemve consimilia
320   faciendi concessit habere facultatem, quo semper sed in secunda
precipue satis sufficienter anime tam commendabili reuocacione
Deo supplicantis confidenter hominis notes inmortalitatem.

Liber Vndecimus[3]

Est Deus et dominus super omnia iure colendus,
Cui mors seua simul crebro fallatur et ultro
Vita suum venit ad libitum, dum viuere viuum
Vis sua summa facit finali funere functum.

---

[1] proposito *ed.*
[2] *S ad.* in *before* anime
[3] Sequitur *S,* liber vndecimus *R*

situation the altogether human healer Elisha supplicated the supreme Healer about whom we presume to speak at present.

[22.] I do not believe that the true Healer's third revivification of one who had relinquished life, worthy as it is of frequent repetition, should be passed over in ignorant silence by the current of our discourse, since it pertains to our present topic. When in the course of His travels, Jesus, the supreme savior, judge and arbiter of those who breathe under the sun, entered the city of Naim with his disciples and a multitude of followers, the only son of a certain widow was being carried away dead, attended by a great number of people. But when this merciful and powerful prelate saw the widowed mother bedewed (as often happens) by weeping and lamentation, He was moved to mercy and said to the wailing woman: "Woman, do not weep." Then He approached the dead boy and touched the bier, and as the bearers halted, He said: "Young man, I say to thee arise." And immediately he that was dead sat up and began to speak, and Jesus returned him alive to his mother, who no longer mourned. This remarkable deed compelled all those who were present to feel extreme fear and amazement. And they always devoutly glorified this admirable God for so many great deeds and marvels.

[23.] In fact, subtle investigators may take this extraordinary act of recalling the soul to a dead body as an effective proof of the immortality of the soul, which remains capable of being recalled even after the body has been deprived of all vital vigor. However, Christ, man and God, did not keep this great power to recall the soul to a dead body for himself alone; instead, He allowed many others to possess the ability to do such things in His name. So you may always note with confidence the immortality of the man who sufficiently supplicates God, but especially in the case of His second restoration of a soul.

BOOK ELEVEN

The lord God is by right to be worshipped above all things,
By whom savage death is often deceived, while further
Life comes at His pleasure, since His supreme power
Causes those who have endured their obsequies to live again;

5   Si summa virtute valens, mirabile non est
    Magna facit, quia sola decent magnalia magnos;
    In magno tamen est mirum si seria soluat
    Nature consueta, scienter et ad noua vadat:
    Hoc satis esse nouum satis et michi censeo mirum
10 Quod sua nature variare potens homo iura
    Infirmus tam firma fuit, quod et ad sua natos
    ffatali sibi consimiles a fine vocaret.
    Non equidem virtute sua vel viribus ulli
    Tale licet licuitve suis subsidere viuo
15 Solari, nisi sancta Dei paciencia finem
    Prosperet effectu, fini faciendo iuuamen;
    Viribus ergo Dei solis homo talia tantum |53ᵛ|
    Sanctus agit, summo sub plasmatore minister.
    Est igitur virtute valens Deus usque colendus—
20 Ille bonus qui tanta suis sic munera seruis
    Prestat, ut elatos ad conuitale reducant,
    Et pius in partem non dedignatur honoris
    Sponte suum summe dominans admittere seruum,
    Quo domini suus intret ouans in gaudia seruus.

25   [1.] Quod autem Deus solummodo sit vnus, suoque sic¹ solus sit
    in arbitrio licens et absolute licenterque voluntarius, non minus
    variis quam patentissime probabilibus facile satis est et promptum
    declarari sermocinacionibus argumentaliterque cogentibus astruere
    raciocinacionibus. In primis itaque probabile satis Dei dumtaxat
30 vnius est ad argumentum quod hominum sub sole spirancium fere
    iam nunc vniuersitas indifferenter vniuersorum quasi confederaliter
    asserat vnum dumtaxat esse Deum. Fere dixi non citra racionis uel
    alicuius inspeccionem, quo scilicet paucos exciperem borealis ab
    intemperancia glacialis et ob inmensitatem diuturnitatemque frigidi-
35 tatis vix viuentes. Atqui Iudeus omnis, gentilis et quiuis, quilibetque
    Christianus pro sue fidei uel professionis exigencia solum confiden-
    ter vnum suo cuncta pro libito disponentem fatetur constanter et
    asserit Deum, communiter ab omnibus nefariis adnumerandus si
    pluralitates fore serio profiteretur asseueraretue deorum.
40   [2.] Sed et asserciones eciam tales vniuersis indifferenter adeo
    censentur esse detestabiles, quod promptas deorum pluralitates
    simpliciter eciam, serio tamen, scienterque profitentibus, indubias-
    que prestent occasiones fatalitatum, perpetuitates eciam pariant post

    ---

    ¹ sit S

Since He possesses supreme power, it is no marvel that He
Should do great things, for only miracles befit the great;
It is a marvel when a great man overrules Nature's
Customary concerns and knowingly proceeds to the new:
I find it quite novel and marvelous
That infirm man should be able to change the firm laws
Of nature, and call sons similar to himself
Away from a fatal end to his own laws.
Certainly it neither is nor was permitted man
To assuage such a fall by his own virtue or strength,
Unless the holy patience of God furthers
The outcome of his action by helping him;
Thus, only by the strength of God does a holy man
Perform such miracles as a minister to the supreme Creator.
So God, flourishing in strength, is always to be worshipped:
The good God who granted such great gifts to his servants,
That they might restore the dead to life;
The supreme Lord in his mercy did not disdain summoning
His servant to part of His honor, so that
His servant might enter exulting into his Lord's joy.

[1.] It is quite simple to articulate a varied and probable discourse, accompanied by cogent proofs, that shows there is only one
God, and that He alone is absolutely free and unconstrained in His
judgment. To begin with, it is a sufficiently probable proof of God's
oneness that almost without exception all men now assert that there
is only one God. I say "almost" not without some thought, so I
might except a few people who are barely alive due to the intemperance of the north and its long expanses of enduring glacial cold.
But every Jew, pagan, and Christian, because of the requirements of
his faith or creed, constantly professes only one God who orders all
things according to His will; all alike would reckon anyone who
seriously professed a plurality of gods among the wicked.
[2.] Everyone without exception considers such assertions utterly
detestable, because they present immediate and clear-cut occasion
for death and give birth to perpetual infamy after death, even for
those who in their simple wisdom seriously confess a plurality of

fatalitates infamiarum. Pari profecto seueritate criminis ad instar in
45   tali casu lese maiestatis expressa presertim voluntas debet puniri,[1]
qua voluntatis effectum firmissime premencionatorum |54ʳ| fuerat
ut est in institutis et indifferentibus solidatum. Debet itaque cuilibet
sane sensato verisimillimum fore videri quod a tam variis, aliis et in
articulis inter se tam dissidentibus, vnanimiter adeoque constanter
50   astruitur, indifferenterque coasseritur, tanteque tandem penalitatis
sub interminacione concustoditur, ut iam nunc eciam velut invaria-
bilem necessitatis in naturam transisse communiter ab vniuersis
examinetur.

[3.] In paucissimis igitur (et me sanumque sencienti quouis, ut
55   auguror, examinatore) differt ab omnino delirante, qui vano volun-
tatis sue solummodo motu sibi conuiuentibus sublunariter vniuersis
dissimiliter viuere contendit inutiliterque conatur; vnum profecto
Deum viuentibus expediens est esse solum, ne sub inconueniencia
pluralitatum vicia vilitatum subemergerent et dissidiorum: frequen-
60   cius enim firma stabilique descensus ab ciuitate confusionis inconti-
nenciam parit in pluralitate. Queuis enim potestas, sed precipue
summa mediocrisue uel minima, consorcii semper et parilitatis
eciam quodammodo genialiter est et inexorabiliter abhominatiua;
semper viuit sompniculosissime studiosa quo sola suo sit sine
65   comparticipante potestatiua. Consuetudinarium profecto pridem fuit
et adhuc eciam quodammodo naturale peribetur a peritissimis esse
communiter a compossidente compossessum negligi facillime,
suamque corrumpi compossessorem pati partem voluntarie dum
parti perniciter invidet aliene. Restat igitur quod si Deus est, ut
70   indubitanter est, summa solus deitatis in sublimitate sit vnus.

[4.] Quod autem Deus sit, quo tamen racionibus et verbis quasi
mutuo michi (quod fas admittit) uel superficialiter appropriatis uti
libere liceat alienis, sane sencientibus approbatissime constabit
commendabiliterque sensatis. Est enim frequens vniuersaliterque
75   consuetudinatum quod alienis mutuo sepissime quid ad expediens
utatur acceptis, rebusque |54ᵛ| vel ad tempus gaudeat sibique
proficiat in accomodatis, sed et alienis frequentissime contingit ut
licite quis spaciatum pergat in latifundiis.[2] Non minus eciam saga-
cis imitatio frequens et spontanea primi nouitatis in opere nouo
80   commentatoris accedere primo consueuit commentatori probabilis
ad augmentum fame uel commendacionis, si tamen circumspectus

---

[1] expressa ... voluntas debet puniri] expressam ... voluntatem puniri debere S
[2] latifundus S

gods. In such a case, even the express will should be punished with severity equal to that exercised in the case of *lèse-majesté*, to the extent that such blasphemers firmly establish their intent, as is the case with habits and things of no importance. Any sensible person should see that many people, disagreeing among themselves on other articles of faith, have constantly asserted and proved this in unison, and enforced it by the threat of eternal punishment, so it is now considered to have achieved the invariable nature of necessity.

[3.] As I (or any other clear-thinking investigator) see things, the man who strives uselessly at the vain prompting of his will to live differently than everyone else on the face of the earth hardly differs from a madman; indeed, it is expedient for man that there be only one God, lest the burden of a plurality give rise to the vices of baseness and disagreement, for divergence from a firm and stable community quite often gives birth to self-indulgent confusion in plurality. Indeed, powers of any size, great or small, are always inexorably opposed to partnership and equality by nature: they always live wakefully vigilant so that they alone might hold power without a co-possessor. Wise men have always said it is natural for joint possessions to be neglected by one possessor: he will allow his own part to suffer damage while he hastily envies his partner's share. So it remains true that if God exists, as He undoubtedly does, He alone dwells in the supreme sublimity of the godhead.

[4.] Since I may, as is my right, freely employ appropriate arguments developed by others, it appears that knowledgeable and sensible men have confirmed God's existence. It is a universal custom of common occurrence that an author should use arguments he has discovered elsewhere to make a point, and rejoice in availing himself of timely borrowings, and it often happens that one strolls lawfully across the estates of others. Even the deliberate and assiduous imitation of one author's novelties in another author's work normally accrues to the original author, to the increase of his praise and fame, but only if the circumspect imitator makes it a habit to

imitator[1] inculpatam[2] rem prosequi conuenientisque consueuerit in moderacione tutele.

[5.] Sic itaque, quo nostrum[3] sanis et sauciatis ab Ambrosii per-
85 gamus inicium sumere sermonibus, elegantissime sic scribit Ambrosius: Vt Deus, qui sui natura fuit et est inuisibilis, agnosci scirique posset a visibilibus, opus fecit quod sui visibilitate suum demonstraret opificem, quo per certum competentissime peruenirentur ad incerti cognicionem, consequenter et ille Deus omnium fore credere-
90 tur qui tale fecerit opus, quod creature cuilibet efficere videretur funditusque foret inpossibile. Contemplans igitur sensu tam veges homo tantam tamque specialem mundi machinam, nullatenus ab ulla fieri posse creatura fore coniectauit, sed et efficaciter intellexit homine multo valenciorem fore talis opificem speciei uel operis
95 adeo speciosi. Sic ductu racionis efficacissime Dei se certificauit in cognicione, Deique sic inuisibilia per ea que facta sunt intellecta sunt a creatura.

[6.] Sunt eciam quamplures alie raciones sinceris et summis in subtilitatibus adprime commendabiles precipuis, et in subtilitate[4]
100 scientiaque iuris antonomasice commendabilibus,[5] eorumque firmas in fide per subtilitates, racionumque per sinceritates firma fundamentalique soliditate ruinasque citra quaslibet rimasue perpetuo stabiles. Ut igitur autenticas in primis falsitatibus et inpermixtas Aristotilis accedamus ad asserciones, que sub sole sunt vniuersa
105 singularis vir subtilitatis breuitate comprehendit sic sub succinctissima: Quicquid sub sole subsistit aut accidens est aut substancia; |55ʳ| vel ut queque remotius[6] amandetur calumpnia, preponatur accidenti si libet in diuisione substancia. Sumatur et hic accidens habundancius quam sumi consueuit in logica, videlicet omne quod
110 abhorret a per se subsistencia. Substancia profecto, cuius est accidentibus accidentalibusque subsistere, nomen a substando tale subsistendoue conuenienter accepit. Oportuit ergo tale quid mente prompta cogitatuue concipi quod et per se foret et a se, nullo videlicet ab alio, per quod et a quo scilicet omnia forent: illud
115 profecto cui supplicat homo sensatus sane censetur esse Deus, quod et vnum fore uel fuisse dumtaxat eciam propter infinitatis oportet inconuenienciam. Nempe si foret aliud a quo foret et illud, sicque

---

[1] imitor S
[2] inculpare S
[3] nostro S
[4] in subtilitate] ab insubtilitate S
[5] commendabiles S
[6] remotus S

follow an irreproachable source under the control of a suitable guide.

[5.] To take our beginning for healthy and wounded alike from Ambrose's discourse, Ambrose elegantly writes: "So that God, who was and is invisible by nature might be recognized and known from what is visible, He created a work which by its visibility demonstrates its artificer; thus an idea of what is uncertain can suitably be achieved through what is certain. Consequently, He who created such a work, which would be impossible for any created thing to effect, should be believed in as the God of all things." So this man of flourishing sense inferred from contemplating the great and unique fabric of the universe that it could by no means have been created by any created thing, and he understood to good effect that the artificer of such a beautiful image or work must be much more powerful than man. By this line of reasoning he assured himself of the knowledge of God; thus, the invisible things of God are known by creatures through those things which are created.

[6.] Men preeminent for their genuine subtlety and praiseworthy for their subtle knowledge of what is right have advanced many other arguments which are confirmed in faith by the subtle and solid arguments of such men and perpetually established as fundamentally solid without crack or ruin. To begin with the assertions of Aristotle, authentic and unmixed with falsehood, this man of singular subtlety comprehended all things under the sun with the utmost brevity, thus: "Whatever exists under the sun is either accident or substance; or, to exclude any unfounded objection, substance is prior to accident, if you care to distinguish." "Accident" is to be taken here more broadly than it normally is in logic, namely as all that is incapable of separate existence. Indeed substance, which underlies accidents or accidentals, took its name from underlying or subsisting. We should, with prompt mind or thought, conceive of something which exists separately and of itself, that is, by the agency of no other, which is that through which and from which all things exist. That which a sensible man supplicates is clearly to be reckoned God, and it must be (or at least have been) unique because of the discord of a permanent regress. For if it were preceded by another from which it came, and so on, it would be impossible

deinceps, sero vicia numquamue vitarentur infinitatum.

[7.] Sed et alia probatur idem racione non minus approbanda.
120 Quodcumque quidem rerum consistit in vniuersitate mutabilium
uel est totum uel pars, quasiue totum uel quasi pars, proprietasue
tocius uel partis. Quasi totum quidem non sine causa dixi, quia non
omne totum racionis, modiue, uel generis est eiusdem. Nempe
quodque uel est integrale uel vniuersale. Totum profecto quodlibet
125 est corpus integrale, partibus scilicet suis constans ex integralibus.
Pars profecto tocius integralis cuiuslibet pars est corporis. Integrale
quidem quasi totum quilibet est spiritus. Pars vero quasi tocius
cuiuslibet pars est spiritus; partes reuera quasi tocius integralis sunt
ipse virtutes, non autem quantitatiue[1] sed potenciales, vt intelli-
130 gendi potencia, memorandiue, cetereque consimiles. Hec omnia
profecto necesse subtiliter inspicienti patebit esse fore dumtaxat ab
vno. Totum reuera racionis a se ius esse non patitur[2] ullum. Nil eo
nempe quod est a se prius est tempore.

[8.] Preter hec et ad hec: a nullo toto suarum procedit parcium
135 composicio. Pars etenim queuis suo genialiter prior est toto. Sic
itaque non potest aliquid |55ᵛ| totum Deus esse, quia Deum sic
oporteret in existencia aliud precedere; preterea pars nulla Deus est.
Quodlibet totum[3] enim parte sua qualibet dignius est; sic itaque
pars nulla Deus esse potest. De proprietatibus quidem tocius et
140 partis, quod a se non sint ea probatur omnino racione quia superius
probatum constat in accidentibus esse. Sic igitur cum de predictis
omnino nullum, sicut dilucide[4] iam satis preostensum, suam possit
sortiri substanciam (prorsus esse videtur et est impossibile), quin
aliud a quo predicta sint omnia persistens sit in eternitate. Summus
145 illud et solus est Deus.

[9.] Ad hec, cum se sana mens non possit ignorare, se uel aliquando cepisse non potest homo non agnoscere. Nec minus et est
uel esse debet sibi sanissime conscius quod, cum non esset per se,
sibi subvenire non poterat in existencia. Sic igitur ab alio sortitus est
150 ut esset. Illud autem non cepisse constat, quia si quouis ab alio
fuisset, omnium primus actor existencium non esset. Sed et si
cepisset ab alio quod sibi sue dare principium non potuisset essencie, si non ab eterno fuisset, ad aliud ascendere superius oporteret
a quo suam sibi subsistenciam susciperet, quod et ut ab eterno sit

---

[1] quantitati ue S
[2] partitur S
[3] totum *ed.*
[4] dilucido S

to avoid the logical defect of a permanent regress.

[7.] The same thing can be proved by another argument no less worthy of approval. Whatever dwells in the totality of mutable things is either whole or part, or virtual whole or virtual part, or a property of whole or part. I do not say "virtual whole" for no reason, since not every whole is of the same property, mode, or class. For anything is either integral or universal. Any body is an integral whole, constituted from its integral parts. A part of any body is part of an integral whole. Any spirit is an integral virtual whole. Any part of a spirit is a part of a virtual whole. Man's faculties are in fact parts of a virtual whole; however, not the quantitative but the potential faculties, such as the power of understanding or remembering, or other similar faculties. It will be apparent to any subtle investigator that it is necessary that all these things receive existence from one source. No law of reason will allow the whole to exist of itself. For nothing is prior in time because it exists of itself.

[8.] To continue on the same subject: the disposition of its parts never emanated from a whole. Indeed, any part is prior by nature to its whole. Thus no whole can be God, since in that case it were necessary that something else precede God in existence. Nor is any part God: any whole is more worthy than a part; thus, no part can be God. As concerns the nature of whole and part, that they do not exist of themselves can be proven by the argument that was previously applied to accidents. Absolutely not one of the above can determine its own substance, as has already been shown with sufficient clarity (it would, indeed, be utterly impossible), but rather something else, from which all other things derive, which exists in eternity. That is the sole supreme God.

[9.] To continue, since a sound mind cannot ignore itself, man cannot fail to be aware that he came into being at some point. Likewise, he should be aware, as regards himself, that since he does not exist separately, he could not maintain his own existence. Thus he was allotted existence by another. But it is manifest that this other did not come into being, since if it took its existence from another there would be no first creator of all things which exist. And if it took its being from another which itself could not give a beginning to its essence unless it existed from eternity, it would be necessary to ascend further back to another from which it received its subsistence. It is necessary that this being exist from eternity and

155 oportet et ita Deus sit et omnium causa creaturarum. Sin autem
subsequenter aliquam facile monstrabitur ab eterno fuisse creatu-
ram, cum tamen intelligi satis non posset esse creatura que suum
non ab alio fuisset inicium sortita. Sic itaque necessario constare
debebit quod vniuersitatis dumtaxat vnum sit originale, quod Deus
160 est, inicium.

   [10.] Preter hec, quo verba tam commendabili producere pergamus in materia, si qua res est que Deus sit, quin ipsa res sit que
non esse non possit sane nemo negauerit. Sic itaque si quid est
Deus, id non esse non poterit; igitur aliquid quod non esse non
165 potest est Deus. Atqui raciocinacionis huius in hoc uel argumenta-
cionis racio locusue consistit, quod ad huius ypothetice veritatem (si
quid, videlicet, |56ʳ| est Deus, id non esse non poterit) exigitur
quod Deus non possit non esse; cuius opposito posito, iam non
sequitur quod si quid videlicet sit Deus quod id non possit non
170 esse, sed pocius quod possit non esse, sed id necessario sequitur.
Est igitur impossibile Deum posse non esse. Sic itaque quod sit est
necesse. Sed uel ad hec, si libet, sic adhuc: est profecto manifestissi-
mum quia si quid est Deus, eo sine Deo bonum non poterit aliquid
esse; si quid[1] igitur est bonum, Deus est.

175   [11.] Sic multis necessariisque racionibus constat esse Deum,
citraque quamlibet vnum pluralitatem numerositatemue deorum.
Nempe si dii duo principiaue fuissent, uel insufficiens esset vtrum-
que uel superhabundans alterum. Si vero quid alteri deesset quod
haberet alterum, consumata non esset in perfectione solidatum.
180 Siquidem nil haberet vnum quod non haberet et alterum, consumata cum sic omnia posset utrumque superflueret alterum, uel
contemplacione communionis abhominabile sepius inciderent in discidium, presertim cum communio mater studiosius semper euitan-
darum fecundissima sit altercacionum, continuarumque semper et
185 sompniculosa sit incitatrix invidiarum. Sic igitur hoc mundo, moles-
tiarumque tam misero delectabilique conclauio, creatura Dei viuens
omnis homo pro vili communiter a quolibet habendus est subsannabiliter et insensato, qui Deum vnum summo sibi specialique pro
subsidiatore non constituit sufficientique subsidio. Reuera plus iusto
190 pussillanimus[2] animoque bestialiter est imbecillis cui vix vitupera-
biliterque viuenti destinatoque fatalitatis ineuitabiliter ad euentus,
suam sibi sufficiens satis ad salutem non est Deus vnus.

   [12.] Hee quidem, frater, tam speciales, verbalitatis et in luculen-

---

[1] quod *S*
[2] pussillanimis *S*

thus be God and the cause of all created things. Otherwise, it would be easy to demonstrate that some created thing existed from eternity, although it is impossible to comprehend the existence of a creature which was not allotted its beginning by another. Thus it must needs be manifest that there is only one origin of the universe, which is God.

[10.] To continue speaking about such praiseworthy material, if by chance there is anything which proves to be God, surely no one will deny that it must be that which cannot not be. Thus, if anything is God, it cannot not be; whatever cannot not be is God. The logic of the proof is grounded in this: the truth of the hypothesis that if something is God it cannot not be requires that God could not not be. Assuming the opposite, it does not follow that if something is God it could not not be, but rather that it could not be, and this follows as a necessary consequence. It is impossible for God not to exist. Thus it is necessary that he exist. We may even add, if you please, that it is apparent that if something is God, without this God nothing could be good; therefore, if anything is good, God exists.

[11.] So it is manifest for many necessary reasons that God exists and is one, without any multiplicity of gods. For if there were two gods or first principles, either both would be insufficient or one superfluous. If either lacked something the other had, it would not be established in consummate perfection. But if neither had what the other lacked, either would suffice for everything and the other would be superfluous, or they would frequently fall into discord from brooding on their sharing, especially since sharing is a fecund mother of altercations, which are always to be avoided, and an unwearied instigator of continual envy. In this world, this delightful conclave of afflictions, that man, God's living creation, who does not choose one God as his supreme support and unique safeguard should be considered base and senseless by all. In fact, the culpable man who lives inevitably destined to a fatal end, for whose salvation one God will not suffice, is unreasonably mean-spirited and subhumanly feeble in spirit.

[12.] As I noted above, brother, these clever arguments, so de-

cia tam commendabiles argucie mee ruditatis, ut et supra succincta
195   sub breuitate notaui, tam nulle nullatenus ascribende velut iniciali
nec eciam cachinnabiliter sunt inuencioni, sed adeo fundamentaliter
|56ᵛ| effusorum tamque laudabiliter[1] assertorum spontanee dum-
taxat et presumptuose tamen imitacionis dulcedini. Concupiscencie
quidem intemperancia, desideriique vehementis impulsus, delecta-
200   cionisue uel appetitus exuberancia mouere multos consueuere
crebrius audacie non minus quam magnanimitatis ad euentualia,
fortunaliter et ad eueniencia, nedum[2] spei uel aliquantule certitu-
dinis incitacionibus excitatiua. Revera longe facilius est originaliter
alienis ab inuencionibus quid quasi nomine mutui gratis accipere,
205   sibique quadam superficiei sub forma presumpcionis ascribere,
quam quid inicialiter laboribusque studiorum non pretemptatis
adinuenire. Verumptamen non omnino censeri debet a sane sencientibus inappreciabile preinuentum uel aliquibus subornacionum[3]
subtilitatibus conari decorare, formaue uel aliquatenus in superficia-
210   li meliorare. Quodlibet profecto commendabiliter inuentum procedere consueuit ad emendacionis argumentum, si commendabilium
fuerit ab appreciatorum manibus mentibusue sciencialiter exceptum.
Reuera vix est quod[4] inuenciones in utilitatibus subtilitatibusue
merito commendabiles veras vegetesque veniant ad appreciaciones
215   temporum dierumue per diuturnitates.

[13.] Sic itaque, mi consors Philippe, nisi tua tam varia volueris et
adhuc in contradicendi procacitate proteruus perseuerare, quod
anima sit humana non deficientis inmortalitate[5] perpetuitatis priuilegiata tibi certissime debet et omne citra dubium constare. Nec
220   minus vniuersalem citra dubitacionem[6] summipotentis Dei dumtaxat et vnius supreme maiestatiuam circa potenciam prepositas per
probaciones adeo necessarias et in veritatis sinceritate fundamentali
stabilitate tam firma solidatas certissimus, nisi contumax omnino
fueris et exfrons, esse debebis, presertim cum salutare tibi sit id
225   admodum, sit et oneris cachinnabiliter importabilis laudabilissime
|57ʳ| reclamatiuum. Sit eciam plures sustinere simul dominos
numerososue geniculariter adorare deos humane simplicitati condicionis onerosissimum.

[14.] Sis igitur, ni (quod absit) derisibiliter desipere quam sanum

---

[1] laudabiliterque S
[2] ne dum S
[3] subortacionum S
[4] qui S
[5] mortalitate S
[6] dubitacionem *ed.*

tailed and praiseworthy in their verbal splendor, are by no means
to be ascribed (not even as a joke) to my barbarous or rather nonexistent power of invention, as if that were their origin, but only to
deliberate and presumptuous imitation of arguments laudably
espoused and soundly expressed by others. The intemperance of
lust, the compulsion of violent desire, or excess of delight or appetite often chances to move men to brave and generous actions and
their outcomes, not to mention the impulse of hope or a modicum
of certainty. In fact, it is much easier to borrow the original invention of another without acknowledgement as a nominal loan and
after making cosmetic changes ascribe it to oneself than to invent
something for the first time by original scholarly labors. Clear
thinkers should not consider it utterly worthless to decorate what
was previously known with some subtle rewording or to improve
its external form. Any praiseworthy invention normally serves as a
cause of moral improvement if it is knowingly accepted by the
hands and minds of praiseworthy judges. It is hardly the case that
inventions commendable for their utility and subtlety must await
the passage of time to achieve true and invigorating evaluations.

[13.] So, Philip, my companion, unless you still wish to persist in
your disagreeable obstinacy, you should consider it a certain truth
not susceptible to doubt that the human soul is endowed with
unfailing immortality. Likewise, unless you are shamelessly defiant,
you should be completely certain about the supreme power of one
almighty God, prior to all things, according to the proofs already
outlined, which are necessary and established as unalloyed truth by
a fundamental stability. This would be extremely healthy for you
and would be a suitable response to a laughably unbearable burden. It is innately difficult for simple humans to endure several
lords or to adore on bending knee numerous gods.

[14.] So unless (heaven forbid) you prefer acting irrationally to

230   salubriter preelegeris commendabiliterque sapere, vt eciam ab
vniuersitate conviuencium sub sole merito secernibilis esse communiter ab omnibus inexorabiliterque iudiceris eternaliter ignominio-
sus infernalisque perpetuitati penalitatis indubitate debitissimeque
destinatus,[1] libens et ultroneus anime perpetuitatis et inmortalitatis
235   humane constans et assertor, sciencialiter et indubius. Sis eciam, si
viuere volueris et hic (in medio videlicet) et indeficienter indemp-
nis, vlterius si sane salubriterque tibi sapere curaueris, libens adorator inuariabiliterque continuus Dei dumtaxat vnius professorque
spontaneus. Nec indissolubile multominus sane continuacione longe
240   remissius inter animam liguamque (sicut satis et ad habundans
eciam premencionauimus) indissolubiliter obseruandum commen-
dare nisu perpetuato pergas et approbare quasi matrimonium,
perpetuitatisue matrimonialis intellectuale commercium, quo tue
tibique conuiuencium bellissime proficias utilitati, continuis in
245   approbacionibus dilectionibusque medianorum, sed et summum tibi
taliter viuendo saluatorem spei certitudine scias factoque frequencius sencias esse propiciatum.

[15.] Commendabile quidem plurimumque commendandum sane
censetur esse matrimonium duraturos in perpetuum paraturum[2]
250   questus perfunctoriorum leuitate succincta laborum. Reuera felicissime suo sanoque quis ancillari seruiens conatur conamine prelato,
qui licet adprime laborat[3] contemplacione seruicii dominanti, denique congaudet dominantis in gaudio. Semper eciam ibi fructuoso
quiuis ancillans munifici dignissime |57ᵛ| domini cariturus erit
255   obsequio, qui suo dum seruit spontanee segnescit in seruicio,
viliterue suam suo ledere fidem domino non verecundatur in
ancillando ministerio. Wlgare quidem triuialiterque tritum et nunc
est, fuit et in vdo pridem, quod firma vernaliter ancillantis fidelitas
non interpolataque fidelis in exibicione seruicii pertinacitas ingredi
260   dominantis in gaudium seruienti semitas procurare pergant stratas-
que patentissimas.

LIBER DUODECIMUS[4]

Uir renuens reus omnis erit contemptor inanis
Esse Dei dum plura rudis sibi numina querit;

---

[1] I transpose vt . . . destinatus, which S copies before Sis (11.235)
[2] parare S
[3] laboriosi S
[4] R del. Sequitur before Liber duodecimus

showing healthy good sense and so are willing to run the risk that everyone will inexorably judge you different from all other men, subject to eternal ignominy and destined to perpetual punishment in hell, you should be an eager proponent, constant in your certain knowledge, of the permanence and immortality of the human soul. If you wish to live unharmed here on earth, if moreover you care to show some healthy good sense, you will also be willing to worship assiduously only one God and voluntarily profess faith in Him. Likewise, you should continually commend with zeal the virtual marriage or intellectual commerce, as permanent as marriage, between soul and tongue: a union clearly indestructible by time and to be observed without end. In this way you will profit yourself and those who live with you and gain the affectionate approbation of the world at large, knowing your supreme Savior in the certainty of hope and sensing Him to be propitious in his actions.

[15.] We may judge praiseworthy that marriage which demands only perfunctory labors and provides profits which will endure forever. In fact, any servant succeeds in his sensible endeavor to serve his master if, after laboring at first in bondage to his lord, he finally rejoices in his lord's joy. Any servant who willingly slackens in his service or is not afraid to break his faith to his lord will rightfully do without his munificent lord's fruitful deference. It is still a trivial commonplace on everyone's lips that the firm faith and persistent service of a house slave will secure him wide-open roads to enter into his master's joy.

BOOK TWELVE

Every man who denies God's existence, who scoffs idly,
Is guilty of crudely seeking many godheads;

Est vni sub sole probo seruire clienti
Res operosa satis, est ergo deis operosum
5 Pluribus ad placitum dominis seruire ministro;
Nempe minor censetur egens homo numine semper,
Numinis auxilio quod crebro pronus adorat.
Ergo deos delirat homo qui querit inepte
Quisque sibi multos, quia uix consueuit honestum
10 Esse modi quod in excessu numerus viciasset,
Presertim si magna modum res exigat instans,
Et si sufficiens odiosa superflua vitet,
Pondere praua premi, cui non satis est Deus vnus,
Gens cupit usque graues dignissima pendere penas;
15 Sensatis sub sole Deo spirantibus vni
Absque pari par est igitur sua fundere vota,
Omnis ut aspernator homo sit in orbe deorum,
Sitque salutaris sibi subsannator eorum.
Sit tamen usque Deus solus sibi trinus et vnus,
20 Sit genitor, genitusque, simul sit spiritus almus,
In deitate Deus summa, sed sic tamen ut tres
Esse deos sub sole scius non senciat ullus; |58ʳ|
Sola salus saluansque fides sacra Christicolarum
Saluat et eternat requiem; soliumque salutis
25 Sufficiens solidare suis est et dare vitam
Lumine conditam lucis finemque fugantem.

[1.] Postquam vero tot et talia sermonibus protractis aliquatenusque diffusis libens satisque licenter effuderam, consors meus iam
secundo bellissime melioratus, iteroque[1] competentissime com-
30 mendabiliterque modificatus, ita wltu prorsus et oculis et animi
motu remocius amandato, morem mecum contra solitum talibus est
sermocinacionibus amicabiliter vsus: Reuera, mi consors Helia, tue
mea sibi iam vendicauere vires, locumque sorciuntur et effectus
allegaciones in consciencia. Nempe michi iam nunc esse sciencialiter
35 eciam fere persuasum sencio, sensatissime probatumque cuilibet est
sanum sensatumque sencienti bellissime, quod anima specialiter
humana racionalitatis sola sit inter animalia preiudicio priuilegiata,
sed et a fatalitatis improperio uel finis omnino condicionaliterque
semota, quodque Deus summipotens vnus, vanis omnino reiectis et
40 a fidei sinceritate remocius amandatis deorum pluralitatibus, spirantibus sub sole solus sit ab hominibus geniculariter adorandus

---

[1] iteraque S

It is sufficiently arduous for an upright client
To serve one earthly master, so it is difficult
To minister to many gods in a way that pleases them all;
For poor man is always reckoned less than the godhead,
Since he often entreats the godhead's aid with bowed head.
Thus any man who foolishly seeks many gods for himself
Raves, since that which is impaired by a sum
In excess of all measure is rarely honorable,
Especially if a great and pressing matter expels measure
And odious superfluity avoids what is sufficient.
A depraved people for whom one God is not enough wants
To be pressed by its burden to the point of grave suffering;
So it is reasonable for those who live their lives sensibly
To make their prayer to one God without equal,
That every man on earth might disdain the gods
And ridicule them to his own salvation.
For you there must be a single God, three and one,
Who is father, son, and fostering spirit:
God in his supreme godhead, but in such a way
That no knowing man perceives there are three gods;
Only the salvation and holy saving faith of Christians
Grants eternal rest: it is sufficient
To consolidate the throne of salvation for its followers
And give life adorned in radiance, dispelling light's end.

[1.] Because I freely uttered all this in my diffuse and protracted discussion, my companion was made a better man for the second time and once again showed a commendable ability to change himself. Suitably restraining countenance, voice, and thought (contrary to his established manner), he spoke these friendly words to me: Elias, my companion, your powers have claimed mine for their own, and your charges have achieved their effect in my conscience. For I am almost persuaded that you have proved to anyone who thinks sanely and sensibly that the human soul, alone among living things, is endowed with rational foresight and remains remote by contract from the reproach of a fatal end. With a vain plurality of gods utterly rejected and banished from the integrity of faith, all men should ceaselessly worship and venerate on bended knee one supremely powerful God, and freely love and fear Him, setting

indesinenterque venerandus, sitque reiecto longius omni cancellaliter et obliterato timore seruili, voluntarie delectabiliterque timendus.
Sit et indigenti moleque molestiarum molestato salutare summum-
45   que refugium, sufficiens sibi solum cuilibet a quolibet examinandus.

[2.] Hec omnia profecto, frater Helia, meo me michi tua salubriter
in animo renouantia,[1] que tam subtiliter retro fudisti tamque laudabiliter inseruisti[2] pectori, verba michi quidem non multominus
approbabilia |58ᵛ| quod velut ab aliis alioue sint sicut asseris
50   mutuata, tibiue quasi nomine mutui superficialiter appropriata.
Refutatis igitur omnibus et abiectissime postergum dimissis, habitis-
que pro derelictis omninoque pro dignissime derelinquendis antiquitatis erroribus adeo ridiculis, humanam sane scius homo nullus
animam dubitet ulterius inmortalitate priuilegiatam, quo spiritus
55   hominis animaue, racionalitatis efficiens causa, brutorum brutis ab
animalium spiritibus specialiter sibi concessam racionalitatis secer-
natur per prerogatiuam, ceterisque dignissime dominetur animalibus homo per consequenciam, concessamque sibi dominatoris
summi voluntate dominacionem suam sepius exerceat ad utilitatem,
60   dum tamen inculpate non excedat in exercicio tutele mensuram uel
exercicii moderacionem. Nec incircumspectius, obliteratis omnino
vetustatis adeo vane tam vilibus ridiculisque deliramentis, subsolari[3] spirans in medio quiuis pertinax sit subsannator tam numerabi-
lium vanitatis antique deorum multitudinis, adeoque numerosorum
65   sub sole numinum tam perniciose pluralitatis.

[3.] Sic itaque mi meritissime, consors michi amantissime, quod
superficiale satis et quasi contemplatiuum retro mencionatorum
michi displicuit, adeoque bilis ad amaritudinem me mouit animi
ligueque matrimonium, tuorum varias verborum vafrecias tamque
70   subtilium allegacionum per argucias mea[4] michi mente bellissime
sedet ut admodum iam nunc approbabile sit[5] sciencialiter et a
sensatis vniuersaliter omnibus approbatum. Nempe nullus sub sole
spirans medianus, ut michi tuis iam nunc videre videor adprime
meliorato sermonibus, virtutis amator esse valebit, vere verus
75   deitatisve cultor sincere sincerus, nisi talis contractus matrimonialis
continuus sit commendator, inuariabiliterque voluntarius |59ʳ|
actualiterque sic affectiuus. Sed nec in vita sibi conviuentibus a

---

[1] renouanti S
[2] inseruerunt S
[3] sub solari S
[4] mee S
[5] sit *ed.*

aside and forgetting all servile fear. He should be salvation and the supreme refuge for those who are poor and troubled by a mass of discomforts; each man should judge Him alone sufficient in Himself for all.

[2.] All these words, brother Elias, which (as I see things) you have uttered subtly so they might insinuate themselves into my mind and restore me to healthy thoughts, are no less worthy of my praise because they are (as it were) borrowed from others, as you claim, or appropriated by you in the guise of a loan. Since you have refuted the absurd errors of Antiquity, and established that they are worthy to be abandoned in neglect, no sensible man can continue to doubt that the human soul is endowed with immortality. So the spirit or soul of man, efficient cause of rationality, is distinguished from the spirits of brute animals by the prerogative of rationality which is granted to man alone. As a result, man rightfully rules the other animals, exercising beneficially the dominion granted to him by the will of the supreme Ruler, as long as he does not exceed the measure of blameless guardianship or duty in performing his task. Since you have utterly obliterated the base raving of vacuous Antiquity, anyone who breathes under the sun should circumspectly ridicule ancient credulity's innumerable multitude of gods and pernicious plurality of earthly deities.

[3.] My most devoted companion, you have by the ingenuity of your words and clever allegations convinced my mind that the marriage of mind and tongue, which previously displeased me and raised my bitter bile as a reflection of the superficiality I spoke of, is worthy of scientific approval and should be endorsed by all sensible people. As I now see for the first time as a result of your edifying discourse, no man who breathes under the sun can love virtue or worship the true godhead purely, unless he constantly praises this matrimonial contract with unchanging will and true emotion. But a praiseworthy or appreciable man is not to be exam-

viris, sibive vicinaliter conuiuantibus a coinquilinis, homo commendabilis uel vir appreciabilis erit examinandus, sed et a sane sensatis
80 indifferenter vniuersis vituperabilis esse censebitur mendax[1] vehe-
mentissimeque vituperandus. Nempe nemo facile fallax consuetudi-
naliterue verba mendaciterque varians virorum gratias appreciato-
rumue perseuerancias promereri[2] valebit de facili valide viriliterue
viuencium.

85 [4.] Tuarum profecto, care mi consors, subtiles sensi per luculencias sermocinacionum quod id quod et triuialiter est tritum, satisque
diouolaliter est in vniuersitate wlgari loquelaliterue wlgatum, mere
veritatis sit sinceritati consonantissimum: solum scilicet sodaliciique
solacio destitutum sanissime censeri miserrimum fore deploran-
90 dumque medianum. Nempe si sodalicii solacio carens ceciderit, sero
senciet subleuatoris auxilium, uel subsidiatoris salutare tempesti-
uumve subsidium. Viuens ergo quiuis, si sane sensatum commendabiliterque circumspectum sapiat, sodalicii[3] studiosissime sibi
conciliare tam decens et adeo salutare subsidium nisu continuato
95 perseueret, casu cariturus exiciali si commendabile sibi feliciter
inuenerit. Huius profecto fidus enunciacionis assertor securus et
astipulator assurgo, quia cui fides est indubitanter habenda iam
sum securificatus, experto salubri tam confusiuo subsidiatus in casu
satis et eleganti verbalitatis in amenitate suffragio.

LIBER TERCIUS DECIMUS[4]

Iam michi me firmum faciunt tua famina frater,
Qui male mouisti per inania verbula bilem
In primis, dum vana vafer variando referres,
Iam tibi conueniens, et in hoc consencio quod sit
5 Res cuiuis operosa satis seruire studenti
Pervalido semper domini pro velle clienti |59ᵛ|
Ad libitum soli, domino si seruiat vni;
Est igitur famulo dominis operosa duobus
Subdere se solum res ancillando clientem,
10 Vix equidem validus eciam seruire duobus
Vir valet ancillans quo sit bene gratus utrique;

---

[1] mendax *ed.*
[2] promeriti *S*
[3] sodalii *S*
[4] R *ad.* liber xiii 9 *in marg.*

ined during his lifetime by those living or sharing meals in common with him. All men who possess sober good sense will without exception vehemently censure a liar. For no one who practices casual deceit or habitually alters his words will claim the thanks or the continued esteem of discerning men who live vigorously and manfully.

[4.] My dear companion, I sensed through the subtle splendors of your discourse that a notion which is a trivial and meretricious commonplace among all commoners is consonant with the unalloyed truth: namely, that the solitary man, destitute of companionship, is clearly to be judged miserable and deserving of tears. When a man who lacks the solace of companionship falls, he is slow to sense timely assistance or support. Anyone alive, if he is of sensible and circumspect understanding, will persist diligently in the effort to win himself the salutary assistance of a companion, and he will avoid a fatal fall if he is fortunate enough to have found one worth his approval. I stand a faithful champion and firm adherent of this pronouncement, since I have already been made secure by Him who deserves undoubting faith, having felt His salutary assistance in my shameful case by the elegant amenity of verbal disputation.

BOOK THIRTEEN

Now, my brother, your words have made me firm;
At first, when you repeated cunningly varied vanities,
Your empty words wrongly provoked my anger;
I agree with you now that if it is
Laborious for anyone eager to serve adequately,
According to the wish of his master,
To serve one lord in an acceptable manner,
Then it is laborious for a servant to place himself
Under two masters by subjecting himself alone as their slave,
Since even a robust servant is unable to serve two lords
So that he is quite acceptable to both;

Nemo quidem dominis famulando placere duobus
15 Sic solet, ut plene placidos sibi senciat ambos,
Seruiat et paribus quod non reprobetur ab vllo.
Est igitur satis insulsum se subdere multis
Sponte sua dominis, dominus cui sit satis vnus:
Iure quidem grauidata premi per pondera quiuis
20 Portitor est nimio quassatus[1] pondere querens,
Omnis enim stolide solum sapit insipientem
Viribus impar onus humeris imponere pergens,
Dum valeat bene, si libeat sibi, sub leuiori
Vtilis esse modo uel pondere lator ad actus;
25 Si sanum sapiat, sibi nemo libens onus optet
Excipiatue suis opus importabile lumbis,
Talia ridiculus ne sic per inania fiat,
Et moueat multis sua sic per facta cachinnum.

[1.] Porro postquam sic sodalis meus, meo bellissime iudicio
30 melioratus, talia sibi tam salubria tam commendabiliter effuderat,
efficacissime statim talia letificatus taliter per effusa, longe licencius
hylariusque solito[2] mea loquelaliter sic cepi laxare labia: Revera
iam sencio, care mi consors, efficacissime quod ad modum vita
viuentibus in mediana sit utile sitque iocundum concordia consortes
35 conuiuere conuenienter in indifferenti, simulque socialiter habitare
commendabiliter et in vnum; bene fidum profecto firmumque
sodalicium fide fraternitatis ad instar et in stabilitate solidatum sibi
sufficiens esse solet et ad expediens in necessitate subsidium. Sana
quidem |60ʳ| iam nunc in veritatis sinceritate michi securissime
40 non dubito solidatum quod adeo commendabili commendabiliter
est a Psalmista dictum[3] velud exclamacionis ad instar enunciatum,
simpliciter tamen ut inculpabilis in modo moderacionem tutele non
excederet exclamacionis. Ait enim sic: Ecce quam bonum quamque
iocundum cohabitare fratres in vnum. Perfecta profecto caritas
45 fratres cohabitare facit indiuisibiliter in vnum commendabiliterque
perfectum. Vir ergo vera vere philosophus[4] in philosophia, fratrum
congaudens de cohabitacione caritatiua, sic est exultanter elocutus,
omnino nil innuens exclamacionis vane vanitatisue de turbulencia, sed
vtilitatis sola iocunditatisque contemplans irreprobabiliter incitatiua.
50 [2.] Sic itaque sodales sana sane conuiuunt in sodalitate si mutua

---

[1] quassati S
[2] solio S
[3] dictum] decendum S
[4] phisicus S

Indeed, no servant can normally please two lords
Enough to sense that both are completely satisfied,
Or serve a pair so as not to be reproved by either one of them.
Thus, a man for whom one lord is enough is stupid
To place himself freely under many lords:
By right, any carrier who brandishes an excessive load
Is asking to be crushed by the burdensome weight;
Indeed, anyone trying to place a load past his strength
On his shoulders stupidly smacks of the fool,
When the carrier would, if he wished to be a useful bearer,
Be fit for the task of lifting a lighter weight;
No sensible person would willingly choose
To take upon himself a load his loins could not bear,
Lest such inanity make him seem absurd
And cause others to laugh at his actions.

[1.] After my companion, whom I judged much improved, had so effectively cheered me by uttering such salubrious sentiments in this manner, I began in good cheer to loosen my lips far more freely than before: I now realize, my dear companion, that it is a source of profit and joy for those who live this earthly life to live together as companions in undivided concord. A faithful partnership, firmly established by fraternal trust, is a sufficient support, indispensable in time of necessity. For my own part, I do not doubt the truth of the praiseworthy Psalmist's straight-forward but properly moderated exclamation: "Behold how good and pleasant it is for brethren to dwell together in unity." Indeed, perfect love causes brothers to dwell together indivisibly in perfect oneness. This man, a natural philosopher of the true philosophy, rejoicing in the charitable cohabitation of brothers, spoke thus in exultation, not implying any turbulent or vain outcry, but with an irreproachable eye on what constitutes utility and charm.

[2.] Companions dwell together in sober companionship if they

conviuant inuariabilique proficiant in caritate. Reuera viuentibus in
50 vnum convenire conviuereve convenit vniuersis, sed sana precipue
salutarique sodalitatis in conueniencia confederatis, et in vnitate
fidei professionis et in ydemptitate consociatis.[1] Pertinaciter igitur
amodo persistere pergamus inuariabilis sinceriterque (licet sero)
solidate societatis in amenitate, quo valida vitam salubrique transi-
55 gamus ulterius sane salutarisque sodalitatis in tranquillitate,[2] fidei-
que saluberrima conviuentes felicissime nobis comproficiamus in
sinceritate. Fida profecto constansque societas dileccionis et in
sinceritate mutua ethnicis eciam quampluribus uel superficialem
fame non deficientis perpetuitatem pridem perpetuauit, perpetuat
60 et adhuc inmortalitatem.

[3.] Si libet itaque nostras iam sane terminatas longas post conten-
ciones, velut invicem pausacionis uel vnum fide societatis exemplum ponendo pergamus succincta sub breuitate deliciari (frequencius enim quasi spaciando delectari iuuat in materia valide
65 viuentibus adeo delectabili, | 60ᵛ | vera profecto falsitatique funditus
impermixta): de fida Damonis est amicicia Phitieque fama, labio-
rumque licet orisue popularis non sit in udo diouolaliterue diducta.
Damon quidem Phiciasque[3] Pitagorice[4] simul secte socialiter in
scolis iniciati, dum disciplinaliter condiscendo scolariter compro-
70 ficerent, indissolubile simul vnanimiterque conviuentes societatis
sibi vinculum sic solidauerunt, quod penitus indifferenti se mutuo
firmaque fidissime dileccionis in continuacione pertinaciter concole-
re perseuerarent, donec fortuna fallax, felicitatibus intempestiue
frequencius euentibus et inopinate prosperis incidens, tam commen-
75 dabiliter confederate tamque pertinacis quietem discussit sodalitatis.
Nempe nullius sub sole spirantis simplicitas est tanta que semper et
ad expediens vitare valeat inuidie venenam.[5]

[4.] Tam solide quidam male liguosus invidens societati, tiranno
Psithiam Siracusano capitali de crimine reum male menciendo
80 detulit coram Dionisio consuetudinaliter ad condempnandum
quocumque modo delatos, sed precipue capitali de crimine semper
vigilantissimeque voluntario. Sicque succinctis facillime motus
facilis in tali casu iudex allegacionibus calumpniose dampnauit

---

1 consocietatis S
2 in tranquillitate] intranquillitate S
3 Phiciasque S, Phintias Valerius
4 Pitagorice Valerius, Pitogarice S
5 venena S

progress together in unvarying charity. It suits all the living to agree to live together as one, especially those who are allied by the salutary concord of companionship, and associated in unity of professed faith. Henceforth, then, we will dwell persistently in the charm of undeviating and sincerely confirmed partnership, so we might live life in the future in the robust tranquillity of salutary sodality, and by dwelling together, delight in the beneficial integrity of faith. Constant partnership in mutual integrity and delight has and still can perpetuate at least a superficially undying fame and immortality, even for pagans.

[3.] Having terminated our long dispute, we will take respite and delight ourselves by giving an example of faithful partnership, for it is often pleasant to stroll (so to speak) in true material, unmixed with falsehood, and pleasurable to vigorous men. The story concerns the faithful friendship of Damon and Pythias, although it has not been meretriciously recounted by the lips of everyone. Initiated at the same time as partners in the teachings of the Pythagorean sect, Damon and Pythias progressed in understanding by learning together according to Pythagorean method and living together indivisibly of one accord. Establishing for themselves a bond of partnership, they persisted in devoting themselves to each other with faithful and unvarying affection, until treacherous fortune, which unexpectedly and out of season assails those who enjoy auspicious fortune and success, shattered the tranquillity of this commendable and unwavering friendship. For no man's lack of guile is so great as always to avoid the poison of envy.

[4.] Someone with a malicious tongue, envying such solid friendship, denounced Pythias as guilty of a capital crime before the Syracusan tyrant Dionysius, who was accustomed to condemn those denounced in whatever manner, but was especially arbitrary in judging capital crimes. This hasty and savage judge was easily swayed by the briefest allegations and convicted the falsely accused.

impetitum, iudex preproperus[1] et examinator inmanissimus. Ve-
85 rumptamen in vno uel aliquatenus tandem gratificatus est con-
dempnato, quod ad componendos penates adeo mestos ei concessit
quas mestus peciit inducias, sodali suo Damone si vellet vade
relicto; quod quia suus Damon sodalis animi simul et wltus in
constancia libens admisit, neci subductus uel ad tempus Pithias
90 libere recessit, dum derisus indifferenter ab vniuersis uti sponsor
cachinnabiliter infatuatus et mancipatus[2] uel superficialiter positus
Damon remansit.

[5.] Omnes itaque sed rex ipse Dionisius precipue rei contemplan-
tur et euentus vix ancipitis exitum, Damonisque sponsionem conde-
95 rident condempnantque tam temerariam. Demumque die diffinita
reditus |61ʳ| appropinquante, dum deridetur indifferenter ab
omnibus, se wltu verbisque constanter exibere perseuerat indifferenter indubium, suique sodalis de constancia fidelitatis securissimum.
Nec sua se securum specialis in amicicia fefellit in fine constancia.
100 Nempe Pithias, eadem die quam sibi Dionisius prefixerat et hora
fidissime veniens, se constantissime promptificauit ad fatalia. Tam
constancium tirannus mox admiratus animos Dyonisius tante
supplicium fidei remisit, solito quod retro non consueuit humanior
factus, societatisque tam specialis et tam solide supplicauit ut
105 admitteretur tercius, licet ad animi tantam fidelitatisque constan-
ciam moribus omnino fuisset inabilis viuendique consuetudinibus.

[6.] Nempe penes improbos eciam crebrius vigere consueuit
virtutum racionisque reuerencia, sed et inopinatos eciam sepissime
sortiri mansuescit effectus. Amicicie profecto vis admirabilis est et
110 vigor effecturus que necis naturaliter aspernande genialiter et
abhominande viuencium mentibus crebro pergit inserere contemp-
tus, vitalitatisque condiciones viuendique continuaciones et vite
vices concinnis perseuerat condire conviuendi dulcedinibus. Ad
istorum, mi consors, igitur instar ulterius et ad exemplum, conten-
115 cionibus et rixis remocius amandatis, fide persistamus in concordia
societatis, vitamque continua mutuaque condiamus dulcedine
excellentissime virtutum trium caritatis.

Quam bene iocundum fuerit retro quam sit amenum
Nunc eciam, scius expertis iam sencio factus,
120 Sponte sua sibi concordes habitare sodales,
Longius et rixas viciumque repellere licis,

---

[1] preproperiis S
[2] mancipati S

He did show some mercy to the condemned in one respect, since he granted a period of grace which the unhappy man sought for setting his sad household in order, on the condition that his companion Damon be left behind as surety if he were willing. Damon agreed freely with constant mind and countenance to be led off to death if Pythias failed to return on time. He surrendered himself and remained behind as surety, to be derided by all as laughably deluded.

[5.] Everyone, but especially King Dionysius himself, awaited the outcome of this scarce doubtful matter, and together they heaped scorn on Damon's rash undertaking. Finally, as the day fixed for Pythias's return approached, Damon was derided by all but continued to show himself confident in countenance and speech, sure as he was of his companion's constant fidelity. Nor, in the end, did his constancy betray this man who was so secure in the friendship of his companion. For Pythias returned faithfully on the day and hour that Dionysius had appointed in advance, hastening with constancy to his fate. Soon the tyrant Dionysius, admiring the spirit of such constant friends and having grown more humane than was his custom, remitted their punishment and asked that he be made a third member of this unique partnership, albeit he had been utterly unsuited by his disposition and actions for such constant fidelity of spirit.

[6.] Reverence for virtue and reason often flourishes even among the immoral, and often creates unexpected results. The admirable force and vigor of friendship will achieve what the contempt of death, which all men naturally spurn and abominate by instinct, often places in the minds of the living; it continues to flavor the conditions of vitality, the length of life and its twists and turns, with the sweetness of living together harmoniously. So, my companion, let us follow the example of these two friends and abandon all conflicts and quarrels to persist in the harmony of faithful partnership, flavoring life with the continual sweetness of mutual charity, the most excellent of the three virtues.

How rightfully joyful it was and how pleasant,
Even now, I sense, made wise by experience,
For harmonious companions to live together freely,
Rebuff brawls and vicious disagreement,

Et sibi sensate vitam solidare quietis
Vitales variando vices dumtaxat in vnum.
Turpe quidem satis est sibi dissentire sodales, |61ᵛ|
125 Et varios animis sociari corpore tantum,
Et sibi disiunctos animo conuiuere vili
More viatorum, qui sola diaria curant,
Ceptaque cum cepto sapiant socialia finem,
Primaque concipiunt properam consorcia metam.[1]
130 Quin pocius solidare parant sociale sodales
Solamen, studeantque sibi condire dierum
Decursus morumque modos solamine sano,
Dum fidum bene fidus amet, foueatque fouentem,
Dumque sibi sua sunt communia singula fidis;
135 Est eciam fulgore[2] patens per compita tritum
Quod socio sub sole carens vir vix bene viuat,
Vix eciam si forte cadat iaceatve resurgat;
Ergo simul sine dissensu viuamus et vltro
Viribus a nobis procul amandare paremus
140 Iurgia, quo solide socialia iura geramus
Vt valido vitam condire modo valeamus,
Longius a nobis et ut invidias abigamus;
Nostraque sic solam sapiant socialia pacem,
Vt renuant variata modo conviuere vili,
145 Et valide studeant validam producere vitam.

Explicit Serium senectutis Helye
Rubei Tripolawensis per ffratrem
Bartholomeum Texerii ordinis predicatorum, degentem pro eo tempore
150   Brechonie eiusdem ordinis Conuentu

---

[1] meram S
[2] fulgare S

And sensibly establish for themselves a quiet life
By living life's vicissitudes together.
Indeed, it is quite shameful for companions to disagree,
Divided in spirit, associate only in the flesh,
And live together disconnected in mind in the base
Manner of travellers, who care only for their daily rations,
Whose newly undertaken friendships end at their outset,
And whose first associations conceive a hasty terminus;
Instead, companions establish a source of comfort
In their partnership, and should strive to flavor the passage
Of time and constraint of manners with a sensible solace;
True faith should love faith, and cherish him who cherishes,
While the faithful hold their own things in common;
It is brilliantly apparent, although utterly commonplace,
That a man who lacks friends does not live well:
If he falls or lies prostrate, he will be slow to rise.
So let us live together without dissent, and to the limit
Of our powers banish conflicts far from us;
Let us thoroughly cherish the laws of partnership,
So we might flavor life with a forceful measure
And drive dislikes far from us;
Our partnership will know only peace,
So we will, once altered, refuse to live basely,
And strive forcefully to live a fit life.

Here end *The Grave Thoughts in Old Age* of Elias
Rubeus of Thriplow, copied by brother
Bartholomew Texerii, O.P., while dwelling
in the convent of the same order at Brecon.

Commentary

For the sake of precision, I cite prose sources by both their place in the original text (book, chapter, section, or line) and their page and line location in the edition to which I refer. I have tried to distinguish between certain or near certain sources, on the one hand, and possible sources or analogues, on the other, by introducing all references to the latter by "cf." Abbreviated titles for books of the Bible are those used by Robert Weber et al. in their edition of the Vulgate. This commentary also employs the following abbreviations:

Beiträge	Beiträge zur Geschichte der Philosophie des Mittelalters
CL	classical Latin
CSEL	Corpus scriptorum ecclesiasticorum Latinorum
MLD	*Dictionary of Medieval Latin from British Sources*
OLD	*Oxford Latin Dictionary*
TLL	*Thesaurus linguae Latinae*

Full publication data for works cited here are available in the bibliography.

Book One

1–28 This poem on the marriages of the gods is inspired by the invocation of Hymen with which Martianus Capella begins his *De nuptiis Philologiae et Mercurii* 1.1 (ed. Willis 1.4ff). For surveys of Martianus's influence, see C. Leonardi, "Nota introduttiva per un'indagine sulla fortuna di Marziano Capella nel Medievo," and Gabriel Nuchelmans, "Philologia et son mariage avec Mercure jusq'à la fin du xiie siècle." Willis provides extensive bibliography in his Teubner edition (Leipzig, 1983). Books 1 and 2 often circulated apart from the rest of the work in the thirteenth and fourteenth centuries; see Leonardi, "I codici di Marziano Capella." Elias also imitates Martianus by continuing his sense units from pentameter to hexameter in violation of the classical norm for elegiac verse.

2 *felici federe*: Cf. Catullus, *Carmina* (ed. Mynors) 64.373.

4–9 Elias echoes Martianus 1.3 (2.17ff.).

4 *verata*: Such a word is attested by Aulus Gellius, *Noctes Atticae* 18.2.12 (ed. Marshall, 540.24–26): "Secundum ea hoc quaesitum est, uerbum 'uerant,' quod significat 'uera dicunt,' quisnam poetarum ueterum dixerit." But it is inconceivable that a grammarian would scan *vĕrātā*. *Verita* would fit the meter but does not yield an acceptable sense unless Elias means the perfect to have a passive sense. The translation assumes such a sense, equivalent to that of *verenda*, "to be held in awe or reverence."

6 The Abderite and Coan are Vulcan and Venus respectively.

7 For Argiona ("the Argive"), cf. Martianus 1.4 (3.11).

11–12 For Admetus and Alcestis, see below 1.89–93.

13 *ceteris cupido*: The classical idiom would be better served by emending to *ceteri*, but the dative shows signs of encroaching on the genitive elsewhere in

Elias (see 3.381–82 below). Or should we take *cupido* as comparative—"more lustful than others"?

19 *coniuga*: Martianus 1.4 (3.9–11): "similique persuasione transduci Ope coniuga Cybeleque permulsa maestissimum seniorem deorum."

29–53 Philip's objections and much of their wording are based on Martianus's son's similar objections, *De nuptiis* 1.2 (2.5ff.).

34 *nasove vigilanti stertendo*: Juvenal, *Saturae* (ed. Clausen) 1.57: "doctus et ad calicem uigilanti stertere naso"; echoed in *De disciplina scolarium* 6.14 (ed. Weijers, 127.6) and *Petronius rediuiuus* 3, 124 (ed. Colker, 196, 225).

35–36 *decuriatus ... computacionibus*: Cf. Remigius of Auxerre, *Commentum in Martianum Capellam* 1.2 (ed Lutz, 70.12–14): "DECURIATUM LUSTRALIBUS INCREMENTIS hoc est provectu aetatis simul et morum maturitate curiae honore dignum. Lustrum enim dicebant antiqui quinquennium."

44 *epithalamicis ... cantilenis*: Cf. 6.17–18 below.

53 *in vdo*: Persius, *Saturae* (ed. Clausen) 1.105.

75 *sub lodice*: This phrase, which Elias uses with nearly adverbial force, comes from Juvenal 6.195–96: "[verbis] modo sub lodice relictis / uteris in turba." It is also used in the *Petronius rediuiuus* 47, 79, 135 (206, 214, 228).

77–80 For Cybele as the earth, see Remigius (73.12–13) *in Martianum* 1.4: "CYBELE dicta est quasi cubele a soliditate. Ipsa est enim terra qua nihil solidius est in elementis."

80–84 *ut sibi ... venustet*: Cf. 4.270–77 below.

82 *desiccet*: Cf. Plautus, *Truculentus* 585 (ed. Lindsay).

84–86 For the allegorical sense behind the marriage of Janus and Argiona, see Remigius (73.17–20) *in Martianum* 1.4: "IANUS deus anni. IANUS dictus est quod ianuam pandit anni. Hinc et mensis Ianuarius bifrons depingitur propter ingressum et egressum anni; a nonnullis quadrifrons propter quattuor anni tempora vel propter quattuor caeli climata."

89–93 *Admeto ... animositatem*: The general sense of this sentence is clear enough, although the syntax could be simplified by emending *aliquid* (91) to *aliquis*, agreeing with *sensatus* (91). Otherwise, construe *vix aliquid humanitatis accedere negaret ad vtilitatem* as meaning "will deny that [the marriage of Alcestis to Admetus] is of practically no use to humanity"; that is, it is of considerable utility. Fulgentius's account of how Admetus won the hand of Alcestis, *Mitologiae*, chap. 22 (ed. Helm, 33.20ff.), is repeated more or less verbatim by all three Vatican Mythographers (ed. Kulcsár, 39, 236; ed. Bode, 1.31.14–26, 128.33–129.10, and 247.26–248.6). Elias's mention of healthy ardor or courage (*salubrem ... animositatem*) echoes the Third Mythographer's allegorical exposition of this marriage (ed. Bode, 1.247.38ff.). According to all four accounts, Admetus represents the mind and Alcestis the truculence (*petulancia*) which the mind must acquire to overcome its fear and function successfully. Elias parallels the marriages of Mercury and Philology, Admetus and Alcestis, because of the similarity of their allegorical significances rather than any literal similarity of circumstance. *Phicii* and *Tirincii* render Pythius and Tirynthius, common epithets of Apollo and Hercules. Ovid is particularly fond of the latter.

100–104 The notion that wisdom should be conjoined with eloquence finds its first definitive expression in Cicero's portrait of the ideal orator, *De inventione* 1.1–5 (ed. Stroebel, 1–6). Cicero later treats *ratio* and *oratio* as the essential bonds of human society at *De officiis* 1.50 (ed. Atzert, 18.7–16). The theme is also made available to the Middle Ages by Quintilian, Marius Victorinus, Augustine of Hippo, and Cassiodorus (Nuchelmans, "Philologia et son mariage," 85–89).

Nevertheless, the source of this theme most important to the Middle Ages was Martianus's mythological treatment in *De nuptiis*, books 1 and 2, which Elias would have understood in the allegorical sense expounded by Remigius of Auxerre in terms borrowed from the *De inventione*: "Philologia ergo ponitur in persona sapientie et rationis, Mercurius in similitudine facundiae et sermonis. Ut autem Cicero dicit, eloquentia, id est sermonis copia, sine ratione et sapientia nocet aliquando, raro aut numquam prodest; sapientia vero sine eloquentia prodest semper, numquam obest. Cum ergo in sapiente haec duo convenerint, et acumen videlicet rationis et facundia sermonis, tunc quodam modo sociantur Mercurius et Philologia, tuncque promptissimum est unicuique ad scientiam VII liberalium artium accedere" (*in Martianum* 1.1 [66.22–29]). Rehandlings of Martianus's allegory are extremely widespread (Nuchelmans, "Philologia et son mariage," 92–107). But besides Remigius's *Commentum*, which he certainly knew, the treatment Elias is most likely to have known is that of John of Salisbury, who treats the marriage as an allegory of proper education, *Metalogicon* 4.29 (ed. Webb, 195.9ff.) or intellectual maturity, *Entheticus de dogmate philosophorum* (ed. van Laarhoven) 167–222. Note also *Metalogicon* 1.1 (7.13) and *Policraticus* 2.19 (ed. Webb, 109.5–7). It is clear from John's account that the marriage served, particularly in the twelfth century, as a rallying point for defenders of humanism. Notice, however, that Elias both literalizes (or demythologizes) and explicitly Christianizes the theme in the course of the *Serium senectutis*.

104–14 Ps. 14. Elias paraphrases the entire psalm.

119–24 Cf. Ps. 5.17; 13.3ff.; 77.36–37.

124–30 Augustine, *De mendacio* 1.3 (ed. and trans. Combès, pp. 242–45), repeated by Vincent of Beauvais, *Speculum doctrinale* 9.94 (Douay ed., 833A–B). Peter Lombard, *Sententiae* 3.38.3–4 (2.215.6–216.13) covers the same ground more exhaustively with quotations from Augustine's *Contra mendacium* and *Enchiridion*.

131–35 Ps. 33.13–14.

Book Two

21–22 "Antonomasice, id est excellenter," John of Salisbury, *Metalogicon* 2.16 (90.18–19). For *antonomasia* as rhetorical figure, see Matthew of Vendôme, *Ars versificatoria* 1.60–61 (ed. Faral, 132) and Geoffrey of Vinsauf, *Poetria nova* (ed. Faral) 923–35, 1775–80, 1807–9.

28–29 *tam rudis . . . vel adeo cornea*: Persius 1.47 (cf. 4.32–33, 454–55 below).

44–50 Cf. Ps. 24.4; 30.6–7 (as well as the references at 1.119–24 above). The soliloquizer is, of course, David. See Minnis, *Medieval Theory of Authorship*, 44, who traces the idea back via the *Glossa ordinaria* to Augustine's *Enarrationes in psalmos*.

48 *licentis*: Elias seems to substitute *licentis* for *licentie* in a desperate attempt to avoid hiatus.

53 *vanos . . . stateris*: Ps. 61.10.

77–87 *Triuiale . . . redegerit*: Expands on Ps. 7.12–13. Construe *quod* (77) . . . *quod* (78) followed by the subjunctive *spernat . . . spreuerit . . . redigat . . . redegerit* (86–87) as indirect discourse. For similar constructions, see 2.28–40, 50–60.

82 *diouolariter*: Paulus Diaconus, *Epitome Sexti Pompei Festi De verborum significatu* (ed. Lindsay, 65.8–9): "DIOBOLARES MERETRICES dicuntur, quae duobus obolis ducuntur." TLL also cites examples from Plautus, Varro, and Fulgentius.

85–86 *arcusque . . . conuertentes*: We might approximate to the meaning of this phrase by emending to *arcumque facile remissibilem in se prauitate sua conuertentes,* which yields the sense assumed by the translation. The use of final *-em* before *in* (*remissibilem in*), while rare in the *Serium senectutis*, is not unacceptable (cf. 11.199: *quidem intemperancia*). But the phrase as emended seems too threadbare to be authorial. Most likely, one or more words have fallen out of the text, which has subsequently been altered by a copyist to yield better sense.

89–90 *delinquencium . . . vlcionis*: Elias violates classical usage, which allows an objective genitive of the person upon whom vengeance is taken with *ultor* but not *ultio*. Cf. 3.152–55 below.

100–107 Lv. 24.10–16.

104–5 *Quam . . . productam*: Sc. *proles* (101, 109).

128–29 *non minus quam . . .* : The first term of this comparison has fallen out of the text.

147–53 Nm. 10.33–11.3.

154–73 Nm. 11.4ff.

155 *quo recordata*: As with *ver[i]ta* (1.4), we might almost discover an acceptable sense by assuming that the perfect here has a passive sense. If so, the subject is *vis diuinitatis* in line 155.

174–80 Nm. 12.

181–203 Nm. 13.

222–70 Nm. 16.

224 *prenominatorum*: Sc. "qui tempore concilii per nomina vocabantur" (Nm. 16.2).

271–302 Ex. 32.

274 *ut michi videre videor*: cf. John of Salisbury, *Policraticus* 5.16 (1.350.23–24): "Quos quotiens diligentius intueor, concussores mihi potius uideor uidere quam iudices."

285 *caduceator*: Huguccio of Pisa, *Magnae derivationes*, s.v., *caduceum, caduceatores*: "caduceum uirga Mercurii cum qua faciebat cadere discordiam [in] pacem [et] somnium. Vnde caducifer, -a, -um, quia ferens caduceum, et hic caduceator, -toris. Caduceatores dicuntur legati pacis, scilicet qui gratia pacis ferunt legacionem pacis inter aliquos" (MS Bodley, e Mus. 96, p. 50). Here, as in other quotations from Huguccio, bracketed words are supplied from the verbatim account in John Balbus, *Catholicon*, s.v.

287 *tante prauitatis . . . prauitate*: The pleonasm seems rather excessive, even in light of Elias's great fondness for *paronomasia*, and may well result from eye skip or anticipation.

288 *proteruiter*: The manuscript reading *prudenter* makes sense if taken to modify *perseuerauit*, but such a reading strains the syntax, the more so as there is no enclitic linking *prudenter* and *efficaciter* (289) in the manner of *adeo peruersis adeoque . . . pertinacibus* (288). However, the obvious emendation to *imprudenter* causes hiatus.

303–14 *Policraticus* 4.7 (1.260.22–29).

314–21 *Policraticus* 5.15 (1.344.27–345.3).

320 *calamitosorum*: We might defend the MS reading *calamosorum* as meaning "tearful," from *calamus*, "water pipe" (MLD 2b).

Book Three

1–2 *Uix . . . Deum*: Contrue: *Vir desipiendo suum Deum usque volet [ea] que quis sponte mouet uix validam plebem dicere.* The unnamed *quis* is probably Chore.

23ff. John of Salisbury devotes a chapter of the *Policraticus*, 8.21 (2.379–96), to the subject of divine vengeance on tyrants, with a long account of Julian the Apostate as its centerpiece.

29–54 Ovid, *Metamorphoses* (ed. Anderson) 2.680ff.

30 *lippis . . . cecucientibus*: See note to 3.85 below and introduction, 28.

33 *Maiugena* is Mercury's frequent appellation in Martianus Capella; see the index to Willis's edition, s.v.

39 *presagum*: *Presagatorem* would better parallel *prenosicicatorem* in the previous member.

45 *poronati*: See the note to 7.41 below.

82–97 Ovid, *Metamorphoses* 3.511–731.

83 For the form *Tioneus (*Tionei* . . . *Tioneo*), we can assume that Elias was misled by MS corruption in a passage such as Isidore of Seville, *Etymologiae* 8.11.44 (ed. Lindsay): "Iste [Liber] et Graece Διόνυσος a monte Indiae Nysa, ubi dicitur esse nutritus."

85 *nec lippos latet, luscosue nec tonsores*: by adding those blind in one eye (*lusci*), Elias overgoes Horace's account of Persius's vengeance on the outlaw Rupilius Rex, "omnibus et lippis notum et tonsoribus" (*Sermones* [ed. Garrod] 1.7.3).

89–90 *Pentheum . . . pertinacissimum*: According to Ovid (*Metamorphoses* 3.514), Pentheus was "contemptor superum."

90–91 *genialis . . . Bachus*: For Elias's phrasing here, and the epithet *Leneus* in line 88 above, see Ovid, *Metamorphoses* 4.11–14.

91 *macescens*: Cf. Ovid, *Metamorphoses* 3.607, where the kidnapped Bacchus is described as a boy with girlish figure ("virginea puerum ducit per litora forma").

98–151 Justinus, *Epitoma historiarum Philippicarum* 39.1.4ff. (ed. Seel, 269.10ff.).

117–22 According to Justinus 29.1.9 (270.1–4), Grypos (Antiochus, son of Demetrius Nicanor) had already been established as figurehead king by his mother after his father's death. Either Elias misread Justinus's statement that Ptolemy "mittit igitur ingentia Grypo auxilia" (29.2.3 [270.10–11]), or his manuscript of Justinus was corrupt.

126 *consensu . . . communi*: cf. 3.636 and 7.64 below. Elias also employs this phrase in his *De vita scolarium*, where he concludes a passage associating various virtuous pagans with the countryside (*rus*) rather than city by writing: "et, vt collectiue loquamur ad summam, suas reuera in rure sedes quasi consensu confederato communi omnes iam pridem posuere virtutes" (British Library, MS Arundel 11, fol. 175ʳ). We may either construe the phrase as hypallage ("allied common consent" for "[men] allied by common consent"), or take *(pre-)confederato* in the loose sense of "agreed upon." The use of *confederate* at 13.75 corroborates the latter interpretation.

129–31 *Sed . . . inedia*: The basic sense is clear from Justinus's account at 29.2.5 (270.18–20): "Ibi inops pecuniae, cum stipendia militibus dessent, in templo Iovis solidum ex auro signum Victoriae tolli iubet." Construe: *Sed ibi effectus inops pecunie sibi minus tempestiue, [et] male molestatus inedia, cum [Allexander] moraretur debita de more stipendia castrorum*, etc. ("But now having become destitute of the money no longer easily available to him, and sorely afflicted by hunger, when Alexander withheld the payments due by custom to his troops," etc.)

134 *[v]afreciis*: Cf. *vafrecias* (12.69). The classical form is *vafritia*.

134–35 *tyranni . . . Syracusani*: The Syracusan tyrant was, of course, Dionysius the Elder, who ruled from 405 to 367 BC. Cf. 13.79–113 below.

139–47 *Paucis . . . interfectus*: Texerii begins a new sentence at *denique* (146), but continuing the same sentence provides a finite verb for what precedes. It may be that another *est* has fallen out of the phrase *magnaque subsequenter vi tempestatis oppressus* (143–44).

144–45 *Iouisque . . . inmanitatem*: Elias adds to Justinus here, transforming a story of the Fall of Princes variety into a tale of divine vengeance, as befits Philip's argument in this passage. The two causes of Alexander's downfall embody in miniature Elias's two basic styles: a relatively straightforward narrative style (*magna . . . vi tempestatis* [143–44]) and a convoluted style for comment or reflection (*Iouisque . . . inmanitatem*).

148 *ingratus [est]*: sc. *hominibus [et] numinibus* (150–51).

149 *compendiario*: "sc. *iter*" (OLD). Cf. Seneca, *Epistolae morales* 73.12 (ed. Reynolds, 1.223.13).

152–80 Justinus 1.9.1ff. (12.24ff.).

152–55 *Cambisis . . . ulcionem*: Construe: *Memorat vetustatis auctoritas . . . ulcionem diuinitatis mote per iniurias criminis Cambisis cachynnabilis commisi in iniuriam Hamonis*. For the objective genitive of the person upon whom vengeance is taken with *ultio*, see note to 2.89–90 above.

164–67 For an analysis of this passage, see above, 39.

169–70 *Nempe . . . vidisset*: Justinus 1.9.4–5 (12.29–13.1) makes it clear that this was a dream.

170–72 *hec . . . procurante*: Again Elias, or his speaker Philip, adds divine causation to Justinus's strictly historical account, as also at 176 below.

171 *facillitas*: While CL *facilitas*, "indulgence; excessive clemency," would make sense here, the doubling of the *ll*, the similar phrase *facillantis ingenii* (4.455), and Texerii's *f/v* confusion elsewhere suggest that we should take *facillitas* as equivalent to *vacillitas* (from *vacillo*) or "wavering inconstancy."

172–73 *vehementer . . . non formidauit*: It is possible that *vehementissime* is intended as a correction for *vehementer*, but given Texerii's care elsewhere to underline deleted words, we may conclude that Elias intended a chiastic arrangement of adverbs and verbs in this line.

176 *paricidas . . . manus*: *Paricidas* is better taken as an adjective than a noun in apposition. Although the form is unattested, corruption from *paricidales* is unlikely.

187–88 The MS reading *confortunalium*, while unattested, may stand. Its sense would be "sharing the same fortune or prosperity." But emending to *consortium* might yield better sense in the context of Cambyses's parricide.

188 *genialiterque consimilium*: Perhaps Elias means "those related by marriage," but "products of the same marriage bed" seems more likely in context. For Genius, see below 10.56 and note.

191–275 Justinus 2.10.2ff. (30.9ff.).

198 *naues . . . numero*: The consensus of MS classes used by Seel in his edition of Justinus reads "naues quoque decies centum milium dicitur," which yields no acceptable sense. In his second edition, Seel adopts Ruehl's emendation, based on the account given by Orosius, *Historiae aduersum paganos* 2.9.2 (ed. Zangemeister, 45.29–30): "naues quoque rostratas mille ducentas, onerarias autem tria milia numero habuisse dicitur." His details indicate that Elias follows Justinus rather than the more summary account of Orosius here, but Elias seems to have used a MS of Justinus which at this point preserved a notice of the three thousand cargo ships mentioned by Orosius but already missing from the MSS used by Seel.

208 *connexa*: *conuexa* ("concavities"), the reading in Justinus, would yield better sense. But Seel does record the reading *connexa* from his D (= Vat. lat. 1860; s. xiv.).

216 *angustias*: The pass is, of course, Thermopylae; Justinus 2.11.2 (31.15–16).

218 *prehabita ... pugna*: The earlier battle was Marathon (490 BC).

227–33 *Sed ... vniuersa*: According to Justinus, this was on the fourth day of fighting, after the Persians had occupied the heights above the pass.

249–50 *dum ... condiducunt*: Cf. 228–29 above, which is closer to Justinus's original (2.11.6 [31.26]): *plura patrie quam vitae deberi*.

253 *se proficisci*: OLD offers no examples for reflexive forms of *proficiscor*.

275–86 Justinus 2.12.8ff. (33.11ff.).

281–82 *debitas ... penas preinfligente*: Again the divine causation is Elias's addition to Justinus.

291–92 *perniciter est ... pungnatum*: Cf. Caesar, *De bello Gallico* 1.26.1 (ed. Du Pontet), "Ita ancipiti proelio diu atque acriter pugnatum est."

292–342 Justinus 2.13.1ff. (35.1ff.). According to Justinus, the intimate (*familiaris*) was Mardonius.

303 *parte*: *parte maiore* would better suit Justinus's account.

308 *bellissime discretus ... quidam*: Sc. Themistocles, Justinus 2.13.6 (35.14).

335–37 *dierum ... ingerebat*: The sense in Justinus is rather different (2.13.12 [36.4–5]): "Multorum deinde dierum inopia contraxerat et pestem." For *dies* as "a day's provision of food," see the *index verborum*.

343–53 Justinus 3.1.1ff. (39.1ff.).

343–44 It is Hercules, the implied subject of *prosequeretur*, who crowns Xerxes's injustice with the murderous misdeed of Artabanus and not Xerxes himself.

349 Justinus gives the prefect's name as Artabanus.

354–80 Justinus 20.2.3ff. (168.29ff.).

381–89 Valerius Maximus, *Facta et dicta memorabilia* 1.1.17 (ed. Kempf 9.11–20).

381–82 *detracte religioni sue ... perhibetur exegisse penam*: It is tempting to emend to *religionis*, which is in accord with classical usage and the reading in Valerius, but the MS reading *religioni* is surely authorial and shows again the dative encroaching on the genitive (see note to 2.89–90 above).

390–97 Valerius 1.1.18 (9.21–24).

397 *ut ... securus*: Sc. *esset*.

398–408 Valerius 1.1.19 (10.1–13).

402 *Doleret* agrees with *dolens* in Kempf's *deteriores* and fills the lacuna in his principal MSS.

403–4 *manifestis ... viribus*: Here the divine causation is supplied by Valerius.

406–8 *superstitibusque ... redintegraret*: This passage was probably a crux in Elias's MS of Valerius, as it is in ours. I take *arbores superstites* as the subject of *habuera[n]t*.

408 *Redintegraret*, while it may not be what Valerius wrote, makes better sense than Kempf's *dis multiplicauit* or the other *lectiones* he supplies.

409–545 Justinus 24.1.8ff. (193.3ff.).

471 *quod*: Although Seel prints *quid* here, five of his MSS read *quod*.

482–84 *Ioue ... vindicta*: Justinus (24.3.10 [195.4]) attributes vengeance on Ptolemy to the *diis immortalibus*.

489–90 *auguriis ... premonstrantibus*: "ducibus avibus," Justinus 24.4.3 (196.13).

528–29 *gallorum ... gloriancium*: From Seneca, *Apocolocyntosis* 7.3 (ed. Eden, 40.20–21), echoed by *Petronius rediuiuus* 100 (219). For the medieval circulation of the *Apocolocyntosis*, see Eden's edition, 20–21, and L. D. Reynold's article in *Texts and Transmission*, ed. L. D. Reynolds, 361–62. Colker, *Analecta Dublinensia*, 245, notes that this saying is cited by William of Malmesbury and appears as entry 10154 in Hans Walther, *Proverbia sententiaeque latinitatis Medii Aevi*, 2:215. A pun on the two senses of *gallus* ("rooster" and "Gaul") is intended in the *Apocolocyn-*

tosis and *Serium senectutis* but not in the other works, which would suggest that Elias knew Seneca's work directly.

546–673 Justinus 24.6.1ff. (197.3ff.).

550–51 *Dux ... Brennius*: According to Justinus, Brennus was in Greece while the Gauls under Belgius defeated Ptolemy. He led a successful raid on Macedonia in an attempt to win himself a share of the booty from the prior engagement. Elias conflates Belgius and Brennus so as to tighten the chain of human transgression and divine vengeance which binds together Ptolemy and Belgius-Brennus.

563–65 *Est ... conueniunt*: Elias probably worked from a MS of Justinus which was defective at this point. The full text of Justinus reads: "Templum autem Apollinis Delphis positum est in monte Parnasso, in rupe undique inpendente; ibi civitatem frequentia hominum fecit, qui admiratione maiestatis undique concurrentes in eo saxo consedere." But "inpendente ... undique" are omitted by Seel's MSS groups τ and ι (11 of 19 MSS).

572 *solus acciderit aduenticius*: Seel's reading, which he bases on MSS classes τ and ι, makes better sense: "accedit tubarum sonus." But he cites a variant "accidit turbarum sonus" from his C (= Laurentianus 66, 21) which points us in the direction of Elias's lone wanderer.

591–92 *ducibus ... duobus*: Justinus gives the names of the two partners as Aenianus and Thessalorus.

594 The delay in question was to have lasted for one night: "Igitur Brennus cum in conspectu haberet templum, diu deliberavit, an confestim rem adgrederetur an vero fessis via militibus noctis spatium ad resumendas vires daret" (Justinus 24.7.1 [198.15–18]).

617 *verpo*: that is, his middle finger. See Huguccio, *Magnae derivationes*, s.v. *digitus*: "Tertius [digitus] medius uel impudicus, quia per eum probri insectatio exprimitur. Idem et uerpus a uerrendo podicem. Percussit enim [Deus] Iudeos in posteriora et obprobrium sempiternum dedit eis. Nam singulis annis in crucifixione Domini emittunt sanguinem per posteriora, que cum medio reponunt et [uerrunt] eo digito podicem. Et inde uerpus dictus est quasi [uerrens] podicem. Vnde ille digitus adhuc ostenditur obprobrium in Iudeis, quoniam si ali[c]ui Iudeo ostenderis nunquam te postea diliget. Hinc Iuuenalis: medium quia ostendere unguem. Hoc faciebat Democritus [fortune]; scilicet pretendebat ei medium digitum in obprobrium, sicut fit Iude[i]s, per hoc eam contemptibilem esse ostendit. Et hinc est quod uerpus inuenitur pro Iudeo; uidelicet Iuuenalis: quod si cum est ad fontem soles deducere uerpos; id est Iudeos glosandum est" (p. 113). Cf. the identical account in Balbus, *Catholicon*, s.v. Why Elias attributes such a gesture to Brennus is not clear. Perhaps he means to suggest no more than a generalized obscenity.

674–92 Valerius 1.1.20 (10.14–11.8).

684–86 *Quin ... recepisset*: According to Valerius, at the same time as he learned of one son's death, Fulvius learned that the other had been severely injured: "alterum decessisse, alterum grauiter audisset adfectum" (1.20 [10.20–21]).

693–705 Valerius 1.1.ex.1 (11.9–17).

713 *censende*: The various punishments of the two previous sentences (*penalitates ... puniciones ... vindictas ulcionumve varietates*) serve as implied subject here.

715–18 *contumaciter ... officiis*: The severe ellipsis which makes the syntax if not the sense of this passage difficult to follow is unusual, since Elias elsewhere bases his style on consistent elaboration. Texerii treats 716–18 (*res ... officiis*) as a separate sentence, but its infinitive verbs (*coniungere ... addicere*) are dependent upon *valeant* (714).

735–36 *vota ... matrimonialia*: This is a strange phrase, but almost certainly authorial, as it finds a deliberate echo at 4.60–61 below: *desideria ... ad contubernalia*. Construe: *liguam uel animum velle migrare ad vota matrimonalia*, and similarly below. Such a reading is supported by 3.738–39.

736–38 *Conueniens ... conuenienti*: Philip's point, as the next sentence makes clear, is that tongue and mind are not well suited to each other.

747–48 *ut mores habent ... consuetudine*: We can take this as evidence for Elias's long career as a writer before composing the *Serium senectutis*.

756–58 *aut ... paginas*: Horace, *Ars Poetica* 333–44.

Book Four

32–33 *rudem ... memoriam*: See note to 2.28–29 above.

42ff. Cf. 3. 730ff. above.

80ff. For similar discussions by theologians of figurative language in secular and scriptural poetry, see Minnis, *Theory of Authorship*, 139–45.

91–94 *quam ... colloquio*: The reference here is to the Song of Songs (especially 1.1) and its allegorical interpretations.

104 *agni stantis in monte*: Apc. 21.

106–8 *quo ... osculum*: Construe: *quo sponsus, coniunctionis dulcedine ... contactus adeoque salutaris, pacis interuenire faceret et oris osculum. Vtraque faciens vnum* ("conjoining the two") is parenthetical.

113–14 *Quia ... fragranciora*: Ct. 1.1–2 (Vulgate: Quia meliora sunt ubera tua vino, Fragrantia unguentis optimis).

128–29 *Ciuitatem ... ornatam*: Apc. 21.2 (Vulgate: sicut sponsam ornatam viro suo).

132–33 *Sponsus ... iusticiaque*: Os. 2.19.

138–39 *Tota die ... dolum*: Ps. 51.4.

141 *Ligua ... iusticiam*: Ps. 34.28; 70.24 (Vulgate: iusticiam tuam).

142 *Os ... sapienciam*: Ps. 36.30.

143 *Protector ... mee*: Ps. 17.3.

144 *Deus ... virtute*: Ps. 17.33.

144–45 *Beatus ... paruulos*: Ps. 136.9 (Vulgate: parvulos tuos).

145–46 *Ligna ... plantauit*: Ps. 103.16 (Vulgate: saturabuntur ligna campi et cedri Libani).

152–53 *te ... submurmurandum*: The subjunctive is potential; cf. 4.431–33.

162–73 *Tota ... asserenti*: Elias's readings of these verses from Psalms are derived from the *glossa ordinaria*. The reading of this verse is based on the *glossa marginalis ad* Ps. 51.4 (*Biblia Latina cum glossa ordinaria*, 3:467ᵛ): "COGITAUIT. Cassiodorus: Leuis mens, preceps dictio non ante cogitat quam loquatur, unde Solomon: In ore stultorum est cor eorum." The quotation from Solomon is Sir. 21.29.

168–70 *qui ... diiudicari*: Elias has claimed in 165–67 that the Psalmist meant Ps. 51.4 to imply a criticism of hasty and unconsidered speech; in 170–73, he follows the *glossa ordinaria* in concluding that David agrees with Solomon, Sir. 21.29, that "the heart of fools is in their mouth." By transposing *qui ... preexaminatum* (168–69) so it appears before *Ligue ... diiudicari* (169–70), we supply an antecedent for *qui* (*perperam circumspecti*, [167]) and clarify the logic of the paragraph. Construe: *Ligue vel oris officium pre cogitatu sanissime censetur diiudicari ridiculum esse.*

174–80 *Talium ... cogitatu*: *Glossa interlinearis ad* Ps. 51.4 (*Biblia cum glossa,*

3:467^v): "COGITAUIT. Augustinus: Si non potest facere, loquitur saltem malum, et si hoc nequit, cogitat."

180 We might wish to emend *Quid* to *Cui*, although doing so would not alter the sense significantly.

181–82 *Sicut . . . facilitate: Glossa interlinearis ad* Ps. 51.4 (*Biblia cum glossa*, 3:467^v): "SICUT NOUACULA. Augustinus: ita expedite."

183–89 *Sequitur . . . testamenti: Glossa marginalis ad* Ps. 34.28 (*Biblia cum glossa*, 3:452^r): "ET LINGUA MEA. Cassiodorus: Lingua eius meditata est iusticiam quando nouum testamentum populis predicauit."

188–89 *cuius . . . testamenti:* Alternatively, "His tongue is said to have meditated justice in preaching a saving God and the New Testament."

190–91 *Subinde . . . instruccionem: Glossa interlinearis ad* Ps. 36.30 (*Biblia cum glossa*, 3:454^r): "ET LINGUA EIUS LOQUITUR IUSTICIAM. Instructioni aliorum quid deus precepit tenere vel fugere." I preserve the substitution of *sapienciam* for *iusticiam* (141 above) as possibly authorial.

194–96 *Subicitur . . . amandata: Glossa marginalis ad* Ps. 17.3 (*Biblia cum glossa*, 3:434^v): "PROTECTOR. Augustinus: Quia de me non presumpsi quasi cornu superbie contra te erigens, sed celsitudinem salutis inueni quod vt inuenirem suscepisti me."

197–202 *Subsequitur . . . intellecta: Glossa interlinearis ad* Ps. 17.33 (*Biblia cum glossa*, 3.436^r): "PRECINXIT. Augustinus: Ne fluentes sinus cupiditatis impediant gressus, id est bona opera."

199–202 *quo . . . intellecta:* Grammatically, the concord is held suspect; logically, the belt is. Perhaps we should take this as hypallagy.

203–27 *Subinde . . . apparencia: Glossa marginalis ad* Ps. 136.9 (*Biblia cum glossa*, 3:554^v): "BEATUS QUI TENEBIT. Augustinus: Quam retributionem, ut babylonia natos in mundo dum parui sunt parentum et seculi suffocat erroribus. Ita quod iam iuuenes data agnitione dei paruulos babylonis elidunt, id est, nascentes cupiditates antequam robur accipiant sic facilius vincuntur, sed et maiores ad petram occidende sunt."

208 *ad . . . allidit: Glossa interlinearis ad* Ps. 136.9 (*Biblia cum glossa*, 3:554^v): "AD PETRAM. Christum."

224–26 *beatitudinis . . . inconueniencia:* Elias's characteristic refusal to say just what specific objections Philip might raise to Ps. 136.9 complicates the task of construing this phrase. I read: *inconueniencia beatitudinis [cum] perempcione propriorum paruulorum* ("the incompatibility of beatitude with the slaughter of one's own children"). A less drastic emendation of the manuscript reading *improperiorum* would yield *improperium*, which Elias uses elsewhere only with an appositive genitive and not a subjective genitive (see *index verborum*).

240–44 *Saturabuntur . . . contumaces: Glossa interlinearis ad* Ps. 103.16 (*Biblia cum glossa*, 3:517^v): "SATURABUNTUR LIGNA CAMPI plebes, humiles prius ET CEDRI, scilicet diuites, scilicet potentes in seculo, etiam postea quia prius electi sunt contemptibiles [contentibiles *ed.*] et ignobiles quam sapientes et nobiles."

244 *nobilitateve vana contumaces:* Should we detect here a gesture towards Elias's *Contra nobilitatem inanem*? For the notion that virtue and not birth provides the only true basis for nobility, see George McGill Vogt, "Gleanings for the History of a Sentiment: *Generositas virtus, non sanguis*," and Marvin L. Colker, ed., "De nobilitate animi," 47–49.

245 *Libani . . . candidati: Glossa interlinearis ad* Ps. 103.16 (*Biblia cum glossa*, 3:517^v): "LIBANI candidacio interpretatur QUAS fide PLANTAUIT." Cf. "Laban candidus," in Jerome's *Liber interpretationis Hebraicorum nominum*, ed. de Langarde, p. 68 and passim. For the availability of this work in the thirteenth century, see Rouse and Rouse, "*Statim invenire*," in *Renaissance and Renewal in the Twelfth Century*, ed. Robert L. Benson and Giles Constable, 221.

256–57 *Namque ... maritas*: Martianus 1.1 (1.7).

260–61 *presertim ... examinares*: Elias does not normally use *examino* transitively; however see 11.53, 12.45, and 12.79, where he uses passive forms. But the sense here ("judge" rather than the customary "examine") seems strained. Perhaps we should retain the manuscript reading *vicium non fore* and emend *examinares* to *hesitares*. However, that would force us to supply another infinitive, as *attribuere* is surely part of the phrase *ligamina ligaminum vicibus attribuere*.

270–73 *vicibus ... producuntur*: Cf. Remigius *ad loc.* (68.13–17); Alan of Lille, *De planctu Naturae* 8.50–52 (ed. Häring, 834).

274–77 *Sed ... exicat*: Cf. 1.80–84 above. The absence in the third clause of an object equivalent to *progenita* and *matura* in the first two and the resultant treatment of Saturn as object suggest that our text is corrupt at this point. Perhaps read: *dum grauia Saturni brumalis sub turbulenciis exiciat*.

282–85 *seminudum ... Cillenium*: Martianus 1.5 (3.20–22): "ac iam pubentes genae seminudum eum incedere chlamidaque indutum parva, invelatum cetera, umerorum cacumen obnubere sine magno risu Cypridis non sinebant."

298–99 *eloquencie ... prelatum*: Cf. John of Salisbury, *Metalogicon* 4.29 (195.16): "Mercurius, eloquentie presul"; also *Policraticus* 2.19 (1.109.5).

299 *discussorem*: One is tempted to emend to *discursorem*, "outrider," especially in light of Martianus 1.5 (3.18–19), describing Mercury's young body as "palaestra crebriusque discursibus exercitum," and Remigius's commentary *ad loc.* (74.18–19): "CREBRIS DISCURSIBUS nam ipse est cursor deorum."

307–9 *nudus ... utraque*: *Metalogicon* 4.29 (195.21–23). John also alludes to Mercury's naked buttocks at *Entheticus de dogmate philosophorum* 217–18.

312–17 Martianus 1.8–9 (5.15–24).

317 Elias's mistaken notion that Mercury's *petasus* ("broad-brimmed hat") was a form of winged sandal comes from Remigius's *Commentum* (82.27–31) *in Martianum* 1.9 (5.24–25). Elias also found the notion that Mercury's sandals are, or should be, silver in Remigius's *Commentum* (82.29–31): "Melius autem dixisset argentea talaria; aurum enim ad puritatem sensus, argentum ad eloquii refertur claritatem."

322–23 *contemplandamque ... subintelligendam*: Sc. *racionem*.

324 *Volatilem ... annexam*: Remigius (82.15) *in Martianum* 1.9 (5.21–22).

325–26 *sermonis et eloquencie ... deus*: Cf. the preface to Remigius's *Commentum* (66.22–23): "Philologia ergo ponitur in persona sapientiae et rationis, Mercurius in similitudine facundiae et sermonis."

334–36 *Nempe ... apposite*: Remigius *ad loc.* (82.19–20).

338–40 *quo ... velocitatem*: Remigius (82.27–31) *in Martianum* 1.9 (5.23–24).

346–49 *summitas ... vltimo*: Mythographus Tertius, ed. Bode, 1.215.39–216.1. The Third Mythographer attributes this to Remigius, but it is not to be found in his *Commentum in Martianum*.

349–54 *Sic ... gratia*: Remigius *ad loc.* (82.15–18).

355–65 Martianus 2.142 (44.2–8). For the sense of this passage, which Willis labels "obscurissimus," see the commentary of Luciano Lenaz, *Martiani Capellae de nuptiis Philologiae et Mercurii liber secundus*, 17–19, 75–77.

361–62 *nec Vedium ... igne*: See the textual note for a passage from Martianus which is lacking from the manuscript but is assumed by Elias in the discussion which follows.

371 *Inmortalitatis*: Elias substitutes the Latin equivalent for Athanasia; cf. Remigius (173.18) *in Martianum* 2.134 (42.2): "HUIC ATHANASIAE NOMEN FUIT. Athanasia Grece, Latine immortalitatem sonat."

377–79 *Reuera ... intrinsecam*: For help with the proper sense and construction of this passage, see 4.394–401. There, Elias first states what he anticipates will be Philip's objections, with the main verb in the imperfect subjunctive (*causari presumeres*) as throughout this book. Then Elias suggests, as an unreal past condition, how Philip's judgment would have been improved by considering the author's underlying intention; the verbs of both protasis and apodosis are pluperfect subjunctive. Most likely, 4.377–85, which is one sentence in Texerii's copy, should be three. Elias would then first rebuke Philip's infatuation. Then, in a conditional clause which has lost its apodosis, he would explain how Philip could do better. Finally, he would explain the proper sense of the passage in question. Note also that Elias places apodosis before protasis only in his verse and nowhere else in his prose. *Fuisses* (*fueris* S) in line 378 seems to stand in for the imperfect subjunctive *esses*, which Elias nowhere uses, so as to avoid hiatus.

380 *racionis amor ... uel sapiencie*: Isidore, *Etymologiae* 2.24.3: "Ipsud autem nomen [philosophiae] Latine interpretatum amorem sapientiae profitetur." Cf. Remigius 66.20 on Philology as "amor vel studium rationis" (repeated by Mythographus Tertius, 9.1 [1.213.40]), and John of Salisbury's account of the three sisters Philology, Philosophy and Philocaly, *Metalogicon* 4.29 (196.7–15).

385–86 *purgacio ... consecracio*: Cf. Remigius (177.13–15) *in Martianum* 2.140 (43.9–13): "APOTHEOSIS deificatio vel consecratio interpretatur. Quae bene mater est Athanasiae quia purgatio mater est immortalitatis."

403–14 Elias's exegesis of this whole passage depends heavily on Remigius *ad loc.* (178.26–179.24).

429–35 The general sense here is clear enough: Elias expects Philip to object to the notion that eternal life can be achieved through death, so he forestalls the objection by arguing that remedies (one thinks of modern vaccines) often use the ailment they are meant to cure to achieve their effect. But the passage seems unusually corrupt, and my piecemeal emendation may obscure larger lacunae.

454–55 *cornei ... ingenii*: Cf. 2.28–29 and note above.

460 Construe *eorum* with *confederacionem* (463) rather than *examine* (460).

Book Five

11–16 For Zambri and his slayer Phinees, see Nm. 25.

17–18 For Dathan and Abyron, see Nm. 16.

19–22 For Mariam, see Nm. 12.

48–50 *Reuera ... impetitus*: Echoes Juvenal 3.288–89, cited by Alan of Lille, *De planctu Naturae* 2.153–54 (814) and *Petronius rediuiuus* 107 (221).

Book Six

13 The marginal rubric *prosa hec Responsus* will alert us to an unannounced change of speakers between the previous book (Philip) and this book (Elias).

14 *Senio ... confecto*: Cf. *De disciplina scolarium* 6.27 (132.2). For *silicernium* as "drybones," see Terence, *Adelphi* 4.2.48.

17–18 *Epithalamicis ... cantilenis*: Cf. 1.44 above.

20–21 *sermonum ... sesquipedalitates*: Horace, *Ars Poetica* 97.

23–26 Elias now proposes to write in the low style. For the *genera dicendi*, see

Rhetorica ad Herennium 4.8.11 (ed. Caplan, 252–55) and Servius's accessus to the *Aeneid* (Harvard Edition, 2.4.81–83), cited by Minnis, *Theory of Authorship*, 15, 49. The standard work is F. Quadlbauer, *Die antike Theorie der genera dicendi.*

27–38 For legislation on dowry (*dos*) and dower (*donatio propter nuptias*), see Gregory IX, *Decretales* 4.20 (ed. Friedberg, 2.725–30), De Donationibus inter Virum et Uxorem, et de Dote post Divortium Restituenda. Notice that the letters of Innocent III in columns 726–30 treat the *dos* in its earlier Germanic sense of a marriage gift from husband to wife.

39–44 Peter Lombard, *Sententiae* 4.28.1.4 (ed. Brady, 2.433.3–14): "Illi etiam sententiae, qua dictum est solum consensum facere coniugium, videtur contraire quod Evaristus Papa ait: 'Aliter legitimum non fit coniugium, nisi ab his qui super feminam dominationem habere videntur et a quibus custoditur, uxor petatur, et a parentibus sponsetur, et legibus dotetur, et a sacerdote ut mos est benedicatur, et a paranymphis custodiatur, ac solemniter accipiatur'.... Hoc autem non ita intelligendum est, tamquam sine enumeratis non possit esse legitimum coniugium, sed quia sine illis non habet decorem et honestatem debitam." Cf. Gregory IX, *Decretales* 4.1.1 (2.661): "Matrimonium solo consensu contrahitur, nec invalidatur, si consuetudo patriae non servetur. EX CONCILIO TRIBURIENSI. De Francia nobilis quidam homo nobilem mulierem de Saxonia lege Saxonum duxit in uxorem, tenuitque eam multis annis, et ex ea filios procreavit. Verum quia non eisdem utuntur legibus Saxones et Francigenae, causatus est, quod eam non sua, id est Francorum lege desponsaverat, vel acceperat, *vel dotaverat*, dimissaque illa aliam superduxit. Diffinivit super hoc sancta synodus, ut ille transgressor evangelicae legis subiciatur poenitentiae, et a secunda coniuge separetur, et ad priorem redire cogatur." (My italics.) On this whole subject, see Brundage, *Law, Sex, and Christian Society*, especially 114 on the status of the dowry in Roman law before Justinian and 275 on its treatment by the decretists of the second half of the twelfth century.

43 *liberis ex eo natis*: Gratian, *Decretum* 2.32.4.15 (ed. Friedberg, 1.1131): "Liber dicti sunt, qui ex libero matrimonio sunt orti." Cf. Gregory IX, *Decretales* 4.17 (2.709–17), Qui filii sunt legitimi.

44–49 *Honeste ... coniunctorum*: *Honestate* may go with either *firmatum* or *est, eritque.* The translation assumes the former.

46 *ipsorum consensu*: For the central role of consent in medieval theories of marriage, see Gratian, *Decretum* C.27, q.2 (1.1062): "Sunt enim nuptiae siue matrimonium uiri mulierisque coniunctio, individuam uitae consuetudinem retinens.... Fuit enim inter eos consensus, qui est efficiens causa matrimonii, iuxta illud Ysidori: 'Consensus facit matrimonium,'" and Gregory IX, *Decretales* 4.1.1 (2.661): "Matrimonium solo consensu contrahabitur." Cf. idem, 4.1.25 (2.670); Peter Lombard, *Sententiae* 4.27.3 (2.422–23) and 4.28.3 (2.434–35). Brundage, *Law, Sex, and Christian Society*, 235–38, distinguishes between a French model of marriage based on consent and an Italian model based on consent and consummation; their major exponents are the Lombard and Gratian respectively. For later emphasis on consent, see Brundage, 333–35, 352–55, and John T. Noonan, Jr., "Power to Choose."

48 *condicione ... et die remocius amandatis*: Gregory IX, *Decretales* 4.5.1 (2.682): "Defectus turpis conditionis, in contractu matrimonii appositae, non vitiat matrimonium, sed vitiatur. EX CONCILIO AFRICANO. Quicunque sub conditionis nomine aliquam desponsaverit, et eam postea relinquere voluerit, dicimus quod frangatur conditio, et desponsatio irrefragabiliter teneatur." Cf. idem, 4.5.6 (2.683).

65–69 Cf. Gaius, *Institutes* 2.193–96 (ed. de Zulueta, 1.120–22); Justinian, *Institutiones* 2.20.8, 31 (ed. Krueger, 1.23, 25).

75 The standard medieval account of Hymenaeus was provided by Servius, *in Aeneida* 1.651 (Harvard ed. 1.276–77) and, more fully, 4.99 (Harvard ed., 2.286–87); it was repeated by all three Vatican mythographers: 1.74 (ed. Kulcsár 33), 2.263 (287–88); 1.75 (ed. Bode, 1.26.17–35), 2.219 (1.148.9–36), and 3.11.3 (1.229.3–230.12). According to this euhemeristic account, Hymenaeus was a young Athenian of humble origins who won his noble beloved by rescuing her and the maidens who accompanied her from pirates who abducted them on their way to the Eleusinian mysteries.

77 Genius figures below at 10.56 as the progenitor of each human soul; see Horace, *Epistulae* 2.2.187–89 and Nitzsche, *The Genius Figure*, 15–20. However, it was customary to consider Hymenaeus, if not a mortal Athenian, the son of Venus and Bacchus (Servius, *in Aeneida* 4.127 [Harvard ed. 2.294] and Mythographus Tertius 11.2 [1.229.35–37]). Hymenaeus is the husband of Venus and father of Cupid in Alan of Lille's *De planctu Nature*, where he delivers Nature's summons to Genius. In lieu of any source naming Genius as the father of Hymenaeus, we may speculate that Elias has conflated confused memories of Servius and Alan.

79 Hermaphroditus was the son of Venus and Mercury: Ovid, *Metamorphoses* 4.285–308. While the general sense of this passage is clear enough—Elias refuses to be carried away by his own fictions—it is not easy to make sense of in detail. The hedonistic mother of Hermaphroditus is Venus, the mother of Hymen (see the note to 6.75): does Elias mean to refer twice in different terms to Venus for the sake of emphasis, or should we emend the ultimate clause to refer to Hermaphroditus's father, Mercury? The latter might be thought to shatter Elias's controlling fiction of Mercury as god of eloquence, but by twice offering accounts critical of Mercury's deception by Battus and subsequent revenge Elias shows that he is neither blind to Mercury's faults nor unaware of the limits of fictions.

90–93 *Remocius . . . sonitus*: Elias's renunciation of the Muses draws its inspiration from the scene in which Philosophy banishes them from the sickbed of Boethius at the beginning of the *Consolation*, 1 pr. 1 (ed. Bieler, 2.23–3.3); for verbal parallels, see Martianus 2.117 and 127 (33.16–19 and 40.20).

Book Seven

1–2 *Seria . . . ludis*: The contrast between serious matters and games (*seria ludo*) is commonplace in classical literature; cf. Vergil, *Eclogae* (ed. Mynors) 7.27; Horace, *Sermones* 1.1.27, *Ars poetica* 226. Also John of Salisbury, "Entheticus in Policraticum" (ed. van Laarhoven) 95–96. For medieval background, see Glending Olson, *Literature as Recreation in the Later Middle Ages*. For the mixture of seriousness and sport as a hallmark of the Menippean genre, see the introduction above, 32.

6 *odiosa senectus*: Elias varies a frequent formula; cf. Ovid, *Tristia* (ed. Owen) 3.7.35.

8 *pigra . . . etas*: Cf. Horace, *Sermones* 2.2.88; Vergil, *Aeneis* 9.610; Ovid, *Metamorphoses* 10.396.

10 *virtutis opus*: Lucan, *Bellum ciuile* (ed. Housman) 7.381; Statius, *Thebais* (ed. Garrod) 8.421.

20–24 Cf. Gratian, *Decretum* 32.2.12 (1.1123): "Nuptiarum autem federa inter ingenuos sunt legittima, et inter coequales. . . . Itaque aliud est uxor, aliud concubina."

22–23 *personis . . . comparatis*: For unequal social status (*conditio*) as a ground for annulment, see Peter Lombard, *Sententiae* 4.30.1.1-2 (2.437-38) and 4.36.1-3 (2.473-74).

24–25 *tabule . . . commercium*: Cf. the Lombard, *Sententiae* 4.27.3 (2.423.10-12), quoting Chrysostom's Sermons on Matthew: "matrimonium quidem non facit coitus, sed voluntas," and Justinian, *Codex* 5.17.11 (ed. Krueger 2:213): "non enim dotibus, sed adfectu matrimonia contrahuntur." On the relation of affection to consent (6.39-44 and note), see John T. Noonan, Jr., "Marital Affection in the Canonists."

31 There seems to be a gap in the text here. Elias's opening paragraph on marriage belongs with the full treatment of that topic in the preceding book; of the three stories he now tells to exemplify divine vengeance on human lies, two (Battus and Mercury, and the scouts sent to the Promised Land) have already been recounted by his interlocutor, Philip (cf. 3.29ff. and 2.181ff. above). In fact, Elias does not so much retell the two tales here as allude to them while expounding their moral content.

31 *venerande vetustatis*: Lucan 9.987, 10.323.

35 *ad restringendas mendaciorum laxitatis habenas*: Cf. Vergil, *Aeneis* 12.499; Walter of Châtillon, *Alexandreis* (ed. Colker) 2.371; Alan of Lille, *De planctu Naturae* 12.149, 18.113 (857, 877); John of Salisbury, *Policraticus* 7.25 (2.219.11-13), "Entheticus in *Policraticum*" 227; Geoffrey of Vinsauf, *Poetria nova* 111.

37–53 Ovid, *Metamorphoses* 2.680-707.

41 *aratorque peronatus*: Persius 5.102, cited by John of Salisbury, *Policraticus* 7, prologue (2.91.12).

54–76 Nm. 13.

81–116 Dn. 13.

81–82 *tam lippis eciam quam tonsoribus*: see note to 3.85 above.

90 *veraci vetustate*: true (*verax*) inasmuch as this story comes from the Old Testament rather than a pagan source.

122–23 *os . . . animam*: Sap. 1.11 (cf. Ps. 5.7), cited by Augustine, *De mendacio* 6 (254).

Book Eight

46 *anime de situ uel existencia*: Although Philip promises to speak of the location or existence of the soul, the passage from Macrobius which follows concerns its nature or composition.

58–80 Macrobius, *Commentarii in somnium Scipionis* 1.14.19-20 (ed. Willis, 58.30-59.12).

76–78 *Uirgilius . . . ymago*: Elias's own addition to Macrobius's list, from *Aeneis* 6.730 (with *ymago* for *origo*).

81–85 *Verumptamen . . . consenciunt*: Macrobius, *Commentarii* 1.14.20 (59.12-13). The rather strange logic by which this claim about the philosophers' agreement on the immortality and incorporeality of the soul follows immediately upon claims that it is composed of blood, earth, fire and water is to be attributed to Macrobius, although Elias accepts the juxtaposition without comment.

87–93 Cf. Vincent of Beauvais, *Speculum naturale* 23.62-74 (1695E-1703D).

94 *Ramnusie*: Nemesis was styled Rhamnusia or Rhamnusia virgo because she was worshipped at Rhamnus in Attica (cf. Ovid, *Metamorphoses* 3.406).

96 Man's *donum speciale* is, as Philip announces in the next sentence, his superior intelligence.

98–110 Vincent of Beauvais, *Speculum naturale* 21.2 (1560B) offers a different list: "quaedam audacia vigent, vt leo, *quaedam astutia, vt serpens,* quaedam mansueta vt vacca, quaedam iracunda vt aper, *quaedam cito domesticantur,* vt elephans, et quaedam etiam hominibus applaudunt vt canis."

120–31 Cf. Vincent of Beauvais, *Speculum naturale* 23.26 (1670E), citing Hugh of St. Victor, *Liber de spiritu et anima*: "Sensum quidem et imaginationem cum ceteris animalibus communia habemus, vident siquidem visibilia, et visorum recordantur. In quibusdam etiam sensibus nos superant, quoniam iustum fuit, vt quibus nihil dandum erat in intellectu, aliquid amplius daretur in sensu. Et econtrario tanto maior necessitas inducitur homini exercendae rationis, quanto maiorem defectum patitur sensualitatis. Ratio autem inde incipit, vnde aliquid occurrit, quod nobis cum animalibus non sit commune."

135 *archigenes*: Juvenal thrice mentions a fashionable physician named Archigenes. Elias uses the name here as a generic term for physicians.

141–44 *Reuera ... fidelissimus*: The phrase "ut et alias scripsi" is strange, inasmuch as Philip is speaking here and not the author Elias. There is nothing in the *Petronius rediuiuus* or the surviving fragments of Elias's other works which corresponds closely to the claim advanced here.

145–52 For a more orthodox discussion of why bodily injury can cause the soul to cease from intellectual activity, see Vincent of Beauvais, *Speculum naturale* 23.39 (1679B–D), citing Avicenna and Algazel as sources.

152–57 *Corporis ... prerogatiua*: Cf. Vincent of Beauvais, *Speculum naturale* 23.27 (1671E): "Si vero magnitudo corporis magnipenda esset, plus nobis saperent elephanti" (repeated at 23.31 [1674A]).

Book Nine

19–20 *Dei ... substancias*: Elias replies definitively to this claim that there may be more than one god at 11.175ff.

20–22 *Euandau*: Charles Burnett suggests that this might be Abraham Ibn Dāūd, the Spanish-Jewish philosopher of the mid-twelfth century. Ibn Dāūd may be the same person as the Avendauth who collaborated with Dominicus Gundissalinus on translating portions of Avicenna's *Shifā'* into Latin. For Ibn Dāūd's life and works, see M. T. d'Alverny, "Avendauth?" However, I am unable to find this quotation in their translation of Avicenna, *Liber de anima* (ed. van Riet), or Gundissalinus, *De anima* (ed. Muckle), which is based on it.

39–45 *Deus ... illuminacionum*: Asclepius 23 (Nock-Festugière, 325.6–10); Augustine, *De civitate Dei* 8.23 (ed. Dombart and Kalb, 1.355.9–12).

46–55 *Species ... temperarios*: Asclepius 23 (325.20–326.8); not in Augustine.

46–47 *Species ... sumit*: For the source and a possible explanation of the peculiar syntax here—*Species* governs a singular verb (*sumit*) but agrees with a plural pronoun (*quas*)—see Nock's apparatus *ad loc.*

56–58 *statuas ... subicientes*: Asclepius 24 (326.11–15); *De civitate Dei* 8.23 (1.355.19–23).

59–62 *Terrenis ... simulachro*: Asclepius 37 (348.8–10); *De civitate Dei* 8.26 (1.365.21–23).

61 *videlicet ... angelo*: This gloss on the text of the *Asclepius* contradicts the account offered at the beginning of this paragraph (9.48–49 above) of the two natures, divine and mortal, conjoined in created gods. It does, however, agree with Augustine (1.365.23–25), who glosses the two natures as body and soul, which is to say daemon and statue. Not all of Elias's citations from the *Asclepius* appear in *De* *civitate Dei*, but the verbal parallel here should clinch the case that Elias worked from Augustine as well as the *Asclepius*.

66–69 Ex. 32.

85–89 3 Rg. 12.28–30.

90–97 3 Rg. 11.1–8.

109–10 *fimbrias . . . dilatauit*: Cf. Mt. 23.5.

113–20 Ovid, *Metamorphoses* 15.626–744.

114 *Mercurius*: Elias's confusion of Mercury and Aesculapius here may have its root in a misreading of Augustine's account of the *Asclepius* (*De civitate Dei* 8.26 [1.365.3–7]): "Ecce duos deos dicit homines fuisse, Aesculapium et Mercurium. Sed de Aesculapio et Graeci et Latini hoc idem sentiunt; Mercurium autem multi non putant fuisse mortalem, quem tamen iste avum suum fuisse testatur."

121–31 Elias could have found accounts of Apis in the First Vatican Mythographer (= Remigius of Auxerre?), chap. 78 (ed. Kulcsár, 34–35); chap. 79 (ed. Bode, 1.27.28–41), Solinus, *Collectanea rerum memorabilium* 32.17–21 (ed. Mommsen, 158.17–159. 21), Pliny, *Natural History* 8.184–85 (ed. and trans. Rackham, 3.128–29), Isidore, *Etymologiae* 8.11.85–86, and Vincent of Beauvais, *Speculum doctrinale* 17.10 (1556C). The first two offer the most verbal parallels, but none provides a source for Apis's apotheosis (*in aere leuabatur*). The image of Apis appearing from a stream also does not appear in these authorities but might arise from a medieval reinterpretation (of the type studied by Panofsky in *Renaissance and Renascences in Western Art*, 87–100, albeit not informed by any christianizing tendency) of the killing of the bull representing Apis in a sacred well, as described by the First Mythographer, Solinus, and Pliny.

Book Ten

15ff. Elias begins his reply to Philip's twin claims that the human soul is not immortal and that there is not one omnipotent God.

42–50 For syzygies, see Remigius (67.26–68.10) *in Martianum* 1.1 (1.7). For a different discussion of the mean uniting body and soul, see Vincent of Beauvais, *Speculum naturale* 23.44–48 (1682Eff.).

56 For Genius as god of generation, see Remigius (118.8–10) *in Martianum* 1.49 (18.17): "GENIUS deus naturalis qui omnium rerum generationibus praeest. Genios enim dicimus qui singulis nascentibus tribuuntur" (repeated with attribution by the Third Mythographer, 1.185.1–5). Remigius also treats Genius as a moral voice or type of conscience (119.31–32), and as a tutelary spirit (184.4–14, *in Martianum* 2.152 [46.14–20]).

67–72 *Sic . . . Israeliticis*: Texerii copied this sentence without a main verb, which I have supplied by deleting *quo* before *progredi* (67) and construing the subjunctive *pergamus* (67) as potential. However, as *quo progredi pergamus* is one of Elias's favorite formulae for introducing purpose clauses, my sense is that a main clause has fallen out of the sentence after the two purpose clauses (*quo . . . pergamus, ut . . . procuremus*). Note also the gap in the sense between this sentence and that which follows.

77–118 3 Rg. 17.

112 *Ionas . . . propheta*: The notion that the boy revivified by Elijah became the prophet Jonah derives from Jerome's Prologue to Jonah: "Sanctum ionam hebrei affirmant filium fuisse mulieris vidue sareptane quem helias propheta mortuum suscitauit, matre postea dicente ad eum: Nunc cognoui quia vir dei es tu, et verbum dei in ore tuo est veritas" (*Biblia cum glossa*, 4.935ʳ).

121–70 4 Rg. 2; 4.8ff.

127 *propter cultus edicularum*: Cf. Petronius, *Satyrica* 85.1 (ed. Müller and Ehlers, 174.18–19).

171–84 4 Rg. 13.20–21.

199–209 Macrobius, *Commentarii* 1.1.9 (3.16–24): "Sed ille Platonicus secretorum relator Er quidam nomine fuit, natione Pamphylus. . . ." It is easy to see that Elias's mistaken notion that Er and "Pamphilus" were two different people has its germ in this passage, but it is hard to see how he could have made the mistake by misreading only these lines.

213–19 Cf. Servius, *in Georgica* 1.166 (ed. Thilo-Hagen, 3.1.171.10–14): "ET MYSTICA VANNVS IACCHI. . . . hinc est quod dicitur Osiridis membra a Typhone dilaniati Isis cribro superposuisse: nam idem est Liber pater . . . quem Orpheus a gigantibus dicit esse discerptum." This account is repeated by the Second Vatican Mythographer, chap. 114 (ed. Kulcsár, 184); chap. 92 (ed. Bode, 1.106.26–32). Cf. Mythographus Tertius, 12.5 (ed. Bode, 1.246.5–8): "habet fabula, Gigantes Bacchum inebriatum invenisse, et discerpto eo per membra, frustra sepelisse, et eum paulo post vivum et integrum resurrexisse."

230–36 *Asclepius* 37 (347.20–348.3); *De civitate Dei* 8.26 (1.364.20–26). This sentence likewise lacks a finite verb in its source.

239–50 *Ad Lucilium epistolae morales* 86.1 (ed. Reynolds, 1.297–98).

249 *deesse*: Although Reynolds prints *esse* in his edition of Seneca, he records *deesse* as a variant in his class δ = BN latinus 8658A and 8539.

266–70 Jo. 11.

281–91 Mt. 9.18–26.

295–311 Lc. 7.11–17.

Book Eleven

14 *Tale . . . subsidere*: Construing the infinitive *subsidere* as the object of *Solari* (15) is a desperate remedy, but otherwise it is hard to preserve either the sense or the meter of the line.

32–35 *Fere . . . viuentes*: Cf. Milton, *Paradise Lost* 9.41–46, and the preface to book 2 of *The Reason of Church Government* (ed. Haug, p. 814).

86–91 Ambrosiaster on Romans 1.19 (CSEL 81.88) *apud* Peter Lombard, *Sententiae* 1.3.1.2 (ed. Brady, 1.69.10–14).

106 *Quicquid . . . aut accidens est aut substancia*: The Old Logic provided ample precedent for dividing all that is into substance and accident: cf. Aristotle's *Categories* 1a20–1b10, 1b25–2a4, 2a34–2b6, Isidore, *Etymologiae* 2.26.10–11, as well as Boethius, *De trinitate*, 4, where Boethius discusses God in terms of the Aristotelian categories and concludes that while normal predications are called *accidentia secundum rem*, predications made of God are named *secundum substantiam rei praedicatio* (ed. and trans. Stewart et al., pp. 24–25). I am grateful to Professor Eleonore Stump for these references.

For a metaphysical rather than epistemological framework more in keeping with Elias's treatment here ("sumatur et hic accidens habundancius quam sumi consueuit in logica" [108–9]), see: *Physics* 242a50–243a31, 256a4–21, 256b21–25, 258b10–11, 259a14–15; *Metaphysics* 1007a21–b18 (cf. Avicenna, *Liber de philosophia prima*, 2.1 [ed. van Riet, 1.65.13–66.23]), *Metaphysics* 1034a31, 1034b16–18, 1045b28–29, 1072b10–12, 1072b26–31. However, perusal of these passages in either the old or new Latin versions printed in *Aristoteles Latinus* will convince any reader that, despite his claim to use the real Aristotle, Elias did not follow any of these passages directly.

For more direct verbal echoes, see Alfarabi, *De ortu scientiarum* (ed. Baeumker, 17.5–6): "scias nihil esse nisi substanciam et accidens et creatorem substantiae et accidentis benedictum in saecula" (cf. idem, 17.19–21 and 22.33–34); Gundissalinus, *De processione mundi*: "si est aliquid, aut substantia aut accidens" (Beiträge 24.3; cited by Sharp, *Franciscan Philosophy at Oxford*, 66); and Gundissalinus, *De anima* 2 (ed. Muckle 37.13): "Item [Plato] quicquid est, aut est substantia aut accidens."

107–8 *preponatur accidenti ... substancia*: Aristotle, *Metaphysics* 1069a18–21 (*Aristoteles Latinus* 25.2.204.3–6): "De substantia quidem theoria est. Nam substantiarum principia et cause queruntur. Et enim si ut totum quoddam omne, substantia est prima pars; et si deinceps, et ita primum substantia, deinde qualitas aut quantitas." Cf. Algazel, *Metaphysica* 1.1.1 (ed. Muckle, 5.13–14): "prima divisio esse est in substantiam et accidens" (repeated at 2.1.1 [130.3–4]); Avicenna, *Philosophia prima* 2.1 (1.66.21–23): "unde substantia est constituens esse accidentis, nec est constituta ab accidente; igitur substantia est praecedens in esse." Robert Kilwardby, *De ortu scientiarum*, chap. 26 (ed. Judy, 82.6–9): "Cum enim quantitas sit accidens, in subiecto est, substantia ex necessitate. Sed illa substantia, cum sit prior quantitate et mobili secundum quod huiusmodi, nondum nota est per physicam neque per mathematicam."

108–10 Cf. Alfarabi, *De ortu scientiarum* (23.4–7): "Existens autem per se est id quod vocatur substantia.... Quod autem est non per se existens, est id quod vocamus accidens." Sten Ebbesen suggests that Elias's discussion of the broad and narrow senses of substance, with his distinction between *per se subsistere* and *accidentibus substare/subsistere*, may derive ultimately from Boethius's *Opuscula* (see note to 11.106 above), most likely by way of discussions of the Trinity in theological *quaestiones* on Peter Lombard. For example, in discussing the Boethian definition of "persona," Stephen Langton writes: "Item, aut ponitur ibi [sc. in Boethius's definition] substantia prout est vel significat genus generalissimum in primo praedicamento, aut prout purificatur huic termino 'res per se existens' " (Cambridge, St. John's MS C 7, fol. 188[ra]). Notice that Elias's proofs of God's unique omnipotence begin, at 11.86ff., from the Ambrosiaster as cited in an important passage early in the Lombard's *Sentences*.

110–12 Isidore, *Etymologiae* 2.26.11: "Substantia autem dicitur ab eo, quod omnis res ad se ipsam subsistit." Huguccio, *Magnae derivationes*, "Unde hec substantia quia substat accidenti" (50). Balbus, *Catholicon*, s.v.

112–17 Cf. Gundissalinus, *De scientiis*, ed. Alonso, 128–29: "Tertio vero pars [scientiae divinae] inquirit de essentiis, que nec sunt corpora, nec in corporibus. De quibus in primis inquirit, an sint essentie, an non. Et demonstratione probat quod sunt essentie. Deinde inquirit de eis, an sint plures, an non. Et demonstrat quod sunt plures. Postea inquirit an sint finite, an non. Et demonstrat quod sunt finite. Deinde inquirit an ordines earum in perfectione earum sint equales, an inequales. Et demonstrat quod inequales. Deinde probat quod ipse secundum suam multitudinem surgunt de minore ad perfectiorem et ad prefectiorem, quousque perveniunt ad postremum perfectum, quo perfectius nihil esse potest, nec in esse potest ei aliquod simile, nec equale, nec contrarium, usquequo pervenitur ad primum, quo nihil potest esse prius, et ad precedens quo nihil potest esse magis procedens, et ad esse quod impossibile est adquiri ab alia re; et quod illud esse est unum absolute, precedens et primum."

120–33 Aristotle, *Metaphysics* 1007a33–b18 (*Aristoteles Latinus* 25.2.69.1–19); cf. idem 993a30–994b31 (*A. L.* 25.2.36.2–39.24). Avicenna, *Philosophia prima* 8.1 (2.376–81). See van Riet's edition, 1.164*–66* for variants from a manuscript dated circa

1240 which belonged to Richard of Fournival. For the existential thrust of Avicenna's proof, see Michael E. Marmura, "Avicenna's Proof from Contigency," 337–52.

134–39 Aristotle, *Metaphysics* 1035b14–21, 1036a14–25: the parts of the soul are prior to the concrete animal. Algazel *Metaphysica* 1.1.5 (37.8–9): "Quod autem pars sit prior suo toto in tempore manifestum est."

139–41 Above, 11.106ff.

146–60 Algazel discusses human self-knowledge in the context of divine self-knowledge at *Metaphysica* 1.3.2 (64.9–20). For a contemporary proof which ascends to an eternal creator by way of cognition, see Kilwardby, *De ortu scientiarum*, chap. 26, esp. 82.24–28.

161–74 Anselm, *Proslogion* 2–3 (ed. Schmitt, 1.101.1–103.11). Elias states Anselm's central proposition but seems singularly incapable of developing it into a logical proof. Clearly, Elias approaches philosophy as a writer and grammarian, not a logician.

177–85 Cf. *Metaphysics* 1072b10–13.

193–215 Cf. 11.74–83 above. For similar disclaimers by other *compilatores*, see the many references assembled by Minnis, *Theory of Authorship*, 191–99, and for the compiler's own contribution to such works, *Theory of Authorship*, 200. An important discussion not mentioned by Minnis but known to Elias is John of Salisbury, *Policraticus* 1, prologue (1.16.4–17.20).

230–34 *vt eciam ... destinatus*: Since Texerii treats this clause as a separate sentence, it may be that the main clause upon which it depends has fallen out of the text. But Elias surely did not mean it to describe the fate of one who asserts the immortality of the human soul (*anime ... humane ... assertor*, 234–35) as it does in the manuscript. Better to read it as a result cause following from *ni ... preelegeris* (229–30) and developing the fate of one so foolish as to deny the soul's immortality.

Book Twelve

58–59 *concessam ... dominacionem*: Gn. 1.28.

71 *sit*: I supply the verb, but we may preserve the manuscript reading by taking it as understood.

90–92 *Nempe ... subsidium*: Ecl. 4.10.

Book Thirteen

8–14 Lc. 16.13.

41–42 *Ecce quam bonum ...* : Ps. 132.1 (Vulgate: *habitare*).

66–106 Valerius 4.7.ex.1 (207.20ff.).

67 *in udo*: Cf. 1.53 above.

Appendices

Appendix 1. Elias's Cotland

De Cotariis[1]

(220^r) Theobaldus Birihewen tenet unam cotariam, et debet qualibet ebdomada per totum annum duas operaciones, et tassabit bladum domini sine operacionibus; et si tasset per totum diem[2] integrum, tunc habebit ad uesperum unam garbam de blado quod tassauerit; et triturabit /220^v/ uigintiquatuor garbas frumenti uel triginta garbas[3] ordei et auene pro una operacione; et habebit unam legiam straminis; et debet seminare in quadragesima totam terram domini et habere ad uesperum tres pongnatas eiusdem bladi quam seminauerit; et debet metere pro una operacione die lune dimidiam acram, et die ueneris unam rodam, et ligabit set non carriabit; et fatiet unum quartam brasei, et triturabit dimidiam quartam auene ad prebendam domini; et debet aueragium sine equo. Et sciendum quod debet sarclare per totum diem integrum pro una operacione.

Helyas le mastre tenet unam cotariam eodem modo.

Walterius Porcarius tenet unam cotariam eodem modo. Ailwinus longus tenet unam cotariam eodem modo. Willelmus filius Alani tenet dimidiam cotariam per dimidium servicium et consuetudines.

Sciendum quod quidam predictorum consuetudinariorum moriatur femina sua dabit de Herieth sexdecim denarios. Et debent esse quieti de operacionibus in Natali, in ebdomada Pasche, in ebdomada Pentecoste, et Die sanctae Parasceue et in quolibet die cuius vigilia Ieiunata.

Theobald Birihewen holds one cotland, and owes two days' labor every week for the entire year, and will stack the lord's corn besides the day-works; and if he stacks continuously for an entire day, then he will receive at dusk one sheaf of the corn which he stacked; and he will thresh twenty-four sheaves of wheat or thirty sheaves of barley and oats for one day's labor; and he will have one leas of straw; and he must sow all the lord's land during Lent and receive at dusk three handfuls of the same corn as he sowed; and he must reap half an acre on Mondays for one day's labor, and one-quarter acre on Fridays, and he will bind it but not carry it; and he will make a quarter of malt and thresh a quarter of oats for the lord's fodder; and he owes carrying service without a horse. And be it known that he must hoe for an entire day as one day's labor.

Elias the master holds one cotland under the same conditions.

Walter the pigman holds one cotland under the same conditions. Alwin Long holds one cotland in the same way. William son of Alan holds half a cotland by half the service and customary dues.

---

[1] British Library, Cotton Tiberius B. ii, fol. 220^{r-v}. I am extremely grateful to Dr. Chris Lewis for checking and correcting my transcription of this document.

[2] MS *deletes* annum *before* diem.

[3] MS *adds* frumenti ... garbas *in margin*.

Be it known that when one of the said customary tenants dies, his widow shall give 16d. as heriot. And they ought to be quit of works at Christmas, in Easter week, in Whit week, and on Good Friday, and on any day of which the vigil is a feast.

Appendix 2. Elias and the "Petronius Rediuiuus"

The main implications of the *Petronius rediuiuus* for understanding Elias of Thriplow's life and works have been addressed in the introduction to this edition. The purpose of this appendix is to outline the evidence for Elias's authorship of that work. Readers seeking further discussion are directed to an article on this topic by Marvin Colker.[4]

There are, to begin with, a number of lexical similarities between the *Petronius rediuiuus* and the *Serium senectutis*, the only work by Elias to survive intact with attribution. Among the words cited by Colker in the *index uerborum uel significationum inuisitatiorum* to his edition of the *Petronius rediuiuus*, the following appear in the *index verborum* to this edition of the *Serium senectutis*: *diovolaris (diobolaris)*, *diovolariter*, *edictaliter*, *preconfederato* and *promptificare*. Colker's index also lists *arans (sensu uenerio)*, which occurs at *Serium senectutis* 5.11. With *caduceatrix*, which also occurs in Colker's index, compare *caduceator* and *caduceatores* (*Serium* 2.285, 4.352).

Among the words which Colker notes are repeated particularly often in the *Petronius rediuiuus*, *coniectura* and *indifferens* appear in my *index verborum*.[5] Almost all the other words noted by Colker appear frequently in the *Serium senectutis* as well: *coniectare* (*Serium* 3.165, 423, 446–47, 523, 4.285, 312, 7.98, 9.123, 10.139, 11.93), *coniecturaliter* (2.215, 4.365–66), *consternatus* (1.32, 3.172, 204, 271, 318, 576–77, 594), *consternatio* (8.82), *feruens* (3.745, 10.268), *indifferenter* (1.70, 2.333, 3.262, 451–52, 4.482, 8.88–89, 9.104, 10.309, 11.31, 40, 50, 12.80, 13.90, 96, 97–98), *petulans* (2.131, 4.477), *petulanter* (7.85), *petulcus* (5.13), *sagax* (3.21, 492, 525, 4.7, 11.78–79), *sagacitas* (8.98, 143, 9.78, 103), *sagaciter* (3.40, 317 [*sagacissime*], 607, 7.60, 10.163), *subtilis* (1.124, 2.343, 4.423, 8.112, 135, 12.70, 85), *subtilitas* (2.333, 3.114, 116, 315, 316, 689, 7.109, 8.111, 116, 10.239, 11.99 [twice], 101, 105, 209, 213), and *subtiliter* (2.344, 3.39, 4.438, 10.314, 11.131, 12.47). Notice also *subtilius* (*Serium* 2.334, 4.323, 8.111, 116, 10.107).

Among words not mentioned by Colker but frequent or striking in both works, we might note:[6] *c(a)ecutire* (*Pet.* 44, 150; *Ser.* 3.30, 4.326), *commilito* (*Pet.* 1, 71, 89, 106, 107; *Ser.* 10.207 [cf. *commilitans*, *Ser.* 10.207]), *communiter* (*Pet.* 23; *Ser.* 1.94, 3.542, 621, 11.38, 52, 67, 187, 231–32), *efferatus* (*Pet.* 5, 18, 133; *Ser.* 10.104, 161), *exaudire* (*Pet.* 20, 71; *Ser.* 2.72, 76, 5.31, 44, 10.81, 85, 117, 285), *exinanire* (*Pet.* 21, 22, 34, 38, 60, 132; *Ser.* 3.268, 10.75–76), *prepropere* (*Pet.* 50; *Ser.* 2.320–21, 3.219), *subinferre* (*Pet.* 20; *Ser.* 3.239, 241, 298, 4.64, 10.307), and *tritum* in the sense of

---

[4] Colker, "New Light," 200–209. Although Colker read the dissertation on which this edition of the *Serium senectutis* is based, he and I have worked independently and without sharing our conclusions in any but the most general terms.

[5] See *Petronius rediuiuus*, ed. Colker, 187 for documentation.

[6] I cite the *Petronius rediuiuus* by paragraph and the *Serium senectutis* by book and line throughout.

"trite" (*Pet.* 29, 51, 147; *Ser.* 1.106, 2.204, 3.30, 85, 7.26, 39, 54, 8.38, 10.30, 62, 11.257, 12.86, 13.135). As the following shared words appear in the *index verborum* to this edition, I give references only to paragraphs in the *Petronius rediuiuus*: *consuetudinaliter* (88), *consuetudinarius* (34), *genialiter* (77), *inexorabiliter* (12), *priuilegiatus* (65), *promptificare* (39), and *sompniculosus* (3, 13, 66, 157). Note also the shared legal terms: *assertor* (*Pet.* 162; *Ser.* 11.235), *astipulator* (*Pet.* 82; *Ser.* 1.132, 2.52, 78, 4.171, 12.97), and *contubernium* (*Pet.* 54, 87, 126; *Ser.* 7.22).

Next, we may note some similarities of word formation. Elias's fondness for verbs and participles beginning with *pre-* is extensively, albeit not fully, documented in the *index verborum* to this edition. In the *Petronius rediuiuus* we find *preadquisitum* (22), *preconceptum* (31), *predesiderato* (157), and *preinterposita* (95). However, the *Petronius rediuiuus* does not share the related fondness for verbs beginning with *con-* and *re-* which Elias displays in the *Serium senectutis*. Elias is also fond of adjectives and substantives terminating in *-iuum*. In the *Serium senectutis* we find *abanimatiuum* (3.58), *affectiuus* (12.77), *contemplatiuum* (12.67), *derogatiuum* (4.69), *effectiuum* (10.314), *excitatiuum* (3.570, 4.18), *festiuum* (3.460), *incentiuum* (2.298, 3.543), *incitatiuum* (3.753, 4.20), *infinitiuum* (1.104), *innuitiuum* (4.119, 8.43), *intempestiuum* (4.356), *motiuum* (4.388), *primitiuum* (8.100), *reclamatiuum* (11.226), *repetitiuum* (8.88), *subsecutiuum* (3.25), *tempestiuum* (12.91–92), and *transitiuum* (6.67). In the *Petronius rediuiuus* we find *extensiuum* (132), *extinctiuum* (31), *freqentatiuus* (96), *incentiua* (83), *optatiuum* (92), and *substentatiuo* (68). However, only *incentiua, -um* is common to the two lists, and the *Petronius rediuiuus* lacks the many derisive adverbs in *-iter* which do so much to set the tone of the *Serium senectutis*.

Next, we come to a group of words and phrases, mostly adverbial in function, which appear for the most part frequently in both works: *ad expediens* (*Pet.* 7; *Ser.* 2.65, 3.202, 4.202, 8.120, 11.75, 13.36, 77), *ad modum* (*Pet.* 78, 119; *Ser.* 2.360, 3.212, 303, 602, 4.467, 6.22, 7.119, 8.16, 9.71, 10.211, 11.225, 12.71, 13.31), *ad summam* (*Pet.* 24, 52, 54, 109, 154, 162; *Ser.* 2.346, 3.64, 343), *de facili* (*Pet.* 21, 29, 62; *Ser.* 1.116, 2.323, 3.187, 4.281, 312–13, 408, 420, 10.90, 12.83), *euestigio* (*Pet.* 22, 29, 57, 86, 99, 137; *Ser.* 1.61, 3.259, 594, 4.97, 258, 432, 8.15), *subsequenter* (*Pet.* 7, 9, 53, 58, 97, 98, 106, 114, 117, 130, 134, 140, 151, 161; see *index verborum* for use in the *Serium senectutis*), *uel in hoc* (*Pet.* 71; *Ser.* 2.35, 3.48, 260, 7.21), and *ut moris est* (*Pet.* 3, 16, 21, 44, 69, 97, 132, 142; *Ser.* 10.100).

Four shared phrases are particularly significant, as they echo classical sources. The first three, *naso uigilanti stertere* (*Pet.* 3, 125; *Ser.* 1.34), *nec ubi tu pulsas et ego uapulo, sane censetur esse pugna* (*Pet.* 107) or *pugnam probe committi serissime contingit, ibi pulsante dumtaxat impetitore, solus subsannabiliter vapulat impetitus* (*Ser.* 5.48–50), and *sub lodice* (*Pet.* 47, 79, 135; *Ser.* 1.75, 4.452, 6.79), derive from Juvenal, *Saturae* 1.57, 3.288–89, and 6.195 respectively. The fourth, *Quiuis suo superbit gallus in sterquilinio* (*Pet.* 100) or *gallorum more suis in sterquiliniis supreme glorianciun* (*Ser.* 3.528–29), derives from Seneca, *Apocolocyntosis* 7. These quotations are to be found in other medieval works.[7] But the appearance of all four in both the *Petronius rediuiuus* and the *Serium senectutis* constitutes strong evidence of shared authorship or, at the very least, shared sensibility and training.

Among many other shared phrases, the following seem particularly notable: *communi consensu (preconfederato)* (*Pet.* 42, 103; *Ser.* 3.126, 636, 7.64; this phrase also

---

[7] See commentary *ad loc.* for documentation.

appears in Whethamstede's *tabula* to the *De vita scolarium*), *esculentum poculentumque* (*Pet.* 27; *Ser.* 2.205, 3.604, 10.141–42), *fame perpetuitas* (*Pet.* 107; *Ser.* 3.755, 13.59 and related phrases at 3.494, 7.114, 11.43), *funditus infatuatus* (*Pet.* 43; *Ser.* 7.94), *gladio ... euaginato* (*Pet.* 124; *Ser.* 3.177), *matrimonialiter copulata* (*Pet.* 44, 47, 52, 146; *Ser.* 4.92 and related phrases at 1.72, 2.25, 3.450, 6.72–73), *membratim dilacerata* (*Pet.* 145) and *membratim discerptus ... letaliterque dilaceratus* (*Ser.* 10.216–17), *non ignarus* (*Pet.* 31, 44, 118; *Ser.* 2.296, 311), *sapiens quiuis* (*Pet.* 96, 102; *Ser.* 5.46 and related phrase at 9.3), *sub breuitate succincta* (*Pet.* 110; *Ser.* 7.89–90, 121–22, 11.105, 194–95, 13.63), and *sub sole (spirantes)* (*Pet.* 31, 92, 149, 152, 162; *Ser.* 1.71, 2.353, 3.286, 4.20, 482–83, 8.98, 134, 10.58, 298–99, 11.30, 104, 106, 231, 12.3, 15, 65, 72–73, 13.76, 136).

More extended phrases shared by or resembling each other in the two works include *bellice cladis indifferenter decurrunt ad remedium* (*Pet.* 108) and *bellice sibi cladis et confusionis peremptorie precipicium primiciare procurant* (*Ser.* 3.220–21), "*Predidicisse, frater,*" ait, "*si saperes, debuisiti*" (*Pet.* 43) and *quod si sensatum saperes predidicisse debuisses* (*Ser.* 1.65), *saluo recte loquendi modo* (*Pet.* 154) and *recti ... saluo sermonis scemate* and *recto ... oracionis tramite* (*Ser.* 3.720, 4.334–35), *si sanius saperet* (*Pet.* 160) and related phrases in the *Serium senectutis* (1.65, 4.28, 265, 472–73, 11.229–30, 237), *ut michi uidere uideor* (*Pet.* 154; *Ser.* 2.274, 3.33, 4.318, 9.121, 10.42–43, 12.73), and *ut sit ad unum dicere* (*Pet.* 150; *Ser.* 1.52, 6.27).

The two works share a number of characteristic grammatical constructions: *fatigatus* plus the ablative (*Pet.* 105, 109; *Ser.* 3.266, 667, 10.79–80, 159–60), *improperium* plus the genitive (*Pet.* 36, 154; *Ser.* 2.114, 3.334, 549–50, 8.118, 12.38), *male* modifying an adjective or participle (*Pet.* 20, 33, 81, 102; *Ser.* 2.34, 50, 81, 161, 167, 319, 3.19, 424, 521, 4.8, 152, 5.21, 7.38–39, 93, 98–99, 126, 8.1, 10.45, 13.78, 79), *more* plus a genitive plural (*Pet.* 37, 84, 95; *Ser.* 3.130, 272, 13.127), *non erubescere* plus a verb phrase (*Pet.* 151; *Ser.* 4.259, 370–71, 7.46–47, 10.20), and an adjective or substantive, frequently terminating in -*iuum*, plus *admiracionis* (*Pet.* 138; *Ser.* 2.349–50, 3.570, 4.17–18, 388, 8.81–82, 87–88, 10.310–11).

Besides this considerable mass of shared vocabulary, phrases and constructions, no reader could fail to notice the more general similarities of style, syntax, prose rhythm and versification shared by the *Petronius rediuiuus* and *Serium senectutis*. Indeed, Colker's remarks on style in his edition of the *Petronius rediuiuus* and those that appear above in the section of the introduction entitled "Language and Style" are virtually interchangeable.[8] Both works employ frequent *paronomasia* or *agnominatio* along with almost obsessive alliteration. Both separate adjectives and participles from the nouns and pronouns they modify. Both go to great lengths to avoid vowels in hiatus. Both tend to articulate several tenses of the copula at once (*Pet.* 15, 42, 92). Neither employs the *cursus*, and both restrict themselves to dactylic hexameters and elegiac couplets in their *metra*.

Nor will similarities elude us when we turn to matters of genre, subject and theme. Both works are *prosimetra*, although the *metra* are somewhat less conspicuous in the *Petronius rediuiuus* than they are in the *Serium senectutis*. Both works display a knowledge of theology and the two laws.[9] The defense of humor in

---

[8] See *Analecta Dublinensia*, ed. Colker, 183–86 and section 8 of the introduction to the present edition for documentation of the generalizations that follow.

[9] *Analecta Dublinensia*, ed. Colker, 185, and sections 2 and 6 of the introduction to the present work. Notice also, in this regard, the entry s.v. *malus* in Whethamstede's *tabula* to the *De vita scolarium*: "Infelicissimus malus est cuius factum malum sit exempli contempla-

paragraph 63 of the *Petronius rediuiuus*—"Ludicra qui spernit, qui non nisi seria querit, / Sero spei seruus sero timoris erit"[10]—sorts well with the entry for *fabula* in Whethamstede's *tabula* to the *De vita scolarium*: "Uaria fabularum ludicra et interdum commixta seriosa, vide libro quarto per totum."[11] The meter at the beginning of book 7 of the *Serium senectutis*, which follows and reflects a line of argument developed by the moral rigorist Philip, rejects *ludicra* as appropriate only to youth: "Ludicra ludenti iuueni sua sunt sibi menti, / Seria sola senis sunt conueniencia cordi."[12] But Philip himself characterizes the sort of moral fable he wishes Elias to write as a *ludicrum* (3.751), and the *Serium senectutis* as a whole conforms to the mock serious tone of Menippean satire, at least in its verbal exuberance and its mockery of paganism and other forms of ignorance.

We might infer from this evolving discussion of *ludicra* that if all three works are by the same author, the *De vita scolarium* and *Petronius rediuiuus* are earlier works and the *Serium senectutis* a later work. There is some other evidence to support such an inference. The *Petronius rediuiuus* and *De vita scolarium* share a virulent antifeminism which is little in evidence in the *Serium senectutis*, which instead devotes itself to the allegorical and legal defense of pagan hierogamies and especially the marriage of Philology to Mercury in Martianus Capella.[13] The *Petronius rediuiuus* and *De vita scolarium* also share an emphasis on rural virtue which is not apparent in the double retelling of the Ovidian story of Battus and Mercury or elsewhere in the *Serium senectutis*.[14] On the other hand, the *Petronius*

---

cione diucius duratiuum. Vnde Marcellus iuris consultus malum quamuis non animo puniendum tamen censuit ne res mali fieret in exemplo" (British Library, MS Arundel 11, fol. 174ʳ). The entries s.v. *iudex, ius,* and *lex* also contain legal material.

[10] *Analecta Dublinensia*, ed. Colker, 210.

[11] British Library, MS Arundel 11, fol. 172ᵛ.

[12] *Serium senectutis* 7.3–4. Note the internal rhyme in the hexameter line of both this couplet and that already cited from the *Petronius rediuiuus*.

[13] Pieces 7–9 of the *Petronius rediuiuus* all turn upon the alleged sexual insatiability and moral debility of women. Piece 12, a character sketch "De feminis," points the moral bluntly: "Ad tria principaliter suam queuis femina dirigit intencionem: ut caducum curet corpus et ornet, ut mares circumueniat, ut eis placens maribus uenerie succumbat" (ed. Colker, 233). Similar sentiments can be found in Whethamstede's *tabula*, s.v. *coniunx, femina, mechus,* and *vxor*. In fact, the similarity is close enough that the author's remark in paragraph 73 of the *Petronius rediuiuus*, "Atqui ut et alias asserere non formidaui, mas omnis rudissime delirat qui feminas ab errore per custodias . . . a furoribus per rationes auertere sperat" (ed. Colker, 213) may be a reference to the material which Whethamstede summarizes s.v. *femina* in this fashion: "De dolis feminarum ac fallaciis, vide libro quarto, prosis 7, 8, and 9 per totum" (MS Arundel 11, fol. 172ᵛ). However, the entries under *coniunx, mechus,* and *uxor* make it clear that Elias is concerned mainly with the wiles women use to excuse their illicit relations after the fact. And there is nothing in Whethamstede's *tabula* to indicate that the *De vita scolarium* contained the sort of obscene material, derived from Petronius, which is sufficient cause for the *Petronius rediuiuus* to lack any authorial attribution.

[14] Compare piece 14, "De ruricolis," in the *Petronius rediuiuus* with the entry s.v. *rus* in Whethamstede's *tabula* to the *De vita scolarium*. The former contains the author's claim that he himself was born to farmers: "De his [sc. ruricolis] profecto, non minus ut reor uerax quam libens assertor, assero, eoque libentior forte quod a talibus natiuam natus originem traho, quod inter homines sub sole soli uita uiuant minus uiciis abili" (ed. Colker, 234). The latter embellishes the theme of rural virtue with classical exemplars: "In rure vel nusquam sub luna lucet Lucrecie castitas, Semelis simplicitas, illaritas Cereris, sedulitas Penelopes.

rediuiuus and the three works which survive only in fragments do not show the acquaintance with academic philosophy and the new Aristotle, in however mediated a form, which has caused us to date the *Serium senectutis* as late as possible in Elias's career.[15]

Besides its understandable lack of an attribution to Elias or any other author, the *Petronius rediuiuus* does differ significantly from the *Serium senectutis* and the fragmentary works in at least two aspects. First, although the *Petronius rediuiuus* does use Suetonius as a source for its account of the death of Nero in piece 3, the bulk of its anecdotal material is medieval (for example, piece 5 on Robert Guiscard and his daughter) or even contemporary with the author (pieces 1 and 4). There is ample precedent for such anecdotes in Walter Map's *De nugis curialium* and John of Salisbury's *Policraticus*.[16] And we find similar anecdotes in the tabula to the *De vita scolarium*, s.v. Arthurus, where Arthur is treated as a just king,[17] and in the tale from the *Contra nobilitatem*, repeated at some length by Ringstede, of a British knight in Norway.[18] But all the other *exempla* in the two fragmentary works come from Roman literature and history, especially Valerius Maximus.[19] And it is Valerius and Justinus who supply virtually all the exemplary material for the *Serium senectutis*. Second, the *Petronius rediuiuus* displays an interest in businessmen and their need to deceive their customers in order to sell their goods which does not recur in the *Serium senectutis* and the other works attributed to Elias.[20]

Are there any borrowings from Petronius in the *Serium senectutis* and the lost works to match those in the *Petronius rediuiuus*? The only resemblance between the *Serium senectutis* and the *Satyrica* is merely verbal. *Propter cultus edicularum* (*ediculorum* S [10.127]) seems a fairly clear echo of *propter cultum edicularum* (*Satyrica* 85.1).[21] But Whethamstede's entry for *magister* in his *tabula* to the *De vita scolarium* reveals a more substantial indebtedness to Petronius. According to Whethamstede, the opening prose of the *De vita scolarium* argued the following:

> Cum delirantibus delirant hii magistri qui seueritati discipline derogantes nil legunt discipulis nilve dicunt nisi quod ipsi commendant ymmo vt adulacionibus placeant. Ad instar vilium viuunt parasitorum qui dum suis friuolis ad mensam diuitis procurant ingressum, eas solummodo vt hillariter excipiantur prolaturi sunt nugulas que placent (British Library, MS Arun del 11, fol. 174ʳ).

Inter ruricolas eciam viget prudencia Dedali, industria Tritoloni, Vlixis paciencia, Scipionis moderancia, Enee pietas, Herculis virilitas, sobrietas Romuli, fidelitasque Pompei" (MS Arundel 11, fol. 175ʳ).

[15] See sections 2 and 6 of the introduction to the present edition.

[16] *Analecta Dublinensia*, ed. Colker, 182.

[17] MS Arundel 11, fol. 171ᵛ.

[18] Oxford, Lincoln College, MS latin 86, fol. 198ʳᵇ–198ᵛᵃ.

[19] For example, the anecdotes concerning Calpurnius Piso, Pyrrhus of Epirus, and Mucius Scaevola recounted by Ringstede, *In proverbia Solomonis*, lectiones 121 and 131 (Lincoln College, MS latin 86, fols. 194ᵛᵇ, 207ᵛᵇ–208ʳᵃ). These anecdotes come, respectively, from Valerius Maximus, *Facta et dicta memorabilia*, 4.3.10, 7.3.14, and 4.1.11.

[20] See *Petronius rediuiuus*, paragraphs 25, 159–61 (ed. Colker, 200, 234).

[21] Petronius, *Satyrica*, ed. Konrad Müller and Wilhelm Ehlers (Munich: Heimeran, 1965), 174.18–19. This passage is preserved only by L (the augmented text of the sixteenth century). For the textual tradition of the *Satyrica*, see the edition of Müller and Ehlers, 381–430, and M. D. Reeve in *Texts and Transmission*, 295–300.

The thought, even more than the wording, here is extremely close to *Satyrica* 3.3–4 (10.27–12.5):

> sicut ficti adulatores cum cenas divitum captant nihil prius meditantur quam id quod putant gratissimum auditoribus fore (nec enim aliter impetrabunt quod petunt nisi quasdam insidias auribus fecerint), sic eloquentiae magister, nisi tamquam piscator eam imposuerit hamis escam, quam scierit appetituros esse pisciculos, sine spe praedae moratur in scopulo.[22]

There are no knockdown arguments here for Elias's authorship of the *Petronius rediuiuus*. But the cumulative weight of the evidence is considerable. If Elias did not write the *Petronius rediuiuus*, then whoever did must almost certainly have been known to our author. If Elias did write the *Petronius rediuiuus*, how does this new attribution alter our sense of the author and his other works? Perhaps most strikingly, the legal material, especially the material derived from civil law, in the *Petronius rediuiuus* brings into sharper focus the legal material in the *Serium senectutis* and *De vita scolarium*. And I think it makes the possibility that Elias had undertaken at least some formal legal studies something closer to a probability. Certainly, authorship of the *Petronius rediuiuus* would cause Elias's oeuvre to loom larger in bulk and importance, and that work's knowledge and use of Petronius would reinforce the sense we should already have from the *Serium senectutis* and the fragmentary works that Elias was widely read in classical literature and history. Finally, the obscene passages in the *Petronius rediuiuus* would give the presumably elderly author of the *Serium senectutis* a youth and frivolity which should increase his appeal to modern readers, even if the antifeminism of the *Petronius rediuiuus* and *De vita scolarium* tends in another direction.

Appendix 3. Corrections to the Manuscript not Recorded in the Textual Apparatus

The first group of corrections not recorded in the apparatus comprises Texerii's additions, deletions, and corrections while copying the text. He customarily marks with a pair of slashes (//) where additions are to be placed. He also uses the slashes to indicate deletions, although he more commonly expunctuates letters and underlines words to be deleted. Corrections are by expunctuation and superscription or by overwriting. All these corrections were made with the pen Texerii used to copy the surrounding text. 1.111 *del.* -ve *before* nec, 2.32 *ad.* -nauerit *in top marg.*, 2.48 *del.* moderacionem *before* moderatorem, 2.53 *del.* me *before* vanos, 2.78 *del.* astipulator *before* assertor, 2.144 *del.* fort- *before* fontis, 2.261 *del.* m[ur]m[ur]is *before* ordinarie, 2.292 *ad.* tam *in marg.*, 2.306 *corr.* decuerit *to* decuit, 2.328 *ad.* -ve *in marg.*, 2.353 *del.* preambulatione *before* preambulatorie, 3.25 *del.* principio *before* propinquo, 3.87 *del.* modus uel forma *before* superficialiter, 3.88 *corr.* inv- *to* infatuata, 3.129 *corr.* C[um] *to* Sed, 3.156 *corr.* Egipto[rum] *to* Egiptum, 3.179 *del.* tam *before* tempestiuissime, 3.189 *corr.* aspersnari *to* aspernari, 3.190 *del.* personarum *before* potestatum, 3.193 *del.* wlgatum *before* wlgaris, 3.251 *corr.* militum *to* milium, 3.255 *corr.* canaturi *to* cenaturi, 3.283 *del.* tumultuantibus *before* invndantibus, 3.300 *corr.* v- *to* euentus, 3.420 *corr.* sorores *to* sororis, 3.452 *corr.*

---

[22] This passage is preserved by L, O (the *excerpta vulgaria*) and Φ (the *Florilegium Gallicum*).

vocato *to* convocato, 3.471 *corr.* iubendo *to* nubendo, 3.491 *corr.* penetrant *to* penetrauit *in marg.*, 3.494 *corr.* lac- *to* laudisque, 3.509 *corr.* patrat[i] *to* patrarentur, 3.682 *ad.* subsequenter *after* pena, 3.745 *corr.* impericies *to* impericiis, 4.63 *del.* malo malum *before* congruo congruum, 4.114 *del.* et *before* sunt et, 4.169 *del.* me[n]dacii *before* meditacione, 4.225 *del.* pauidorum *before* paruulorum, 4.291 *ad.* sub *in marg.*, 4.405 *corr.* Proserpinam *to* Proserpina, 6.9 *ad.* tua *after* si, 7.53 *del.* secundum *before* vires, 7.79 *ad.* punicionis *after* mendaciorum, 7.90 *del.* wlgata (S^1 diwlgata) *before* wlgariterque, 7.92 *ad.* deambulans *after* pomerio, 8.14 *corr.* seni- *to* segnificare, 8.82 *corr.* i[ncitatiuum] *to* consternacionisque, 8.126 *ad.* ex *in marg.*, 8.139 *ad.* satis *in marg.*, 10.66 *corr.* argumentis *to* argumenta, 10.78 *ad.* tenui *in marg.*, 10.105 *del.* factus *before* sanctus, 10.109 *ad.* subsequenter *after* fudit, 10.185 *corr.* vereneranda *to* veneranda, 11.8 *corr.* et *to* scienter, 11.66 *corr.* ēciam *to* eciam, 11.69 *del.* feli-*before* perniciter, 11.106 *ad.* substancia *in marg.*, 11.107–8 *ad.* preponatur ... substancia *in marg.*, 11.115 *del.* m- *before* profecto, 11.199 *del.* autem *before* quidem, 12.37 *ad.* preiudicio *after* priuilegiata, 12.82 *corr.* morum *to* virorum *in marg.*, 13.10 *del.* cu[m] *before* eciam, 13.19–20 *ad.* Omnis ... pergens *in marg.*, 13.25 *del.* ne ridi[cu]lus *before* ridiculus ne, 13.41 *ad.* excederet *in marg.*, 13.50 *del.* Sic itaque *before* Reuera, 13.56 *corr.* sob- *to* sodalitatis, 13.75 *corr.* frequenter *to* frequencius, 13.81 *corr.* contempnandum *to* condempnandum, 13.86 *corr.* glorificatus *to* gratificatus, 13.120 *del.* factis *before* factus, 13.145 *ad.* variata *after* vili.

A second group of corrections not recorded in the apparatus has been made with a thin pen in a fluent hand here denoted by the siglum S^1. It is almost certainly Texerii's. Additions are by superscription and are usually marked by a caret. Deletions are marked by a slash, underlined, or crossed out. Corrections are by expunctuation and superscription. While these changes generally appear to have been made at the proofreading stage, some (e.g., that recorded at 9.49 below) may have been made during copying. At 7.91, S^1 corrects *wlgata* to *diwlgata* before the corrected word is deleted by Texerii as he copies the text. Here, at least, we have a correction by S^1 which was almost surely executed during copying rather than proofreading. 1.84 S^1 *ad.* et, 2.174 S^1 *ad.* sed, 2.282 adoracio] oracio *S*, 3.67 S^1 *ad.* in *before* inmutando, 3.147 et] est *S*, 3.149 S^1 *del.* et *before* ad, 3.216–17 preinuestigauerat] inuestigauerat *S*, 3.345 tamque] tam *S*, 3.347 quibus] qui *S*, 3.428 S^1 *ad.* quod, 3.596 vino] vno *S*, 3.618 directo] erecto *S*, 3.684 S^1 *ad.* per, 4.43 deteccionem] teccionem *S*, 4.310 S^1 *ad.* non, 4.446 commendacione] commendaciones *S*, 7.108 intelligenciam] indulgenciam *S*, 7.122 asseritur] asserit *S*, 8.93 S^1 *ad.* ad, 8.132 blandiatur] blandiat *S*, 9.49 versatur] versat *S*, 10.85 S^1 *ad.* ad, 10.274 S^1 *ad.* per, 11.72 S^1 *del.* est *before* admittit, 11.171 S^1 *del.* est *before* esse, 11.172 S^1 *ad.* uel, 12.66 mi] in *S*, 13.57 comproficiamus] proficiamus *S*, 13.65 valide] valde *S*.

Another group of corrections, marked with the siglum S^c, is by superscription and shows evidence of careful reading of Texerii's text. However, there is no compelling reason to think that these corrections arise from a comparison of the Sloane manuscript with another copy of the *Serium senectutis*. A number of these corrections (e.g., those recorded for 4.2, 4.176, and 10.46 below) are in a small, neat hand which closely resembles Texerii's. Others (e.g., 2.322) are in a shaky hand which does not. But I have not felt able to distinguish in every case between hands and have felt the less need to do so as most of these corrections are obvious and could have been supplied by any perceptive reader. Here it is only necessary to note the readings in Texerii's original hand which have been replaced by corrections in this group. 1.69 sinceritate *S*, 2.3 loquenda *S*, 2.70 contrarietas *S*, 2.70 inconcinnitatis *S*, 2.74 locutus *S*, 2.254 egssus *S*, 2.261–62

diminuerunt *S*, 2.314 Sensassime *S*, 2.322 indices *S*, 2.333 perpense *S*, 3.149
infatuassimi *S*, 3.216 angustas *S*, 3.230 parie *S*, 3.337 ingebat *S*, 3.409 illas *S*, 3.624
Dolio *S*, 4.2 ridicolosus *S*, 4.114 fragranciara *S*, 4.176 affectum *S*, 4.352 caducatores
S, 4.367–68 fastidisndo *S*, 4.399 procacitas *S*, 6.4 proferet *S*, 9.110 tange *S*, 10.46 fit
S, 10.286 affectui *S*, 11.30 homini *S*, 11.105 breue *S*, 12.77 affectus *S*, 13.75 invidens
S, 13.127 disiunctis *S*.

Another group of corrections which should almost surely be attributed to
Texerii, either during copying or proofreading, involves changes by expunctuation. The readings before correction are: 3.292 pungnantium *S*, 3.501 adicere *S*,
4.135 psalmistita *S*, 12.76 commendatorque *S*.

A similar group involves corrections by overwriting. The uncorrected readings
are: 1.50 mollis *S*, 3.2 de<r>ipiendo *S*, 3.243 suppicantibus *S*, 3.314 vincē *S*, 10.136
deorsum *S*, 10.166 elato *S*, 11.85 innicium *S*, 11.92 nulletenus *S*.

Another group involves corrections by erasure. While I have in every instance
accepted these corrections, I am less sure that they are by Texerii, who elsewhere
uses underlining or expunctuation to remove words or letters. 3.1 *eras.* suam
before mouet, 3.335 fame *S*, 3.594 consternatis *S*, 10.79 *eras.* expers *before* exceptus,
10.196 libeuerit *S*, 11.4 *eras.* mos *before* finali, 13.79 societate *S*, 13.131 sociales *S*.

A final, mostly miscellaneous group, contains those corrections which look
most likely to have been made by later readers. One subgroup involves erasure
and overwriting in a hand which is almost surely not Texerii's. 3.295 dimississo
S, 3.443 *ad.* secundam *in marg. and over eras.*, 4.318 videre] videtur *S*, 4.356
intempestiue *S*, 5.10 *ad.* interitum *over eras.*, 7.17 *del.* per *before* pergere.

I have also omitted from the apparatus some manifest slips of the pen and
faulty abbreviations. 1.32 effussa *S*, 1.90 adlatari *S*, 1.109 pmeruerit *S*, 1.121–22
pituram *S*, 1.122 dōloseve *S*, 2.23 excogitas *S*, 2.23 presuuas *S*, 2.24 sollepnitates
S, 2.192 pollubiliter *S*, 2.231 fanctissime *S*, 2.233 iure iure *S*, 2.298 rederelinquendi
S, 2.340 voluntaro *S*, 3.91 macescē *S*, 3.134 nafreciis *S*, 3.144 vi] in *S*, 3.166 vi] in
S, 3.221 subsequentur *S*, 3.244 commendalius *S*, 3.494 immortatalitatisque *S*, 3.569
ue … ue] ne … ne *S*, 3.569 potestiua *S*, 3.609 ue] ne *S*, 4.20 insolenue *S*, 4.24
inge/ *S*, 4.42–43 impicie *S*, 4.71 preeximianisses *S*, 4.81 exfrontus *S*, 4.162 soli-
loqus *S*, 4.184 incompetentur *S*, 4.236 subintēlligendum *S*, 4.255 meditats *S*, 4.297
Merculialis *S*, 4.318 aggarites *S*, 4.358 Philo/gia *S*, 4.425 menibus *S*, 4.448 consui
S, 5.1 sana] saa *S*, 6.48 ppetuitate *S*, 6.88 suffragarere *S*, 7.39 triuiliter *S*, 8.32
cachynnaliter *S*, 8.128 delectiones *S*, 9.18 p/phisicorum *S*, 9.75 de-/re *S*, 10.1 Uit
S, 10.55 pprie *S*, 10.83 farinnula *S*, 10.154 fellit *S*, 10.169 rediuinum *S*, 11.72
appropiatis *S*, 11.111 accidentilibusque *S*, 11.165 ratiocinacinacionis *S*, 11.190–91
vituperaliterque *S*, 13.31–32 vita viuentibus *twice S*, 13.99 suique sodalis *twice S*,
13.145 rennuant *S*.

Bibliography

1. Manuscripts

Bale, John. *Angliae descriptio et collectiones manu proprie*. London: British Library, MS Cotton Titus D. x. 2.

Cartulary of the Hospital of St. John the Evangelist. Cambridge: St. John's College.

Ely Coucher Book (1222). London: British Library, MS Cotton Tiberius B. ii.

Ely Old Coucher (or *Liber R*, 1251). Cambridge: Ely Diocesan Record G. 3. 27.

Huguccio of Pisa. *Magnae derivationes*. Oxford: Bodleian Library, MS e Musaeo 96.

Leland, John. *Collectanea et Commentarii de scriptoribus Britannicis*. Oxford: Bodleian Library, MSS Top. gen. c. 1–4.

Ringstede, Thomas. *In proverbia Solomonis*. Oxford: Bodleian Library, MS Bodley 829; Lincoln College, MS latin 86.

Whethamstede, John. *Pabularium poetarum*. London: British Library, MS Egerton 646.

———. Tabula to Elias of Thriplow, *De vita scolarium*. London: British Library, MS Arundel 11.

2. Printed Works and Secondary Sources

A. Gellius. *Noctes Atticae*. Ed. P. K. Marshall. 2 vols. Oxford: Clarendon Press, 1968.

Adelard of Bath. *De eodem et diverso*. Ed. Hans Willner. Beiträge zur Geschichte der Philosophie des Mittelalters, 4, 1. Munich: Aschendorffschen, 1903.

Alan of Lille. *Anticlaudianus*. Ed. R. Bossuat. Textes Philosophiques de Moyen Age, 1. Paris: Vrin, 1955.

———. *De planctu Naturae*. Ed. Nikolaus M. Häring. In *Studi medievali*, third series, 19 (1978): 797–879.

Alexander, J. J. G., and M. T. Gibson, eds. *Medieval Learning and Literature: Essays Presented to R. W. Hunt*. Oxford: Clarendon Press, 1976.

Alfarabi. *De ortu scientiarum*. Ed. Clemens Baeumker. Beiträge zur Geschichte der Philosophie des Mittelalters, 19, 3. Munich: Aschendorffschen, 1916.

Algazel. *Metaphysics: A Medieval Translation*. Ed. J. T. Muckle, C.S.B. Toronto: St. Michael's College, 1933.

Allen, Judson Boyce. *The Ethical Poetic of the Later Middle Ages: A Decorum of Convenient Distinction*. Toronto: University of Toronto Press, 1982.

Anselm [of Canterbury]. *Opera omnia*. Ed. Franciscus Salesius Schmitt. 6 vols. Edinburgh: Nelson, 1946–61.

Aquinas, Thomas. *Commentaria in octo libros physicorum Aristotelis*. Opera omnia iussu impensaque Leonis XIII. P. M., 2. Rome: Typographia polyglotta, 1884.

———. *In duodecim libros metaphysicorum Aristotelis expositio*. Ed. M.-R. Cathala, O.P.; rev. Raymundus M. Spiazzi, O.P. 3d ed. Turin: Marietti, 1964.

Aristotle. *Opera cum Averrois commentariis*. Venice, 1562–74; repr. Frankfurt: Minerva, 1962.

Aristoteles Latinus. Ed. L. Minio-Paluello and G. Verbeke. Corpus Philosophorum Medii Aevi Academiarum Consociatarum Auspiciis et Consilio Editum.

I. 1–5. *Categoriae vel Praedicamenta*. Ed. Laurentius Minio-Paluello. Leiden: Brill, 1961.

I. 6–7. *Categoriarum supplementa: Porphyrii Isagoge et Liber sex principiorum*. Ed. Laurentius Minio-Paluello. Leiden: Brill, 1966.

XXV. 1–1ª. *Metaphysica I-IV. 4: Translatio Iacobi sive "Vetustissima" et Translatio composita sive "Vetus."* Ed. Gudrun Vuillemin-Diem. Leiden: Brill, 1970.

XXV. 2. *Metaphysica I-IX, XII-XIV: Translatio anonyma sive "Media."* Ed. Gudrun Vuillemin-Diem. Leiden: Brill, 1976.

Asclepius. Ed. A. D. Nock, trans. A.-J. Festugière. Corpus Hermeticum, 2. Paris: Les Belles Lettres, 1945, 257–401.

Aston, T. H., G. D. Duncan, and T. A. R. Evans. "The Medieval Alumni of the University of Cambridge." *Past and Present* 86 (1980): 9–86.

Augustine of Hippo. *De civitate Dei*. Ed. Bernardus Dombart and Alfonsus Kalb. 5th ed. 2 vols. Stuttgart: Teubner, 1981.

———. *De mendacio*. Ed. and trans. Gustave Combès. Opuscules 2. Problèmes Moraux. Oeuvres de Saint Augustin. Paris: Desclée de Brouwer, 1948.

Ayscough, Samuel. *A Catalogue of the Manuscripts Preserved in the British Library Hitherto Undescribed ... Including the Collections of Sir Hans Sloane, bart. ...* 2 vols. London: J. Rivington, 1782.

Avicenna Latinus. *Liber de anima seu sextus de naturalibus*. Ed. S. van Riet. 3 vols. Louvain: Peeters; Leiden: Brill, 1968–72.

——. *Liber de philosophia prima sive scientia divina*. Ed. S. van Riet. 3 vols. Louvain: Peeters; Leiden: Brill, 1977–83.

Bakhtin, Mikhail. *Problems of Dostoevsky's Poetics*. Trans. R. W. Rostel. [Ann Arbor]: Ardis, 1973.

Balbus, Joannes. *Catholicon*. Mainz, 1460; repr. Farnborough: Gregg, 1971.

Bale, John. *Acta Romanorum Pontificum a dispersione discipulorum Christi usque ad tempora Pauli quarti*. Basel: Oporinus, 1558.

——. *A declaration of Edmonde Bonners articles, concerning the cleargye of London dyocese whereby that excerable Antychriste, is in his righte colours reueled*. London: Tysdall, 1561.

——. *Index Britanniae scriptorum*. Ed. Reginald Lane Poole and Mary Bateson. Anecdota Oxoniensia, medieval and modern series, 9. Oxford: Clarendon Press, 1902.

——. *Illustrium Maioris Britanniae scriptorum ... Summarium*. Wesel: Plataneum, 1549 [recte 1548].

——. *Rhithmi vetustissimi de corrupto ecclesiae statu*. [Cologne]: Ioannes Kempensis, 1546.

——. *Scriptorum illustrium Maioris Brytannie ... Catalogus*. 2 vols. Basel: Oporinus, 1557–59.

——. *The vocacyon of Johan Bale to the bishoprick of Ossorie in Irelande his persecucions in the same and finall delyuerance*. Rome: S. Angell, 1553.

Benson, Robert L. and Giles Constable, eds. *Renaissance and Renewal in the Twelfth Century*. Cambridge, Mass.: Harvard University Press, 1982.

Bentham, James. *The History and Antiquities of the Conventual and Cathedral Church of Ely from the Foundation of the Monastery, AD 673 to the Year 1771*. Cambridge: Cambridge University Press, 1771.

Bernard, Edward. *Catalogi librorum manuscriptorum Angliae et Hiberniae in unum collecti*. 2 vols. in 1. Oxford: E theatro Sheldoniano, 1697.

Bernardus Silvestris. *Cosmographia*. Ed. Peter Dronke. Textus Minores, 53. Leiden: Brill, 1978.

Biblia Latina cum glossa ordinaria et postillis Nicolai de Lyra. 5 vols. Venice: Paganinus de Paganinis, 1495.

Biblia sacra iuxta vulgatam versionem. Ed. Robertus Weber, O.S.B. et al., 2 vols. Stuttgart: Wurttembergische Bibelanstalt, 1975.

Blund, Iohannes. *Tractatus de anima*. Ed. D. A. Callus, O.P. and R. W. Hunt. London: Oxford University Press for The British Academy, 1970.

Boas, M. "De librorum Catonianorum historia atque compositione." *Mnemosyne* 42 (1914): 17–46.

Bode, Georgius Henricus, ed. *Scriptores rerum mythicarum Latini tres Romae nuper reperti*. 2 vols. Celle, 1834; repr. Hindesheim: Olms, 1968.

Boethius, Anicius Manlius Severinus. *Commentarii in librum Aristotelis "ΠΕΡΙ ΕΡΜΗΝΕΙΑΣ."* Ed. C. Meiser. 2 vols. in 1. Leipzig: Teubner, 1877–80.

———. *Philosophiae consolatio*. Ed. Ludwig Bieler. Corpus Christianorum, series latina, 94. Turnholt: Brepols, 1957.

———. *Theological Tractates and Consolation of Philosophy*. Ed. and trans. H. F. Stewart, E. K. Rand, and S. J. Tester. Loeb Classical Library. Cambridge, Mass.: Harvard University Press, 1973.

[Pseudo-] Boethius. *De disciplina scolarium*. Ed. Olga Weijers. Studien und Texte zur Geistesgeschichte des Mittelalters, 12. Leiden and Cologne: Brill, 1976.

Boyle, Leonard E., O.P. "The Beginnings of Legal Studies at Oxford." *Viator* 14 (1983): 107–31.

Brundage, James A. *Law, Sex, and Christian Society in Medieval Europe*. Chicago: University of Chicago Press, 1987.

Burley, Walter. *Liber de vita et moribus philosophorum*. Ed. Hermann Knust. Tubingen: Litterarischer Verein, 1886.

Butterfield, H. "Peterhouse." In *The City and University of Cambridge*, ed. J. P. C. Roach, 334–40. A History of the County of Cambridge and the Isle of Ely, vol. 3. Victoria History of the Counties of England. London: Institute of Historical Research, 1959.

Caesar, C. Iulius. *De bello Gallico*. Ed. Renatus du Pontet. Oxford: Clarendon Press, 1900.

Calendar of the Charter Rolls Preserved in the Public Record Office. 6 vols. London: H. M. S. O., 1903–27.

Calendar of the Liberate Rolls Preserved in the Public Record Office: Henry III. 6 vols. London: H. M. S. O., 1917–64.

Callus, D. A., O.P. "Introduction of Aristotelian Learning to Oxford." *Proceedings of the British Academy* 29 (1943): 229–81.

———, ed. *Robert Grosseteste: Scholar and Bishop*. Oxford: Clarendon Press, 1955.

Catalogus librorum manuscriptorum bibliothecae Sloanianae. 19 vols. London: British Library, 1837–40.

Catto, J. I., ed. *The Early Oxford Schools*. The History of the University of Oxford. Ed. T. H. Aston, vol. 1. Oxford: Clarendon Press, 1984.

Catullus, C. Valerius. *Carmina*. Ed. R. A. B. Mynors. Oxford: Clarendon Press, 1958.

Chartularium universitatis Parisiensis. Ed. Henricus Denifle, O.P. and Aemilius Chatelain. 4 vols. Paris: Delalain, 1889–97.

Chevallier, Philippe, O.S.B., ed. *Dionysiaca: Recueil donnant l'ensemble des traductions latines des ouvrages attribués au Denys de l'Aréopage.* 2 vols. Paris: Desclée, de Brouwer, 1937–49.

Cicero, M. Tullius. *Academicorum reliquiae cum Lucullo.* Ed. O. Plasberg. Scripta quae manserunt omnia, 42. 1922; repr. Stuttgart: Teubner, 1980.

———. *De officiis.* Ed. C. Atzert. Scripta quae manserunt omnia, 48. Leipzig: Teubner, 1971.

———. *Rhetorici libri duo qui vocantur de inventione.* Ed. E. Stroebel. Scripta quae manserunt omnia, 2. 1915; repr. Stuttgart: Teubner, 1977.

Close Rolls of the Reign of Henry III Preserved in the Public Record Office. 14 vols. London: H. M. S. O., 1902–38.

Coffey, Michael. *Roman Satire.* London: Methuen; New York: Barnes and Noble, 1976.

Colker, Marvin L., ed. *Analecta Dublinensia: Three Medieval Latin Texts in the Library of Trinity College Dublin.* Medieval Academy of American Publication, 82. Cambridge Mass.: Medieval Academy, 1975.

———. "New Light on the Use and Transmission of Petronius." *Manuscripta* 36 (1992): 200–9.

———. *Trinity College Library Dublin: Descriptive Catalogue of the Mediaeval and Renaissance Latin Manuscripts.* 2 vols. Aldershot: Scolar, 1991.

———, ed. "De nobilitate animi." In *Mediaeval Studies* 23 (1961): 47–79.

Corpus Iuris Canonici. Ed. Aemilius Ludouicus Richter and Aemilius Friedberg. 2 vols. Leipzig, 1879; repr. Graz: Akademische Druck, 1955.

Cross, F. L. and E. A. Livingstone, eds. *The Oxford Dictionary of the Christian Church.* 2d ed. Oxford: Oxford University Press, 1974.

Curia Regis Rolls Preserved in the Public Record Office. 16 volumes (to date). London: H. M. S. O., 1922–.

Curtius, Ernst Robert. *European Literature and the Latin Middle Ages.* Trans. Willard R. Trask. Bollingen Series, 36. Berne, 1948; Princeton: Princeton University Press, 1973.

d'Alverny, M. T. "Avendauth?" In *Homenaje a Millás-Vallicrosa,* 19–43. Barcelona: Consejo Superior de Investigaciones científicas, 1954.

Davies, W. T. "A Bibliography of John Bale." *Oxford Bibliographical Society, Proceedings and Papers* 5 (1936–39): 201–80.

A Descriptive Catalogue of Ancient Deeds in the Public Record Office. 6 vols. London: H. M. S. O., 1890–15.

de Zulueta, Francis and Peter Stein. *The Teaching of Roman Law in England around 1200.* Seldon Society, supplementary series, 8. London: Seldon Society, 1990.

Diener, Ronald Ernst. "The Magdeburg Centuries: A Bibliothecal and

Historiographical Analysis." D.Th. dissertation, Harvard Divinity School, 1978.

Disticha Catonis. Ed. Marcus Boas and Henricus Johannes Botschuyver. Amsterdam: North-Holland, 1952.

Du Cange, Charles du Fresne. *Glossarium mediae et infimae latinitatis.* Ed. with the supplements of Carpenter and Henschel by Leopold Favre. 10 vols. Niort: Favre, 1883–87.

Dyer, Christopher. *Standards of Living in the Later Middle Ages: Social Change in England c. 1200–1520.* Cambridge Medieval Textbooks. Cambridge: Cambridge University Press, 1989.

Eckhardt, Caroline D. "The Medieval *Prosimetrum* Genre (from Boethius to *Boece*)." *Genre* 16 (1983): 21–38.

Eliot, T. S. *The Sacred Wood.* 3d ed. London: Methuen, 1932.

Emden, A. B. *A Biographical Register of the University of Cambridge to 1500.* Cambridge: Cambridge University Press, 1963.

——. *A Biographical Register of the University of Oxford to AD 1500.* 3 vols. Oxford: Clarendon Press, 1957–59.

Faral, Edmond. *Les arts poétiques du xiie et du xiiie siècle: Recherches et documents sur la technique littéraire du moyen âge.* Paris: Champion, 1924.

Festus, Sextus Pompeius. *De verborum significatu quae supersint cum Pauli epitome.* Ed. Wallace M. Lindsay. Leipzig: Teubner, 1913.

Firth, Katharine. *The Apocalyptic Tradition in Reformation Britain 1530–1645.* Oxford Historical Monographs. Oxford: Oxford University Press, 1979.

Fischer, Bonifatius, O.S.B., ed. *Novae concordantiae Bibliorum sacrorum iuxta vulgatam versionem critice editam.* 5 vols. Stuttgart: Frommann-Holzboog, 1977.

Flacius Illyricus, Matthias. *Antilogia papae; hoc est, de corrupto ecclesiae statu et totius cleri papistici perversitate, scripta aliquot veterum authorum ante annos plus minus CCC et interea.* Basel: Oporinus, 1555.

——. *Catalogus testium ueritatis, qui ante nostram aetatem Pontifici Romano, eiusque erroribus reclamarunt.* 2d ed. Strassburg: Apud Paulum Machaeropoeum, sumptibus Ioannis Oporini, 1562.

——. *Varia doctorum piorumque virorum de corrupto ecclesiae statu poemata ante nostram aetatem conscripta.* Basel: Lucius, 1557.

Fowler, Alastair. *Kinds of Literature: An Introduction to the Theory of Genre.* Cambridge, Mass.: Harvard University Press, 1982.

Frye, Northrop. *Anatomy of Criticism: Four Essays.* Princeton: Princeton University Press, 1957.

Fulgentius, Fabius Planciades. *Opera.* Ed. Rudolfus Helm. Leipzig: Teubner, 1898.

Fuller, Thomas. *The History of the Worthies of England.* London: J. G. W. L. and W. G., 1662.

Gaius. *Institutes*. Ed. and trans. Francis de Zulueta. 2 vols. Oxford: Clarendon Press, 1946–53.

Galterus de Castellione. *Alexandreis*. Ed. Marvin L. Colker. Pavia: Antenore, 1978.

Garrett, Christina Hallowell. *The Marian Exiles: A Study in the Origins of Elizabethan Puritanism*. Cambridge: Cambridge University Press, 1938.

Gibson, Margaret, ed. *Boethius: His Life, Thought and Influence*. Oxford: Blackwell, 1981.

Glare, P. G. W., ed. *Oxford Latin Dictionary*. Oxford: Clarendon Press, 1982.

Glorieux, P. *La faculté des arts et ses maîtres au xiiie siècle*. Études de Philosophie Médiévale, 59. Paris: Vrin, 1971.

Grabmann, Martin. *I divieti ecclesiastici di Aristotele sotto Innocenzo III e Gregorio IX*. Miscellanea Historia Pontificiae, 5. Rome: Typis Pontificiae Universitatis Gregorianae, 1941.

Gradon, Pamela. *Form and Style in Early English Literature*. London: Methuen, 1971.

Gray, Arthur. *The Priory of Saint Radegund Cambridge*. Cambridge Antiquarian Society, octavo series, 31. Cambridge: Cambridge Antiquarian Society, 1898.

Grosseteste, Robert. *Commentarius in VIII libros physicorum Aristotelis*. Ed. R. C. Dales. Studies and Texts in Medieval Thought. Boulder: University of Colorado Press, 1963.

――――. *Die philosophischen Werke des Robert Grosseteste, Bishofs von Lincoln*. Ed. Ludwig Baur. Beiträge zur Geschichte der Philosophie des Mittelalters, 9. Munich: Aschendorffschen, 1912.

Gruber, Joachim. *Kommentar zu Boethius "De consolatione Philosophiae."* Texte und Kommentare, 9. Berlin-New York: de Gruyter, 1978.

Gundissalinus, Dominicus. *De anima*. Ed. J. T. Muckle, C.S.B. In *Mediaeval Studies* 2 (1940): 23–103.

――――. *De divisione philosophiae*. Ed. Ludwig Baur. Beiträge zur Geschichte der Philosophie des Mittelalters, 4, 2–3. Munich: Aschendorffschen, 1903.

――――. *De processione mundi*. Ed. G. Bulow. Beiträge zur Geschichte der Philosophie des Mittelalters, 24, 3. Munich: Aschendorffschen, 1925.

――――. *De scientiis*. Ed. P. Manuel Alonso Alonso, S.J. Madrid: Maestre, 1954.

Hackett, M. B., O.S.A. *The Original Statutes of Cambridge University: The Text and Its History*. Cambridge: Cambridge University Press, 1970.

Hall, Jennifer. *Lucian's Satire*. Monographs in Classical Studies. New York: Arno, 1981.

Hallam, H. E., ed. *The Agrarian History of England and Wales: Volume*

II, 1042–1350. Cambridge: Cambridge University Press, 1988.

Hamesse, Jacqueline. *Les auctoritates Aristotelis: Un florilège médiéval, étude historique et édition critique*. Philosophes Médiévaux, 17. Louvain: Publications Universitaires; Paris: Béatrice-Nauwelaerts, 1974.

Hammond, N. G. L. and H. H. Scullard, eds. *The Oxford Classical Dictionary*. 2d ed. Oxford: Clarendon Press, 1970.

Hampson, Ethel A. "Schools." In *The Victoria County History of the County of Cambridgeshire and the Isle of Ely*, vol 2, ed. L. F. Salzman, 319–56. London: Institute of Historical Research, 1948.

Happé, Peter. "Recent Studies in John Bale," *English Literary Renaissance* 17 (1987): 103–13.

Hathaway, Neil. "*Compilatio*: From Plagiarism to Compiling." *Viator* 20 (1989): 19–44.

Hinnesbusch, William A., O.P. *The Early English Friars Preachers*. Dissertationes Historicae, 14. Rome: Ad S. Sabinae, 1951.

Hirzel, Rudolf. *Der Dialog: Ein literarhistorischer Versuch*. 2 vols. Leipzig: Hirzel, 1895.

Horatius Flaccus, Q. *Opera*. Ed. Edward C. Wickham and H. W. Garrod. Oxford: Clarendon Press, 1912.

Howlett, D. R. "Studies in the Works of John Whethamstede." D.Phil. thesis, Oxford University, 1975.

Hugh of Trimberg. *Registrum multorum auctorum*. Ed. Karl Langosch. Germanischen Studien, 235. Berlin, 1942; repr. Nendeln: Kraus, 1969.

Hunt, R. W. "English Learning in the Late Twelfth Century." *Transactions of the Royal Historical Society*, fourth series, 19 (1936): 19–42.

———. *The History of Grammar in the Middle Ages: Collected Papers*. Ed. G. L. Bursill-Hall. Amsterdam Studies in the Theory and History of Linguistic Science, third series, 5. Amsterdam: Benjamins, 1980.

Illingworth, W. *Rotuli hundredorum tempore Henrici III et Edwardi I in turre Londoniensi et in curia receptae scaccarii Westmonasterii asservati*. 2 vols. London: George Eyre and Andrew Strahan, 1812–18.

Isidore of Seville. *Etymologiae sive origines*. Ed. W. M. Lindsay. 2 vols. Oxford: Clarendon Press, 1911.

Janson, Tore. *Prose Rhythm in Medieval Latin from the 9th to the 13th Century*. Acta Universitatis Stockholmiensis: Studia Latina Stockholmiensia, 20. Stockholm: Almqvist and Wiksell, 1975.

Jerome. *Liber interpretationis Hebraicorum nominum*. Ed. P. de Lagrande. Corpus Christianorum, series latina, 72. Turnholt: Brepols, 1959.

Johannes de Hauvilla. *Architrenius*. Ed. Paul Gerhard Schmidt. Munich: Fink, 1974.

John of Salisbury. *Entheticus maior et minor*. Ed. Jan van Laarhoven. 3

vols. Studien und Texte zur Geistesgeschichte des Mittelalters, 17. Leiden: Brill, 1987.

——. *Metalogicon*. Ed. Clemens C. J. Webb. Oxford: Clarendon Press, 1929.

——. *Policraticus, sive de nugis curialium et vestigiis philosophorum*. Ed. C. C. J. Webb. 2 vols. London, 1909; repr. Frankfurt: Minerva, 1965.

Jones, Norman L. "Matthew Parker, John Bale, and the Magdeburg Centuriators." *Sixteenth Century Journal* 12, 3 (1981): 35–49.

Iustinianus, Flavius Petrus Sabbatius. *Codex*. Ed. Paulus Krueger. 10th ed. In *Corpus Iuris Civilis*, vol. 2. Stereotype Edition. 3 vols. Berlin: Weidmann, 1928–29.

——. *Institutiones*. Ed. Paulus Krueger. 15th ed. In *Corpus Iuris Civilis*, vol. 1. Stereotype Edition. Berlin: Weidmann, 1928–29.

Iustinus, M. Iunianus. *Epitoma historiarum Philippicarum Pompei Trogi*. Ed. Otto Seel. Stuttgart: Teubner, 1972.

Iuuenalis, D. Iunius. *Saturae*. Ed. W. V. Clausen. Oxford: Clarendon Press, 1959.

Kaepelli, Thomas, O.P. *Scriptores Ordinis Praedicatorum Medii Aevi*. 3 vols. Rome: Ad S. Sabinae, 1970.

Keeling, S. M. "Thriplow." In *Armingford and Thriplow Hundreds*, ed. A. P. M. Wright, 239–42. A History of Cambridgeshire and the Isle of Ely, vol. 8. The Victoria History of the Counties of England. London: Institute of Historical Research, 1982.

Ker, N. R. *Medieval Libraries of Great Britain: A List of Surviving Books*. 2d ed. Royal Historical Society Guides and Handbooks, 3. London: Royal Historical Society, 1964.

——. "Sir John Prise." In *Books, Collectors and Libraries: Studies in the Medieval Heritage*, ed. Andrew Watson, 471–96. London and Ronceverte: Hambledon, 1985.

Kilwardby, Robert. *De ortu scientiarum*. Ed. Albert G. Judy, O.P. Auctores Britannici Medii Aevi, 4. [London]: British Academy; Toronto: Pontifical Institute, 1976.

Kindermann, Udo. *Satyra: Die Theorie der Satire im Mittellateinischen; Vorstudie zu einer Gattungsgeschichte*. Erlanger Beiträge zur Sprach- und Kunstwissenschaft, 58. Nuremberg: Hans Carl, 1978.

King, John N. *English Reformation Literature: The Tudor Origins of the Protestant Tradition*. Princeton: Princeton University Press, 1982.

Kirk, Eugene P. *Menippean Satire: An Annotated Catalogue of Texts and Criticism*. New York: Garland, 1980.

Knoche, Ulrich. *Roman Satire*. Trans. Edwin S. Ramage. Bloomington-London: Indiana University Press, 1975.

Kretzmann, Norman et al., eds. *The Cambridge History of Later Medieval Philosophy: From the Rediscovery of Aristotle to the Disintegration of*

Scholasticism, 1100–1600. Cambridge: Cambridge University Press, 1982.

Kulcsár, Péter, ed. *Mythographi Vaticani I et II*. Corpus Christianorum, series latina, 91C. Turnholt: Brepols, 1987.

Lapidge, Michael. "The Hermeneutic Style in Tenth-Century Anglo-Latin Literature." *Anglo-Saxon England* 4 (1975): 67–111.

Latham, R. A., ed. *Revised Medieval Latin Word-List from British and Irish Sources*. London: Oxford University Press for the British Academy, 1965.

Latham, R. A. and D. R. Howlett, eds. *Dictionary of Medieval Latin From British Sources*. (In progress.) London: Oxford University Press for The British Academy, 1975–.

Leader, Damian Riehl. *The University to 1546*. A History of the University of Cambridge, 1. Cambridge: Cambridge University Press, 1988.

Leland, John. *Commentarii de scriptoribus Britannicis*. Ed. Antony Hall. 2 vols. Oxford: E theatro Sheldoniano, 1709.

——. *The laboryouse journey and serche of Johan Leylande, for Englandes Antiquitees, geuen of hym as a newe yeares gyfte to Kynge Henry the viii. in the .xxvii. yeare of his reyne, with declaracyons enlarged: by Johan Bale*. London: Bale, 1549.

——. *De rebus Britannicis collectanea*. Ed. Thomas Hearne. 6 vols. Oxford: E theatro Sheldoniano, 1715.

LeMoine, Fanny. *Martianus Capella: A Literary Re-evaluation*. Münchener Beiträge zur Mediävistik und Renaissance-Forschung, 10. Munich: Bei der Arbeo-Gesellschaft, 1972.

Leonardi, C. "I codici di Marziano Capella." *Aevum* 33 (1959): 433–89, and 34 (1960): 1–99, 411–524.

——. "Nota introduttiva per un'indagine sulla fortuna di Marziano Capella nel Medievo." *Bullettino dell' Istituto storico italiano per il medio evo e Archivio muratoriano* 67 (1955): 265–88.

Lerer, Seth. *Boethius and Dialogue: Literary Method in "The Consolation of Philosophy."* Princeton: Princeton University Press, 1985.

Lewis, Charlton T. and Charles Short. *A Latin Dictionary Founded on Andrew's Edition of Freund's Latin Dictionary*. Oxford: Clarendon Press, 1879.

Liber de causis. Ed. R. Steele. In *Opera hactenus inediti Rogeri Baconi*, vol. 12. Oxford: Clarendon Press, 1935.

Liber feodorum: The Book of Fees Commonly Called Testa de Nevill Reformed from the Earliest Manuscripts. 3 vols. London: H. M. S. O., 1920–31.

Lombard, Peter. *Sententiae in IV libris distinctae*. [Ed. I. Brady.] 2 vols. in 3. Grottaferrata: Collegii S. Bonaventurae ad claras aquas, 1971–81.

Lucanus, M. Annaeus. *Bellum Ciuile.* Ed. A. E. Housman. Oxford: Blackwell, 1926.

Luscombe, David. "The Reception of the Writings of Denis the Pseudo-Areopagite into England." In *Tradition and Change: Essays in Honour of Marjorie Chibnall...*, ed. Diana Greenway, Christopher Holdsworth, and Jane Sayers, 115–43. Cambridge: Cambridge University Press, 1985.

———. "Some Examples of the Use Made of the Works of the Pseudo-Dionysius by University Teachers in the Later Middle Ages." In *The Universities in the Late Middle Ages,* ed. Jozef Ijsewijn and Jacques Paquet, 228–41. Louvain: Louvain University Press, 1978.

Macrobius, Ambrosius Theodosius. *Commentarii in somnium Scipionis.* Ed. Iacobus Willis. Leipzig: Teubner, 1970.

Maitland, Frederic William. *Township and Borough.* Cambridge: Cambridge University Press, 1898.

Marmura, Michael E. "Avicenna's Proof From Contingency for God's Existence in the *Metaphysics* of the *Shifā'.*" *Mediaeval Studies* 42 (1980): 337–52.

Martianus Capella. [*De nuptiis Philologiae et Mercurii.*] Ed. James Willis. Leipzig: Teubner, 1983.

———. *De nuptiis Philologiae et Mercurii liber secundus.* Ed. and trans. Luciano Lenaz. Padua: Liviana Editrice, 1975.

McCusker, Honor C. *John Bale: Dramatist and Antiquary.* 1942; repr. Freeport: Books for Libraries, 1971.

McKisack, May. *Medieval History in the Tudor Age.* Oxford: Clarendon Press, 1971.

Miller, Edward. *The Abbey and Bishopric of Ely: The Social History of an Ecclesiastical Estate from the Tenth Century to the Early Fourteenth Century.* Cambridge Studies in Medieval Life and Thought, new series, 1. Cambridge: Cambridge University Press, 1951.

——— and John Hatcher. *Medieval England—Rural Society and Economic Change 1086–1348.* Social and Economic History of England. London and New York: Longman, 1978.

Milton, John. *Complete Prose Works.* 6 vols. in 8. New Haven: Yale University Press, 1953–73.

Minnis, Alastair J. *Medieval Theory of Authorship: Scholastic Literary Attitudes in the Later Middle Ages.* London: Scolar, 1984.

——— and A. B. Scott with David Wallace, eds. and trans. *Medieval Literary Theory and Criticism c. 1100–c. 1375: The Commentary Tradition.* Revised ed. Oxford: Clarendon Press, 1991.

Mortier, R. P. *Histoire des maîtres généraux de l'ordre des Frères Prêcheurs.* 8 vols. Paris: Picard, 1903–20.

Mras, Karl. "Varros Menippeische Satiren und die Philosophie." *Neue Jahrbücher für Klassiche Altertum* 33 (1914): 390–420.

Mynors, R. A. B. "The Latin Classics Known to Boston of Bury." In *Fritz Saxl, 1890–1948: A Volume of Memorial Essays from His Friends in England*, ed. D. J. Gordon, 192–217. London: Nelson, 1957.

Neckam, Alexander. *De naturis rerum*. Ed. T. Wright. Rolls Series, 34. London, 1863; repr. Nendeln: Kraus, 1967, 1–354.

Nitzsche, Jane Chance. *The Genius Figure in Antiquity and the Middle Ages*. New York: Columbia University Press, 1975.

Noonan, John T., Jr. "Marital Affection in the Canonists." *Studia Gratiana* 12 (1967): 481–509.

———. "Power to Choose." *Viator* 4 (1973): 419–34.

Norberg, Dag. *Introduction à l'étude de la versification latine médiévale*. Stockholm: Almqvist and Wiksell, 1958.

———. *Manuel pratique de latin médiéval*. Connaissance des Langues, 4. Paris: Picard, 1968.

Norden, Eduard. *Die antike Kunstprosa vom VI. Jahrhundert vor Christ bis in die Zeit der Renaissance*. 2 vols. Leipzig-Berlin: Teubner, 1909.

Nuchelmans, Gabriel. "Philologia et son mariage avec Mercure jusq'à la fin du xiie siècle." *Latomus* 16 (1957): 84–107.

Olson, Glending. *Literature as Recreation in the Later Middle Ages*. Ithaca and London: Cornell University Press, 1982.

Olson, Oliver K. " 'Der Bücherdieb Flacius'—Geschichte eines Rufmordes." *Wolfenbütteler Beiträge* 4 (1981): 111–45.

———. "Matthias Flacius Illyricus (1520–1575)." In *Theologische Realenzyklopädie*, ed. Gerhard Krause and Gerhard Muller, 11:206–14. (In progress.) Berlin-New York: de Gruyter, 1977–.

Orme, Nicholas. *English Schools in the Middle Ages*. London: Methuen, 1973.

Orosius, Paulus. *Historiae aduersum paganos*. Ed. Carolus Zangemeister. Leipzig: Teubner, 1889.

Ovidius Naso, P. *Metamorphoses*. Ed. William S. Anderson. Leipzig: Teubner, 1977.

———. *Tristia*. Ed. S. G. Owen. Oxford: Clarendon Press, 1915.

Owen, Dorothy M. *Ely Records: A Handlist of the Records of the Bishop and Archdeacon of Ely*. Cambridge: Heffer, [1971].

——— and Dorothea Thurley, eds. *The King's School Ely: A Collection of Documents Relating to the History of the School and Its Scholars*. Cambridge Antiquarian Records Society, 5. Cambridge: Cambridge Antiquarian Records Society, 1982.

Owens, Joseph. *The Doctrine of Being in the Aristotelian "Metaphysics."* 3d ed. Toronto: Pontifical Institute, 1978.

Panofsky, Erwin. *Renaissance and Renascences in Western Art*. Stockholm: Almqvist and Wiksell, 1960.

Parker, Matthew. *Correspondence*. Ed. John Bruce and Thomas Thomason Perowne. Parker Society, 33. Cambridge: Cambridge University Press, 1853.

Parkes, M. B. *English Cursive Book Hands 1250–1500*. Oxford, 1969; repr. Berkeley: University of California Press, 1980.

Patent Rolls of the Reign of Henry III Preserved in the Public Record Office. 6 vols. London: H. M. S. O., 1901–13.

Payne, F. Anne. *Chaucer and Menippean Satire*. Madison: University of Wisconsin Press, 1981.

Persius Flaccus, A. *Saturae*. Ed. W. V. Clausen. Oxford: Clarendon Press, 1959.

Petronius. *Satyrica*. Ed. Konrad Müller and Wilhelm Ehlers. Munich: Heimeran, 1965.

Pignon, Laurentius. *Catalogi et chronica; accedunt catalogi Stamsensis et Upsalensis scriptorum O.P.* Ed. G. Meersseman, O.P. Monumenta ordinis fratrum praedicatorum historica, 18. Rome: Socii Instituti Historici Fratrum Praedicatorum, 1936.

Pits, John. *Relationes historicae de rebus Anglicis*. Paris: Thierry and Cramoisy, 1619.

Plautus, Titus Maccius. *Comoediae*. Ed. W. M. Lindsay. 2 vols. Oxford: Clarendon Press, 1904.

Plinius Secundus, C. *Natural History, VIII–XI*. Ed. and trans. H. Rackham. Loeb Classical Library. Cambridge, Mass.: Harvard University Press, 1940.

Postan, M. M. *The Medieval Economy and Society: An Economic History of Britain in the Middle Ages*. 1972; repr. Harmondsworth: Penguin, 1975.

———. *The Agrarian Life of the Middle Ages*. 2d ed. The Cambridge Economic History of Europe, 1. Cambridge: Cambridge University Press, 1966.

Powicke, Sir F. Maurice and E. B. Frye, eds. *Handbook of British Chronology*. 2d ed. Royal Historical Society Guides and Handbooks, 2. London: Royal Historical Society, 1961.

Prise, John. *Historiae Brytannicae defensio*. London: Impressum in aedibus H. Binneman, 1573.

Quadlbauer, F. *Die antike Theorie der genera dicendi im lateinische Mittelalter*. Sitzungberichte der Osterreichische Akademie der Wissenschaft, Philosophisch-Historische Klasse, 241, 2 Abh. Vienna: Bohlaus, 1962.

Quetif, Jacobus and Jacobus Echard. *Scriptores Ordinis Praedicatorum*. 2 vols. Paris, 1719–21; repr. Torin: Botega d'Erasmo, 1961.

Raby, F. J. E. *A History of Secular Latin Poetry in the Middle Ages*. 2d ed. 2 vols. Oxford: Clarendon Press, 1957.

Rashdall, Hastings. *The Universities of Europe in the Middle Ages.* Ed. F. M. Powicke and A. B. Emden. 3 vols. Oxford: Oxford University Press, 1936.

Relihan, Joel C. "A History of Menippean Satire to AD 524." Ph.D. dissertation, University of Wisconsin, 1985.

Remigius of Auxerre. *Commentum in Martianum Capellam.* Ed. Cora E. Lutz. 2 vols. Leiden: Brill, 1962.

Rhetorica ad Herennium. Ed. and trans. Harry Caplan. Loeb Classical Library. Cambridge, Mass.: Harvard University Press, 1954.

Reynolds, L. D., ed. *Texts and Transmission: A Survey of the Latin Classics.* Oxford: Clarendon Press, 1983.

Riessner, Claus. *Die Magnae Derivationes des Uguccione da Pisa und ihre Bedeutung für die romanische Philologie.* Temi e Testi, 11. Rome: Edizioni di Storia e Letteratura, 1965.

Rye, Walter, ed. *Pedes finium: Or Fines, Relating to the County of Cambridge, Levied in the King's Court from the Seventh Year of Richard I to the End of the Reign of Richard III.* Cambridge Antiquarian Society, octavo series, 26. Cambridge: Cambridge Antiquarian Society, 1891.

Schmidt, Paul Gerhard. "Elias of Thriplow—A Thirteenth-Century Anglo-Latin Poet." In *Papers of the Liverpool Latin Seminar, Third Volume,* ed. Francis Cairns, 363–70. ARCA Classical and Medieval Texts, Papers, and Monographs, 7. Liverpool: Cairns, 1981.

———, ed. *Lateinische Sprichwörter und Sentenzen des Mittelalters und der fruhen Neuzeit in alphabetischen Anordnung.* Carmina Medii Aevi posterioris Latina, II, 7. Gottingen: Vandenhoeck and Ruprecht, 1982–.

Schumann, Otto. *Lateinisches Hexameter-Lexikon: Dichterisches Formelgut von Ennius bis zum Archipoeta.* Monumenta Germaniae Historica, Hilfsmittel, 4, 1–5. Munich: MGH, 1979–82.

Seneca, L. Annaeus. *Apocolocyntosis.* Ed. P. T. Eden. Cambridge: Cambridge University Press, 1984.

———. *Ad Lucilium epistolae morales.* Ed. L. D. Reynolds. 2 vols. Oxford: Clarendon Press, 1965.

Servius Grammaticus. *Servii Grammatici qui feruntur in Vergilii carmina commentarii.* Ed. Georgius Thilo and Hermannus Hagen. 3 vols. in 4. Leipzig: Teubner, 1881–1902.

———. *Serviani in Vergilii carmina commentarii.* Ed. E. K. Rand et al. Editio Harvardiana. 2 vols. (in progress). Lancaster and Oxford: American Philosophical Society, 1946–65.

Shanzer, Danuta. *A Philosophical and Literary Commentary on Martianus Capella's "De nuptiis Philologiae et Mercurii" Book 1.* University of California Publications: Classical Studies, 32. Berkeley: University of California Press, 1986.

Sharp, D. E. *Franciscan Philosophy at Oxford in the Thirteenth Century.*

1930; repr. New York: Russell and Russell, 1964.

Skeat, T. C. "Two 'Lost' Works by John Leland." *English Historical Review* 65 (1950): 505–8.

Smalley, Beryl. *English Friars and Antiquity in the Early Fourteenth Century*. New York: Barnes and Noble, 1960.

Solinus, C. Iulius. *Collectanea rerum memorabilium*. Ed. Th. Mommsen. Berlin: Nicolaus, 1864.

Souter, Alexander. *A Glossary of Later Latin to 600 AD* Oxford: Clarendon Press, 1949.

Southern, R. W. *Robert Grosseteste: The Growth of an English Mind in Medieval Europe*. Oxford: Clarendon Press, 1986.

Statius, P. Papinius. *Thebais*. Ed. H. W. Garrod. Oxford: Clarendon Press, 1906.

Steinmann, Martin. *Johannes Oporinus: Ein Basler Buckdrucker um die Mitte des 16. Jahrhunderts*. Basler Beiträge zur Geschichtswissenschaft, 105. Basel and Stuttgart: Helbing und Lichtenhahn, 1967.

Stokes, H. P. *The Medieval Hostels of the University of Cambridge: Together with Chapters on Le Glomery Hall and the Master of Glomery*. Cambridge Antiquarian Society, octavo series, 49. Cambridge: Cambridge Antiquarian Society, 1924.

———. *Outside the Trumpington Gates before Peterhouse Was Founded: A Chapter in the Intimate History of Medieval Cambridge*. Cambridge Antiquarian Society, octavo series, 44. Cambridge: Cambridge Antiquarian Society, 1908.

Strype, John. *The Life and Acts of Matthew Parker*. 2 vols. London: John Wyat, 1711.

Tanner, Thomas. *Bibliotheca Britannico-Hibernica; sive de scriptoribus qui in Anglia, Scotia, et Hibernia ad saeculi xvii initium floruerunt, literarum ordine juxta familiarium nomina dispositis Commentarius*. London: Impensis Societatis ad literas promovendas, 1749.

Terentius Afer, P. *Comoediae*. Ed. Robert Knauer and Wallace M. Lindsay. Oxford: Clarendon Press, 1926.

Thery, Gabriel. "Scot Érigène traducteur de Denys." *Bulletin du Cange* 6 (1931): 185–278.

Thesaurus linguae Latinae. (In progress.) Leipzig: Teubner, 1900–.

Thomson, David. "The Oxford Grammar Masters Revisited." *Mediaeval Studies* 45 (1983): 298–310.

Thurot, Charles. *Notices et extraits de divers manuscrits latin pour servir à l'histoire des doctrines grammatical au Moyen Age*. Paris: Imprimerie Impériale, 1868.

Titow, J. Z. *English Rural Society 1200–1350*. Historical Problems: Studies and Documents, 4. London: Allen and Unwin; New York: Barnes and Noble, 1969.

Valerius Maximus. *Facta et dicta memorabilia.* Ed. Carolus Kempf. Leipzig: Teubner, 1888.

Van Steenberghen, Fernand. *La philosophie au xiiie siècle.* Philosophes Médiévaux, 9. Louvain: Publications Universitaires; Paris: Béatrice-Nauwelaerts, 1966.

Vaux, R. de. *Notes et textes sur l'Avicennisme latin aux confins des xiie–xiiie siècles.* Bibliothèque Thomiste, 20. Paris: Vrin, 1934.

Vergilius Maro, P. *Opera.* Ed. R. A. B. Mynors. Oxford: Clarendon Press, 1969.

Vincent of Beauvais. *Speculum quadruplex, sive speculum maius: naturale, doctrinale, morale, historiale.* 4 vols. Douay, 1624; repr. Graz: Akademische Druck, 1964.

Vogt, George McGill. "Gleanings for the History of a Sentiment: *Generositas virtus, non sanguis.*" *Journal of English and German Philology* 24 (1925): 102–24.

Von Moos, Peter. *Geschichte als Topik: Das rhetorische Exemplum von der Antike zur Neuzeit und die "historiae" im "Policraticus" Johann von Salisbury.* Ordo: Studien zur Literatur und Gesellschaft des Mittelalters und der frühen Neuzeit, 2. Hildesheim and New York: Olms, 1988.

Walter of Wimborne. *Poems.* Ed. A. G. Rigg. Studies and Texts, 42. Toronto: Pontifical Institute, 1978.

Walther, Hans. *Proverbia sententiaque latinitatis Medii Aevi.* Carmina Medii Aevi posterioris Latina, 2, 1. 6 vols. Göttingen: Vandenhoeck and Ruprecht, 1963–69.

Watson, Andrew G. *Catalogue of Dated and Datable Manuscripts c. 700–1600 in the Department of Manuscripts, the British Library.* 2 vols. London: British Library, 1979.

———. *Catalogue of Dated and Datable Manuscripts c. 435–1600 in Oxford Libraries.* 2 vols. Oxford: Clarendon Press, 1984.

Welti, Manfred Edwin. *Der Basler Buchdruck und Britannien: Die Rezeption Britischen Gedankenguts in den Basler Pressen von den Anfängen bis zum Beginn des 17. Jahrhunderts.* Basler Beiträge zur Geschichtswissenschaft, 93. Basel: Hebling und Lichtenhahn, 1964.

Winterbottom, Michael. "Aldhelm's Prose Style and Its Origins." *Anglo-Saxon England* 6 (1977): 39–76.

Indices

Index verborum

This index lists all post-classical words or senses of words, along with *rariora* and technical terms of any provenance, appearing in the *Serium senectutis*. It treats as post-classical words or senses which do not appear in the *Oxford Latin Dictionary* (OLD), but for matters of documentation or interpretation, the OLD has been consulted in tandem with the *Thesaurus linguae Latinae* (TLL). The OLD, TLL and *Dictionary of Medieval Latin from British Sources* (MLD) have been consulted for every word they cover. However, only the OLD is complete. In the *Thesaurus linguae Latinae*, I have been able to consult volumes 1–9 and volume 10, part 1, fascicules 1–4, and part 2, fascicules 1–5 (A-M, O-pastor, porta-praepotens). In the *Dictionary of Medieval Latin from British Sources*, I have been able to consult fascicules 1–4 (A-inconsonans).[1]

For all words outside the scope of the TLL and MLD as published to date, I have consulted Alexander Souter's *Glossary of Later Latin* (S) and R. E. Latham's *Revised Medieval Latin Word-List from British Sources* (L) respectively. These books supply reliable corpora of late and medieval Latin and are usefully related to the larger works they stand in for. Souter admits his debt to the *Thesaurus linguae Latinae*, to which he contributed material, in his preface, and the *Revised Word-List* was compiled from an earlier version of the data base now being used to write the MLD. However, readers should note a slight difference in my use of S and L. Because Souter carefully outlines the independent reading program which underlies his *Glossary*, I sometimes cite S when the TLL is silent; however, since the editors of the *Medieval Latin Dictionary*, beginning with Latham himself, have scrutinized anew all the material in the *Word-List*, I never cite L when MLD is silent.

For words and senses which do not appear in the OLD, TLL/S or MLD/L, I sometimes suggest analogues or probable sources. Normally, I do not cite senses not used by Elias, even when those senses are documented and the sense employed by Elias is not. However, I stretch this rule somewhat in the case of words having technical senses related to the trivium, where it seems likely that Elias' usage might have been influenced or triggered by his knowledge of the technical term.

---

[1] I am grateful to D. R. Howlett, editor of the *Dictionary of Medieval Latin*, for collating this index against the contents of fascicule 4 in advance of publication.

Numerical references are to book and line in the *Serium senectutis*. I distinguish between word forms but not between different cases with the same termination. In the case of classical words which develop post-classical senses, I do not provide references for Elias' use of classical senses. Orthography follows Sloane 441. As a result, I follow Texerii in treating *u/v* and *t/c* as interchangeable, likewise *i/y*, except when *y* represents Greek upsilon. Since the various dictionaries observe different spelling conventions, I supply references to lemmata wherever confusion seems likely to arise. In both definitions and documentation, commas divide synonyms or closely related senses, while semicolons divide distinct or unrelated senses. Because the *Dictionary of Medieval Latin from British Sources* provides the most detailed evidence for Elias' immediate lexical environment, I have recorded its division of senses within lemmata whenever that seemed useful; otherwise I document senses only by reference to the lemmata under which they appear.

In addition to dictionary titles, this index employs the following abbreviations:

CL	classical Latin
LL	late Latin (c. 200–600 AD)
ML	medieval Latin (c. 600–1500 AD)
adj.	adjective
adv.	adverb
f.	feminine
gram.	grammatical
leg.	legal
lit.	literal
log.	logical
m.	masculine
n.	neuter
pl.	plural
rhet.	rhetorical
sb.	substantive
sing.	singular
theo.	theological
trans.	transferred or metaphorical
vb.	verb

abanimatiuum, *adj. as sb.*, disincentive; argument against; *-um*, 3.58 (cf. TLL, *animatus*, inclined towards).

abhominabilis, *adj.*, abominable, outrageous; *-is*, 3.213, 9.114; *-e*, 7.83, 11.182; *-ia*, 3.482 (TLL, MLD).

abhominabiliter, *adv.*, abominably; 3.475–76 (TLL, MLD).

abhominacio, *sb.*, abominable or outrageous act; *-onem*, 2.278, 7.120; *-onibus*, 2.59, 3.481–82 (TLL, MLD 3).

abhominatiuus, *adj.*, adverse to; *-a*, 11.63.

abhorribilis, *adj.*, horrible; to be shunned; *-is*, 10.27.

ablacto, *vb.*, wean; *-ato*, 10.156 (TLL, MLD).

abscisio, *sb.*, act of cutting off, mutilation; *-onis*, 3.396 (TLL, MLD).

accidentalis, *adj. as sb.*, accidental (log.); *-ibus*, 11.111 (TLL, MLD).

actualiter, *adj.*, actually, in practice; 10.70, 12.77 (TLL, MLD).

ad expediens, *adv. phrase*, sufficiently, quite; 3.202, 4.202, 8.120, 13.77; *adj.*, useful; 2.65, 11.75. 13.36 (L, *expediens*).

adinuencio, *sb.*, invention; novelty; *-onis*, 2.279; *-onibus*, 4.404 (TLL, MLD).

adinvito, *vb.*, invite, entice; *-at*, 7.97.

adlaterabilis, *adj.*, capable of being set beside; concordant with; *-e*, 2.140 (cf. MLD, *allaterare*).

adlateracio, *sb.*, partnership; juxtaposition; *-o*, 3.733.

adlatero, *vb.*, be or place beside, accompany; *-are*, 9.31, 10.24; *-auerit*, 2.240; *-atum*, 3.26; *-atis*, 3.607; *-ari*, 1.90 (MLD, *all-*).

admissibilis, *adj.*, admissible; *-e*, 10.223 (MLD).

adorator, *sb.*, worshipper; *-or*, 11.237–38 (TLL, MLD).

affectiuus, *adj.*, (1) effective, resulting in (=CL *effectiuus*); *-as*, 3.415; (2) concerned with the affections; *-us*, 12.77 (TLL, MLD).

aggar(r)icio, *sb.*, chatter, idle talk; *-one*, 4.484.

aggar(r)io, *vb.*, jabber about; *-ire*, 4.231; *-ires*, 4.318 (TLL, citing Mart. Cap. 1. 2 [2. 7]).

alatilitas, *sb.*, wingedness; *-atem*, 4.319–20.

aliquantulus, *adj.*, very little; *-e*, 11.202; *-o*, 10.172 (TLL; cf. MLD *aliquantillulus*).

allego, *vb. intr.*, allege, claim; *-abat*, 3.562 (TLL, MLD 4).

alludo, *vb.*, allude, refer; *-ere*, 10.227; *-ens*, 4.128, 130 (TLL, MLD 3–4).

amicabiliter, *adv.*, in a friendly manner; 12.32 (TLL, MLD).

amodo, *adv.*, henceforth; 13.53 (MLD, TLL).

analogice, *adv.*, by analogy; 4.151, 6.81 (TLL, MLD).

analogisticus, *adj.*, analogical; *-ice*, 3.715 (TLL, MLD).

angustia, *sb.*, distress; *-as*, 3.653 (TLL, MLD).

animalitas, *sb.*, animal nature; *-atem*, 8.96 (TLL, MLD).

animositas, *sb.*, courage; *-atem*, 1.93, 3.310; *-ates*, 3.525–26 (TLL, MLD).

anomale, *adv.*, abnormally; 3.733 (TLL [gram.], MLD).

anomalus, *adj.*, anomalous, abnormal; *-e*, 3.84, 4.225; *-um*, 4.356 (TLL,MLD).

antidotizo, *vb.*, recompense; *-are*, 10.146.

antidotum, *sb.*, recompense; *-a*, 10.145 (MLD 2).

antonomasice, *adv.*, preeminently, *par excellence* (gram.); 2.21–22, 120, 4.185, 11.100 (TLL, MLD, s.v., *antonomastice*).

apparencia, *sb.*, appearance (of truth); *-a*, 4.227 (MLD 3).

appreciabilis, *adj.*, worthy of esteem; *-is*, 12.79 (MLD, assessable).

appreciacio, *sb.*, appraisal; *-ones*, 11.214 (TLL, MLD).

appreciator, *sb.*, appraiser; *-orum*, 11.212, 12.82–83 (MLD).

approbabilis, *adj.*, commendable; *-e*, 12.71; *-ia*, 12.49 (MLD, TLL).

approbate, *adv.*, in the approved manner; *-issime*, 11.73 (TLL, MLD).

approprio, *vb.*, appropriate, make one's own; *-ata*, 12.50; *-atis*, 11.72 (TLL, MLD 2).

archigenes, *sb. pl.*, physicians; *-es*, 8.135 (TLL, from Archigenes, a physician mentioned by Juvenal).

argumentalis, *adj.*, serving an argument or proof; *-e*, 3.57; *-alibus*, 7.27, 9.137 (TLL, MLD [log.]).

argumentatiuus, *adj.*, acceptable as proof; *-a*, 7.36, 10.213 (TLL, *fabulae argumentum exponens*).

articulus, *sb.*, article, clause; *-is*, 11.49 (TLL, MLD 3).

artificialis, *adj. as sb.*, artifice; *-ia*, 3.567; *-ium*, 3.210 (TLL, MLD).

aspernator, *sb.*, disdainer; *-or*, 3.187, 12.17 (TLL, MLD).

assercio, *sb.*, assertion; *-o*, 8.22; *-onis*, 4.54, 402, 8.143; *-one*, 4.51–52, 171, 8.34; *-ones*, 2.128, 4.252, 8.92, 10.192, 201, 212, 227, 11.40, 104; *-ibus*, 2.47, 3.621, 4.79, 123–24, 128, 446, 7.31–32, 8.44 (TLL, MLD).

assercionalis, *adj.*, in the form of an assertion; *-ibus*, 10.194.

assertiue, *adv.*, as a proposition; 8.24 (MLD).

assertor, *sb.*, one who states or affirms a proposition; *-or*, 1.125, 2.78, 8.30, 11.235, 12.96; *-orem*, 1.68, 4.402 (TLL, MLD).

assiduo, *vb.*, to be busy, practice; *-atos*, 3.355 (TLL, MLD).

associabilis, *adj.*, contingent upon (?); *-es*, 6.52.

astruo, *vb.*, assert, prove; *-itur*, 11.50; *-ere*, 8.26, 10.225, 11.28 (TLL, MLD 2–3).

auctrix, *sb.* (=*f. of auctor*), paragon; *-ix*, 7.14; *autricem*, 8.147 (TLL, MLD).

augurizo, *vb.*, practice augury (=CL *auguro*); *-izando*, 3.490.

autentico, *vb.*, authenticate, confirm; *-at*, 10.186; *-atus*, 9.118; *-atum*, 7.38; *-atos*, 4.476; *-orum*, 10.198 (MLD).

autenticus, *adj.*, authoritative, authentic; *-e*, 7.49; *-as*, 4.253, 11.103; *-is*, 4.185, 7.121; *-os*, 4.253; *-orum*, 8.55–56 (TLL, MLD).

beatifico, *vb.*, bless, make blessed; *-atis*, 4.395 (TLL, MLD).

bellice, *adv.*, in battle; 3.279 (MLD, conveniently for war).

bestialiter, *adv.*, like a beast; 2.359, 8.145, 11.190 (TLL, MLD).

blasphemo, *vb.*, abuse, blaspheme; *-are*, 2.103, 112 (TLL, MLD).

bouinus, *adj.*, ox-like; *-o*, 9.70; *-am*, 9.83 (TLL, MLD).

bubalinus, *adj.*, of a wild ox or buffalo; *-um*, 8.155 (MLD).

cachynnabilis, *adj.*, deserving of laughter, risible; *-is*, 3.152; *-e*, 4.52; *-em*, 2.310 (OLD, boisterous).

cachinnabiliter, *adv.*, in a manner worthy of derisive laughter; 2.23, 4.415, 9.90, 11.196, 225, 13.91; *cachynnabiliter*; 2.37, 3.27, 8.32.

cachinnator, *sb.*, mocker, scoffer; *cachinnator*, 4.230; *cachynnator*, 4.280–81.

cancellaliter, *adv.*, by cancellation or crossing out; 12.42–43 (cf. MLD, *cancellare* 4).

candidacio, *sb.*, whiteness; *-o*, 4.245 (TLL, MLD).

capesco, *vb.* (=CL *capesso*), enter on, engage in; *-ere*, 3.219 (TLL, MLD).

capio, *vb.*, come into being (=CL *incipio*); *cepisse*, 11.147, 150; *cepisset*, 11.152 (TLL, MLD 15e).

captiualiter, *adv.*, as a captive; 3.93.

caritatiuus, *adj.*, charitable; *-a*, 13.45 (MLD).

castralis, *adj. as sb.*, soldier; *-ium*, 3.131.

casualiter, *adv.*, by chance, accidentally; 3.335, 10.37 (TLL, MLD).

cateruo, *vb.*, assemble, amass a multitude; *-auerat*, 3.197.

cauillatorius, *adj.*, specious, sophistical; *-a*, 3.43; *-as*, 6.44 (TLL, MLD).

causor, *vb.*, complain (about); *-aretur*, 2.160; *-ari*, 2.260, 4.286, 370, 394, 10.263 (TLL, MLD).

cautela, *sb.*, trick, device; *-as*, 6.44 (MLD 3).

cecucio, *vb.*, to be blind; *-ientibus*, 3.30, 4.326 (OLD, TLL, MLD)

celebritas, *sb.*, celebration; *-as*, 6.41 (TLL, MLD 3).

celsitudo, *sb.*, eminence; *-inis*, 1.103 (TLL, MLD 1c).

cerebratus, *adj.*, intelligent; *-o*, 2.350;

-*um*, 4.28; -*is*, 4.387 (cf. CL, *cerebrum*).
certifico, *vb.*, assure, establish in faith; -*auit*, 11.95 (TLL, MLD).
certitudo, *sb.*, certainty, security; -*inis*, 11.202–3; -*ine*, 11.246 (TLL, MLD).
circumcido, *vb.*, purify (trans.); -*ere*, 1.134 (TLL, MLD 2b).
circumscribilis, *adj.*, capable of limitation, limited; -*is*, 3.164 (MLD).
coacerbo, *vb.*, to aggravate at the same time; -*at*, 8.82 (TLL).
coadmoneo, *vb.*, admonish, urge together; -*ere*, 3.646.
coaduersor, *vb.*, oppose a foe; -*ancium*, 3.626.
coadultero, *vb.*, commit adultery with a partner; -*ante*, 7.100; -*antem*, 7.100–101.
coambulo, *vb. intr.*, accompany; -*et*, 2.65–66 (TLL, MLD).
coambulus, *adj. and sb.*, accompanying; companion; -*us*, 2.300; -*o*, 10.157; -*um*, 3.25; -*as*, 3.709.
coamplexor, *vb.*, embrace together; -*os*, 3.361.
coassero, *vb.*, assert jointly; -*itur*, 11.50.
cognicionaliter, *adv.*, with certainty; 8.48 (TLL; MLD, with full cognizance [leg.]).
cohabitacio, *sb.*, proximity, dwelling together; -*o*, 2.311–12; -*onem*, 10.133; -*one*, 13.45 (TLL, MLD).
cohabito, *vb.*, dwell together; -*are*, 13.42, 43; -*ando*, 10.105 (TLL, MLD).
coinquilinus, *sb.*, cotenant, one who shares the same dwelling; -*is*, 12.78 (TLL).
colludium, *sb.*, love play; -*ium*, 1.79, 4.454 (TLL).
commendabiliter, *adv.*, commendably, rightfully; 2.20, 272–73, 307, 315, 3.32, 182, 4.172, 251, 427, 7.56, 59, 112, 8.16, 77, 9.76, 10.224–25, 11.74, 210, 230, 12.29–30, 92–93, 13.28, 34, 38, 43, 74–75; -*ius*, 4.449 (MLD).
commentator, *sb.*, (1) author; -*oris*, 11.80 (TLL, MLD 1); (2) commentator; -*ori*, 11.80 (TLL, MLD 2).
commenticie, *adv.*, fictitiously; 2.92, 3.99, 4.38, 415, 6.89–90.
commenticius, *adj. as sb.*, fictions; -*iis*, 3.111 (TLL, MLD).

comparticipo, (-**or**), *vb.*, share; -*ante*, 11.65 (TLL, MLD).
compassibilis, *adj.*, capable of suffering with others; -*is*, 10.78 (TLL, MLD).
compersono, *vb.*, sound together; -*antibus*, 3.572.
compitaliter, *adv.*, commonly; 7.80, 8.38, 9.111 (cf. CL, *compitalis*).
compossessor, *sb.*, joint possessor; -*orem*, 11.68; -*orum*, 9.33 (TLL, MLD).
compossideo, *vb.*, hold a joint tenancy; -*idente*, 11.67; -*essum*, 11.67.
comproficio, *vb.*, share success; -*iamus*, 13.56; -*erent*, 13.69–70 (MLD).
comproficiscor, *vb.*, set out together; -*icescencium*, 2.149; -*ecturos*, 3.252 (MLD).
compromptifico, *vb.*, make ready together; -*icati*, 2.248.
concepte, *adv.*, formally; -*issime*, 3.440 (cf. OLD, 1 *conceptus*).
concessor, *sb.*, giver; -*ori*, 8.112 (TLL, MLD).
conclauium, *sb.*, conclave (?); -*io*, 11.186 (cf. MLD, *conclaue*).
concolo, *vb.*, (1) worship together; -*uere*, 9.37 (TLL); (2) mutually cultivate a friendship; -*ere*, 13.72–73.
conconsidero, *vb.*, consider together; -*are*, 3.237.
concupiscencia, *sb.*, lust, desire; -*ia*, 1.47, 2.171; -*ie*, 11.198; -*iam*, 2.162; -*iarum*, 2.24 (TLL, MLD).
concupiscibiliter, *adv.*, lustfully; 4.61 (TLL, MLD).
condempnabilis, *adj.*, worthy of condemnation; -*es*, 7.109 (TLL; MLD, liable to be mulcted [leg.]).
conderideo, *vb.*, deride together; -*ent*, 13.94–95.
condux, *sb.*, co-commander; -*ibus*, 3.655.
confederacio, *sb.*, league; compact; -*io*, 1.102, 2.225; -*ionis*, 4.470; -*ionem*, 4.463 (TLL, MLD).
confederaliter, *adv.*, in a league; 8.83, 146, 9.127–28, 11.31.
confedero, *vb.*, ally oneself, join in a league; -*ant*, 3.668; -*ato*, 3.126, 636; -*ate*, 13.75; -*atis*, 13.51 (TLL, MLD).
confedus, *sb.*, compact, treaty; -*ere*, 1.23 (MLD).

conferencia, *sb.*, discussion; -*iis*, 5.37 (TLL, MLD 2).

conferueo, *vb.*, share ardor (=CL *conferuesco*); -*entes*, 3.358 (TLL).

conflatilis, *adj.*, made of cast metal; -*em*, 9.69 (TLL, MLD).

confortunalis, *adj. as sb.*, sharing the same fate; -*ium*, 3.187–88.

confusio, *sb.*, ruin, undoing; -*onis*, 3.220; -*onem*, 3.138 (MLD 2b).

confusiuus, *adj.*, shameful, confusing; -*o*, 12.98 (MLD).

congaudeo, *vb.*, rejoice greatly or together; -*et*, 11.253; -*eat*, 8.133; -*ens*, 13.45 (TLL, MLD).

coniectura, *sb.*, plot, stratagem; -*a*, 3.123 (MLD 2).

coniuga, *sb.*, wife; -*a*, 1.19 (OLD, TLL).

coniunctim, *adv.*, jointly (leg.); 1.115, 4.437 (OLD, TLL, MLD).

coniunctiuus, *adj.*, capable of partnership; -*orum*, 7.27–28 (TLL; MLD, subjunctive [gram.]).

coniungibilis, *adj.*, capable of being joined to another; -*ia*, 10.45; -*ium*, 4.464.

conresono, *vb.*, resound together; -*antibus*, 3.573.

conrudesco, *vb.*, bray along with; -*escenti*, 6.26.

consanccio, *vb.*, duly appoint; -*ieuere*, 9.29 (TLL, *consancio*).

consciencialiter, *adv.*, cognitively (?); 9.23.

consedeo, *vb.*, settle together (=OLD, *sedeo*, 9); -*it*, 3.488, 492.

consternabilis, *adj.*, capable of befuddlement; -*em*, 3.317–18; -*ibus*, 4.408.

consternabiliter, *adv.*, with amazement; 3.580–81.

consubsidior, *vb.*, act as an allied reserve; -*ancium*, 3.625.

consubstantialis, *adj.*, consubstantial; -*em*, 3.68 (TLL, MLD).

consuetudinaliter, *adv.*, according to custom, habitually; 1.105–6, 2.299, 312, 3.109, 202, 4.299–300, 7.91, 8.122, 9.125–26, 10.33, 12.81–82, 13.80 (MLD).

consuetudinarius, *adj.*, customary, usual; -*ium*, 4.175, 11.65; -*io*, 4.233;

-*iorum*, 3.746; -*ios*, 10.131 -*iis*, 4.68 (TLL, MLD 1).

consuetudino, *vb.*, habituate; -*atum*, 3.61, 11.75.

contemplatiuus, *adj.*, reflective of; -*um*, 12.67 (cf. CL, *contemplacione* + gen.).

contencionaliter, *adv.*, contentiously; 5.33–34, 36 (cf. MLD, *contencionalis*).

contignacio, *sb.*, act of framing or contriving; -*ones*, 3.210 (OLD, a horizontal structure of joists and boards erected to form a roof or floor of an upper story).

continuatiuus, *adj.*, continuative; -*as*, 5.47 (TLL [gram.], MLD).

contradictorie, *adv.*, in opposition or contradiction; -*ius*, 10.16 (TLL, MLD).

contrarietas, *sb.*, opposition; -*atis*, 2.70, 4.100 (TLL, MLD).

controuersialis, *adj.*, disputed, in dispute; -*em*, 5.52–53; -*es*, 5.57 (TLL).

controuersionalis, *adj.*, disputed; -*ibus*, 5.34 (cf. above).

contubernalis, *adj.*, intimate; involving cohabitation; -*e*, 4.53; -*i*, 1.78; -*ia*, 4.61 (TLL).

conuencionaliter, *adv.*, by covenant; 3.736 (cf. CL, *conuentio*).

conuitalis, *adj. as sb.*, shared life (?); -*e*, 11.21.

cooccisus, *adj.*, one killed at the same time as another; -*os*, 10.209.

cooperor, *vb.*, work together; -*etur*, 1.110 (TLL, MLD).

copulatiuus, *adj.*, copulative, coordinating (gram. and log.); -*as*, 4.458 (TLL, MLD).

corealiter, *adv.*, in a dance style; 6.19.

cornicularis, *adj.*, horn shaped; -*ari*, 9.124–25 (cf. CL, *corniculatus*).

corrixacio, *sb.*, squabble, dispute; -*onis*, 10.27–28; -*onum*, 8.47, 9.34 (cf. LL, *corrixor*).

corrixatiue, *adv.*, in a squabble; 5.37, 38 (cf. above).

corruptibilis, *adj.*, perishable; -*e*, 2.81, 10.51 (TLL, MLD).

crapulor, *vb.*, intoxicate; surfeit; -*atus*, 4.127 (TLL, MLD).

creatura, *sb.*, created thing, creature; -*a*,

11.93, 97, 157, 186; -e, 11.90; -am, 11.156–57; -arum, 4.268–69, 11.155 (TLL, MLD 2).

crescencia, sb., growth; -iam, 4.207, 209 (TLL, MLD).

cruciatrix, sb., female tormenter; -ices, 4.410 (MLD).

cursilis, adj., swift; -is, 1.88 (TLL, ML, fluid).

dampnabiliter adv., culpably; in a manner worthy of damnation; 7.125 (TLL, MLD).

dampnifico, vb., harm; damn; -ari, 1.137; -etur, 1.111; -andum, 2.57; -atus, 7.44; -ato, 8.119; -ati, 2.197; -atos, 2.256 (TLL, MLD).

debite, adv., duly; -issime, 11.233 (TLL, MLD).

decurio, vb., make worthy of court (Remigius of Auxerre ad Mart. Cap. 1. 2 [2. 7]); -atus, 1.35 (TLL, increase tenfold; MLD, put out of court).

de facili, adv. phrase; 1.116, 4.281, 312–13, 408, 10.90, 12.83; defacili; 2.323, 3.187, 4.420 (MLD).

defectiuus, adj., defective (gram. and trans.); -os, 2.91 (TLL, MLD).

deificacio, sb., apotheosis; -o, 4.385; -onis, 4.389; -one, 4.327 (TLL, MLD).

deifico, vb., deify; -atus, 4.327 (TLL, MLD).

deitas, sb., the deity, divine nature; -as, 2.164; -atis, 1.12, 2.59, 108, 145, 150, 160, 281, 3.84, 4.297, 326, 8.147, 9.23, 119, 133, 10.276, 11.70, 12.75; -ate, 3.591, 12.21 (TLL, MLD).

delecio, sb., destruction; -onis, 3.549 (OLD, TLL, MLD, s.v., deletio).

delicior, vb., delight in; -ari, 13.63 (TLL, MLD).

delire, adv., madly; 2.18, 89, 103, 4.323, 7.47, 50; -issime, 7.123 (MLD).

deprecacio, sb., expression of disapproval; -ones, 2.313 (TLL, curse).

derisibilis, adj., worthy of ridicule, deplorable; -is, 3.549; -ibus, 2.35 (TLL, MLD).

derisibilitas, sb., that which deserves derision; -ates, 4.55.

derisibiliter, adv., in a manner worthy of laughter, deplorably; 1.117, 2.228, 362, 3.65, 159, 214, 329, 724, 726, 4.51, 321, 7.43, 11.229.

derisorie, adv., in a manner worthy of derision; 2.266, 4.403 (TLL, MLD, derisively).

derogacio, sb., calumny; -ones, 2.314; -ibus, 3.747 (TLL, MLD).

derogatiuus, adj., derogatory; -um, 4.69 (TLL, MLD).

desipio, vb. tr., make a fool of; -endo, 3.2 (TLL).

detecte, adv., openly, explicitly; -ius, 6.59.

detectio, sb., revelation; -ctione, 4.27; -ccionem, 4.43 (TLL, MLD 3).

deterioro, vb. tr., make worse; -aret, 4.99; -atus, 3.184 (TLL, MLD).

detestabiliter, adv., abominably, execrably; 2.281 (TLL, MLD).

devio, vb., go astray; -ante, 2.139 (TLL, MLD).

deuoratrix, sb., devourer; -icem, 7.71 (TLL, MLD).

deuote, adv., devoutly, zealously; -cius, 9.18; -tissime, 9.120, 126, 10.312 (TLL, MLD).

diduccio, sb., conduct (of a legal case), course (of an argument) (=CL, deductio); -onis, 2.334; -onem, 5.53; -ones, 8.53, 162; -ibus, 5.36 (MLD 4–5).

diduco, vb., deduce, propose (=CL, deduco); -it, 2.91; -itur, 1.52; -ere, 3.274, 8.162, 9.1; -encium, 8.40; -cta, 10.33, 13.67 (MLD 4–5).

dies, sb., day's provision of food; -erum, 3.335 (MLD 10d).

differentialiter, adv., on the basis of some difference or distinction; 8.139.

diiudico, vb., judge; -asses, 1.63; -ari, 4.170 (TLL, MLD).

dilectio, sb., Christian love; -ctionis, 7.87; -ccionis, 13.57, 72; -ctionibus, 11.245 (TLL; cf. MLD 2).

diminuo, vb., diminish; -erint, 2.261–62 (MLD 2).

diouolariter, adv., meretriciously; 2.82, 3.192, 7.81; diouolaliter; 8.44, 9.121, 10.30, 62, 12.87, 13.67 (MLD).

directorium, sb., prescribed route; -io, 2.328 (TLL).

disciplinaliter, *adv.*, wisely, in accordance with a discipline; 13.69 (TLL, MLD).

discrecio, *sb.*, power of discretion or making distinctions; -*onis*, 3.727, 8.151 (TLL, MLD).

discrete, *adv.*, prudently, discreetly; -*ius*, 1.62–63 (TLL, MLD 2).

discretus, *adj. and sb.*, discreet; of good judgment; -*us*, 3.308; -*o*, 4.152; -*is*, 8.37 (TLL, MLD, s.v., *discernere* 4).

discussor, *sb.*, messenger; -*orem*, 4.299; -*ore*, 10.157 (TLL, MLD, investigator).

discutio, *vb.*, discuss; examine; -*ere*, 8.111; -*ssis*, 1.136 (TLL, MLD 3).

disiunctim, *adv.*, separately (leg.); 1.115 (OLD, TLL, MLD).

disposicio, *sb.*, disposition, nature; -*onem*, 8.137 (TLL, MLD 3).

dissidium, *sb.*, strife, disagreement (=CL, *discidium*); -*orum*, 11.59 (TLL, MLD).

dissonancia, *sb.*, disagreement, discrepancy; -*a*, 4.98 (TLL, MLD).

diuarico, *vb.*, stray; -*antes*, 2.82 (TLL, diverge; MLD, vary).

diuersifico, *vb.*, vary, differentiate; -*ata*, 3.586; -*atis*, 5.38 (MLD).

diuisim, *adv.*, severally; 4.437 (TLL, MLD).

doctrinaliter, *adv.*, as doctrine; 4.416 (cf. TLL, *doctrinalis*; MLD, instructively).

dogmatizo, *vb.*, proclaim as doctrine; -*abat*, 4.412; -*are*, 4.424; -*andi*, 4.419 (TLL, MLD).

donarium, *sb.*, votive offering; gift; -*ia*, 3.585 (TLL, MLD).

dulcor, *sb.*, sweetness; -*ore*, 5.59 (TLL, MLD).

duplico, *v.*, copy, duplicate; -*auerat*, 10.121 (TLL, MLD 3)

ecclesiasticus, *adj.*, ecclesiastical; -*us*, 1.109, 2.45–46 (TLL, MLD).

edictaliter, *adv.*, by edict; 2.123, 143 (cf. TLL, *edictalis*).

edulitas, *sb.*, famine; -*atis*, 3.334 (MLD, food supply).

effectiue, *adv.*, effectively; 7.106 (TLL, MLD).

efficacia, *sb.*, strength, efficacy; -*ie*, 3.714 (TLL, MLD).

endelichia, *sb.*, entelechy (=*entelechia*); -*iam*, 8.61 (TLL, MLD).

enormis, *adj.*, outrageous; -*e*, 3.682; -*es*, 3.546; -*ia*, 4.34 (MLD 1).

enormitas, *sb.*, wickedness, outrage; -*as*, 2.225; -*atem*, 2.279; -*ate*, 2.230; -*atibus*, 2.38 (MLD 2).

enormiter, *adv.*, outrageously; 1.137, 3.43, 365, 7.44, 45 (TLL, MLD 2).

enunciator, *sb.*, speaker; -*or*, 1.126 (TLL).

epithalamicus, *adj.*, epithalamic; -*is*, 1.44, 6.17 (MLD).

equilibriliter, *adv.*, in balance, equally; 9.77 (MLD).

erasio, *sb.*, removal, excision; -*one*, 4.293 (MLD).

ergastulum, *sb.*, dungeon; -*o*, 2.105 (TLL, MLD 2).

erratus, *sb.*, error, sin; -*us*, 8.32 (TLL, MLD).

erroneus, *adj.*, false, heretical; -*ea*, 3.27; -*ee*, 4.402; -*eas*, 8.19 (TLL, MLD 2).

eternaliter, *adv.*, eternally; 7.115, 125, 11.232 (TLL, MLD).

ethnicus, *adj. as sb.*, pagan, heathen; -*orum*, 10.192; -*is*, 13.58 (TLL, MLD 2).

euagino, *vb.*, unsheathe; -*ato*, 3.177 (TLL, MLD).

euentualis, *adj. as sb.*, outcome (=*euentus*); -*ia*, 11.201.

euexia, *sb.*, good health; -*ie*, 8.123 (TLL, MLD).

examen, *sb.*, examination, judgment; -*inis*, 4.400; -*ine*, 2.334, 3.66, 4.80–81, 118, 167, 225, 235, 397, 460 (TLL, MLD).

examinator, *sb.*, judge; -*or*, 2.32, 13.84; -*oris*, 2.216; -*ore*, 2.145, 11.55; -*orum*, 7.102 (TLL, MLD).

exauditus, *sb.*, favorable hearing; -*um*, 10.285; -*u*, 10.117 (TLL, MLD).

excellencio, *vb.*, make preeminent; -*iata*, 8.134.

excessus, *sb.*, excess; -*u*, 12.10 (TLL, MLD 4).

excicatrix, *sb.*, inciter; -*ix*, 9.34 (TLL, MLD).

excitatiuus, *adj. and sb.*, stimulating; stimulant; -*um*, 3.570, 4.18, 388, 8.82; -*a*, 2.350, 11.203; -*as*, 3.757, 5.45 (MLD).

excrescencia, *sb.*, increase, excess; *-iis*, 4.216 (TLL, MLD).

exercicium, *sb.*, use, work, administration; *-ium*, 2.201, 8.64; *-ii*, 12.61; *-io*, 2.291, 8.98, 12.60; *-iis*, 8.36 (MLD 4).

exercitor, *sb.*, practitioner; *-orem*, 2.317 (MLD).

exfrons, *adj.*, shameless; *-ns*, 11.224 (TLL, MLD, *eff-*).

exfronter, *adv.*, shamelessly; 2.116–17, 4.42, 81, 428; *-issime*, 7.66, 8.30, 10.15 (TLL, MLD, *eff-*).

exibicio, *sb.*, display, performance; *-one*, 11.259; *-ones*, 2.356; *-ibus*, 9.85 (TLL, MLD).

exigencia, *sb.*, exigency, demand; *-ia*, 3.753, 11.36 (MLD).

existencia, *sb.*, being, existence; *-ie*, 8.55; *-ia*, 8.46, 51, 9.23, 11.137, 149 (TLL, MLD, *exs-*).

expedienter, *adv.*, usefully, conveniently; *-issime*, 4.456 (MLD, quickly).

experimentaliter, *adv.*, by experience; 8.31 (MLD).

expertum, *sb.*, attempt; *-um*, 3.284 (TLL).

expressio, *sb.*, express mention, statement; *-one*, 4.396 (TLL, MLD 3).

extrinsecus, *adj.*, external; *-e*, 2.218; *-is*, 3.197 (TLL, MLD).

facillitas, *sb.*, propensity, indulgence (OLD 5, MLD 1b); fickleness (influenced by *vacillo* ?) *-as*, 3.171.

falsiloquium, *sb.*, lie; *-io*, 7.47 (TLL, MLD).

falsitas, *sb.*, false opinion, error; *-atis*, 1.70, 5.41, 8.41; *-ati*, 13.65; *-atum*, 1.140; *-atibus*, 2.100, 11.103 (TLL, MLD).

famen, *sb.*, speech, language; *-ine*, 2.6, 14, 5.55; *-ina*, 2.11, 4.157, 6.1, 8.3, 9.2, 10.3, 13.1; *-ibus*, 5.37–38 (TLL, MLD).

farinula, *sb.*, meal, flour; *-a*, 10.83, 92 (TLL, MLD).

fatalitas, *sb.*, destiny; death; *-as*, 3.338, 10.158; *-atis*, 2.183, 3.416, 550, 10.75, 11.191, 12.38; *-ati*, 2.113, 3.403, 506; *-atem*, 3.468, 10.170; *-ate*, 2.172, 262, 10.98, 290; *-ates*, 11.44; *-atum*, 11.43 (TLL, destiny; MLD, death).

fataliter, *adv.*, fatally; 2.38, 103, 3.155, 10.268 (OLD, by destiny).

fedamentum, *sb.*, filthiness, depravity; *-is*, 2.33.

federalis, *adj.* as *sb.*, article of union; *-ia*, 4.110.

fermento, *vb.*, corrupt (trans.); *-atus*, 3.183 (TLL, MLD).

figuraliter, *adv.*, figuratively; 4.173 (TLL, MLD 4).

figurate, *adv.*, figuratively (theo. and gram.); 4.120, 154, 157 (TLL, MLD).

figuratiue, *adv.*, as a figure (theo.); 2.352 (TLL, MLD 1b).

finalis, *adj.*, ultimate, final; *-is*, 4.346 (TLL, MLD).

finalitas, *sb.*, termination (gram.); *-atem*, 4.429 (TLL, MLD).

fortunaliter, *adv.*, by chance or fortune; 11.202.

forulus, *sb.*, bag kept by marshall in Exchequer; *-us*, 1.113 (MLD 1 *forulus* 2).

fructuose, *adv.*, profitably; 2.212 (TLL, MLD).

frustratim, *adv.*, piecemeal (=CL, *frustatim*); 10.218 (TLL, MLD, s.v., *frustatim*).

fundamentalis, *adj.*, basic, fundamental; *-ali*, 10.70–71, 11.101–2, 222 (TLL, MLD 2).

fundamentaliter, *adv.*, basically, fundamentally; 8.33, 11.196 (TLL, MLD 2).

genialis, *adj.*, natural, innate; *-is*, 8.54; *-em*, 8.137–38; *-i*, 8.51 (MLD 3).

genialiter, *adv.*, by nature; 2.124, 3.188, 4.451, 6.82, 8.138, 9.106, 10.55, 11.63, 135, 13.110.

geniculariter, *adv.*, on bended knee, while kneeling; 2.282, 9.84, 11.227, 12.41.

globatim, *adv.*, as a group; 2.242 (TLL, MLD 1b).

glorifico, *vb.*, glorify; *-abant*, 10.312 (TLL, MLD).

grauido, *vb.*, become heavy; *-ata*, 13.17 (TLL, MLD 2).

hylariter, *adv.*, joyfully; 4.461, 10.183 (TLL, MLD).

(h)ystrionaliter, *adv.*, in a manner appropriate to the stage, theatrically; 3.556 (MLD).

horripilaliter, *adv.*, with hair standing on end; 4.368 (cf. CL, *horripilo*).

(h)ymeneicus, *adj.*, pertaining to the wedding song; -*is*, 1.44, 6.18 (TLL).

(h)ypotheticus, *adj. as ab.*, hypothesis; -*e*, 11.166 (TLL, MLD).

ydemptitas, *sb.*, sameness, oneness; -*ate*, 6.25, 13.52 (TLL, MLD).

ignoranter, *adv.* ignorantly; 4.81–82 (TLL; MLD, unawares).

impetitor, *sb.*, attacker, assailant; -*ore*, 5.49; -*oribus*, 10.207–8 (TLL, MLD).

importabilis, *adj.*, unbearable; -*is*, 11.225; -*e*, 13.24 (TLL, MLD).

improperium, *sb.*, reproach, taunt; -*ium*, 3.334, 550; -*io*, 2.114, 8.118, 12.38 (TLL).

inanicio, *sb.*, emptiness (of stomach); -*onem*, 1.34 (TLL).

inappreciabilis, *adj.*, worthless; -*e*, 11.208 (L, inestimable).

incensum, *sb.*, incense; -*o*, 2.248 (MLD 1a).

incentiuum, *sb.*, instigation, enticement; -*um*, 2.298, 3.543, 10.311 (TLL, MLD).

incircumscribilis, *adj.*, illimitable; -*is*, 10.283–84 (cf. TLL, MLD, *incircumscriptibilis*).

incircumspecte, *adv.*, rashly, heedlessly; -*ius*, 4.141, 12.61 (TLL, MLD).

incircumuenibilis, *adj.*, incapable of being cheated; -*is*, 1.104, 2.151, 188–89; -*em*, 2.47–48 (cf. TLL, *incircumueniendus*).

incitatiuum, *adj. as sb.*, incentive; -*um*, 3.753, 4.20–21, 8.81–82; -*o*, 3.749; -*a*, 2.349, 13.47 (MLD).

incitatrix, *sb.*, arouser; -*ix*, 11.185 (TLL).

inclinatiuus, *adj.*, inclined, tending towards; -*a*, 3.364 (MLD; TLL, enclitic [gram.]).

incompetens, *adj.*, unsuited; -*ntes*, 4.457 (TLL, MLD).

incompetenter, *adv.*, inappropriately, wrongly; 4.80, 184, 397; -*cius*, 4.143 (TLL, MLD).

inconcinnus, *adj.*, inappropriate, disso-

nant; -*a*, 2.142, 3.734, 4.234; -*um*, 4.118; -*e*, 4.119; (TLL, MLD).

inconsciliabilis, *adj.*, irreconcilable; -*is*, 4.101 (cf. TLL, *inconciliatus*).

inconsonans, *adj.*, dissonant; -*cius*, 3.735, 4.90 (TLL).

inconueniencia, *sb.*, incompatability, disagreement, discord; -*ia*, 4.196, 226, 236, 11.58; -*iam*, 5.41–42, 11.117 (TLL, L).

inconuenienter, *adv.*, inappositely; -*cius*, 4.142 (TLL).

incorporeitas, *sb.*, immateriality; -*ate*, 8.83–84 (L).

inculpabilis, *adj.*, blameless; -*is*, 13.40 (TLL).

incussio terroris, *sb.*, intimidation; *terrorum ... incussionibus*, 3.713–14 (cf. L, *incussio timoris*).

indefectus, *sb.*, inexhaustibility; -*u*, 10.83 (cf. CL, *indefectus, adj.*).

indeficiens, *adj.*, unfailing; -*ns*, 2.119; -*nti*, 4.127; -*ntibus*, 8.118 (TLL, L).

indeficienter, *adv.*, unfailingly; 11.236 (TLL, L).

indifferens, *adj.*, without difference of degree, equal; -*ns*, 2.312; -*nti*, 7.29, 13.33, 71; -*ntia*, 2.58; as *sb.*, equivalence; -*ntia*, 9.133–34 (TLL, L).

indifferentialis, *adj.*, without distinctions according to degree; -*is*, 2.311 (cf. L, *differentialis*).

indiscretus, *adj.*, indiscreet, undiscriminating; -*us*, 4.281 (TLL, L).

indissolubiliter, *adv.*, indissolubly; 11.241 (TLL, L).

indistincte, *adv.*, indiscriminately, without exception (leg.); 1.126; (OLD, TLL).

indiuidualiter, *adv.*, indivisibly; 3.120 (L).

indiuiduitas, *sb.*, indivisibility; -*atem*, 4.468, 7.28 (TLL; L, individuality).

indiuisibiliter, *adv.*, indivisibily; 13.43 (TLL).

inductiue, *adv.*, inductively; -*issime*, 7.26 (TLL, L).

ineuitabiliter, *adv.*, inevitably, unavoidably; 3.496, 11.191 (TLL).

inexorabilitas, *sb.*, unyieldingness; -*as*, 4.100 (TLL).

inexorabiliter, *adv.*, inexorably; 2.235, 256, 3.741, 11.63, 232 (TLL, L).

infauste, *adv.*, unpropitiously; 2.102 (TLL, L).

infernalis, *adj.*, hellish, infernal; *-is*, 11.233 (TLL, L).

infinibilitas, *sb.*, everlastingness; *-atem*, 4.429, 7.116 (cf. CL, *infinitas*).

infinibiliter, *adv.*, unendingly; 2.32.

infinitiuus, *adj.*, unending; *-um*, 1.104; *-e*, 2.349 (TLL, infinitive [gram.]).

inflexibilitas, *sb.*, constancy; *-atem*, 4.345 (L).

infrigido, *vb.*, cool, chill; *-atum*, 10.39 (TLL, L).

ingratificatus, *adj.*, ungrateful; *-i*, 9.86 (cf. CL, *ingratificus*).

ingratitudo, *sb.*, ingratitude; *-inis*, 3.110, 147 (TLL, L).

inhumatio, *sb.*, burial; *-onem*, 10.269 (L).

inicialiter, *adv.*, originally; 11.206 (TLL, L).

iniunctum, *sb.*, command; *-o*, 2.268 (L).

innuitiue, *adv.*, implicitly, tacitly; 4.396 (L).

innuitiuum, *sb.*, hint, implication; 4.119, 8.43 (L).

innuo, *vb.*, intimate, insinuate; *-uit*, 4.115; *-ere*, 4.53; *-ens*, 13.46; *-erem*, 4.466 (TLL, L).

inopinate, *adv.*, unexpectedly; 13.74 (TLL).

inquilinatus, *sb.*, sojourn; *-u*, 10.97 (TLL).

insensate, *adv.*, senselessly; 8.117 (TLL).

insensatus, *adj.*, senseless, stupid; *-o*, 11.188 (TLL, L).

insinuacio, *sb.*, report, notification; *-onis*, 6.36; *-one*, 6.29 (TLL, L).

insufficiens, *adj.*, insufficient; *-ns*, 11.177 (TLL, L).

integralis, *adj.*, integral; *-is*, 11.126, 128; *-e*, 11.124, 125, 126; *-ibus*, 11.125 (L).

intellectualis, *adj.*, of the mind, mental; *-e*, 11.243 (TLL, L).

interminabilis, *adj.*, endless, eternal; *-is*, 4.35–36 (TLL, L).

interminacio, *sb.*, threat, anathema; *-one*, 11.51 (TLL, L).

interpolate, *adv.*, at intervals; 4.25 (L).

interpolo, *vb.*, interrupt; *-ata*, 8.124, 11.259 (TLL, L).

intrinsecus, *adj.*, internal, intrinsic; *-e*, 4.448; *-am*, 4.379 (TLL, L).

intumulo, *vb.*, bury; *-ati*, 10.181 (L).

invariabilis, *adj.*, invariabile, unchangeable; *-is*, 13.53; *-em*, 11.51–52; *-i*, 13.49 (S, L).

inuariabiliter, *adv.*, invariably; 11.238, 12.76 (L).

inuenticius, *adj.*, fictitious; *-iis*, 9.38 (TLL, L).

Iouialis, *adj.*, of or pertaining to Iuppiter; *-e*, 3.138, 165.

irregularis, *adj.*, disorderly, uncanonical; 4.226 (TLL, L).

irregularitas, *sb.*, irregularity; *-ate*, 6.86 (L).

irreprobabiliter, *adv.*, irreproachably; 13.47 (TLL).

irreprobatus, *adj.*, unreproved; *-um*, 4.313.

itero, *adv.*, again, repeatedly (=CL *iterum*); 12.29 (TLL, L).

itinerarius, (1) *adj.*, of or for a journey; *-ias*, 3.728; *-iis*, 9.68 (TLL); (2) *sb.*, traveler, *-ius*, 10.301 (L).

iuuamen, *sb.*, help, aid; *-en*, 11.16 (TLL, L).

lacesco, *vb.*, provoke, harass (=CL, *lacesso*); *-enda*, 2.131 (TLL, s.v., *lacesso*).

lator, *sb.*, bearer, carrier; *-or*, 13.22; *-oribus*, 10.306 (TLL, L).

laxitas, *sb.*, moral slackness; *-atis*, 7.35 (TLL).

legisticus, *adj.*, legal, lawyerly; *-i*, 2.327 (cf. L, *legista*).

libramen, *sb.*, a weighing, balancing; *-ibus*, 2.54 (TLL).

lignulum, *sb.*, stick; *-a*, 10.82 (L).

limphatice, *adv.*, in a frenzy; 10.101 (cf. CL, *lymphaticus*).

litteralis, *adj.*, pertaining to letters or books; *-ibus*, 3.354; *-ium*, 4.71 (TLL).

litteralitas, *sb.*, the literal sense; *-atis*, 4.151 (TLL, literature).

loculus, *sb.*, coffin; *-um*, 10.306 (TLL, L).

logica, *sb.,* logic; *-a,* 11.109 (L).
loquelaliter, *adv.,* orally, in speech; 2.80, 3.615, 4.177, 444, 5.61, 6.31–32, 7.40, 12.87, 13.30 (cf. TLL, L, *loquelaris*).
lubricitas, *sb.,* lubricity, lewdness; *-atem,* 2.124–25 (TLL, L).
luculencia, *sb.,* distinction, brilliance; *-ia,* 2.304, 8.51, 11.193–94; *-ias,* 4.253, 12.85–86; *-iis,* 4.104 (TLL).
lupanaliter, *adv.,* in the manner of a prostitute; 4.148.

madido, *vb.,* wet, moisten; *-atam,* 10.304 (TLL).
magnalia, *sb. n. pl.,* miracles; 11.6 (TLL, L).
maiestatiuus, *adj.,* majestic; *-a,* 2.120; *-am,* 11.221 (L).
malignor, *vb.,* entertain an evil purpose; *-andum,* 3.434 (TLL).
maneries, *sb.,* manner, method; 3.84 (L).
mansuesco, *vb.,* make a habit of, become familiar with (=CL, *consuesco*); *-uescit,* 4.212, 333, 13.109; *-ueuit,* 2.306; *-uescat,* 2.326, 9.31; *-uescunt,* 3.587, 665, 4.125–26, 157, 6.15, 58–59; *-ueuisses,* 4.379; *-ueta,* 2.182.
manualiter, *adv.,* by hand; 3.566, 9.105–6 (L).
manubialiter, *adv.,* for the sake of booty; 3.278, 392, 552 (cf. CL, *manubiae*).
manubiator, *sb.,* plunderer; *-oris,* 3.395.
mastigo, *vb.,* chew, ruminate (=LL *mastico*); *-ancibus,* 2.170 (cf. TLL, L).
materialiter, *adv.,* from matter, materially; 9.49 (S, L).
maternaliter, *adv.,* maternally; 3.473, 10.304.
matrimonialitas, *sb.,* state or condition of marriage; *-atis,* 4.464–65.
matrimonialia, *adj. as sb.,* marriage; *-ia,* 1.98, 3.736, 4.254; *-ibus,* 1.101, 4.67, 445; *-ium,* 4.66, 110 (TLL, *matrimonialis*).
matrimonialiter, *adv.,* in marriage; 1.72, 3.120, 4.53, 92, 452, 6.49, 72, 7.19 (L).
medianus, *adj.,* earthly, human; *-us,* 1.96, 10.293; *-a,* 4.382, 13.32; *-orum,* 1.85–86; *sb.,* man as dweller on earth; *-us,* 10.7, 12.73; *-um,* 12.90; *-os,* 2.53; *-is,* 1.71, 100; *-orum,* 11.245.
medio, *vb.,* mediate; *-atorum,* 10.51 (TLL, L).
meditatiue, *adv.,* in meditation; 6.31.
melificacio, *sb.,* music making; *-onibus,* 6.91–92.
menciono, *vb.,* mention; *-atorum,* 12.67 (L).
mendacitas, *sb.,* habitual lying; *-atis,* 7.51, 8.42 (TLL).
mendaciter, *adv.,* falsely; 7.66, 12.82 (TLL).
mendositas, *sb.,* falsehood (=CL, *mendacitas*); *-atis,* 7.119 (TLL).
mercurialis, *adj.,* quicksilver; *-i,* 2.156 (L).
meridionalis, *adj.,* midday-; *-is,* 7.91 (OLD, southern).
(merite), *adv.,* deservedly (=CL, *merito*); *-issime,* 1.50, 2.197, 7.111, 118, 8.99, 10.147, 12.66 (TLL).
ministerialiter, *adv.,* officially, in the line of work; 4.300 (cf. TLL, *ministerialis*).
ministro, *vb.,* minister as priest; *-antes,* 2.241 (TLL, L).
miraculose, *adv.,* miraculously, *-issime,* 10.173 (L).
mitificacio, *sb.,* mitification; reduction; *-ones,* 2.188 (cf. CL, *mitifico*).
morigeratus, *adj.,* of good character; *-i,* 3.44–45; *-os,* 2.319 (TLL, L).
mortifico, *vb.,* mortify; *-ando,* 8.4 (TLL, L).
motiuum, *sb.,* motive, reason; *-um,* 4.388 (L).
musco, *vb.,* become covered with moss (?); with flies(?); *-antem,* 5.21 (OLD, strip of moss).

nausealiter, *adv.,* with nausea; 4.259.
nausito, *vb.,* disgust, bore; *-aret,* 10.98 (L).
nitor, *sb.,* support, underpinning (?); *-ori,* 2.217 (cf. CL, *nitor, vb.*).
nouercacio, *sb.,* hostility; *-onem,* 8.126 (cf. S, L, *nouercor,* act like a stepmother).
nouiter, *adv.,* recently, newly; 4.407, 10.158 (S, L).
nuditas, *sb.,* nakedness; *-atis,* 8.118, 119 (S, L).

nugula, *sb.*, little trifle; *-is*, 3.750 (queried in OLD).

nullatenus, *adv.*, by no means, not at all; 4.88, 7.98, 8.50, 11.92, 195 (S, L).

numerositas, *sb.*, abundance, multitude; *-atem*, 11.176; *-ates*, 7.68 (S, L).

numinaliter, *adv.*, by the power of (one's) godhead; 3.94.

obliterabilis, *adj.*, forgettable; *-i*, 4.87.

oleatus, *adj.*, made with olive oil; *-i*, 2.163 (TLL).

opitulo, *vb.*, remedy (=CL, *opitulor*); *-are*, 4.442 (OLD, citing Livius Andronicus, *Trag.* 22).

opposicio, *sb.*, opposition, contradiction; *-o*, 4.101 (TLL, L).

oppugno, *vb.*, capture, storm (=CL, *expugno*); *-ata*, 3.392 (TLL, s.v., *expugno*).

optate, *adv.*, in accordance with one's wishes (=CL, *optato*); 3.258 (TLL).

optatiue, *adv.*, optatively (gram.); as a wish; 1.52 (TLL, L).

oracio, *sb.*, prayer; *-onem*, 10.109 (TLL, L).

ordinarie, *adv.*, in a due or orderly fashion; 1.67, 2.21, 233, 261, 306 (TLL).

ordinarium, *sb.*, directive; injunction; *-ia*, 2.343 (cf. L, s.v., *ordo*).

originaliter, *adv.*, originally; 11.203 (TLL, L).

palestraliter, *adv.*, like a wrestler; 4.301.

parafernalis, *adj.*; res parafernales, married woman's property; *-ibus*, 6.75 (L, s.v., *paraphernalia*).

paranimphalis, *adj.*, of bridesgrooms and bridesmaids; *-ibus*, 6.19 (cf. TLL, *paranymphus*).

paricidus, *adj.*, parricidal (=CL, *parricidalis*?); *-as*, 3.176.

parificabilis, *adj.*, equal, worthy of comparison; *-em*, 3.75–76 (L).

particularitas, *sb.*, character or status of a part; *-ate*, 6.22–23 (TLL, L).

paruiloquium, *sb.*, disparaging remarks (=*prauiloquium*?); *-io*, 4.477 (cf. S, *prauiloquium*; L, *parviloquium*).

pastoraliter, *adv.*, in the manner of a shepherd; 3.36 (L; S, as a bishop).

patenter, *adv.*, openly, publicly; 3.119,

4.115, 7.65; *-issime*, 9.125, 11.27 (L).

paternaliter, *adv.*, as a father; 10.216 (S, L).

pausacio, *sb.*, rest, pause; *-onis*, 13.62 (S, L).

peccamen, *sb.*, sin; *-um*, 2.40 (S, L).

peccatrix, *sb.*, female sinner; *-ix*, 10.105 (S).

pecualiter, *adv.*, like livestock; 4.394 (cf. S, L, *pecualis*).

penalitas, *sb.*, punishment; *-atis*, 1.138, 3.545, 548, 7.30, 48, 115, 11.50, 233; *-atem*, 2.270, 7.111–12; *-ate*, 3.50; *-ates*, 2.123–24, 357–58, 3.709, 4.36, 7.33, 53; *-atibus*, 2.59–60 (L).

penaliter, *adv.*, by way of punishment; 2.39, 126, 176, 235, 3.67, 83, 695, 4.411, 7.76, 77 (S, L).

penitentialis, *adj.*, penitential; 2.179 (L, S).

penulaliter, *adv.*, in the manner of a cloak; 4.282 (cf. CL, *penula*).

perceptibilis, *adj.*, capable of receiving; *-em*, 8.136–37 (S).

perempcio, *sb.*, slaughter, destruction; *-one*, 4.224–25 (S, L).

perfeccionaliter, *adv.*, perfectly; 4.18 (cf. L, *perfectionalis*).

perfunctorius, *adj.*, perfunctory, superficial; *-ia*, 6.50; *-ias*, 2.120; *-orum*, 11.250 (S).

perhenniter, *adv.*, forever, eternally; 2.190, 9.136 (S, L).

perhenno, *vb. tr.*, make permanent; *-at*, 5.15, 8.6; *-auerit*, 4.36 (queried in OLD).

perpetualiter, *adv.*, perpetually; 2.191, 6.47, 72 (S, L).

perplacitus, *adj.*, utterly pleasing; *-e*, 3.304.

perproperus, *adj.*, in haste (=CL, *preproperus*); *-um*, 1.66 (cf. L, *perpropere*).

persecutor, *sb.*, persecutor; *-ibus*, 3.472 (S).

persisto, *vb.*, (1) exist, continue to exist; *-ens*, 11.144; *-ere*, 13.53; *-amus*, 13.115; (2) persist, persevere; *-eres*, 4.258 (L).

perspicacitas, *sb.*, clear vision, perspicacity; *-ate*, 8.115.

pertero, *vb.*, grind thoroughly; *-tritas*, 2.163.

pertinacitas, *sb.,* obstinacy; *-as,* 11.259; *-ati,* 4.160; *-ate,* 10.135 (L).

pervalidus, *adj.,* extremely strong; *-o,* 13.6 (S).

peticio, *sb.,* postulate (log); *-onum,* 8.26 (L).

philozophaliter, *adv.,* philosophically; 8.50.

philosophicus, *adj.,* philosophical; *-o,* 1.131; *-e,* 8.85; *-is,* 8.36 (S, L).

phisicalis, *adj.,* physical, medical; *-es,* 10.41 (L).

phisicus, *sb.,* physician; *-us,* 10.284 (L).

pilescencia, *sb.,* hairiness; *-ie,* 4.304 (cf. L, *pilesco*).

placite, *adv.,* pleasingly, graciously; 10.27 (S, L).

plaga, *sb.,* plague; *-a,* 2.172; *-e,* 2.269 (S, L).

plasmator, *sb.,* creator, maker; *-ore,* 11.18 (S, L).

platealiter, *adv.,* publicly; 3.84.

pluralitas, *sb.,* multitude, plurality; *-atis,* 12.65; *-atem,* 11.176; *-ate,* 3.23, 153, 11.61; *-atum,* 11.59; *-ates,* 9.17, 36, 11.39, 41; *-atibus,* 2.36, 12.40 (S, L).

poculentum, *sb.,* drink; *-o,* 2.205 (cf. L, *poculenta*).

podium, *sb.,* staff; support; *-io,* 2.214 (L).

portitor, *sb.,* porter; *-or,* 13.18 (TLL, L).

posicio, *sb.* thesis (rhet.), proposition (log.); *-ones,* 4.77 (TLL, L).

possibilitas, *sb.,* (1) power, ability; *-atis,* 6.22; *-ate,* 3.626, 4.180, 6.85 (TLL, L); (2) possibility, plausibility; *-atis,* 5.42 (L).

potencialis, *adj.,* possessing power; *-es,* 11.129 (TLL, L).

potencialiter, *adv.,* in power; potentially; 10.266–67, 291 (TLL, L).

potestatiuus, *adj.,* invested with power; *-a,* 3.569, 11.65 (TLL, L).

pragmatice, *adv.,* pragmatically; 2.334.

preabigo, *vb.,* rustle cattle beforehand; *-actas,* 3.39.

preabscondo, *vb.* conceal previously; *-erant,* 7.94; *-itas,* 3.41.

preambulatorie, *adv.,* in advance, prophetically; 2.353 (cf. S, *preambulus,* and L, *preambulum*).

preambulus, *adj.,* preliminary; *-arum,* 8.25 (L).

preassero, *vb.* assert beforehand; *-tis,* 1.68 (L).

preassigno, *vb.,* appoint beforehand; *-auerat,* 3.331–32; *-atum,* 3.384 (cf. L, *preassignatus*).

precipicium, *sb.,* (1) first shock (of battle); *-ium,* 3.220; (2) precipice; *-ia,* 3.566 (TLL).

precircumuenio, *vb.,* deceive with foresight; *-erit,* 1.38.

precommendo, *vb.,* commend beforehand; *-aui,* 4.460.

preconcipio, *vb.,* preconceive; *-cepta,* 3.123; *-ceptam,* 1.107 (L).

preconfedero, *vb.,* form an alliance in advance; *-ato,* 7.64.

preconfirmo, *vb.,* reassure in advance; *-auerat,* 3.252–53.

precontemplor, *vb.,* examine beforehand, scout; *-ati,* 2.187.

preculpo, *vb.,* censure beforehand; *-are,* 2.207 (TLL).

predampnifico, *vb.,* harm beforehand; *-auerit,* 3.43 (cf. S, L, *damnifico*).

predelinquo, *vb.,* commit an offense beforehand; *-entem,* 3.676.

predesignatiuus, *adj.,* signifying in advance; *-a,* 2.353 (cf. TLL, *praedesigno*).

predestino, *vb.,* foreordain; *-ato,* 1.29 (TLL, L).

predissemino, *vb.,* disseminate beforehand; *-auerat,* 4.416.

prediuido, *vb.,* divide beforehand (rhet.); *-diuisis,* 3.499 (TLL).

predo, *vb.,* give beforehand; *-dederat,* 3.254 (TLL).

predogmatizo, *vb.,* dogmatize earlier; *-auerat,* 4.417.

preeffundo, *vb.,* pour out earlier; *-fuderat,* 10.182 (cf. TLL, *praefundo*).

preeligo, *vb.,* choose, prefer; *-eris,* 11.230; *-erit,* 3.729–30, 9.97; *-erant,* 9.35 (TLL [s.v., *prelego*], L).

preexamino, *vb.,* consider beforehand; *-atum,* 4.169 (TLL, L).

preexcipio, *vb.,* receive earlier; *-ceptis,* 3.539 (L, previously excepted).

preexcogito, *vb.,* think up, contrive in advance; *-ata,* 4.415 (L, premeditate).

preeximio, *vb.*, excell; *-iauisses*, 4.71.

prefastido, *vb.*, scorn in advance; *-ire*, 2.207.

prefigo, *vb.*, prearrange, set in advance; *-fixerat*, 13.100 (TLL, L).

pregratificor, *vb.*, show grace to beforehand; *-atus*, 9.93; *-ato*, 9.89 (cf. S, L, *pregratus*).

prehabitus, *adj.*, previously held; *-a*, 3.218 (L).

preignarus, *adj.*, previously without experience of; *-a*, 3.209.

preimpero, *vb.*, order beforehand; *-ati*, 3.179.

preinanimo, *vb.*, vivify previously; *-atum*, 10.75 (cf. TLL, L, *inanimo*).

preinfigo, *vb.*, impale beforehand; *-fixum*, 3.542.

preinfligo, *vb.*, inflict in advance; *-ente*, 3.282.

preingredior, *vb.*, enter before, precede into; *-gressa*, 3.459.

preinstruo, *vb.*, advise, instruct beforehand; *-ctus*, 2.106; *-ctis*, 7.55 (TLL, L).

preinuenio, *vb.* discover beforehand; *-tum*, 11.208.

preinuestigo, *vb.*, examine beforehand; *-auerat*, 3.216–17; *-andum*, 4.266.

preiudicium, *sb.*, forethought, ability to think ahead; *-io*, 12.37.

preiungo, *vb.*, ally in advance; *-iunxerat*, 3.592 (TLL).

prelatus, *sb.*, ruler, lord; *-us*, 10.303; *-um*, 4.299; *-o*, 11.251 (L).

premenciono, *vb.*, mention previously; *-auimus*, 1.118, 10.99, 11.241; *-ata*, 4.445–46; *-atorum*, 11.46 (cf. L, *premencionatus*).

premereo, *vb.*, to be particularly deserving of; *-itum*, 7.52 (L).

prenomino, *vb.*, name beforehand; *-atorum*, 2.224 (TLL, L).

prenoscicator, *sb.*, prognosticator, one who predicts; *-orem*, 3.37.

prenoto, *vb.*, notice previously; *-ata*, 4.366 (TLL, L).

preoffero, *vb.*, offer in advance; *-optulerint*, 3.535 (L).

preoptineo, *vb.*, acquire beforehand; *-uerant*, 3.384–85 (cf. L, *preobtentus*).

preostendo, *vb.*, mention earlier; *-sum*, 11.142; *-so*, 3.171 (TLL, show beforehand).

preperpetro, *vb.*, perpetrate beforehand; *-ati*, 3.180.

preperscrutor, *vb.*, examine thoroughly beforehand; *-ari*, 4.399.

preplaceo, *vb.*, please previously; *-uere*, 2.164 (L, please greatly).

preprocuro, *vb.*, procure, bring about in advance; *-ante*, 3.289 (cf. S, L, *procuro*).

prepromitto, *vb.* promise in advance; *-missi*, 4.105.

presagus, *sb.*, diviner; *-um*, 3.39 (S).

presentencio, *vb.*, pass sentence beforehand; *-antis*, 2.195–96.

presencialiter, *adv.*, immediately; face to face; 6.60, 82, 10.262 (L).

presocio, *vb.*, unite beforehand in alliance; *-auerat*, 3.234.

presubstituo, *vb.*, establish beforehand; *-tis*, 3.655 (L).

presumo, *vb.*, act rashly or arrogantly; *-o*, 10.264, *-it*; 3.511, 8.22; *-imus*, 10.292–93; *-as*, 2.23, 4.230; *-at*, 2.329, 3.148; *-psi*, 4.464; *-psisses*, 1.64; *-pserit*, 2.111, 206; *-eres*, 4.91, 394; *-eret*, 3.280; *-entem*, 10.264; *-ere*, 2.19 (S, L).

presumpcionalis, *adj.*, presumptuous; presumptive; *-is*, 8.42–43; *-i*, 3.59.

presumptuose, *adv.*, presumptuously; 2.228 (S, L).

presumptuosus, *adj.*, presumptuous; *-a*, 4.54; *-um*, 3.689, 10.263; *-e*, 11.198; *-os*, 3.94; *-orum*, 2.236, 249, 252 (S, L).

pretaxo, *vb.*, mention previously; *-auimus*, 7.122; *-atum*, 4.251 (L).

preuaricacio, *sb.*, transgression, sin; *-onis*, 2.354; *-onum*, 2.39–40, 296, 356–57 (S, L).

preuaricator, *sb.*, sinner; *-ibus*, 2.289 (S).

preuaricor, *vb.*, transgress, sin; *-anti*, 2.347 (S).

preuideo, *vb.*, provide for; *-it*, 7.106, 8.119 (L).

preuisio, *sb.*, foresight; *-onis*, 7.107 (S, L).

preuitupero, *vb.*, criticize beforehand; *-are*, 2.206.

primicio, *vb.*, initiate; *-are*, 3.221 (L).

primitiuus, *adj.*, preeminent; *-um*, 8.100.

priuilegio, *vb.*, privilege, grant a privilege; *-auerit*, 8.95; *-ari*, 9.78; *-atus*, 4.122–23, 8.28; *-ata*, 8.27, 10.238, 11.218–19, 12.37; *-atam*, 8.90–91, 12.54; *-atum*, 10.59; *-atas*, 10.252–53; *-atorum*, 4.84 (L).

probamentum, *sb.*, proof, evidence; *-um*, 2.285, 10.73 (S, L).

procommendo, *vb.*, commend previously; *-aui*, 4.450.

procuro, *vb.*, (1) (+ infinitive) endeavor, *-o*, 6.33, 7.18; *-ant*, 3.221; *-auit*, 2.296, 3.689–90, 10.148; *-es*, 9.139; *-emus*, 10.71, 258–59; *-ent*, 4.178 (L); (2) procure; *-are*, 2.201–2, 3.138, 11.260; *-ata*, 3.31; *-auit*, 3.494, 549 (S, L).

proditor, *sb.* revealer; *-or*, 2.323 (S).

professionaliter, *adv.*, avowedly; 3.45–46, 56.

professor, *sb.*, one who professes a belief; *-or*, 11.238; *-ores*, 10.256 (L).

promptificacio, *sb.*, haste; *-one*, 6.17.

promptifico, *vb.*, make ready, hasten; *-are*, 2.292, 7.9; *-auit*, 2.292–93, 3.472, 13.101; *-ares*, 4.153, 322; *-atus*, 4.281.

propicior, *vb.*, act favorably towards; *-ato*, 9.86 (L).

prorimor, *vb.*, cast about; *-areris*, 4.152.

protelacio, *sb.*, delay, prolongation; *-one*, 2.229; *-ones*, 3.664–65 (S, L).

protelo, *vb.*, prolong, protract; *-atas*, 3.606 (S, L).

protensus, *adj.*, long, extended (=CL, *protentus*); *-um*, 10.36 (L).

proteruio, *vb.*, mock impudently; *-ire*, 4.230 (S, L).

proteruiter, *adv.*, impudently; 2.288, 4.231, 474, 5.26 (OLD, citing Ennius, *scen.* 374, L).

pruinose, *adv.*, frostily; 4.303.

psallo, *vb.*, hymn, chant; *-entes*, 9.128 (S, L).

psalmista, *sb.*, the psalmist, David; *-a*, 4.135 (S, L).

pungitiuus, *adj.*, poignant, goading; *-o*, 3.747; *-am*, 4.343; *-orum*, 3.756 (L).

punibilis, *adj.*, punishable; *-ium*, 4.48 (L).

punitiuus, *adj.*, punitive; *-a*, 7.118; *-e*, 7.33, 53 (L).

purgatiuus, *adj.*, cleansing, purgative; *-a*, 4.412 (S, L).

purgatorius, *adj.*, purgatorial; *-ia*, 2.180 (S, L).

pusillanimus, *adj.*, faint hearted, discouraged; *-us*, 11.190; *-orum*, 3.272 (S).

putatiuus, *adj.*, putative, alleged; *-a*, 6.89 (S).

qualifico, *vb.*, cause to become; *-facit*, 3.75 (L, qualify, modify).

quamplures, *adj. and sb.*, some, many (=CL, *complures*); *-es*, 2.39, 3.497, 4.250, 475, 10.202, 208, 11.98; *-a*, 2.99, 7.77, 10.210; *-ibus*, 2.99, 147, 10.319, 13.58; *quam plurima*, 7.117; *-imis*, 3.539.

quantitatiuus, *adj.*, quantitative; *-e*, 11.129 (L).

quietas, *sb.*, state of repose; *-atis*, 7.125.

quoniam, *rel. adv.*, that; 10.292 (S, L).

racionalitas, *sb.*, power of reason; *-as*, 10.25, 189; *-atis*, 8.147, 153, 157, 12.37, 55, 56; *-atem*, 8.138–39 (S, L).

recedo, *vb.*, return; *recessit*, 10.181, 13.90 (L).

recenter, *adv.*, recently, newly; 2.22, 10.35, 172.

receptibilis, *adj.*, admissible, worth entertaining; *-ium*, 10.196–97 (S, L).

reclamatiuus, *adj.*, responsive to; *-um*, 11.226.

recongratulor, *vb.*, congratulate anew; *-atus*, 10.184.

reconuiuo, *vb.*, live together again; *-ere*, 10.184.

reconuiuus, *sb.*, restored companion; *-is*, 10.184 (cf. S, *conuiuus*, living along with).

rectitudo, *sb.*, uprightness, rectitude; *-inis*, 2.82; *-inem*, 4.345 (S, L).

rededuco, *vb.* lead anew; *-ctus*, 3.349 (L, put back).

redelinquo, *vb.*, sin again; *-endi*, 2.298.

rediuiuum, *adj.*, restored to life; *-um*, 10.169, 208–9 (S).

refocillo, *vb.*, revive, refresh; *-ari*, 10.81 (S, L).

regularis, *adj.*, canonical, according to rule; *-is*, 3.716; *-i*, 2.340; *-es*, 6.86 (S, L).

reinfatuo, *vb.,* make foolish anew; *-atus,* 8.18.

remissibilis, *adj.,* capable of being relaxed or unstrung; *-is,* 2.85 (L).

repetitiuum, *sb.,* repeated cause; *-um,* 8.88.

repositio, *sb.,* requital; *-ciones,* 5.45; *-ibus,* 5.35.

reprobabilis, *adj.,* blameworthy; *-em,* 4.74 (S, L).

reprobabiliter, *adv.,* disgracefully; 2.280, 4.174 (L).

reprobacio, *sb.,* reproof; *-onis,* 4.389; *-ones,* 2.61; *-onibus,* 4.136 (S, L).

reprobator, *sb.,* critic, one who disapproves; *-orem,* 4.297.

reproduco, *vb.,* produce again (leg.); *-ere,* 10.258 (L).

resuscitacio, *sb.,* a raising from the dead; *-onem,* 10.296 (S, L).

retractator, *sb.,* one who repeats or rehandles; *-orem,* 4.403.

retransitiue, *adv.,* in return; 9.44 (S, with a reflexive sense [gram.]).

retribucio, *sb.,* reward, punishment; *-onem,* 2.90–91 (S).

retro, *adv.,* previously; 2.87, 3.110, 596, 4.29, 49, 460, 476, 10.13, 12.47, 67, 13.103, 118.

retrotempus, *sb.,* time past; *-orum,* 10.198 (L).

reuegeto, *vb.,* revivify; *-at,* 10.75; *-atus,* 10.182.

reuigoro, *vb.,* return to life; *-atus,* 10.181–82.

reuiuus, *adj.,* restored; *-us,* 10.184 (L).

ridiculose, *adv.,* comically, absurdly (=CL, *ridicule*); *-issime,* 3.73, 10.22–23 (S, L).

ridiculosus, *adj.,* absurd (=CL *ridiculus*); *-us,* 1.50, 4.2; *-os,* 10.288; *-is,* 2.36; *-issima,* 1.40 (S).

ruditas, *sb.,* lack of skill or polish; *-atis,* 6.25, 11.194; *-ate,* 4.292 (L).

ruralitas, *sb.,* rusticity; *-atis,* 3.50.

ruraliter, *adv.,* in the fashion of the countryside; 3.44 (S).

rusticaliter, *adv.,* like a rustic; 3.45 (cf. L, *rusticalis*).

rutilo, *vb.,* drip, exude; *-abit,* 10.39 (cf. L, *rutilans*).

sacrilege, *adv.,* sacrilegiously; 3.278 (S).

salebrositas, *sb.,* roughness, unevenness; *-ates,* 4.278 (cf. CL, *salebritas*).

saluator, *sb.,* savior; *-or,* 10.299; *-orem,* 11.246 (S, L).

saluo, *vb.,* save; *-at,* 12.24; *-ans,* 12.23 (S, L).

sanccio, *vb.,* enact, decree (=CL, *sancio*); *-ita,* 9.16, 27; *-ite,* 2.341; *-am,* 10.19 (L, s.v., *sanxio*).

sanum, *adv.,* soundly, well; 5.1 (S, L).

saturacio, *sb.,* fullness, satiety; *-o,* 4.232 (S, L).

sciencialiter, *adv.,* with knowledge; 9.37, 11.212, 235, 12.35, 71 (S, L).

scolariter, *adv.,* in school; 13.69.

scrupulositas, *sb.,* jagged roughness; *-ates,* 3.495.

secernibilis, *adj.,* distinguishable; *-is,* 1.117, 11.231.

seculariter, *adv.,* in a worldy fashion; 4.243 (S, L).

secundo, *adv.,* for a second time; 12.29 (S).

securifico, *vb.,* make secure; *-atus,* 10.91, 12.98.

segnesco, *vb.,* become slow or lazy; *-it,* 11.255 (S).

segnifico, *vb.,* slow, make slow; *-are,* 1.11, 7.7, 8.14; *-ato,* 6.13–14.

sensate, *adv.,* sensibly; 2.94, 324, 350, 3.40, 4.140, 190–91, 236, 246, 306, 329, 343, 382, 5.43, 10.3, 13.132; *-issime,* 2.105, 290, 314, 3.309, 4.111, 134, 213, 10.168, 12.35 (S, L).

sensatus, *adj. and sb.,* sensible, intelligent (person); *-us,* 1.25, 91, 4.423, 7.1, 8.1, 13, 9.56, 10.144, 172, 11.115; *-o,* 1.116, 136, 9.4, 14, 11.48; *-um,* 1.65, 3.49, 4.27, 265, 473, 12.36, 92; *-i,* 2.214, 3.726, 4.127, 155, 6.14, 8.50; *-is,* 2.349, 4.387, 11.74, 12.15, 72, 79; *-issimus,* 8.99, 9.90–91 (S, L).

sentencialiter, *adv.,* (1) in the form of a judicial sentence; 2.339, 4.406 (L); (2) as an opinion; 8.59 (cf. L, *sententio*).

sentencio, *vb.,* pronounce sentence; *-auit,* 2.108; *-anti,* 2.330; *-ando,* 2.328 (S, L).

sermocinacio, *sb.,* preaching; discourse; *-onis,* 4.446–47, 5.25; *-ones,* 4.368; *-oni-*

bus, 4.126, 11.28 (L).

sermocinalis, *adj.*, of or concerning speech; *-i*, 5.63 (L).

sermocinanter, *adv.*, in speech; 4.155 (S).

sermocinor, *vb.*, speak, declare; *-antis*, 4.397–98; *-ante*, 2.251–52; *-ancium*, 4.378; *-andi*, 4.254 (L).

sero, *adv.*, rarely, only under extraordinary circumstances; 3.185, 5.5, 6.52.

seruicium, *sb.*, service, devotion; *-ia*, 3.11 (S, L).

sesquipedalitas, *sb.*, unit of one and one-half feet (=five syllables); *-ates*, 6.21.

silenciarius, *adj.*, silent; *-ius*, 8.15; *-ium*, 7.51 (cf. S, L, *silenciarius*, papal secretary).

silicernialis, *adj.*, pertaining to an old man; *-i*, 6.14 (cf. L, *silicernius*).

sinceriter, *adv.*, sincerely; 13.53 (L).

siquidem, *adv.*, indeed, without doubt; 3.181 (L).

socialia, *sb.*, friendships; *-ia*, 13.128, 143.

solaciator, *sb.*, one who consoles; *-orem*, 10.167.

solacio, *vb.*, solace, console; *-ari*, 4.93; *-ata*, 9.83 (L).

solicanus, *adj.*, singing alone; *-is*, 6.91 (S, citing Mart. Cap. 2. 127 [40. 20]).

solidus, *adj. as sb.*, solid earth; *-o*, 8.128, 131 (OLD, L).

soliloquus, *adj. and sb.*, one who speaks a soliloquy; *-us*, 2.45, 4.134, 162 (L).

sompniculose, *adv.*, tirelessly, *-sissime*, 11.64.

sompniculosus, *adj.*, tireless; inventive; *-a*, 3.694, 4.76, 212, 11.185; *-is*, 3.117, 412, 754, 4.70, 147 (L, fanciful).

specialitas, *sb.*, special quality or nature; *-ate*, 6.28 (S, L).

spiritualis, *adj.*, spiritual; *-is*, 2.45, 4.103, 162; *-i*, 4.85 (S, L).

spiritualitas, *sb.*, spiritual intercourse; *-ate*, 7.107 (S, L).

spiritualiter, adv. spiritually; *-issime*, 9.88–89 (S, L).

sponsalicius, *adj.*, of marriage; *-ia*, 6.35; *-ie*, 6.28 (S).

spontanee, *adv.*, voluntarily; 11.255 (S, L).

spontaneus, *adj.*, voluntary, willing; *-eus*, 2.360, 4.171, 11.239; *-ee*, 11.197; *-ea*, 9.41, 11.79 (S, L).

status, *sb.*, equilibrium; *-u*, 2.214 (L).

stellaris, *adj.*, of the stars; *-is*, 8.67 (S).

strata, *sb.*, paved street; *-e*, 3.727 (S, L; OLD, *strata uiarum*).

subcinctura, *sb.*, underfastening; *-a*, 4.201.

subcinericius, *adj.*, baked under ashes; *-ium*, 10.86–87 (S).

subditus, *sb.*, underling; *-orum*, 2.309 (S, L).

subemergo, *vb.*, emerge as a consequence; *-erent*, 11.59.

subiaceo, *vb.*, be subject to; *-ere*, 2.133 (L).

subintelligencia, *sb.*, implied or hidden meaning; *-ia*, 4.247, 277; *-ie*, 4.449 (S).

subintelligo, *vb.*, understand as implied; *-as*, 4.339, 10.273; *-ere*, 4.344; *-i*, 4.158, 166, 329; *-endum*, 2.67, 4.165, 236, 247, 266–67, 306; *-endam*, 4.323 (S, L).

subiunctiuus, *adj.*, subordinate (gram.); *-a*, 4.113 (S, L).

subleuator, *sb.*, one who gives assistance; *-oris*, 12.91 (L).

sublucio, *sb.*, bath, washing; *-ones*, 4.373, 395.

sublunaris, *adj. and sb.*, sublunar (being); *-is*, 2.125; *-em*, 9.102; *-i*, 7.113, 9.99; *-ia*, 4.382; *-ibus*, 1.77 (S, L).

sublunariter, *adv.*, in the sublunar world; 11.56.

subornacio, *sb.*, decoration; *-onum*, 11.208.

subpedito, *vb.*, trample under foot, subdue; *-ari*, 7.68 (L).

subpodiatio, *sb.*, propping (of a mine gallery); *-oni*, 2.218 (L).

subpodio, *vb.*, support from beneath; underpin; *-are*, 9.138; *-atus*, 4.309, 8.35; *-ata*, 2.215, 343–44 (*supp-*) (L).

subpono, *vb.*, assume; *-ere*, 8.43 (L).

subpuncto, *vb.*, expunctuate (=CL, *expungo*); *-etur*, 4.201 (cf. L, *punctuo*).

subsannabilis, *adj.*, deserving of mockery or laughter, ridiculous; *-is*, 2.36, 331, 3.214; *-e*, 2.201, 3.70, 555; *-i*, 3.24,

thurifico, *vb.*, burn incense; -*are*, 2.249, 10.18 (S, L).

tortula, *sb.*, roll, cake; -*as*, 2.164 (S).

totaliter, *adv.*, totally, entirely; 3.702 (L).

transcursio, *sb.*, passage (of time); -*onibus*, 10.198 (S, L).

transgressio, *sb.*, transgression, sin (against); -*onis*, 2.292; -*onem*, 5.42; -*onum*, 2.34, 3.712 (S, L).

transitiuus, *adj.*, transferrable; -*um*, 6.67 (S, L, transitive [gram.]).

transitorius, *adj.*, transitory, passing; -*ias*, 2.121 (S, L).

transmissor, *sb.*, sender; -*or*, 3.176.

tribunaliter, *adv.*, judicially; 2.293 (L).

tripudialis, *adj.*, of a dance (in triple time); -*ibus*, 6.119 (cf. CL, *tripudium*).

triuialiter, *adv.*, in the manner of a commonplace; 3.29–30, 85, 6.53, 7.26, 39, 54, 8.37–38, 10.29, 11.257, 12.86 (S).

turbulencia, *sb.*, trouble, difficulty; -*a*, 10.178, 13.46; -*as*, 4.351, 8.84; -*arum*, 3.131–32 (S, confusion, disturbance).

variabilis, *adj.*, changeable; -*is*, 6.49 (S, L).

uditas, *sb.*, drunkenness; -*ate*, 1.113 (cf. CL, *udus*).

veges, *adj.*, vigorous; -*es*, 2.291, 3.9, 315, 7.12, 11.91; -*eti*, 6.16; -*etes*, 11.214 (L).

vegete, *adv.*, vigorously; -*ius*, 3.645, 7.15 (cf. above).

velocifico, *vb.*, hasten someone on their way; -*atum*, 4.338.

venenosus, *adj.*, poisonous, deadly; -*a*, 4.342; -*as*, 9.107 (S, L).

veneria, *sb.*, sexual intercourse; -*is*, 1.41, 51 (S, s.v., *venerea*; L, lust).

venusto, *vb.*, beautify; -*et*, 1.83–84; -*ata*, 7.90; -*atis*, 10.69 (S, L).

veraciter, *adv.*, truly; 10.288; -*issime*, 3.273 (S).

vero, *vb.*, speak the truth; -*ata*, 1.4 (OLD).

verbalis, *adj.*, expressed in words, oral; -*is*, 2.141, 4.292; -*e*, 10.265; -*i*, 3.60, 4.396, 8.22; -*es*, 2.121, 127; -*ibus*, 4.89, 106, 5.35 (L; S, of a word or verb [gram.]).

verbalitas, *sb.*, (1) oral disputation; -*atis*, 11.193, 12.99; (2) verbiage, mere words; -*atum*, 8.162.

verbaliter, *adv.*, in words, orally; 1.64, 2.175, 346–47, 4.115, 155, 166, 176, 444, 10.16 (L; S, as a verb [gram.]).

verbula, *sb.*, verbiage; -*a*, 13.2 (L).

verisimillime, *adv.*, plausibly (=CL, *verisimiliter*); 3.446, 10.87–88.

vernaliter, *adv.*, obsequiously (=CL, *veniliter*); 3.76–77, 11.258 (S).

verpus, *sb.*, middle finger; -*o*, 3.617.

vicinaliter, *adv.*, in proximity; 12.78 (L).

vicissitudinaliter, *adv.*, by turns; 5.37 (L).

victualia, *sb.*, victuals, food; 2.208 (S, L).

vigoro, *vb.*, invigorate; -*et*, 7.11 (S).

vilifico, *vb.*, debase, abuse; -*antibus*, 2.92; -*atus*, 2.1 (S, L).

villa, *sb.*, small town, village; -*as*, 3.599 (S, L).

vinaliter, *adv.*, concerning the vine; 3.86 (cf. L, *vinealiter*, S, *vinalis*).

virtuosus, *adj.*, potent; -*am*, 10.274 (S, L).

visibilitas, *sb.*, visibility; -*ate*, 11.87 (S, L).

vituperabiliter, *adv.*, culpably; 11.190–91 (S, L).

vituperium, *sb.*, blame, censure; -*ium*, 4.480, 5.43 (S, L).

vlcionalis, *adj.*, pertaining to vengeance; -*es*, 2.357.

vlcionaliter, *adv.*, as vengeance; 3.283.

vnanimiter, *adv.*, with one spirit or purpose; 3.256, 9.35–36, 11.49, 13.70.

vnificus, *adj.*, unifying; -*is*, 6.76 (L).

volatilitas, *sb.*, wingedness, ability to fly; -*atem*, 4.319 (L).

vsualis, *adj.*, ordinary, usual; -*e*, 10.62 (S, L).

zelotipo, *vb.*, guard zealously; -*ando*, 5.14 (L, cuckold).

zinzugia, *sb.* syzygy, union; -*ia*, 10.43 (S, L, s.v., *syzygia*).

Index auctorum

Only definite or highly probable sources are noted here. Possible sources, analogues, and later citations can be located by using the *index nominum et rerum* and the commentary. References to prose sources are by book, chapter, and section. Those to verse sources are by book, poem, and line. References to the *Serium senectutis* are by book and line.

1. The Bible

Genesis
  1.28: 12.58–59
Exodus
  32: 2.271–302, 9.66–69
Leviticus
  24.10–16: 2.100–107
Numeri
  10.33 ff.: 2.147–73
  12: 2.174–80, 5.19–22
  13: 2.181–203, 7.54–76
  16: 2.222–70, 5.17–18
  25: 5.11–16
3 Regum
  11.1–8: 9.90–97
  12.28–30: 9.85–89
  17: 10.77–118
4 Regum
  2, 4.8 ff.: 10.121–70
  13.20–21: 10.171–84
Psalmi
  5.17: 1.119–24
  7.12–13: 2.77–87
  13.3: 1.119–24
  14: 1.104–14
  17.3: 4.143
  17.33: 4.144
  24.4: 2.44–50
  30.6–7: 2.44–50
  33.13–14: 1.131–35
  34.28: 4.141
  36.30: 4.142
  51.4: 4.138–39
  61.10: 2.53
  70.24: 4.141

  77.36–37: 1.119–24
  103.16: 4.145–46
  132.1: 13.41–42
  136.9: 4.144–45
Ecclesiastes
  4.10: 12.90–92
Canticum canticorum
  1.1: 4.91–94
  1.1–2: 4.113–14
Sapientia
  1.11: 7.122–23
Osee
  2.19: 4.132–33
Danihel
  13: 7.81–116
Secundum Mattheum
  9.18–26: 10.281–91
  23.5: 9.109–10
Secundum Lucam
  7.11–17: 10.295–311
  16.13: 13.8–14
Secundum Iohannem
  11: 10.266–70
Apocalypsis
  21: 4.104
  21.2: 4.128–29
Glossa ordinaria
  ad Ps. 17.3: 4.194–96
  ad Ps. 17.33: 4.197–202
  ad Ps. 34.28: 4.183–89
  ad Ps. 36.30: 4.190–91
  ad Ps. 51.4: 4.162–82
  ad Ps. 103.16: 4.240–45
  ad Ps. 136.9: 4.203–27

2. Other Authors and Works

Index nominum et rerum

This index covers introduction, text, translation, commentary and appendices. However, modern scholars are indexed only when they appear in the text of the introduction or appendices. Biblical passages cited in the text of the *Serium senectutis* are all accessible through the *index auctorum* and so are not indexed here. Other ancient and medieval authors and works are indexed here because many of them are cited in the introduction and commentary but are not direct sources for the *Serium senectutis* and so do not appear in the *index auctorum*. Names are normally cited in the normalized forms used in the translation, although I have usually followed the Douay-Rheims Bible in rendering the names of Old Testament figures and so add the more familiar name forms of the Revised Standard Version in parentheses. Rhetorical figures are indexed according to their Latin names. References to the *Serium senectutis* are to the Latin text; all references are to pages in this edition.

Elias of Thriplow: Serium senectutis is an edition and translation of Elias of Thriplow's only surviving work. *Serium senectutis,* or "Grave Thoughts in Old Age," is a prosimetrum, or Menippean satire, cast in the form of a dialogue between Elias and his friend Philip. Composed as an assemblage of excerpts from other authors which Elias has embellished and arranged to suit his argument, this dialogue attempts to marry the encyclopedism and mannered style of Martianus Capella to the stricter design and heavenly telos of Boethius' *Consolation of Philosophy.* Its contents range from a hymn praising the marriages of pagan gods to Aristotelian proofs of God's existence; its sources include poets, historians, and standard medieval authors.

This edition offers a critical text with full apparatus; a translation; an introduction to matters of historical, literary, philological and codicological interest; notes on sources and interpretation; an *index verborum*; an *index nominum*; and a bibliography.

Roger Hillas is Assistant Professor of English at Howard University and has published on the writings of Elias of Thriplow.

CRTS

CEDIEVAL & RENAISSANCE TEXTS & STUDIES
is the publishing program of the
Center for Medieval and Early Renaissance Studies
at the State University of New York at Binghamton.

CRTS emphasizes books that are needed —
texts, translations, and major research tools.

CRTS aims to publish the highest quality scholarship
in attractive and durable format at modest cost.